The Time-Life Book of Family Finance

TIME
LIFE
BOOKS ®

The Time-Life Book of Family Finance

by Carlton Smith, Richard Putnam Pratt
and the Editors of TIME-LIFE BOOKS

Illustrations by Lionel Kalish

TIME-LIFE BOOKS, NEW YORK

About the authors

Carlton Smith and Richard Putnam Pratt have collaborated since 1966 on the nationally syndicated newspaper column, "Your Personal Finance." Mr. Smith earned his M.A. at the University of Chicago after serving as a Navy pilot in World War II, then won a Ford Foundation fellowship for further study in the social sciences. He began his writing career as a Chicago newspaper reporter and has since been both a newspaper and magazine editor. He lives with his wife in New York City. Mr. Pratt, a graduate of the University of Illinois, also began his career in newspaper work, later specializing in the economics of medicine. Since 1963 he has been on the staff of the American Bankers Association. He and his wife and two daughters live in New Jersey. Both authors have contributed articles to various publications.

TIME-LIFE BOOKS

EDITOR: Maitland A. Edey
EXECUTIVE EDITOR: Jerry Korn
TEXT DIRECTOR: Martin Mann
ART DIRECTOR: Sheldon Cotler
CHIEF OF RESEARCH: Beatrice T. Dobie
PICTURE EDITOR: Robert G. Mason
ASSISTANT TEXT DIRECTORS: Ogden Tanner, Diana Hirsh
ASSISTANT ART DIRECTOR: Arnold C. Holeywell
ASSISTANT CHIEF OF RESEARCH: Martha T. Goolrick

PUBLISHER: Walter C. Rohrer
ASSISTANT PUBLISHER: Carter Smith
GENERAL MANAGER: John D. McSweeney
BUSINESS MANAGER: John Steven Maxwell
PRODUCTION MANAGER: Louis Bronzo

SALES DIRECTOR: Joan D. Manley
PROMOTION DIRECTOR: Beatrice K. Tolleris
MANAGING DIRECTOR, INTERNATIONAL: John A. Millington

The Time-Life Book of Family Finance

EDITOR: Robert M. Jones
ASSISTANT EDITOR: Marian Gordon Goldman
ILLUSTRATIONS EDITOR: Sheila Osmundsen
DESIGNER: John Newcomb
TEXT EDITORS: David S. Thomson, George Constable, John M. Dille, Anne Horan, Edmund White, Peter Wood
STAFF WRITERS: Ethel Strainchamps, Peter Yerkes
RESEARCHERS: Sondra Albert, Rhea Finkelstein, Monica O. Horne, Ellen Leiman, Shirley A. Miller, Louise Samuels, Melissa Wanamaker
ART ASSISTANT: Herb Quarmby

EDITORIAL PRODUCTION
COLOR DIRECTOR: Robert L. Young
ASSISTANT: James J. Cox
COPY STAFF: Rosalind Stubenberg, Barbara Fairchild, Florence Keith
PICTURE DEPARTMENT: Dolores A. Littles
TRAFFIC: Arthur A. Goldberger

The following individuals and departments of Time Inc. helped to produce this book: Editorial Production, Robert W. Boyd Jr.; Editorial Reference, Peter Draz.

CONTENTS

1
Money

How to keep more
of what you make
and make more of
what you keep

Save your money, spend it sparingly and wisely, work hard and get
to bed early, said Poor Richard.

How times have changed since Ben Franklin's day—or even since
World War II, for that matter. To an American of 1900, or 1935, today's economic universe would seem like a psychedelic hallucination.

Two great new forces have altered our horizons—vastly increased
incomes and near-limitless credit. If many of us have financial problems—and many do—it is largely because we have not yet developed
the navigational systems we need to adjust to our new surroundings.

By 1950, only 2 per cent of U.S. families had reached what was
then considered the first rung of the ladder to the economic upper class
—an income of $10,000 a year. By 1960, approximately 10 per cent of
all families—8,333,000 in all—were reporting incomes in excess of
$10,000. Toward the end of the decade this level had been reached by
more than one family in three.

This growth is so startling and its effects so profound that it
amounts to a revolution. In previous eras an "affluent society" was
one in which there was enough wealth for the ruling class to live in luxury. The rest of the people lived on a subsistence level. Our affluent society is radically different. Now a great majority of the people can
afford at least some luxuries. The very necessities of life—food, clothing, shelter—assume luxurious forms. Many luxuries—automobiles,
education—have indeed become necessities. And even after such luxurious necessities and necessary luxuries have been bought, ordinary
people have the money for things they know they do not have to have.
There has been an enormous rise in what economists call discretionary
income—money that is left over after "nondiscretionary" expenditures
and can be used at the discretion of the family. It can be spent immediately to fulfill present desires, or put aside for future spending
—"saved." "What is new," says Professor George Katona of the
University of Michigan, "is the common man's sharing in the ways of
living that in the past were reserved for the few. The common man's
ability to use some of his money for what he would *like* to have, rather
than for what he *must* have, represents the revolutionary change."

Part of the reason the common man can now have what he likes
is a second revolution: a tremendous expansion of credit. Today anyone who holds a job can buy almost anything on time—a house, a
boat, a suit, a dinner, a trip to Europe, a college education. Mortgage
credit has become so common since World War II that a majority of
American families have become homeowners. The effects of this revolution have been profound, too—we have been transformed from a
cash-paying society into a credit-using society.

These revolutionary changes, both the cause and the result of a growing economy, have been accompanied by steady inflation. A dollar worth 100 cents in 1949 was worth only 67 cents in 1969. The maxims of money management that once guided the prudent family no longer hold true: the seemingly conservative investments turn out to be risky, their return diminished by inflation; a large down payment on a house sometimes proves uneconomical; short-range life insurance can provide heavier and surer protection than long-range policies; savings accounts and annuities for a child's college education, your own retirement or your heirs' future fail to keep up with rising prices and taxes. The rules have altered so much and so fast that many Americans haven't heard about the changes yet, much less had a chance to get used to them. It's no wonder that, despite a nationwide affluence unmatched in history, most people do not feel rich and happy.

Feeling poor in paradise

Not long ago LIFE magazine reported on how difficult five American families were finding it to get by on annual incomes ranging from $19,000 to $24,000. By any objective standard these people were, if not rich, clearly well off. Yet, said LIFE, "none felt prosperous, most in fact felt poor." Adults in the five families generally shared the wonderment of the $19,000-a-year Minneapolis lawyer who was "mystified by where it all goes." Well, where did it go?

In the case of the young Minneapolis lawyer and his wife a lot of it went for week-end jaunts to sporting events plus theater-going. They did not deny themselves their favorite recreations.

Neither did a Florida architect and his wife. Proclaiming that "We're not going to wait until age 65 to enjoy life," they belonged to a tennis club and collected pottery, but did not save any of his $20,000-a-year salary.

A Manhattan couple, living with two children in a $400-a-month Fifth Avenue apartment, also did not postpone life's pleasures. To supplement his $24,000 a year as a television network executive, they used deficit financing, running $3,500 to $5,000 in debt.

A California delicatessen owner netting $20,000 a year reported family expenditures for the year of $4,400 on entertainment and vacations, $3,389 on food and $2,330 on clothes—the latter made mostly by his wife, who had 30 pairs of shoes. "We prefer the best," they said. They had savings of $1,000.

To a $24,000-a-year television executive in Arkansas, it seemed that aside from the $2,880 a year for entertainment, vacations and hired help, there was nothing much to account for the way the money

went. He and his wife and three children lived in a $35,000 house, but also had a week-end cottage and two cars.

Only one family interviewed by LIFE broke the pattern. The husband and wife belonged to two clubs and led an active social life. They had a $39,000 home, one car and sent two children to private schools. They also put nearly $3,000 a year into stocks and bonds out of the husband's $19,000 salary.

The husband had deliberately picked his employer—a Michigan auto manufacturer—because of the excellent fringe benefits that allowed him to save a good deal on health and life insurance premiums. The family's one car was leased at an advantageous rate from the company, and its tank got filled with gas bought by octane rating—no paying for octane numbers not needed. Social life, while active, was not expensive: about $830 a year. The family waited for sales to buy clothes, often saving 20 to 25 per cent. The wife and her friends babysat for each other. The husband, who had made himself a whiz at tax forms, would often figure taxes for his neighbors—especially the ones who were talented with a plumber's wrench or knew electric wiring. There was no penny pinching—as football fans, the family used $120 worth of tickets a season—just businesslike attention to getting a dollar's worth out of a dollar.

But this family also had a system, a method of control. They had looked at their lives and decided that, as the husband put it, their income should be allocated to three areas: fixed obligations, savings for the future, and savings for present discretionary pleasures. Some such system of control is necessary for anyone who wants to feel comfortable with money. It may divide income up in any of a number of different ways, and it may assign any proportion of income to any purpose. If it's your considered choice that life will be fuller and richer if you concentrate your extra money on present pleasures and defer investments until later, no one is going to argue with you. That's one life style. Just make sure it is a life style you have deliberately chosen, not just a habit you have drifted into. You will need a plan. Not a budget in the old-fashioned sense, allowing 41 cents a month for shoeshines—you're right, budgets like that don't work. Simple, logical plans do, for they tell you where your money is going and help you make sure that it goes where you really want it to.

A new view of money: cash-flow accounting
Planned control over family finance has been made essential by the twin income and credit revolutions that transformed our society. The obvious material changes have been accompanied by far-reaching

Abagail counted the bills and silver in the cookie jar, which provided the Canbys with the "extra" they used for all discretionary purposes. There was $83 in the jar. They bought the Gramophone.

changes in economic concepts. When the consumer of an earlier generation bought a house, for example, it was quite clear what had happened. He had exchanged cash that was already his for real property that then became his. Today a family usually buys a house with a 10 or 20 per cent down payment, the balance coming from a mortgage loan. After using the house for perhaps a decade—the average U.S. family lives in its first home only seven to eight years—the owner turns it in and buys another one, getting the down payment back much as he might get his deposit refunded after returning a rented floor sander. Sometimes he gets back more than he deposited, sometimes less. In any case, it looks more and more as though he were renting rather than acquiring an owned asset. There is an even closer resemblance to renting when we consider the family that never actually owns a car but makes a never-ending succession of monthly payments for the use of a series of cars. The credit revolution has resulted in so many consumer goods being de facto rented rather than owned that our new way of life has been labeled the "rental economy" by economist Peter Drucker.

A credit/rental economy makes a difference that goes deeper than semantics. It changes the way people think of their money and influences the way they manage it:

Enoch the wheelwright and his wife Abagail were debating in the spring of 1919 whether they might buy a new horsehair sofa for the parlor, a washing machine to lighten Abagail's weekly bout with the tubs and washboards, or a Gramophone and some tasteful Schumann-Heink recordings, which would not only give them pleasure of an evening but enhance their social image in the community.

Whether or not they could afford to buy the desired item was settled quickly and simply. Abagail went to the cookie jar and counted the bills and silver she had accumulated by selling eggs and cream to Mr. Osgood, the grocer. There was $83 in the jar, which provided the family with the "extra" they used for all discretionary purchases. They decided on the Gramophone, and that perhaps says something about Enoch and Abagail.

Fifty years later Enoch's grandson, Roger M. the lawyer, was sitting in the patio with his wife Marcia as they discussed, over martinis, whether the family finances would support a vacation in Mexico, or whether they should just spend the summer out at the lake this year. There was, they calculated, the fact that their black-and-white television was beginning to look like an antique, and they would simply have to trade it in on a color set this fall. Roger had learned he could get a good deal just now on a sale at Midtown Radio & TV—around $23 a month, with trade-in. Maybe they should get their set now, at

the sale price. The children, Marcia reminded him, really should have a set of encyclopedias when they started back to school in the fall; she had asked the Hardings about the set they got for their kids last year, and it was $12-something a month. Well, said Roger, they could go to Mexico "fly now, pay later," use one of his credit cards for hotels and meals, and, if necessary, by paying the 1½ per cent a month interest charge, they could let the bills ride until December, when he'd be getting his bonus. For 10 or 12 days they probably wouldn't need more than $150 or $200 cash. So they decided they would vacation in Mexico.

A different question: Can you afford it?

One of the more profound changes from Grandfather's day to Roger's is illustrated by an inconspicuous difference between these two scenes. Roger and Marcia did not count the egg money. Neither of them knew precisely, when they made their decision, how much spending money they could have scraped together to pay cash for anything. They would have guessed, if there was any reason to, that the checkbook balance was under $500. What is significant is not that they sat in the patio and decided to spend at least $1,500 more than they had in the cookie jar at the moment; it is that they didn't bother to count the money in the cookie jar.

Under Enoch's system, which required cash for nearly all consumer goods and services, there was a kind of built-in automatic control on all spending decisions. You simply counted your money. If you had enough, you could buy A or B or C, and if the cash wasn't laid aside somewhere, there was really no decision to make. It was made for you. "Do we have the money?" was a question with a simple answer; you counted it. Under the system in which Roger, like most Americans today, operates, the question is no longer "Do we have the money?" but "Can we afford it?" The latter involves a much more complex equation, and there is no built-in yes or no signal to which you can look for an answer.

There is an answer, of course, and most people get it by applying —consciously or unconsciously—the technique that professional money managers call cash-flow accounting. They try simply to keep the amount of money coming in from every source roughly equal to the amount going out for every purpose (nonessentials and savings as well as essentials). Then it is not so necessary to be concerned with how much cash is on hand before deciding "Can we afford it?" Through the use of credit they can postpone payments, if necessary, to keep inflow adjusted to outflow, rather than, as formerly, letting out-

flow be determined by the amount of inflow that has been retained.

Roger the lawyer calmly committed $1,500 more than he had in his possession—an action that would have horrified Enoch the wheelwright—because he was confident his inflow of money would provide the payments when they had to be made. This system works very well, providing the most comfortable life for the man of average means, if it is applied to all financial needs—insurance savings, major expenses like automobiles and housing, retirement, emergency funds, education—and not merely to trips to Mexico or new TVs. But it must be properly managed. Deciding how much of inflow can be diverted to each of many needs, not simply today but next year and the year after, is indeed much more difficult than counting the cash on hand.

Money and the art of living

Managing money cannot be regarded as a purely mechanical art, like repairing clocks, for it cannot be separated from the art of living. The object is to manage money in a way that will advance the fortunes (broadly understood) of the individuals to whom the money belongs, not to make the individuals conform to some system that seems to suit the requirements of money. Since there is a considerable variety among people, there are no easy formulas that can be prescribed for everyone—14 per cent of your income for this, $9 a month for that. It sounds alluringly simple to divide all the money up into neat piles that way, with simple instructions for making the figures come out even at the end of the month. The trouble with such mechanical systems for moving dollars and dimes around like wooden pegs on a board is that they have us managing, not our lives, but something with an importance of its own. It's too easy to fall into the trap of managing money for the sake of managing money.

The paradox about money is that it's nothing anyone in his right mind wants to have for itself. Money, as money, can't be put to any practical use (with some few exceptions, such as using a dime for a screwdriver). Money is merely, as the classroom definition reminds us, a medium of exchange, and only when it is exchanged for something of value—that is, spent—does it do anything for you.

One facet of the art of managing family finances rests on the ability to discriminate between the various values for which money can be exchanged. Your supply of money is finite and limited. There is not enough for everything, therefore when you use money for A, you eliminate the possibility of using it for B. The need for making choices is not eliminated by increased income. No matter how much you make, there will never be enough for everything.

The second part of money managing concerns the execution of your choices. Once you have decided how you will use your money, you want to be certain you use it most efficiently. An informed buyer gets more for his money. There are ways to increase the value purchased with every expenditure and investment—the calendar date when you buy a new car can make a difference of several hundred dollars, choosing the location of a house wisely may mean thousands, some savings accounts return more than others, the sales charges on certain types of mutual funds may outweigh any profit, even glamorous vacations come in economy packages.

How to get started

The first step, obviously, in any financial plan is to find out exactly how much money you have to work with. If you are going to use your money to best advantage, you have to know how much of it there is. Yet it's a 7-to-1 bet that you cannot set down on a piece of paper within $100 on one side or the other your annual disposable income—the money you have left after taxes, Social Security payments, union dues and those other things that are deducted from your paycheck.

After you have determined that first essential figure, disposable income, the next information you need is a breakdown on where it's going. No guesses, please, or estimates arrived at by doodling on a sheet of paper. You need hard facts. If you don't know where your money goes, you have very little chance of getting it to go where you want it to. Even in the family that feels it is keeping income and outgo in reasonable balance, this exercise can be an eye-opener and lead to greatly improved management. Get out the canceled checks for the past 12 months and reconstruct as best you can what all the money was spent on last year.

(Tip: If this is to be done *en famille*, better make a solemn promise before you begin that there will be no bloodletting over what the totals reveal. What's done is done. The object of this exercise is to improve the family's use of money in the future, and not to indulge in recriminations about what happened in the past.)

If you're a typical family, you will come out at the end with a few major categories that account for much of what you spent during the year, although you will probably also discover that quite a lot of cash just simply slipped through your fingers. These figures—your own personal picture of where the money is going—will tell you a great deal more than any dissertation about what we've been calling discretionary and nondiscretionary spending. As you study your picture, you'll see that a major portion of your so-called disposable income

Text continues on page 18

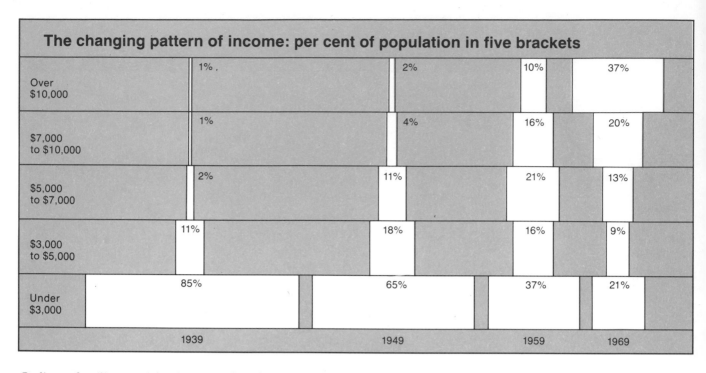

The changing pattern of income: per cent of population in five brackets

	1939	1949	1959	1969
Over $10,000	1%	2%	10%	37%
$7,000 to $10,000	1%	4%	16%	20%
$5,000 to $7,000	2%	11%	21%	13%
$3,000 to $5,000	11%	18%	16%	9%
Under $3,000	85%	65%	37%	21%

Ordinary families got richer in recent decades, reversing income patterns and making sophisticated financial planning more essential for everyone. In 1939, 85 per cent of all families made less than $3,000 a year; by 1969 only 21 per cent were at that level; 37 per cent made over $10,000.

The erosion of inflation and taxes: income required to stay even

1939
$5,000 Gross income
$50 Federal income taxes
$4,950 Income left after taxes in 1939 dollars

1949
$9,450 Gross income
$3,450 Purchasing power lost through inflation
$1,050 Federal income taxes
$4,950 Income left after taxes in 1939 dollars

1959
$12,100 Gross income
$5,350 Purchasing power lost through inflation
$1,800 Federal income taxes
$4,950 Income left after taxes in 1939 dollars

1969
$15,150 Gross income
$7,750 Purchasing power lost through inflation
$2,450 Federal income taxes
$4,950 Income left after taxes in 1939 dollars

Data: National Industrial Conference Board, Inc.

But much of modern affluence has been illusory. Inflation and taxes shrank the value of the dollar so that a family earning $5,000 in 1939 would have had to earn $15,000 in 1969 to maintain its buying power. One reason: federal income taxes for such a family jumped from $50 to $2,450.

WHERE WE ARE AND HOW WE GOT THERE

In a generation the financial profile of the typical American family was transformed, and so was its approach to the management of money, as the graphs on these and following pages show. Mass affluence on a scale never seen before in world history made most of the nation seem rich; by 1969 more than one family in three had achieved the heady status of a five-figure income. Explosive use of credit magnified the effects of affluence; by 1969 installment debt averaged almost $1,500 per household, mortgage debt more than $4,000.

This optimistic picture was clouded, however, by onrushing inflation and growing taxes. The American family had to increase its income faster and faster just to stay even; a family that tripled its income between 1939 and 1969 found itself no better off in terms of real purchasing power.

Nevertheless, savings were stacking up for the down payment on a house, a college education, a secure retirement. Americans had managed to put by nearly $6,000 per family in savings accounts and owned nearly $20,000 in life insurance—but these savings were very unevenly distributed: two fifths of American families had no savings at all, according to one study. Stock holdings grew to average over 250 shares per family.

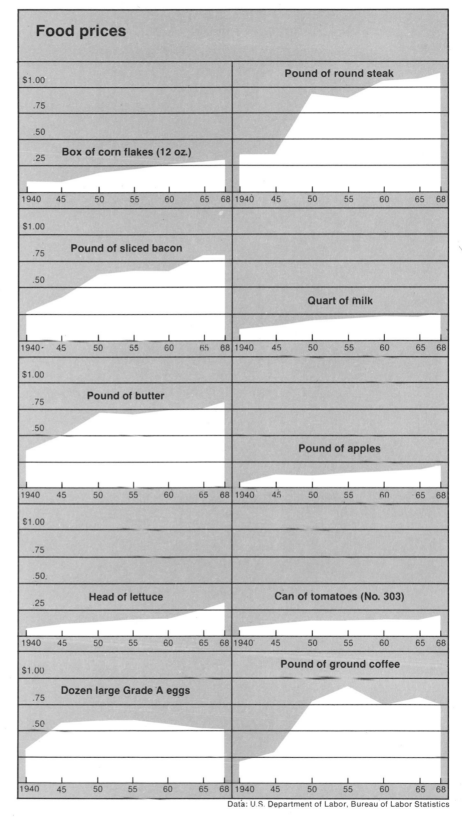

Food prices

Data: U.S. Department of Labor, Bureau of Labor Statistics

Inflation's relentless march is dramatized by the price changes of 10 common foods. Steak more than tripled in cost and most other market produce more than doubled—only eggs, thanks to recently developed chicken-management techniques, sell for less than they did in 1945.

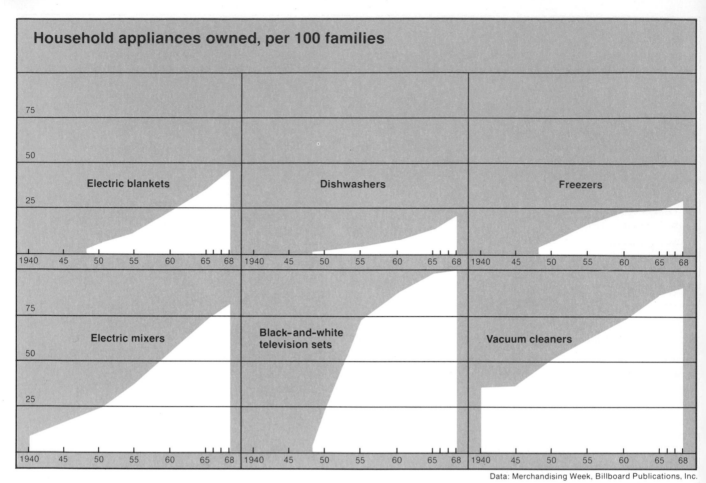

Household appliances owned, per 100 families

Electric blankets

Dishwashers

Freezers

Electric mixers

Black-and-white television sets

Vacuum cleaners

Data: Merchandising Week, Billboard Publications, Inc.

The proliferation of appliances in the American home has introduced a new element in spending, transforming from luxury to necessity such expensive gadgets as television sets, and requiring regular allotments for installment payments, maintenance and eventual replacement. Almost every household has at least one vacuum cleaner. The number of TVs grew even more rapidly—within 20 years after their introduction there were more than enough to supply one to every family in the country.

A nation of two-car families became an obvious reality in the middle 1950s, when the number of automobiles passed the number of families and continued to grow without a pause of any consequence. This testimony to affluence is made even stronger by the fact that in recent years more than 80 per cent of new cars have been factory-equipped with automatic transmissions and radios, three fourths with power steering, and nearly half with air conditioning. The majority also come equipped with installment debts—almost 70 per cent were bought on time.

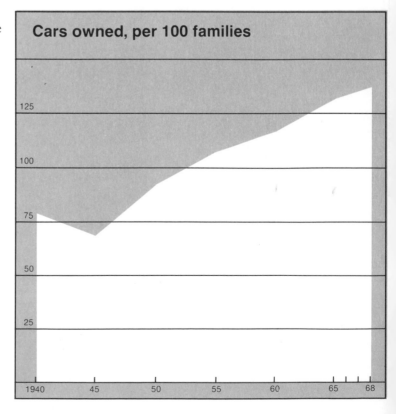

Cars owned, per 100 families

Debt

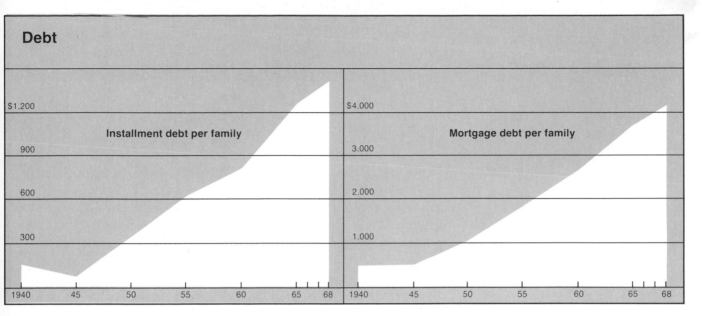

The rapid, steady growth of indebtedness—home mortgages and installment purchases—reflects not only confidence that the money will keep flowing in but also a new way of financing things families need. They are paid for while being used, out of current income. Time payments still owed increased almost 1,000 per cent to about $1,500 per family in three decades. And the ready availability of mortgages—despite periods of tight money—turned America into a nation of homeowners; the number of families renting quarters was cut in half.

Savings and investments

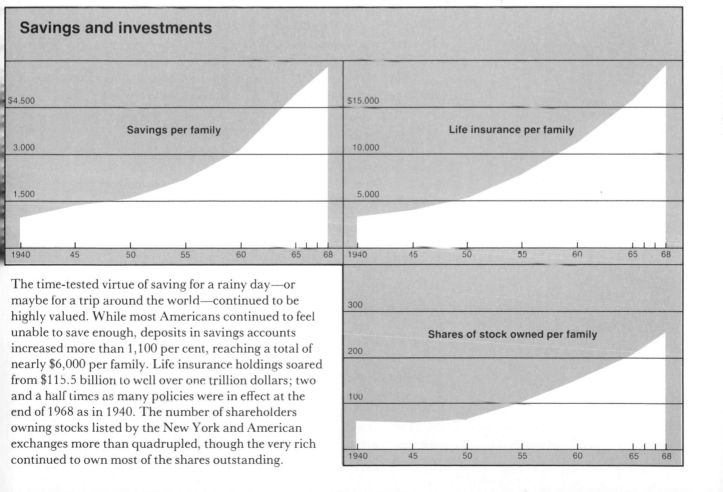

The time-tested virtue of saving for a rainy day—or maybe for a trip around the world—continued to be highly valued. While most Americans continued to feel unable to save enough, deposits in savings accounts increased more than 1,100 per cent, reaching a total of nearly $6,000 per family. Life insurance holdings soared from $115.5 billion to well over one trillion dollars; two and a half times as many policies were in effect at the end of 1968 as in 1940. The number of shareholders owning stocks listed by the New York and American exchanges more than quadrupled, though the very rich continued to own most of the shares outstanding.

is disposed of without your having much choice about it. For this year, at least, you're locked into paying a certain amount for housing. Your commuting costs are not subject to very much change. Contractual payments and installment debts are fixed obligations. Premiums for life and health insurance probably come off the top of your income with almost the inevitability of taxes. When you total up all these, you've blocked out your area of nondiscretionary spending. For the time being, you can do very little to change this.

It is in the area of discretionary spending that you can do something immediately to improve family finances—make your money go further, get more value for what you spend, identify and eliminate the waste of money spent on things you don't really need or want. How much discretion you have about any given expense will vary: it will be (a) absolute, when the item is not a necessity and you can do without it altogether if you choose—a camera, tape recorder or another drink; (b) moderate, for a need that you can postpone, such as a new refrigerator; (c) slight, when the need is variable and your only discretion concerns quantity or quality—shoes from the factory-outlet store or Bond Street? spaghetti or steak?

Among the classically defined necessities of life, food and clothing are generally discretionary in the third sense—and while substantial economies can be effected by a determined household manager, there's obviously a limit to how much cutting can be done. The major items of discretionary spending are automobiles, home improvements and repairs, household durables and entertainment and vacations. In most of these categories a good deal of trimming is possible, but the most that can usually be accomplished is best characterized as economizing. It may make the difference between being $40 short at the end of the month and showing a surplus, an accomplishment in itself but not the way to achieve financial ease.

It is the nondiscretionary expenses, the ones that seem to be immutable, that you can change the most. You can make your housing expenses go up or down radically, if you wish; it's a choice you must face whenever you move. Installment payments are fixed commitments, but the purchases that led to them are discretionary (and often of the first, most adjustable type). Insurance premiums can be altered—and should be as family needs change. Even taxes, while inevitable, are something you can do a lot about by your choice of savings and investment programs. The truth about nondiscretionary expenses is that they are discretionary, and it is precisely in this area that you can make your most important decisions. Much of the rest of this book, in fact, deals with these large areas of choice.

Calculating the true cost of home ownership

Perhaps the best example of the choices involved in financial planning is housing. It takes the biggest bite out of the average family's income. Its selection makes the biggest emotional demands. The ultimate choice has a great influence on the character of family life. And yet so important a step is often taken without a careful, step-by-step analysis of the factors that should go into a rational decision.

The basic choice seems relatively simple. Should you buy a house or rent equivalent living quarters? The notion is widely held that if you pay rent you are just pouring money down a drain. Buying a house, though you must make rent-like mortgage payments for 25 or 30 years, is thought to be wiser. That way, you at least "have something to show" for all those years of payments. The question is how much will you have to show. Let's take a clear-eyed view of the matter—the same clear look required for all economic decisions.

First of all, let's examine the implicit assumption behind that cliché about "having something to show" for those payments. The assumption is that you can buy a house with the same amount of money you would otherwise pay in rent. Real-estate advertisements frequently make this claim. They point out that you can buy a $24,000 house with monthly mortgage payments of only $151 a month. If you've been paying $150 a month in rent, this looks mighty attractive. You can own your own home—or at least make steady monthly steps toward owning it—for only a dollar more monthly.

Unfortunately, as experienced homeowners will tell you, that $151 mortgage payment is far from the only expense you will have. You must add to it the cost of fire and casualty insurance—the bank issuing your mortgage will require this protection. Then there will be real-estate taxes. These can amount to an additional $40 or so a month. So the $151 is now up in the neighborhood of $190.

And this isn't all. Another often formidable item is operating costs. As a renter you generally do not pay for heat, probably aren't charged for water and may have other utilities furnished. But heating and water bills are usually a major expense for a homeowner. Further, you may use two or three times as much electricity for lighting and operating a house as for an apartment. You'll often have to pay for trash and garbage removal. All together, your operating costs can add 20 or 40 or even 50 per cent to your basic monthly payment. Your "rent" has now grown to perhaps $250 a month.

Then there is maintenance. This may sound like a theoretical expense, but eventually you will have to replace the screens or the hot-water heater. The National Housing Conference estimates that over

the years the typical homeowner spends 2 per cent of the value of his house in annual maintenance costs. Another $40 a month, say, and the "rent" is now just under $300.

Innumerable odds and ends add still more. You'll need a lawnmower, for example, plus other tools and supplies for keeping up the grounds. Commuting costs may increase substantially when you move to an area of family homes. Often a second car seems essential.

A home as an investment

So far, so bad. But the expenses listed above are the obvious, visible costs. Another is so well hidden that most home buyers never take it into account, but it's as real as the mortgage payment.

Let's imagine twin brothers, Dan and Sam. Each has accumulated $3,500. It is Dan's theory that owning a home is a family's best investment. So he finds a $24,000 house, makes the down payment with his $3,500, arranges for a 30-year mortgage and moves in. He knows his out-of-pocket expenses will run to $300 a month, but he considers part of this as investment. His brother Sam does not buy a house. He says apartment living suits him fine. He finds a place nearby that meets his needs for $250 a month, and takes his $3,500 to a broker, where he invests it in good long-term growth stocks.

It should be obvious already that home-owning brother Dan has run into another hidden cost. By putting his $3,500 into his house rather than into stock, he loses the money the stock could earn over all the succeeding years. It is not an inconsiderable sum. If apartment-dwelling Sam put his $3,500 into stock with a compound growth rate of 9.3 per cent a year (a modest long-term average), he would have $46,437 at the end of 30 years, when Dan gets his mortgage paid off.

Let's look ahead 30 years and examine the brothers' finances then. Sam has paid out $90,000 in rent, but in his safe-deposit box are stocks worth $46,437. Dan has paid out $111,500 in down payment, mortgage payments, upkeep, taxes and insurance, but he has saved over $10,000 in income-tax deductions. Dan also has a 30-year-old house, which, if we assume normal depreciation and average inflation, is probably worth about $45,000. The brothers have come out with roughly the same nest eggs—but Dan had to spend almost $10,000 more to get his.

Some people, astute and lucky buyers, have done much better than Dan—and he made out almost as well as if he had put his money in the stock market. But an investment in a home is not always as sure-fire as is commonly thought. Even as a hedge against inflation it has limitations. You might be told, "Owning a home protects

you against the landlord's merciless rent increases." But ask anyone who has owned a house for 10 years how much his taxes have increased in that time. Ask him to get out the bills of the last 10 years to see how much more it costs him today to buy a pound of nails or a gallon of paint, to call in a plumber or someone to fix the washer or refrigerator, or to fill up the fuel tank in the basement. The landlord isn't the only one who's raising prices, and the homeowner gets his "rent" raised along with everyone else. Owning a house is an expense as much as it is an investment, and it should be viewed as both.

But that is the economic view, and in deciding how you will live, economics is only one consideration. If you're the kind that needs a lawn and a green tree or two and a basement to putter in, then a house may be a psychological necessity. Most people prefer the privacy, space and amenities of life that come with homes of their own. Such reasons for choosing a house over rented quarters are sufficient. Doing the best job of managing your money requires that you make clear-headed choices, for the right reasons.

When you're thinking of buying a house, don't look only at the mortgage payment figures. Think of the upkeep, the taxes, all the other extra costs. Then see if you really can afford it. Perhaps the best way to do this, one expert suggests, is to follow the plan outlined earlier in this chapter. Go through your canceled checks and see what your expenses really are. See where you've been spending money for things you don't really need or want, and eliminate those sums. Then add up the figures for the discretionary items that you can't really cut far—some vacation is essential, and economizing on food won't really pay for a house. Having done this, add up the nondiscretionary items that cannot be changed in the foreseeable future, but omit current housing expenses. Now, add these discretionary and nondiscretionary expenses together and subtract them from disposable income. What's left over is the figure you *can* spend for housing. Is it enough for *all* the costs of a house?

This first choice about housing—whether to buy or to rent—is only the first in a long series of decisions that require the same kind of balanced consideration. Most people decide to buy. But what kind of house? It may seem more economical to buy an older house—but then the need for increased maintenance must be taken into account. Will the fixing up be fun for you to do yourself? Or must someone be hired to do it? The location of a house is an overwhelmingly important consideration that many families neglect to think clearly about.

These decisions require some insight into the technical details of building, real estate and mortgage financing. It is fairly simple to tell

if a new house is a good value (*see New-House Check List, Chapter 7*), if a community is the kind you want your children to grow up in (*see Location Check List, Chapter 7*), if the mortgage being offered you is a good deal (*see Terms of Mortgages, Chapter 7*). When you inform yourself in advance, you can choose wisely and get the most for your money.

A plan for the modern family's money

This same sort of analysis can put money-saving logic into every financial decision. "Can we afford it?" turns into several manageable questions: "What does it cost when absolutely everything is counted in?" "Do we want it enough to spend that much for it instead of for something else?" "Is it the most economical way to get what we really want?" Asking yourself such questions—and all the subsidiary questions that stem from them—sweeps away the confusion that causes financial waste in the major areas of family finance covered in this book: housing, daily expenses, credit, automobiles, insurance, second incomes, vacations, children, taxes, savings, investments, estate planning and retirement funds.

■ Daily expenses. It is astonishing how little of a family's income can be used for this class of discretionary expenses—typically, it's no more than a third of total income. That means that choosing what you will and will not buy and getting full value for what you spend is all the more important. Some big holes in the family purse are easy to spot if you look for them. Entertainment is one; many families drift into a habit of eating out frequently, for example. But others are not so obvious—most people don't realize they are likely to spend more than they need to on home-heating bills.

■ Credit. Nearly everybody uses it. Those who use it knowingly enjoy fuller lives and save money. Simply having handy a credit card issued by a gasoline company can convert a highway breakdown from an embarrassing frustration into a minor inconvenience. Yet no credit is truly free, and the art of making credit work for you depends on knowing when to use it and which type to use: department-store charge account, credit card, appliance-store installment contract or a bank's personal loan of cash.

■ Automobiles. After a house, an automobile represents the average family's biggest single expenditure. But this outlay is one easily adjusted upward or downward by personal choice and informed buymanship. Will a smaller car serve? (Costs may be halved.) How many extras do you really need? (They can add 25 per cent or more to the cost of a new car.) Can you time your purchase of a car to the dealer's slow seasons? (Then the price will be several hundred dollars

less.) Do you know how to bargain with a salesman? (Discounts of 10 to 20 per cent are common.) Do you know where to look for genuine economies in maintenance? (Switching tires seldom pays.)

■ Insurance. Unless you get a thrill out of living dangerously, you'll want to allocate some of your income to protection against disaster. Oddly, many people buy more of some kinds of insurance—fire and personal liability, for example—than they need but skimp on automobile and life insurance. Heavy protection against suits arising from automobile accidents—damages in staggering amounts are sometimes awarded—can be had by spending only a little more than usual for premiums. The large amount of life insurance that a young family needs is not beyond the young family's resources, provided the insurance program is carefully planned with a knowledge of the many types of policies available and the wide variation of rates.

■ Extra income. The affluent society gets its affluence from the extra money brought in by someone other than the family breadwinner. Usually the other income is the wife's. More women work than ever before, even married women and women with school-age children. They find new and interesting occupations and fairly high pay. The pay shrinks sharply, however, when you figure in all the expenses of not staying home in the kitchen; deciding whether to go out to work requires carefully weighed choices. Husbands, too, are finding ways to fatten the family purse by moonlighting. Part-time clerking may be rewarding for some, but many men find greater profit by taking advantage of the tax benefits that come with small jobs pursued at home.

■ Vacations. You might think that getting the most for your vacation money is simply a matter of giving up the glamour trips in favor of two weeks at a cottage near home. Not necessarily. Today you can fly around the world on a budget—if you know about the clubs and special plans that make seemingly posh tours relatively inexpensive. The increased availability of camping facilities and camping trucks and trailers also enables average families to enjoy new experiences in new places. Even a vacation home of your own may cost less than you are spending now for routine excursions.

■ Children. Allowances often cause dissension because they are handled in the wrong way, serving as rewards or job payments instead of as a child's proper share of family income. The big problems, however, come with the college years. Many parents vaguely assume that they'll be able to pay the costs out of current income. They also seem to believe that scholarships and grants are so plentiful that the kids will almost get a free ride. The hard fact is that college costs get paid for out of family funds, unless you've got a near-genius or an all-state

If you think of savings not as Puritan self-denial but as income earmarked for future spending, you get a clearer view of its true objectives.

quarterback in the family, and trying to pay college expenses out of current income puts the screws on tight. Loan funds are available but are not always as easy to obtain as you might think. Saving tuition funds in advance paves the way, but how the saving is done can be crucial; such traditional methods as endowment insurance policies don't always work very well today.

■ Taxes. The government does not expect you to pay any more taxes than are due, but most people do. They neglect to list all the deductions they are entitled to (some are the kind you'd never think of by yourself). But more often they needlessly pay income taxes on money that isn't really their income—that is, money they never get to use themselves. If you help support a relative, put money by for children's college expenses, or set aside funds for your heirs, you should know about arrangements that help shelter those parts of your income from taxes. Even money diverted for your own retirement may qualify for a boost in the form of special tax treatment.

■ Savings and investments. If you think of savings not as Puritan self-denial but as income earmarked for future spending, you get a clearer view of its true objectives; there are several different ones and they must be provided for in different ways. Some money should be on hand in a quickly available form—as an emergency reserve, and to underwrite sizable purchases for which cash is either necessary (down payment on a house) or advisable (vacations). Savings accounts serve here; they are not all alike, however, and taking the time to seek the best one can mean extra dollars to your credit. For other purposes (retirement, college tuition) you may be willing to tie up funds for some time in order to get protection against inflation and a better return. That means you need to know something about stocks, bonds and real estate: what kinds of risk each involves, how they can be purchased intelligently, and why the choice between them depends on your income and your personality.

■ Estate and retirement. Your estate is probably bigger than you expect. It pays to add it up now, while you can do something about making sure it is neither dissipated by legal fees nor distributed to the wrong people. A will helps accomplish your wishes, but may not be sufficient. It is also wise to prepare a letter of instructions and investigate provisions for special funds that can save your heirs money. Retirement funds usually turn out to be smaller than you expect. "To be old is to be poor," reported a U.S. Senate Special Committee on Aging recently. Social Security seldom provides enough to live on, and attempts to add to that pension with part-time jobs can jeopardize the Social Security payments. For a secure, independent retirement, income from

investments is needed. If you plan the investments prudently, you can build a comfortable nest egg for later years—one that may even continue to grow after you begin to draw on it for your income.

Decisions, decisions, decisions

In every area of money management, the same two ideas appear. You must know enough about the things you buy to get your money's worth, and you must make sensible decisions about what you will and will not buy to be sure your money doesn't run out. There's never enough for everything. The people who forget that find they cannot cope with today's financial world. A curious proof of this is offered by the Tracer Company of America, a firm that tracks down missing husbands. These runaways, according to Tracer Company vice president Edward Goldfader, seldom leave home because of "the other woman." Actually, fewer than 1 per cent do. Nor are they ne'er-do-wells. Many are college graduates with jobs in the $12,000 to $18,000 class. Rather, they are men who mismatched income and outgo. "The typical adult runaway has spent years digging himself into a financial hole," Goldfader says. He has "every expectation of getting himself out"—but he's dug his hole so well that "sometimes it takes just the slightest financial reversal or setback to drive him off, like not getting the Christmas bonus he's been expecting—and spending—since about midyear." Most of the runaways have "an unrealistic approach to their own finances, the desire to give their families 'everything.' "

The formula for staying solvent was never put more succinctly than it was by Dr. Samuel Johnson, the formidable 18th Century writer, critic and compiler of dictionaries. He did it in five words: "Whatever you have, spend less." Dr. Johnson was no pinchpenny. He also said, "It is better to live rich than to die rich." If you make sure your money goes where you truly want it to go, you'll do both.

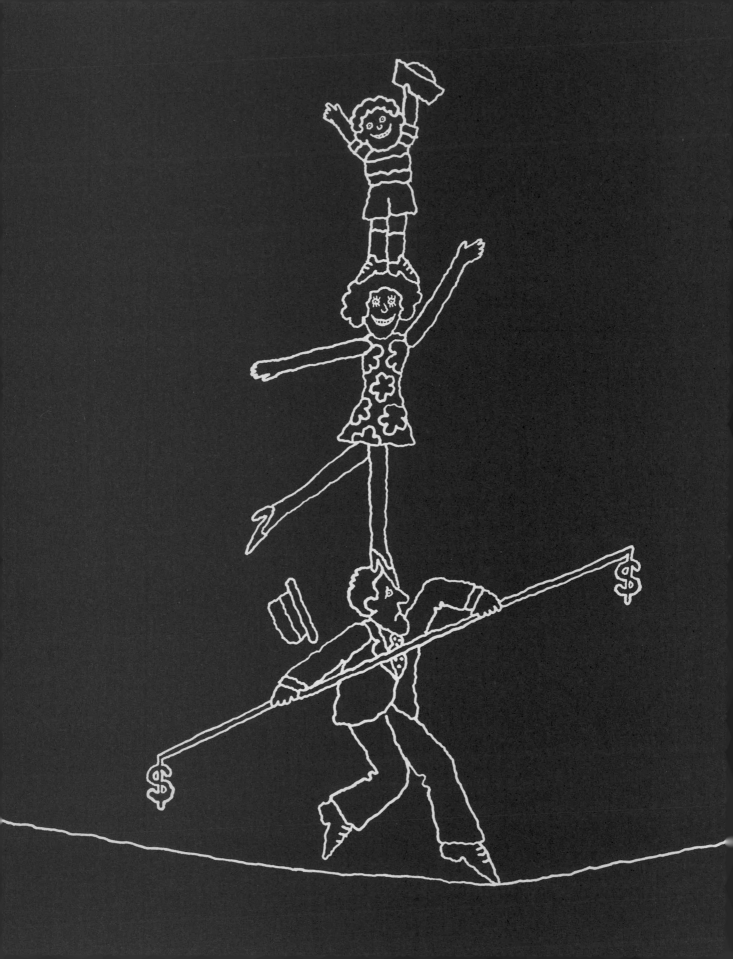

2 Credit

Making the most
of borrowed money

Buy now; pay later. That's the slogan, and that's what credit is. What you buy may be something tangible, like a washing machine; or a service, like a doctor's visit; or money itself, in the form of a loan. Whatever it is, the person who has agreed to wait to be paid will expect some sort of reward for his patience, and some guarantee that he will eventually receive his money. The reward may be nothing more than simple goodwill on the part of his customers, or it may be a finance charge. If a guarantee is demanded, it may be as abstract as your signature, or as concrete as the house you live in.

This simple idea has been aiding everyday life since Sumerian times at least. But never has it been employed in so many forms and so widely as it is today. Intelligently used, it makes possible a life fuller and richer than our grandfathers could have imagined. But to take full advantage of credit—and avoid its pitfalls—you need to recognize its many forms and understand how each works.

High finance for everyday needs

The difference credit has made—both in the way we live and how we must manage our living—can be seen if we look at two families separated by a half century of time. The Pringles lived in Iowa 50 years ago. Mr. Pringle taught mathematics in high school and supplemented his income by keeping the books for a downtown store. Besides the $25 that he still owed the doctor and the grocery bill at Halliday's and the milk bill—if you want to include every last penny—that Mrs. Pringle paid on Friday nights by putting money into one of the empties, he had no outstanding debts. They had bought almost nothing on credit. The corollary was that the Pringles also had almost nothing they could look upon as their own. The ample, Victorian house that they lived in on quiet, tree-lined Elm Street was rented—paid for monthly, in advance. Some of the furniture was theirs, but much of it belonged to the owner of the house. The previous year they had spent their savings on a new icebox, which meant that Mrs. Pringle no longer needed to visit the stores every day but could buy in greater quantity. After the icebox was bought, they earmarked their savings for a car, but they knew that it would be several years at least before they could accumulate $360, the price of a Model T Ford. Meanwhile, they walked or took the trolley. All in all, their life was as comfortable as their neighbors', but so many of their aspirations, it seemed, belonged to a future that remained tantalizingly out of reach.

Although Iowa has changed much in the past half century, the Victorian house on Elm Street still stands. Living there now is a family named Randolf. The Randolfs claim, jokingly, that the bank owns

their house. But what they mean is that they had used their credit to borrow the purchase price, and the bank holds a 15-year, $10,000 mortgage, half of which the Randolfs have already repaid. The house is better equipped and much more comfortable than it was when the Pringles lived there, and the Randolfs take great pride in it.

There are other differences, as well, in the life styles of the two families. Although Mr. Randolf's income as a foreman at a nearby factory represents approximately the same buying power as Mr. Pringle's did five decades ago, the Randolfs lead a far different life. They have two cars, so that both can drive to work—at a job anywhere in the area, not just one located near a trolley route. Mr. Randolf mows his lawn with a power mower, leaving him the free time to do all the maintenance around the house, even the big painting jobs. Mrs. Randolf has no paid help, but she actually puts in fewer hours on housework than Mrs. Pringle did with a hired girl because so many household tasks are automated—it is this fact that enables Mrs. Randolf to work three days a week as a nurse in a doctor's office. Her major appliances include a dishwasher, a range, a clothes washer, a dryer, a self-defrosting refrigerator and a newly bought sewing machine. Only a few of the Randolfs' acquisitions would have been possible if it had been necessary to pay for each with cash.

How the Randolfs make credit work for them so effectively is demonstrated by the case of the new sewing machine. Mrs. Randolf saw it at the Adelphi Department Store one day when she was downtown shopping. A $109 machine, it was on sale for $89. She had neither $89 in cash with her at the time nor that amount in her checking account. However, she did have an active account at Adelphi, so she charged the machine and had it delivered to her home the very next day. Not only did she save $20 by being able to take advantage of the sale, she was now in a position to save a worthwhile sum by making many of her own clothes. By using her charge account, she got a convenient record of her purchase—the Randolfs keep track in a rough way of expenditures, a big help in financial planning *(Chapter 3)*. And she was more certain of having attention paid to a complaint than if she had bought the machine for cash—she could if necessary withhold payment until any dissatisfaction was cleared up.

The Randolfs are as typical of their times as the Pringles were of theirs. By the mid-1960s, at a time when you could charge anything from a tube of toothpaste to an air ticket to Timbuktu, one out of two American families was making time payments on goods of one sort or another, not including home mortgages. One family out of 20 was using one third of its income to retire its debts; and one family out of

33 had somehow managed to commit 40 per cent or more of its income to deficit spending by buying on credit.

That last figure also tells another, sadder story. For all the advantages brought by the modern credit system—convenience, efficiency and a capacity to place so much of the world within immediate grasp—it also brings inevitable vexation and danger. Not all families have learned to manipulate credit without losing control, and those who have not pay a high price for their lack of skill. Those families, one out of every 33, that are in hock to creditors to the tune of 40 per cent or more of their incomes, for all their color TV sets, washer-dryer combinations and new cars, are every bit as limited in their options as the Pringles were a half century ago—perhaps more so. A slight miscalculation, illness or accident could bring disaster. One can be sure, as well, that with 40 per cent or more of a family's income devoted to paying debts, an overly large slice of that money is spent for interest, producing no concrete gain.

With the sewing machine, the Randolfs, who know how to make credit work for them rather than the other way around, called a temporary halt to their credit buying. They were still making payments on one of their cars and on a TV set as well. Earlier that year they

A nation that lives on credit
Borrowing money has become so popular in the U.S. that it almost ranks ahead of baseball as the national sport. In 1968 an astonishing three fourths of all young families were paying off an installment purchase or loan, and so were half of all householders under the age of 54. Older families—who have higher incomes and already own most home furnishings they want—borrow less, as the chart at left shows.

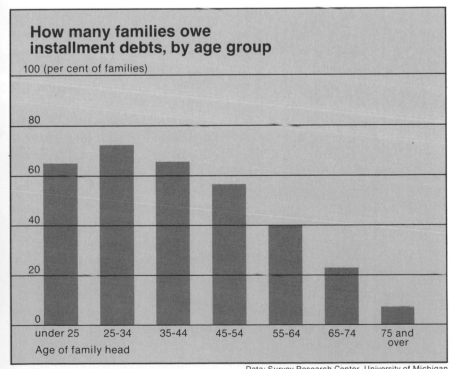

How many families owe installment debts, by age group

100 (per cent of families)

Age of family head: under 25, 25-34, 35-44, 45-54, 55-64, 65-74, 75 and over

Data: Survey Research Center, University of Michigan

What people buy on time

"Big-ticket hardware" like cars and some home appliances are too expensive for many Americans to buy with cash. Fifty-three per cent of all cars are purchased on what the English call the "never-never," as are 39 per cent of all refrigerators and 35 per cent of all cooking ranges. Less essential appliances, such as clothes dryers, are bought on credit about 30 per cent of the time.

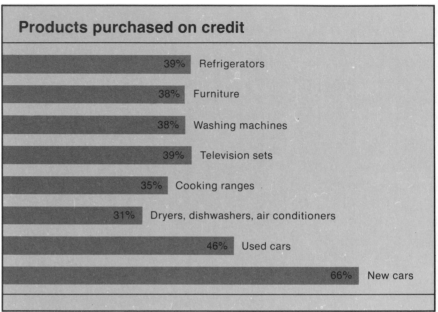

Products purchased on credit

39%	Refrigerators
38%	Furniture
38%	Washing machines
39%	Television sets
35%	Cooking ranges
31%	Dryers, dishwashers, air conditioners
46%	Used cars
66%	New cars

Data: Survey Research Center, University of Michigan

had talked of borrowing money to take their children on a camping trip through the Western parks. But they decided to put this off until the following year, since, as Mrs. Randolf pointed out, they ought to pay for the sewing machine as soon as possible to escape the 1½ per cent monthly charge levied by the store. If they let the bill run too long they would lose all the money saved by buying it on sale.

THE ANATOMY OF CREDIT

Mrs. Randolf was concerned about paying the bill promptly because she tries to spend as little as possible for credit. She knows that the cost of credit varies enormously. Figuring out exactly *how much* used to be a job for a computer because different lenders employed different bookkeeping methods and stated the charges differently. The variations still exist, but you no longer need the computer. The "Truth in Lending" law that went into effect in 1969 requires all finance charges to be stated plainly in dollars and as an "annual percentage rate" —a figure that represents the yearly interest rate on any credit for which a finance charge is levied. Look for the annual interest figure whenever you sign for credit, since it gives an accurate basis for comparing one deal with another. It may be anything from around 12 per cent to more than 40 per cent—or it can be nothing at all.

The kind of credit for which no charge is added is the old-fashioned charge account like the one the Pringles had with their gro-

cer. You get a bill at the end of the month for what you bought over the previous 30 days. There is a cost, of course, but it is hidden in the price you pay for the merchandise or service. If the merchant offers a discount for cash payment, you can calculate just how high the cost is.

This kind of credit is "open account." It is common in any number of situations. You pay for electricity and telephone service on an open account. Your doctor, your dentist and your milkman have come to look on open-account credit as the next thing to natural law.

So common is open-account credit, in fact, that we tend to discount its value in dollars and cents. But it can be calculated. Let's assume that the Adelphi Department Store is willing to allow you up to $200 in open-account credit. You can buy $200 worth of goods on the first of the month and not be billed for it until the 30th. In effect, you have the free use of $200 for 30 days. To borrow $200 for 30 days at typical small-loan-company rates, you would pay $4.50 in interest.

Some retailers, usually those selling furniture or clothing, offer 90-day open-account credit. But most open accounts must be paid in full within 30 days. After that it may stop being free credit and a finance charge may be added to the bill—often about 1½ per cent per month, or 18 per cent annually. Then it becomes the second type of credit, the kind you pay a special charge for.

Merchant credit—for a consideration

Open-account credit is usually good only for limited sums. When the Randolfs bought wall-to-wall carpeting for the downstairs rooms in their house, the bill at Adelphi came to $635, which they were unable to pay in a single lump sum. Credit, however, was still readily available to them—at a price. The store was quite willing to carry the bill over a period of time provided the Randolfs paid for the privilege.

One possibility was the revolving charge account (open-end credit). There are many variations; one type offers the customer a specified amount of credit that he can make use of so long as he makes monthly payments at a specified rate. If you have a $240 account, for example, you may be required to make payments of $20 monthly. You may charge any amount you like so long as you make regular payments and your unpaid balance does not exceed $240. For such an account you pay a charge, usually 1 to 1½ per cent a month on the unpaid balance. This amounts to 12 to 18 per cent a year.

Plastic money—the credit-card proliferation

Not since the advent of paper money has a revolution in finance had greater impact than the one that is presently replacing cash with that

Flying high on a credit card

Credit cards are nearly as good as cash in America today. A 24-year-old blonde from San Francisco lived on one for an entire month recently without spending a cent of cash. Hired by a bank to test its card, Ann Foley first spent two cashless weeks at home. She shopped for everything from a new wig to groceries, had her hair done, went to the dentist, even rented a bicycle. Then she headed south to Los Angeles in a rented car. Staying at a motel on Sunset Boulevard, she toured the city, shopped, visited Disneyland, and went to a baseball game. Back in the real world when the month was over, Ann reported that about the only thing she couldn't get with her credit card was a hot dog at the ball park.

slab of plastic known as the credit card. As a form of all-purpose charge account, it eliminates the need—and danger—of carrying large sums of currency, a dispensation particularly welcome when traveling. It also assures the unarguable itemization of expenditures that may be essential at tax time. There are several types. All provide revolving (open-end) credit—no finance charge if you pay the bill within the stated time, but stiff interest (perhaps 18 per cent annually) thereafter. Some cards also involve a regular yearly fee.

■ The single-use card. Department stores and oil companies have long issued cards to identify credit-worthy patrons. With an oil company card you can charge gas and oil at any of the service stations across the country franchised by the company whose card you hold (a great convenience if you must account to your employer or the tax man for auto expenses). Hotel and motel chains, telephone companies and car-rental agencies are other examples of businesses that issue "single-use" cards. (Some are dual-use, giving you credit at both a service-station chain and a motel chain, for example.) Their purpose, from the point of view of the company that issues them, is to encourage you to use their hotel or their gasoline rather than someone else's. From the consumer's point of view, the card provides all the advantages of an open charge account. You pay nothing to get one. Just send in your application, and if your reputation for paying your debts promptly is intact you will receive one posthaste.

■ The travel and entertainment card. Following the Second World War a new form of credit card was devised to serve travelers and businessmen; it was the "travel and entertainment card" (T&E). It provided credit not with one establishment but with many, particularly hotels and restaurants, and centralized the bookkeeping; all charges, no matter where made, are combined into one bill collected by the company that issued the card—Diners Club, Carte Blanche, American Express. A T&E card quickly became indispensable to anyone who had to conduct business outside his office. A salesman can take a client to lunch in Dubuque or Dallas, flash his card and sign the tab. He does not have to make tedious notes for his expense account, and there'll be no question later whether he did indeed spend $10.74, tax and tip included, for a lunch on July 26. Nonbusiness travelers find the cards equally valuable as a ready substitute for cash.

T&E cards are not free. You pay an annual fee of $10 to $20 for the use of the card, and your financial profile gets a thorough review before it is issued. Once you have obtained the card, however, you will find it acceptable at tens of thousands of places around the world. Chiefly, these will be airlines, hotels, restaurants, summer re-

sorts, nightclubs, and clothing and gift shops. But it can also be put to use at such unusual places as ski schools and boat marinas.

■ Bank credit cards. The phenomenal success of the credit card convinced the banks that they too ought to get into the act, and presently some 2,000 commercial banks across the country are doing so, either singly or as a cooperative venture. The major cooperative plans are the BankAmericard, the Master Charge and Uni-Card. Taking over where the single-use and T&E cards left off, though not averse to poaching on the same territory, the bank card endeavors to service all everyday credit needs. Department stores, specialty shops, beauty parlors, service stations and the like, as well as restaurants and transportation facilities, make up the banks' retail clientele. One advantage over T&E cards is that the bank cards are free (if you pay the bills in full when due). The bank cards in particular make it disarmingly easy to buy (and sell) almost anything on credit. Quiggins receives a bank credit card in the mail. Needing a pair of new tires, but being short of cash, he decides to try out the card. He locates a garage displaying a window decal that says it accepts the card, and he buys two tires for $25 each. He pays for them by offering his bank card and signing the credit slip. At the end of the business day, the garage includes the credit slip with its bank deposit. The bank credits the slip to the garage's account, just as if it were cash, except that it deducts 5 per cent of the amount, or $2.50, as its fee for handling the transaction. The bank then bills Quiggins for $50. (If Quiggins had asked, the garage might have given him a $2.50 discount for cash.)

Whether or not you actually intend to use it, a credit card or two is handy to have with you. (You're 100 miles from home with only $5 in your pocket and a tire on your car blows.) It is a comfort to know that in an emergency you probably can charge what you need. But which should you carry? Nearly every card differs from the others in some respect. What you are looking for is a card, or cards, that will cost you the least amount and that will be honored where you most often trade. Pay particular attention to the amount of the annual charge, if any, and to what charges you are subject to for late payment. Also investigate carefully the extent of your liability should someone use your card fraudulently.

Losing a credit card may be almost as serious as losing a check you have signed but not filled out. The finder could pass it off as his and run up a big bill in your name. If you lose a credit card, immediately notify the issuer both by telephone and by letter. The company will then stop payment on any subsequent charges and will issue you a new card. Some credit cards include insurance to protect you against

fraudulent use of your card, but notify the company immediately anyway (the insurance may not cover all losses). Another hazard arises from the manner that banks have chosen to launch their card plans. While platoons of salesmen are lining up retailers willing to honor the cards, the banks mail out thousands of cards to prospective customers with good credit ratings. If you should receive one of these unsolicited cards with your name on it and you do not intend to use it, destroy it. True, you cannot be held legally responsible for charges made with it by someone else, but you may have to spend considerable time and trouble establishing your case.

You might even receive one of these cards with someone else's name on it. An example of how the computerized society in which we live can go awry took place not long ago when a bank notified customers that they would soon receive a credit card unless they said they didn't want one. Somehow the computer scrambled the first and last names on 150,000 letters, and although the post office managed to intercept most of them before they were delivered, no one is sure what happened to the rest. Had actual cards been sent out, the ensuing mess might have set the "card game" back a good year or two.

Big credit for the big ticket

Charge accounts, whether they are actuated by a credit card or not, most frequently offer credit for soft goods and small appliances, items without much redeemable value. No merchant wants to repossess a cocktail gown, a tankful of gas, a dozen bath towels or a toaster. The creditor has no tangible security to guarantee payment of his loan.

"Big-ticket hardware," ranging up to and including the automobile, is another story. Not only is it expensive, but it can serve as a guarantee for repayment. The merchant who sells you a color TV on time, for example, generally offers credit in a different form. He will ask you to sign a contract in which the TV is pledged as security. Should you fail to keep up the payments, the set could be seized and resold with the proceeds going to retire the debt.

The contract you are asked to sign may have any one of a number of names—installment sales contract, chattel mortgage, bailment lease are the most common. Because the provisions of each vary from state to state and from one credit source to another, it is nearly impossible here to point out all the pitfalls that might trip you up. But be sure you read all the fine print carefully.

To see how one such installment contract might work, let's use a color TV set as an example, purchased in Arizona. Say it cost $500 and you paid $50 down and signed an installment sales contract for

the rest. If you paid off another $300, but then couldn't make any more payments, the merchant could repossess the TV set. He would then have to sell it within 90 days, usually at auction. What he gets for the secondhand set is distributed for three purposes in strict priority: to cover expenses of the repossession and sale, to pay off the remaining indebtedness and to satisfy a secondary claim, if the set had been pledged to guarantee still another debt. If there is money left over, you get it. If the proceeds of the sale exactly satisfy all demands, you come out clean. If the proceeds fail to pay everyone off, you owe the merchant the difference, even though your TV set is gone.

As with all credit, there is a price tag on installment buying. Historically, this price has been euphemistically called the "carrying charge" rather than "interest," because the term encompasses a lot more than just plain interest. It includes the cost of credit investigation, collection costs, bookkeeping expenses and insurance against fire and theft. (Under the Truth in Lending bill, these are all included in the finance charge.) Adding these auxiliary charges to the basic interest rate on the purchase price boosts the ante considerably. How much? You might pay at an annual rate of 12 to 34 per cent for credit from an auto dealer, 18 to 42 per cent on the installment purchase of a major appliance at a retail store.

Despite the steep costs of revolving and installment contract credit, some 40 per cent of such durable goods as furniture and household appliances are purchased this way, 66 per cent of new automobiles, 46 per cent of used cars. As must be abundantly clear, buying on the installment plan is one of the least economical ways known to acquire anything. A less expensive way to achieve the buyer's purpose is readily available: Pay cash for the item, borrowing the money to do it.

Cash for rent

Many people seeking a loan assume that money is money, and the important thing is to find a lender who will say "yes." In fact, there are plenty of people in the business of lending money who are all too eager to say "yes" to most of us. The important thing, if you are going to borrow, is to search out the least expensive source of money. There is a wide difference in costs, partly because of the variations in the way interest is computed.

When a banker is discussing a personal loan, he is thinking in terms of "installment interest." He may say the rate is 6 per cent, but he means 6 per cent of the whole sum, which makes a big difference. If you borrow $100 on January 1 on a one-year installment loan, you will be asked to pay back one twelfth of the loan each month, plus the

Perils of installment buying

Installment purchase contracts can be as full of booby traps as a jungle battlefield. Always read the fine print. Beware especially of these hidden mines: the "wage assignment clause," which allows the store to force your employer to deduct payments from your paycheck; the "add-on" clause, which allows a store to repossess other purchases that have already been paid for if you miss payments on the present purchase; the "acceleration clause," which makes all payments due if one is missed; and the "balloon clause," which demands a very high final payment. And of course, never sign any contract that has blanks in it that are not filled in.

$6 in interest spread over the same period. Since you pay back some of the principal each month, you actually have the use of only about half the money for the full length of time. But since you are paying $6 for the use of what averages out to about $50 over the full year, you are paying at an annual rate of close to 12 per cent on the money you actually have to use.

Banks use installment interest when they lend you money to buy a car, pay for a dishwasher or catch up on your medical bills.

There are two ways to figure such installment interest. One way costs you a little more than the other. The more expensive method is called "discount": the lender subtracts his interest immediately from the amount borrowed. If you ask for $100 and pay interest at the rate of $6 per $100, the lender will deduct the interest when he pays you the money, leaving you with $94 to spend but $100 to be repaid in 12 installments. The other method is "add-on." The $6 interest charge is added to the $100 you borrow and the resulting $106 is paid back in 12 monthly installments.

There is also such a thing as "monthly interest," in common use by some lenders. Monthly interest is paid on the "declining balance." If you borrow $100 at 2 per cent per month, the first month's interest, $2, would be paid on the full $100. If you were repaying the principal at the rate of $10 a month, the second month's interest, levied on the $90 balance, would be only $1.80, and so forth. Each month you pay interest only on the money you've actually had the use of during that month. This is a very fair system—provided the monthly rate is low enough. A rate of 2 per cent a month multiplies into 24 per cent a year. Small-loan and consumer-finance companies are the greatest exponents of monthly interest and are among the most expensive sources of borrowed money. Some credit unions also use it, at rates as low as 2/3 per cent a month (8 per cent annually), making them among the least expensive sources of borrowed money.

Since the "Truth in Lending" law went into effect, direct comparisons of loan costs are more easily made, for the rates, however computed, are now stated in terms of annual interest. Sometimes, though, the rate is not as important as the total cost: a low-rate loan for a long period of time may be more expensive in total interest than a high-rate short-term loan. Check the dollar cost of the loan.

Cost is one factor, the major one, but not the only one. There are half a dozen major sources of short-term loans, and the only way to choose between them is to understand their differences.

■ Commercial banks. Don't let the name fool you. It is a holdover from an earlier time when such banks lent money only to businessmen.

A $500 TV'S ACTUAL COST: THREE COMPARISONS OF CREDIT TERMS

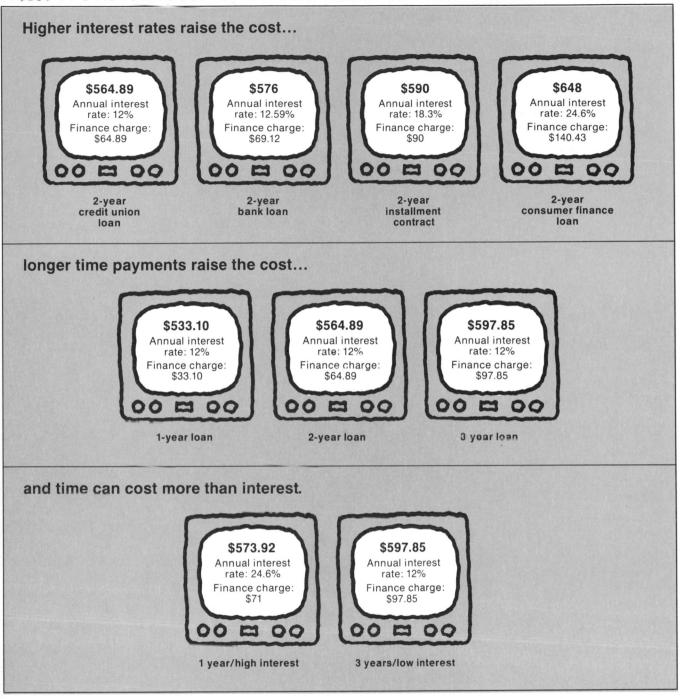

Higher interest rates raise the cost...

$564.89
Annual interest rate: 12%
Finance charge: $64.89
2-year credit union loan

$576
Annual interest rate: 12.59%
Finance charge: $69.12
2-year bank loan

$590
Annual interest rate: 18.3%
Finance charge: $90
2-year installment contract

$648
Annual interest rate: 24.6%
Finance charge: $140.43
2-year consumer finance loan

longer time payments raise the cost...

$533.10
Annual interest rate: 12%
Finance charge: $33.10
1-year loan

$564.89
Annual interest rate: 12%
Finance charge: $64.89
2-year loan

$597.85
Annual interest rate: 12%
Finance charge: $97.85
3 year loan

and time can cost more than interest.

$573.92
Annual interest rate: 24.6%
Finance charge: $71
1 year/high interest

$597.85
Annual interest rate: 12%
Finance charge: $97.85
3 years/low interest

Time makes time payments expensive

How much you pay for something bought on time depends on where and for how long you get installment credit. The top row above compares the costs of a television set financed for two years at four different interest rates. The dearest source of credit (a finance company) costs over $100 more than the cheapest (a credit union). But even a modest rate (constant in the middle row) raises the cost almost $75 if payment is stretched from one year to three. Long-term credit adds so much to cost that a three-year period at a low rate is still dearer than one year at a high rate (bottom).

They still lend money to businessmen, of course, but they also do a thriving trade in personal loans.

Loans negotiated at a commercial bank can range from a couple of hundred dollars to tide you over a Christmas bind to $3,000 to buy a car. At some banks you can keep a loan standing by, ready to use when you want it, but not piling up interest charges until you do use it. When you need money, you just write a check against part or all of that stand-by loan, which is often called check credit.

Bank loans are usually made on the installment basis; interest rates vary depending on the type of loan and, to a lesser degree, on economic conditions at the time, but are usually lower than those of other lenders. Most small loans are secured on your signature alone. When you borrow large amounts, to buy a car for example, the bank may ask for a chattel mortgage as security.

It took commercial banks a long time to decide to make personal loans, but having done so they now handle more than one third of all consumer credit. This figure would undoubtedly be greater if there weren't people around who still are uncertain of their welcome at a bank officer's desk. You needn't be one of them. If you have a job and a halfway decent credit record, your chances of obtaining a loan are excellent. Bankers estimate that they grant 9 out of 10 loan requests.

■ Consumer-finance companies. In some parts of the country these are known as personal finance companies or small-loan companies. They do a large volume of business in small cash loans—as low as $25 or $50 and as high as perhaps $1,500 in most states. The rates are high. Explore other sources before dealing with a personal finance company.

■ Credit unions. A credit union is a voluntary association of individuals with some common bond, such as employment by the same firm or membership in the same church. Members with an excess of money deposit it with the credit union and are paid interest on their savings. These funds are then used to make low-rate loans to other members. Credit unions make many auto loans. A member can usually borrow up to $2,500 on his signature alone, while some form of security is required on larger amounts. Interest charges may range from $2/3$ to 1 per cent per month (8 to 12 per cent annually).

■ Life insurance companies. Anyone with a life insurance policy that has a cash surrender value can borrow up to 95 per cent of that amount, usually at 5 per cent annual interest. This is the biggest bargain in borrowing, but it has serious drawbacks. First, the amount you can borrow may not be enough for your needs. Second, since the policy itself serves as collateral for the loan, there will be no demands for payment of anything but the interest; the temptation to let the

Seller's Name: _____   **Contract #** _____

_____

RETAIL INSTALLMENT CONTRACT AND SECURITY AGREEMENT

The undersigned (herein called Purchaser, whether one or more) purchases from _____ (seller) and grants to _____ a security interest in, subject to the terms and conditions hereof, the following described property.

QUANTITY	DESCRIPTION	AMOUNT	

Description of Trade-in:

	Sales Tax	
	Total	

Insurance Agreement

The purchase of insurance coverage is voluntary and not required for credit. _____ (Type of Ins.) insurance coverage is available at a cost of $_____ for the term of credit.

I desire insurance coverage

Signed _____ Date _____

I do not desire insurance coverage

Signed _____ Date _____

Notice to Buyer: You are entitled to a copy of the contract you sign. You have the right to pay in advance the unpaid balance of this contract and obtain a partial refund of the finance charge based on the "Actuarial Method." [Any other method of computation may be so identified, for example, "Rule of 78's," "Sum of the Digits," etc.]

PURCHASER'S NAME _____

PURCHASER'S ADDRESS _____

CITY _____ STATE _____ ZIP _____

1. CASH PRICE $_____
2. LESS: CASH DOWN PAYMENT $_____
3.   TRADE-IN _____
4.   TOTAL DOWN PAYMENT _____ $_____
5. UNPAID BALANCE OF CASH PRICE $_____
6. OTHER CHARGES:

   _____ $_____

7. AMOUNT FINANCED $_____
8. **FINANCE CHARGE** $_____
9. TOTAL OF PAYMENTS $_____
10. DEFERRED PAYMENT PRICE (1+6+8) $_____
11. **ANNUAL PERCENTAGE RATE** _____%

Purchaser hereby agrees to pay to _____ at their offices shown above the "TOTAL OF PAYMENTS" shown above in _____ monthly installments of $_____ (final payment to be $_____) the first installment being payable _____ 19____, and all subsequent installments on the same day of each consecutive month until paid in full. The finance charge applies from ____ (Date)

Signed _____

Finding the real cost of credit

Before Congress passed the "Truth-in-Lending" bill in 1968 it was often impossible for the consumer buying on time to tell how much interest he was paying. Credit costs were figured in many different ways and labeled on contracts in even more ways. Now, however, they must always be expressed in terms of a "finance charge" and an "annual percentage rate," as shown on the typical documents at left. The top one is a contract used to arrange installments on a large purchase; the other, a department store bill offering time payments. The finance charge, given on the department store bill as $8.10, is the sum of the interest, service charge and all other costs. The annual percentage rate, 18 per cent on the bill, is simply the same cost expressed in percentage terms. This percentage figure makes it easy to compare the rates charged for credit by different banks and stores.

DEPARTMENT STORE 50 MAIN STREET

ACCOUNT NUMBER
10-000-000
TYPE
OPT

Mrs. G. Customer
110 Elm Street
Springfield, Missouri

BILLING DATE
Sept 15, 69
PAYMENT DUE
94.00

Please Detach This Stub And Mail With Your Remittance
OR
Pay In Person At The Cash Office Of Any Of Our Stores
Your Next Statement Will Show Payments And Returns
Received By Us After Billing Date
IF YOU HAVE MOVED PLEASE WRITE
YOUR NEW ADDRESS HERE
IF YOU HAVE ANY QUESTION ABOUT YOUR BILL. PLEASE SPECIFY DATE, STORE AND REFERENCE NUMBER OF ITEM

AMOUNT PAID

DATE	STORE	REFERENCE NUMBER	DEPT	TRANSACTION DESCRIPTION	PURCHASES	PAYMENTS, RETURNS AND OTHER CREDITS
Aug 5	N.Y.	112	056	Drugs	11.50	

PREVIOUS BALANCE	PLUS FINANCE CHARGE	PLUS TOTAL PURCHASES	MINUS TOTAL CREDITS	YOU MAY PAY NEW BALANCE	OR MINIMUM PAYMENT DUE	PAYMENT DUE BY	YOUR ACCOUNT IS NOW IN ARREARS BY
560.00	8.10	11.50	112.00	467.60	94.00	Oct 10	

★ INCLUDES "AMOUNT IN ARREARS" IF ANY

The FINANCE CHARGE represents an ANNUAL PERCENTAGE RATE OF 18% on the previous balance up to $500.00 (subject to a minimum of 50¢) and 12% on that portion of the previous balance over $500.00. (The FINANCE CHARGE is within 7½¢ of the amount computed at the above rates). To avoid additional FINANCE CHARGE, pay the new balance within 10 days of receipt of statement. NOTICE: SEE REVERSE SIDE FOR IMPORTANT INFORMATION.

Sources of installment credit

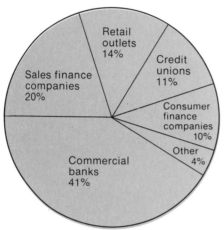

Data: Federal Reserve System

When Americans buy on time, they most often get the bank to help them. Commercial banks, which charge relatively low interest rates, provide more than 40 per cent of installment credit—some $37 billion worth in 1968. Sales finance companies, which specialize in "big-ticket" items like auto loans, account for 20 per cent of consumer credit, and retail-store charge accounts are the next most heavily used source of credit. Credit unions were collecting on more than a tenth of all installment debt; they generally offer the lowest interest, but only members are eligible for their loans. Consumer finance companies are last among the major lenders —perhaps because they are generally the most expensive.

loan run may prove irresistible. Third, the protection provided by the policy is diminished by the amount of the loan—you are giving up essential life insurance to get some cash *(Chapter 5)*.

■ Savings-account loans. If you have funds on deposit in a savings bank or a savings and loan association, you may find it advantageous to take out a "pass-book loan" with your deposit as security. Such loans also carry a low interest rate. Why not simply withdraw the savings, since the loan interest you pay the bank is always going to be more than the savings account interest the bank pays you? If you have an iron will, that is what you should do in most instances. However, most of us find it easier to repay a loan than to rebuild a savings account. There are also times when you actually save money by borrowing instead of withdrawing. Unless your account pays you interest from day of deposit to day of withdrawal, you may lose a big chunk of interest if you withdraw shortly before the end of an interest period. In such a case, a secured loan until the end of the interest period costs less than the potential loss in savings interest. At the end of the interest period, the loan is repaid with a withdrawal from the savings account. At some commercial banks you can use stocks, bonds, insurance policies, even your car as security for a loan.

■ Last resorts. Pawnbrokers have a tradition almost as ancient as lending itself. Borrowing from them is simple, quick and impersonal—and very expensive. The borrower pledges some item of value (jewelry, a camera, a musical instrument) in exchange for a loan. If he returns the sum borrowed, plus interest, within a year, the broker returns the pledged item. If not, the broker sells the item and uses the proceeds to recover his money. The disadvantages of using a pawnbroker are that his rates are high, averaging 36 per cent annually, and he will seldom lend you more than 30 per cent of the value of the item pledged. As for borrowing from friends and relatives, it's commonly done, but such loans often create friction between the parties.

EMERGENCY PROCEDURES

Credit is obtainable so readily from so many sources that it sometimes seems inexhaustible. But there's truth in the old saw about a million dollars being easier to borrow when you're rich than $10 when you're broke. Like the jet pilot who must know how to eject from his plane, each of us needs a plan for handling a financial emergency. We're talking about a head-on, 180-proof, wall-to-wall disaster, the kind of mess in which you have been borrowing money to make payments on money you borrowed earlier. Now, you can't borrow from anybody, and everything is about to come due at once.

It will never happen to you? Probably not. There are plenty of danger signals before you hit this point, and most people see them and take heed. But this kind of problem does happen. Many people go along for years performing a kind of financial brinkmanship and getting away with it. But all disaster requires is one major miscalculation. Perhaps an elderly mother has to be put in a nursing home, or a wife finds she can no longer work, or a child needs extended hospitalization. Whatever the cause, it is the breaking point. Fancy footwork just won't do any more. What now?

Aside from a dash for Brazil, there are two alternatives: bankruptcy, or the long, hard road back to solvency. First let's take a look at the less gloomy course of action.

What to the victim is personal tragedy is to creditors another business problem. They will listen to almost any plan that sounds even remotely like a solution. But if there is no such plan, creditors will feel they must take whatever steps are open to them. This can mean repossession of cars, furniture and appliances, foreclosure of mortgages, even forced bankruptcy if such a course yields some hope of recovery.

But creditors use these weapons only as a last resort. Repossessing a set of dining room furniture is a nasty piece of business, and generally an unprofitable one. The market for used furniture is notoriously bad. Mortgage foreclosure in most states is a cumbersome process, the costs of which make deep cuts in the property's value.

Out of self-interest, if for no other reason, creditors will probably assent to any feasible plan. This plan can be one the debtor develops himself, based on what he knows of his needs and capabilities. Or it can be a plan developed by a third party such as a community counseling service or debt counseling agency. Caution in seeking advice is necessary, however. There are unscrupulous debt counselors who prey on those in trouble, simply adding their fee to an already unmanageable burden. By far the safest arrangement is one made with a community-supported, nonprofit counseling agency.

All the plans for bailing out of debt are based on some method of gaining time. There is all the difference in the world between $3,000 due a week from Friday and $3,000 to be paid back over the next three years. Here are a few of the options:

■ Consolidation loan. This arrangement involves a new loan from one lender, such as a bank, a loan that is big enough to pay off other debts. One large debt is often preferable to several small ones, even when they total the same amount. Monthly payments are smaller since the repayment period has been extended, and the interest rate on a single bank loan may well be less than those on the overdue

A man's credit rating doesn't end until he dies. If he moves from one city to another, it will follow him as soon as he makes a credit application in the new area.

debts. But it is essential to be certain that the terms of any consolidation loan are really an improvement—to wit, that the whole is not greater than the sum of its parts.

■ Debt pooling. To apply this method, a debt counselor examines the family living pattern, decides how much income is needed to keep the family functioning, and puts the rest to work paying off the debts. This means making a small payment to each creditor each month until all debts have been repaid. Most creditors will go along with such a plan only if they feel certain that the debtor will stick to it. Usually, this means that the plan must be created and administered by someone experienced in debt counseling.

■ "Chapter XIII." A third method of debt reorganization is actually a form of bankruptcy known as "Chapter XIII," because it is based on Chapter XIII of the Federal Bankruptcy Law. This is a kind of debt-pooling operation run by a judge of one of the federal district courts that handle bankruptcies. Under "Chapter XIII," debtor, creditors and a referee, supervised by the judge, get together to work out a way for the debtor to settle up on an installment basis.

■ Voluntary bankruptcy. When all else fails, there is still the voluntary petition for straight bankruptcy. To do this, a list of all assets and liabilities is needed, plus $50 for a filing fee. Ordinarily, the rest is routine. Except for clothing, tools and some household goods, all assets are liquidated and the proceeds distributed among the creditors. Once the debtor has been discharged by the court, the slate is clean— except for the bankruptcy record that will dog his footsteps for years.

HOW YOUR CREDIT IS RATED

A far more pleasant companion to take through life's commercial thickets is a "good credit rating." When you apply for a charge account, say, you force someone to judge the extent of your ability and resolve to repay the debt. He has never met you and probably never will. And anyway he'd rather have an objective than a personal measure of your fiscal responsibility. Today he uses methods so thorough that by the time your application is granted (or denied), the grantor will know more about you than you can imagine.

Credit applications ask a lot of questions, but perhaps not the ones you would expect. They don't ask, for instance, whether you pay your bills on time or if you have a lot of money. Instead, they want to know where you work and live, how long you have been there, where you bank and where you have other credit accounts. Your answers will provide guideposts necessary for an investigator to find out what else he wants to know.

Sometimes whoever plans to extend credit will conduct this investigation himself. Usually, however, he will use a credit bureau, an agency that specializes in such information. A credit bureau may be either a profit-making business, run by a proprietor, or a mutual organization supported by a group of merchants. All serve the same purposes: to find out as much as possible about those who request credit, to keep such information on file, to circulate it among clients and to exchange it with other credit bureaus.

A man's record begins the first time he makes a formal request for credit. It won't end until he dies. In between, it will record each new request for credit and keep track of his repayment pattern. But that's not all. It keeps a beady eye on his employment record, and estimates his earnings. It tries to estimate the size and number of his bank accounts. It checks out his references. Less expected are some other activities of the credit bureau. It clips newspapers, it combs police blotters, and it keeps an eye on courthouse records. If a divorce comes to court, the fact will be noted. So will the fact that he's been involved in a property transfer. And when anybody gets picked up by the police as drunk and disorderly, his credit record shows it. In short, a credit bureau collects any information that may bear on willingness or ability to pay debts.

A person's credit record may consist of anything from a file folder to a series of blips on a computer tape. But it's there, ready for perusal by those who have a legitimate interest. Most of these are retail merchants, but banks, mortgage lenders and even prospective employers have been known to patronize credit bureaus. If a man moves from one city to another, his record will follow him as soon as he makes a credit application in the new area.

Ideally, a bureau is supposed to report pertinent facts and let the man on the other end of the line make his own decision about an applicant's responsibility. Sometimes, however, a bureau will report that a man is either a good or a bad risk, leaving the prospective creditor to make his own decision only if the case is marginal.

How to keep your record clean
One of the pitfalls of this system is that credit bureaus make mistakes. Consider the true case of Leon B. Sanders, a television news editor living in Shreveport, Louisiana, who gave the following testimony in 1968 to a Senate subcommittee investigating credit bureaus: In 1964, Sanders had returned to the manufacturer a new car that he claimed, and the company agreed, was a "lemon." However, the transaction was reported to the local credit bureau as a repossession, as if

he had failed to keep up the payments, and it was so recorded in Sanders' file. Unbeknownst to him, this blot remained on his record for nearly a year and, according to Sanders, cost him a newly acquired job. When he eventually did learn of it, in the course of making another credit application, he contacted the automobile manufacturer, and after a lengthy exchange of letters the error was corrected. But meanwhile Sanders had lost a good job and had been denied a mortgage on a house he wanted to buy.

You can usually tell if a credit bureau has made a mistake in your case if you have trouble getting credit although you know your record is clear. Whoever refuses credit will normally tell where he got his information. You should then contact that particular credit bureau and ask to see your record. Most bureaus will cooperate, although they may ask you to sign a waiver agreeing not to sue them for what

What the credit bureau knows about you

You may never know when it is happening but you can be fairly sure that a great number of intimate details about your life will be searched out, recorded and reported by a local credit bureau before you are likely to be given any kind of credit, whether it's a personal loan from a bank, a charge account at a department store or a purchase of a refrigerator or automobile on time. Among the facts the credit investigator has to get about you are:

YOUR IDENTITY
How long you have been in the files, how long you have lived at your present address, the kind of neighborhood you live in, the number of dependents you have, whether or not you are considered "permanent," your age, your race, your parentage.

YOUR HISTORY
How often you have moved, the credit ratings you have left behind you, the reputation of the place where you work.

YOUR CHARACTER
What others—including your employer—think of you and your morals, how given you are to overbuying, how steady you are in your work, whether or not you indulge in liquor or narcotics.

YOUR RESOURCES
The amount of your income and its regularity, what your prospects are, the amount of your wife's income, your sources of income, your estimated worth, what your banker thinks of your financial state, and your financial "involvements."

they have on file about you, accurate or inaccurate. They may also charge a small fee—it shouldn't be more than $5. If you find any errors —a frequent one is getting two people with the same name mixed up —you will be able to point them out to the bureau, and normally the record can be set straight within a matter of days.

A few late bills won't make any blot on your credit escutcheon. However, if you are chronically late, this information will find its way into your file and may influence a prospective creditor to deny your application. If you do not pay a bill for a valid reason—a controversy over merchandise, for instance—it may be a good idea to find out the name of the credit bureau involved and write explaining your side of the case. It may well be that the only entry the bureau has—as in the case of Leon Sanders—is the routine report of nonpayment. And finally, if for any reason you suffer a financial reversal—if you can't pay your bills temporarily because of sickness, say, or some other sudden unforeseen cause—go to your creditors and explain the situation. They will often cooperate and delay reporting you delinquent. It's nonpayment of bills accompanied by an ominous silence that makes your creditors truly uneasy.

Credit is based on trust, and trust requires communication. The best communication of all is to pay your bills promptly—that act speaks louder than any words. But in an emergency, don't remain silent; put your mouth where your money was.

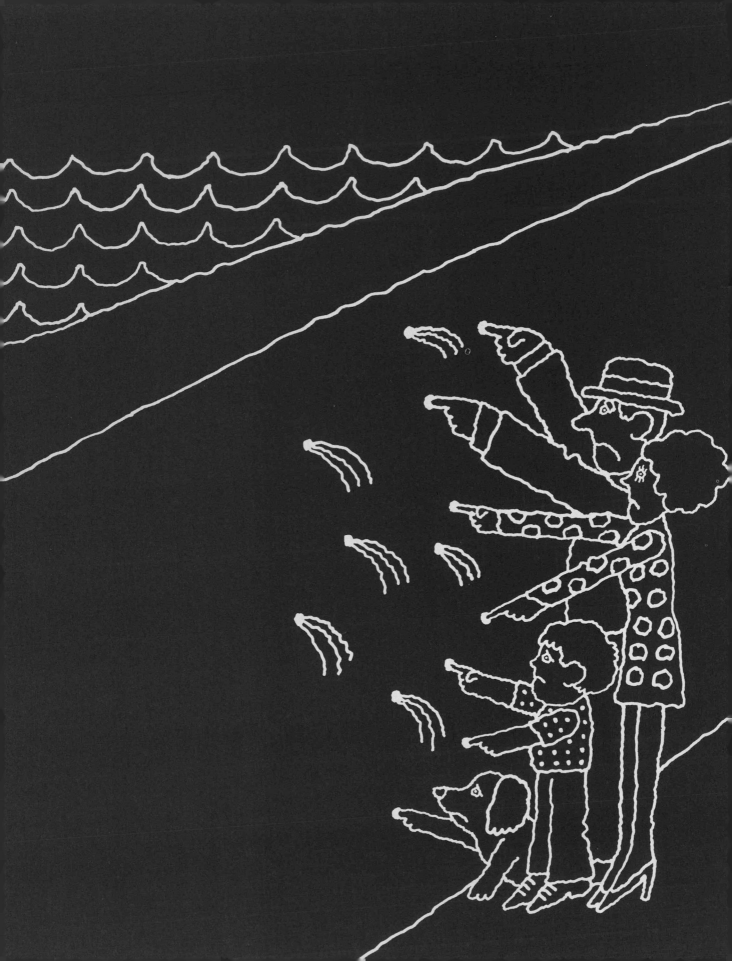

3
Daily expenses

Plugging the leaks
in the
family purse

The most formidable of family finances to manage may well be day-to-day household outlays and family spending. It is here that old-fashioned budgets break down in the effort to keep track of dimes and dollars divided among 15 or 20 accounts, each representing a spending category. The failure is almost always due to some impossibly complicated system that tries to make accounts balance down to the nickel within arbitrary limits for each category, and makes no allowance for the fact that the affairs of man (and woman) seldom proceed with that kind of machinelike precision.

A story told by a family finance counselor illustrates the problem. A young husband and wife were not in real financial difficulty, but they were barely squeaking by from month to month, not much more than making ends meet and feeling harassed and uncomfortable about it. "We've just got to get things under control," they kept telling each other—and finally they got around to it.

"They did their homework well," the counselor related. "Went to the library and got some books on budgeting, made up a detailed list of expense categories that covered everything down to broken shoe-laces, and devised a method of making all this work that appealed to them as scientific and foolproof. For each category there was an envelope, and they had a file box to keep all the envelopes in alphabetical order. Each week they would cash a check for the amount to be distributed among all the envelopes, and then during the week they'd simply spend the cash out of the envelopes as needed.

"Then they saw that it wasn't necessary to put one fourth of the month's rent into the "Rent" envelope in cash every week; they simply wrote a fake check for that amount—subtracting it from the stub balance in their checkbook—and put the check in the envelope. That meant having to replace it the next week with another check representing two weeks' rent—but they got around that by just crossing out the old amount, writing in the new amount, and making the appropriate adjustment to the stub in the checkbook.

"There was a small problem with the envelopes that really had cash in them. They'd go to the 'Laundry and Dry Cleaning' envelope for $1.75 to pay a bill, and find nothing but a $5 bill there. That required making change out of other envelopes, which wasn't always possible—but that could be solved by leaving a slip of paper in the 'Grocery' envelope reading, 'I.O.U. $1.75—Laundry.'

"With remarkable fortitude, they kept this up for more than two months. One evening, after spending more than an hour trying to get all the envelopes to settle up their I.O.U.s with other envelopes, and trying without much success to determine how much they actually

What it costs to live where

Country folk count on living for less than their city cousins, but the larger cities are not invariably the more expensive. New York is the costliest, requiring some $1,600 more per year to support an average family of four than Houston. But Cedar Rapids, Iowa, is just as expensive as Los Angeles, and Detroit and Pittsburgh cost less than the national average.

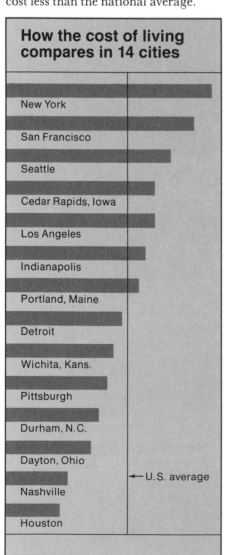

How the cost of living compares in 14 cities

New York
San Francisco
Seattle
Cedar Rapids, Iowa
Los Angeles
Indianapolis
Portland, Maine
Detroit
Wichita, Kans.
Pittsburgh
Durham, N.C.
Dayton, Ohio
← U.S. average
Nashville
Houston

Data: U.S. Department of Labor, Bureau of Labor Statistics

had in their checking account and how much the altered and re-altered checks in the envelopes came to, they decided they'd had it. Charlie grabbed the file box and threw the contents into the air, and for the next 10 minutes or so they happily tore envelopes and fake checks into shreds and threw them in the air. Charlie scooped some change up off the floor, went out and bought a bottle of wine, and they had a wake for their late departed budget.''

Not many people try a system as absurdly complex as this one. But many do attempt budgets that are similar in principle—with similarly discouraging results. It is futile to view the management of the family pocketbook as a mathematical equation that can be precisely balanced. Mathematical symbols are abstractions; peas and hamburgers, underwear and auto tires aren't.

What does work is not the old-fashioned scheme of precise budgets, but a plan for spending—a system for seeing that money is spent the way you want it to be spent, not aimlessly or in such helter-skelter fashion that no one really knows where it's going. You still need careful control, and categories to which income can be allotted for specific purposes, but the categories must be more general than they are in traditional budgets so that you have elbow room. The system must be flexible enough so that it is a servant, not a master.

The need for such a flexible control in today's economy was underlined at a conference of bankers. One, Robert C. Dembergh, president of a Reading, Pennsylvania, bank, reminded his audience that the lack of prudent fiscal management caused distress in all groups in American society. "Let's remember that the overborrowed-family syndrome is not reserved exclusively to those in lower-income levels. We all know of families living quite comfortably, and even able to save something, on incomes at relatively low levels—while others with incomes of $20,000 and more can't quite make ends meet, even when sickness or high education costs aren't plaguing them. You all know the answer as bankers. It's a case of regular saving and planned spending on one hand, versus fumble and bumble on the other.''

Avoiding the fumble and bumble requires self-discipline, not just occasionally but day after day as a regular habit. Two very hard-nosed approaches to spending are essential:

■ You have to care about what your dollars are buying—care enough to really work at it—or you'll find you've been cajoled into buying a gross of Ben Franklin's penny whistles. Contemporary technology and mass production techniques have confronted the consumer with such an avalanche of new products and new materials that informed buying decisions demand educated buymanship. That means time

and effort spent learning to gauge value, recognize real bargains, understand merchandising techniques so that you can tell what to buy, when to buy and where to buy.

■ You must also care deeply whether your dollars are spent on things that mean genuine satisfaction to your family. Since no one ever has enough money to buy everything, each spending decision involves the hard choice between what you may buy now and what you must put off buying until later.

Along with the need for self-discipline, another often-overlooked fact of economic life must be recognized: A system of planned spending will not make the difference between being rich and being poor. It may make the difference between feeling rich and feeling poor. It enables a family to get along comfortably, to avoid the misery of always living on next week's paycheck, no matter what the income. But it cannot make available large amounts of extra money, simply because prudent management of household costs cannot save much money. There isn't much money that you can work with.

How much is manageable?

You'll probably be surprised, when you analyze it, to see how little of the family income is subject to effective day-to-day control. On the one hand, this simplifies your job as day-to-day comptroller, once you understand how family income divides up into (a) manageable cash flow, and (b) relatively unmanageable committed funds. On the other hand, it requires more professionalism of the family comptroller if he is to achieve anything at all this way.

Let's take as an example the Hardin family—they are fictional but as representative of their income level as statistics can make them. The Hardins are about 35 and live with their two children in a $27,000 suburban home. The family income—he's an on-the-way-up personnel manager—is $14,000. Nominally, that makes $1,167 a month for them to manage.

But first of all, there's withholding at the source for federal income tax and Social Security—$150 and $31 a month respectively —which reduces the monthly check to $986. Withholding for state income tax takes another $17 a month. Take-home pay: $969.

Next there's the cost of keeping a roof over the Hardins' head. Most of that cost is just as "unspendable" as what's withheld from the paycheck. The mortgage payment, real-estate taxes and the home-owners' insurance policy add $234 a month. Heating bills and utilities average $57 a month. Repair and maintenance of the kind that won't take no for an answer come to about $180 a year, or another $15 per

Master control plan

Committed expenses	Jan	Feb	Mar	Apr	May	June	July	Aug	Sept	Oct	Nov	Dec	Totals
Taxes	$198	$198	$198	$198	$198	$198	$198	$198	$198	$198	$198	$198	$2,376
Housing	234	234	234	234	234	234	234	234	234	234	234	234	2,808
*House maintenance	15	15	15	15	15	15	15	15	15	15	15	15	180
Spent	0	0	47	17	0								
Utilities	57	57	57	57	57	57	57	57	57	57	57	57	684
Life insurance	29	29	29	29	29	29	29	29	29	29	29	29	348
*Automotive	129	129	129	129	129	129	129	129	129	129	129	129	1,548
Spent	105	137	116	156	120								
*Medical	41	41	41	41	41	41	41	41	41	41	41	41	492
Spent	52	17	98	17	17								
Manageable expenses													
Food	165	165	165	165	165	165	165	165	165	165	165	165	1,980
Spent	178	195	150	155	147								
Personal expenses	75	75	75	75	75	75	75	75	75	75	75	75	900
Spent	65	53	150	70	66								
Clothing	65	65	65	65	65	65	65	65	65	65	65	65	780
Spent	85	57	50	45	60								
Gifts, contributions	25	25	25	25	25	25	25	25	25	25	25	25	300
Spent	25	25	20	25	20								
*Appliances	15	15	15	15	15	15	15	15	15	15	15	15	180
Spent	0	0	27	0	35								
*Furnishings	25	25	25	25	25	25	25	25	25	25	25	25	300
Spent	125	0	0	0	0								
Entertainment	25	25	25	25	25	25	25	25	25	25	25	25	300
Spent	20	22	30	28	20								
Building and grounds	10	10	10	10	10	10	10	10	10	10	10	10	120
Spent	0	0	25	25	10								
Savings	60	60	60	60	60	60	60	60	60	60	60	60	720
Saved	45	55	80	65	60								

Grand total $14,016

* The law of averages makes expenditures for such things as medical bills, auto repairs, furnishings and new appliances inevitable, but they do not occur with predictable regularity.

The Hardins use a special savings account for these funds, so they will be prepared when the day of reckoning comes. If it fails to come on schedule, they'll take an extra vacation.

month (that's a bare minimum; the Hardins spend quite a bit more on the house every year). Added up, the housing costs over which this family has virtually no control come to roughly $306 a month. Income whose spending they can control is now down to $663.

The $20,000 worth of life insurance acquired over the past few years (even with his group insurance in the company, Hardin is underinsured) averages $29 a month for premiums, reducing the spendable income of $663 to $634.

The Hardins are a little untypical in being a one-car family, driving a $3,600 car. It is traded in every three years and the new one is financed for 36 months, so that there is a never-ending $78 a month as a kind of car-rent payment. Auto insurance adds $20; gas, oil, and repairs and maintenance, another $31. So the family auto takes $129 a month out of income just about as inexorably as the tax collector gets his. What's left of the Hardins' income is now down to $505.

Medical and dental expenses can hardly be called manageable. Nor are they generally predictable. But according to the government's Bureau of Labor Statistics, they average $497 a year when you count group health-insurance premiums. That's another $41 a month.

We can stop here, though it's obviously only a partial list of the family's committed monthly expenses. So far we have accounted for 60 per cent of a nominal $14,000 a year. That leaves the Hardins $464 a month or about $107 a week for the manageable family purse, to cover food, clothes, furniture, appliances, household operation, transportation other than by car, school expenses, personal care, entertainment, contributions, gifts, vacations, savings and investments

One family's money management

The trick of planned spending is to establish categories small enough to be watched, yet large enough not to make everyone a full-time bookkeeper. This example of such a master control plan shows how the Hardins manage with an income of $14,000 a year. Committed expenses are largest and offer the greatest room for economies—but only in the long term; they are not subject to month to-month control, hence they are not fretted over month to month. The manageable expenses amount to only 40 per cent of gross income, but they are easily adjusted upward or downward and are watched carefully. The Hardins plan savings, too (not as much as they would like), plus amounts for automotive, appliance and furnishing replacements.

—not to mention the indispensable and insatiable "miscellaneous."

If you'll narrow your own family income down this way, to what is actually available for day-to-day spending, you are likely to find your circumstances not too different. As a national average, reports the National Industrial Conference Board, the consumer has available to him for uncommitted spending 34.7 cents out of each dollar of income. The job of managing income and outgo becomes easier once you've zeroed in on what's actually available for jiggling and juggling; it's a small enough part of the family income to be watched closely and apportioned wisely. The exercise should, at the very least, impress you with how much territory your discretionary dollars have to cover and how necessary it is to make choices, and motivate you to spend this family-purse money to get the most possible mileage out of it.

It also makes clear why you can expect relatively little success in reaching major goals if your management efforts are limited to this family-pocketbook area. For major results you have to make careful, long-range decisions in the area of major expenditures and committed funds. Much of this book is devoted to such decisions. What you can expect from good management of the family-purse money, the subject of this chapter, is better day-to-day living and avoidance of those end-of-the-month pinches.

Some planning principles

But how do you go about it? Most students of the subject would agree that six principles underlie any system for effective management of the family pocketbook:

■ Plan your spending. This simply means organizing your thinking about what your needs are, day to day and year to year. It introduces cohesion and order into making purchases—as opposed to the "spend till there isn't anything left" method of hand-to-mouth living. It will cut down on impulse buying—one of the great wasters of the family dollar. But don't just think about your plan—write it down.

■ Know what you're buying. The informed consumer gets more for each dollar spent by not wasting money on things that don't last, won't work, break down or wear out too soon, or simply don't give full measure. This means spending time acquiring product knowledge, learning the art of reading labels (whether on canned peaches or motor oil) and knowing how to distinguish quality from the cheap and shoddy. It also means knowing when it pays to buy quality and when it doesn't. The past few years' increasing interest in the needs of the consumer has resulted in expanded sources of information; suggestions about where to find it are given at the end of this chapter.

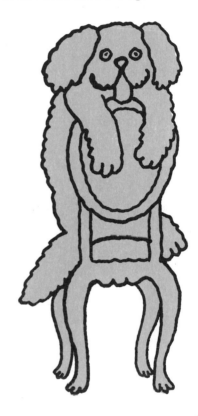

■ Know where and when to buy at the best price. There is often wide variation in price, on a given item or its equivalent, between one retailer and another, from one season to another, and at bona fide, reduced-price sales. You can determine that one store generally has good prices on meat, another on produce; one is especially economical on housewares, another on children's clothes. In sections that follow you'll find suggestions on how to be an effective store-to-store comparison shopper, how to recognize and avoid the phony markdown and the fictitious discount, how to plan buying around the traditional seasonal sales of various items.

■ Know merchandising practices. You can learn a lot by becoming a sophisticated student of advertisements and displays. Reading the ads is one of the best ways to keep informed about the new and useful products that are constantly being developed. You'll find much straightforward, practical information if you read all the copy, particularly the stuff in small print that gives the factual details. But you also have to learn to read a bit between the lines: What's new with one advertiser may be old-hat among his competitors.

■ Know what protection you have. Study those guarantees and service contracts. Consumer losses from merchandise that breaks down —especially among the costly "big-ticket" items—run into millions of dollars every year. Guarantees and warranties are almost always limited in some way, as you'll discover when you read the fine print. Knowing just what you are truly entitled to can help you get your money's worth when a purchase seems unsatisfactory.

■ Analyze your life style. Effective management of family finances must proceed from an understanding of the life style into which a family properly fits. Money spent to build an unreal image of what the family is—or is trying to be—is money wasted. One family moving into a new home felt that at last they could afford to decorate in good style. With the help of a decorator and the support of savings (which dwindled alarmingly), they achieved a French provincial interior that looked just like the illustrations in a magazine. Unfortunately for the chic decor, this family was active. Sam was the kind of guy who was always using some corner of the house to overhaul his fishing tackle. Nancy was the kind of woman who couldn't help leaving a trail of cookbooks, magazines and mail behind her as she progressed through the day. The youngest child collected stray cats; her older brother built model airplanes (usually on the living-room floor); the eldest invited half her high-school class for Coke every afternoon. There was also a dog. The battle to keep the picture-book interior looking like a picture irritated parents and children. After a year and a half, when

You may find a formula that tells you $37.50 a week is right, but if it means feeding your folks on tasty dishes of giblets or salads of dandelion greens . . . well, in some homes there would soon be a movement afoot to lynch the cook.

they'd almost come to hate the place, they were able to admit they had made a major mistake—and one that was so expensive there was little they could do to retrieve it. They had constructed an unreal image of the kind of family they were and the kind of habitat they needed for comfortable living.

The same rules about life styles apply to money you don't spend. Let's say you decide that economy is going to be the new order of things. Your analysis shows that you're spending an extraordinary amount on food, so that comes in for heavy cutting. This could be a mistake. If among life's major pleasures in your family are good food, friends at your table and good talk over a glass of brandy, forget the food bill. Better find another area of expense for heavy cutting—something lower on the scale of your pleasures and satisfactions. Tailor your spending to the life style that fits your family most comfortably, and watch out for false-image spending—or saving.

Each of these six general principles can be applied to any kind of household expenditure, though not always to the same degree. A guarantee is a lot more important on a refrigerator than on a box of cake mix. It pays to study clothing labels for the clear statement of fiber content that indicates washing characteristics, but you won't learn much by reading the chemical analysis printed on a box of detergent. Sale prices are rare at the movies, but you know for sure that sheets will be cheaper in January. Still, to get the most from a scheme of planned spending, all these points must be kept in mind for all expenses. In the sections that follow they are applied to eight major areas of day-to-day expenditures: food, clothing, home furnishings, appliances, maintenance of house and grounds, entertainment, gifts and contributions, and personal expenses.

These eight categories cannot cover every nickel in a family budget, but they include the most flexible expenses, the ones offering the biggest opportunities for effective planning and control. In each category you can buy more value with the dollars you spend, avoid unnecessary or wasteful expenditures, and increase buying efficiency through planned spending.

FOOD: NECESSITY AND LUXURY

Despite all the surveys showing what percentage of the family income is spent on food, there are few useful guidelines to what your family —or any particular family—should spend. You may find a formula that tells you $37.50 a week is just about right for the size of your family and your income. But if feeding your folks on that amount means concocting tasty dishes of giblets or converting dandelion greens into

salad . . . well, in some homes there would soon be a movement afoot to lynch the cook. What some families will tolerate in culinary economizing, others won't.

You have to make your own decisions on how far you want to go in the food department, but there is no denying that a penny here and a nickel there add up. To the extent that a housewife has the temperament for it and the family a tolerance for it, economy-minded grocery shopping and cooking is a useful budget-stretcher.

One hint on where to begin an attack on grocery bills comes from a survey of American shopping habits made by the National Industrial Conference Board. It revealed that 11 per cent of every dollar Americans spent for food and beverages went for sweets—candy, cookies, pies and cakes, gum—and soft drinks. Nutritionists generally frown on a heavy intake of sweets and it is a habit that can often be changed simply by making sweets less available.

Americans also spend a big part of their food allowances on "convenience foods"—those that are sold already prepared or partly prepared—and these are widely considered an expensive luxury, to be avoided if possible. Not so, according to a marketing research report of the Department of Agriculture. It says that of each $100 spent for food in grocery stores, $12.55 was spent for farm products packaged as convenience foods. But it also points out, "An equivalent quantity of fresh or home-prepared items would have cost $12.82—a difference of 27 cents." So don't let your conscience bother you if you depend on convenience foods as timesavers—except for fancied-up varieties, they are not only easier, they are better buys.

Food experts offer these painless ways to cut grocery bills:
■ Always make a list of what you're going to buy before you go to the store. Otherwise you will choose foods that suddenly appeal to you. Merchandisers have made many a scientific study of ways to entice you into loading up your cart with expensive impulse items.
■ Prepare shopping lists from a week of menus. Plan these menus so you can make good use of leftovers. That way you can cut down by 10 to 20 per cent on wasted money that goes out via the garbage can. But keep your planning—and your shopping list—flexible enough to let you take advantage of the food bargains that almost always turn up when you're touring the supermarket.
■ Watch for the lists of seasonal good buys supplied by the Department of Agriculture and reported by newspapers and radio stations. They can be real money-savers. You may spend half again as much for apples in July as you would in November, or on fresh tomatoes in April as you would in September.

Big supply, low price

Certain fresh fruits and vegetables flood into food markets at specific times each year, and when they do, you can be sure that their prices will drop. The month-by-month abundance of those that have 25 per cent or more of their annual supply concentrated in a single month is charted here. As these figures suggest, the first watermelon of the season in April, while tempting, will be too scarce to be an economical buy.

When produce is in season
Per cent of annual supply of fresh fruits and vegetables sold each month

	JANUARY	FEBRUARY	MARCH	APRIL	MAY	JUNE	JULY	AUGUST	SEPTEMBER	OCTOBER	NOVEMBER	DECEMBER
Apricots					2%	55%	37%	5%				
Asparagus		2%	20%	34%	27%	16%	1%					
Blueberries					3%	29%	38%	26%	4%			
Cantaloupes			1%	4%	9%	21%	22%	25%	11%	4%	1%	
Cherries					6%	44%	43%	7%				
Cranberries									8%	19%	52%	21
Mangoes				4%	9%	17%	31%	24%	12%	2%		
Nectarines	1%	4%				11%	33%	38%	13%			
Peaches					3%	24%	33%	27%	12%	1%		
Persimmons	6%	1%							1%	27%	42%	23
Plums—prunes	1%	1%	1%			16%	30%	31%	19%	2%		
Pomegranates									5%	60%	33%	2
Pumpkins	1%	1%	2%	2%	3%	1%	1%	1%	4%	79%	3%	2
Rhubarb	6%	12%	16%	20%	27%	14%	3%	1%				
Strawberries	2%	3%	7%	16%	27%	24%	9%	4%	3%	2%	1%	1
Tangelos	13%	2%								8%	40%	37
Tangerines	21%	6%	3%	1%						1%	22%	45
Watermelons					2%	14%	29%	30%	19%	5%		

Data: United Fresh Fruit & Vegetable Associa

■ Study the weekly supermarket ads in the local paper (usually they appear on Thursday). The "loss leaders"—specials on sale for the weekend—aren't actually being sold at a loss, but they are generally real bargains because they are meant to attract you to the store offering them. If several markets are near each other, so that you don't have to waste a lot of time and gas driving around, it might be worthwhile stopping at each just to pick up its specials.

■ Learn the U.S. Department of Agriculture's system of grade labeling to know what you are getting and to avoid buying a better product than you need. You are really burning money if you buy U.S. Choice beef instead of the cheaper U.S. Good when it's *pot-au-feu* you have in mind, or if you buy U.S. Fancy tomatoes instead of U.S. Standard when you're planning to make spaghetti sauce. There are official grade standards for fresh fruits and vegetables, meats, processed fruits and vegetables, poultry, butter and eggs, and most of these products come in packages clearly labeled with their grades. The Department of Agriculture offers pamphlets explaining the grade system; write to the Publications Division, Office of Information, U.S. Department of Agriculture, Washington, D.C. 20250 for "How to Use USDA Grades in Buying Food."

■ Don't turn a husband loose with a shopping cart. He's all too likely to load it up with the most expensive goodies in the store. Children, too, can be costly shopping partners. Let Father sit with the kids while you shop for groceries alone.

■ Do your shopping after meals, not before. Studies have shown that women who shop after they have eaten spend 9 to 17 per cent less than those who shop while hungry.

■ Watch for new wrinkles in food merchandising; inflation has a way of making price competition newly important. A few cities, for example, now have canned-goods discount houses. They are typically unfancy warehouses—no soft music, no gleaming refrigerator cases filled with meats and dairy products and fresh produce, no solicitous clerks. But you can buy canned goods by the case in these places—at very substantial savings.

Simple steps like these can add up to a real difference in the weekly grocery bill. But such nickel-and-dime savings are insignificant compared to the reductions possible through control of another food expense—eating out. Add up the cost of a good restaurant dinner, a bar bill, tips—including buying your hat and car back—plus your contribution to the portfolio of high-grade stocks the babysitter must be accumulating, and you're well on your way toward paying half or more of a week's grocery bill. If you are among the many who find it easy

to spend $15 for an evening in a restaurant, who like to indulge in a night out maybe once a week—that's a $780-a-year habit.

Such meals, however, are special occasions. In some families, money drains away in a never-ending stream of snacks purchased on the run. Hamburgers, malts, pieces of pie, sundaes, cookies, pizza, pretzels, hot dogs, enchiladas and all the rest do much to increase the drain of food money away from home. Eating out can be one of the worst of the budget-wreckers because it is seldom assigned to any of the usual categories of expenditures. Thus it is not subject to control and there is generally no awareness of how much is being spent by the month or the year. If it's your pleasure to spend $780 a year, or $1,780, or $5,780 on lobsters and steaks with accompanying amenities —fine. No argument. Certainly, eating good food in a pleasant atmosphere with someone else doing the work is one of those joys that ought not be eliminated. Just be sure you know that you are spending substantial amounts and that this spending is a clear decision representing a choice between eating out and something else you want but will not be able to afford.

CLOTHING: THE VALUE OF LOOKING AHEAD

The family wardrobe is an expense most easily managed by planning ahead, a season at a time. That way you can either get what you need for less money or get better clothes for the same money. If you wait until the company's annual dinner-dance is week-after-next before you discover you don't have a thing to wear, the heat's on. There's not much time for shopping around; after some frantic looking, you pay the height-of-the-season price for whatever you must have.

Less dramatic, perhaps, but more instructive is the example of women's stockings. Sylvia gets a run while dressing, finds to her dismay that she's down to her last pair, and hastens to the nearest shop to buy more. She pays the regular price. Barbara stocks stockings. She has found a brand that fits well and wears well, and watches her monthly statement from the department store for an enclosed leaflet announcing the semiannual stocking sale (most brands are on sale in spring and fall). Then Barbara orders a couple of boxes—for $16\frac{2}{3}$ per cent less than Sylvia pays. Furthermore, Barbara has noted that a number of matching pairs last longer than the same number of odd pairs, which have an unnerving tendency to degenerate rapidly into an assortment of unwearable singles.

Nancy is another calendar watcher. For the past 12 years she has bought her winter coats on the day before Christmas. She discovered by accident that on this day—when almost no woman in her

right mind is shopping for a coat—the clerks in the coat department are putting on sales tags for the after-Christmas sale. So Nancy has first pick of the whole selection of winter coats that are going to be cleared out, and she's quite smug about the $140 coat she bought a couple of seasons ago for $93.34.

Susan spends most of the summer at her family's vacation cottage and wears out a bathing suit a year. On the day after the Fourth of July she goes to town to buy this year's bathing suit, when the markdowns are as much as 50 per cent.

Is it really worth your while to plan the accumulation of your wardrobe around seasonal sales? From a hard-eyed, financial analyst's point of view, how much sense does it make? One answer has been provided by Wallachs, a Fifth Avenue men's store known for low-key ads. During a recent summer it ran one of its typically quiet announcements under the heading INVESTMENT OPPORTUNITY:

"Let's say, for argument, that you've got $120 to spare in a checking account or under the mattress. You'd like to have it working for you. Invested at 5 per cent it would earn you $1.50 in three months.

"Now suppose you invested it in an overcoat or topcoat—assuming that you'll be needing a new coat next winter anyway—at our pre-season sale. Let's say that you select a $140 worsted or camel hair or Saxony coat at the August-only price of $119.90. That's a saving of $20.10, or 14 per cent on your investment. Not bad."

You bet it's not bad. It's as good as having your money in a well-managed mutual fund. Pre-season or after-season, you can save a bundle by anticipating your needs. And the seasonal sales aren't the only way to achieve this result. Understanding merchandising practices can also lead you to good buys.

Many of the larger department and clothing stores follow a rule expressed in the slogan: "Sell it, move it or get rid of it." These retailers have calculated that they come out ahead by taking a loss on an item instead of keeping it on a rack to gather dust and occupy valuable space. So they cut its price in stages to try to "move it." The first markdown is typically around 10 per cent, and the dress (let's say) is kept in the same department but moved to an "on-sale" rack. If it doesn't sell then—many retailers will give the item around two weeks —it goes to the bargain basement for successive markdowns that may bring the price to half its original amount.

To make the most from this practice, some determined shoppers haunt the stores, stopping by every few days for an appraisal of the merchandise in various stages of price reduction. You have to enjoy shopping to do this. But it is possible to get a bead on something you

The trick to saving money with home sewing is in knowing when to bother. It makes little economic sense for a woman to invest $10 worth of materials and $30 of time running up a dress that can be picked up in a store for $10.99.

couldn't possibly afford while it is still displayed at full price, and then lie in wait, tracking it from the "special" rack to the "as is" rack to the bargain basement, where—if your aim is true—you nail it just before the price goes so low someone else will beat you to it.

What if it hasn't sold, finally, at the last markdown? "Get rid of it." The quality stores regularly sell, at less than cost, slow-moving items to stores that work at creating a "low, low price" image. Saks Fifth Avenue, in New York, a couple of times a year sells shoes that haven't moved to Gimbels, where they turn up on basement tables at a fraction of the uptown price.

In most cities you'll find clothing stores, men's as well as women's, where the garments for some mysterious reason have the labels removed. Not so very mysterious, really. The makers of prestige-label clothes don't like to advertise the fact that their expensive products turn up in discount stores. So before Uptown Clothiers disposes of merchandise to Harry's Pants & Suits, it's understood that labels will be removed. You can buy top-quality clothing, if you can get along without a label, for 25 to 40 per cent less than you'd pay uptown. Unfortunately, there are people who pretend to be in this business but who are really in the business of selling junk, with no labels, for 25 to 40 per cent more than it's worth. Your eye and your fingers should tell you whether it's a $165 suit for $100 or a $50 suit for $95.

The bargains you find on the basement racks seem overpriced in comparison to those in the second-hand shops. Don't sniff. There is a special kind of used-clothing store, ma'am, to be found in most large cities—any city where people have the kind of money that requires a woman to buy $500 or $600 Diors and Balmains knowing she couldn't possibly be seen twice in the same one. If she tried to wear that wild mink a second season, they'd begin to wonder if Bob's investments had all gone bad or if he was in trouble down at the office. So there are a couple of places—never more than a few—where the Dior or the mink can discreetly be unloaded. A famous one, a stone's throw from Carnegie Hall in New York, keeps some of our most attractive young actresses attractively turned out for dress affairs in used Diors and minks—at perhaps 20 per cent of their original cost.

Possibly the greatest bargain counter of them all, however, is the sewing machine. Experts differ about whether a woman should be urged to become a do-it-yourself couturière if she isn't one already. One school says that if she has not learned to sew by the time she gets married, a sewing machine is likely to sit in the closet and collect dust. The other says that anyone who buys a machine and takes the sewing course offered by the store will find making a dress no more

difficult than baking a cake. The truth lies somewhere in between.

But there's more to it than simply learning how to sew a straight seam. The trick to saving money with home sewing is in knowing when to bother. If you cross-examine the kind of enviably well-dressed woman who casually remarks, "Oh, this is just something I made myself," you discover that the "just something" is really something special. She does not invest $10 worth of materials and three days' worth of time running up a simple dress that can be picked up on special in a department store for $10.99. That's all right for learning, but once she has developed skill, she makes the most of it by turning out $90 suits with $25 worth of materials. Or she shops the remnant counters and stitches up high-style resort clothes that she knows will never be worn again once the vacation is over.

The more general principles of buymanship apply to clothing as they do to other expenses, though perhaps to a somewhat lesser degree. Be an active comparison-shopper. In that way you will know which stores specialize in which items of merchandise. Don't overbuy. Clothing is a poor long-term investment, subject to vagaries of style that can make it useless overnight. And keep a close inventory of your present wardrobe. Men, especially, seem oblivious to the principles of clothing coordination. A man who has been wearing sedate blue and gray for years and has plenty of ties, shoes and whatnot to wear with them will casually purchase a bright brown suit he likes—and discover after he's brought it home that he suddenly needs matching shoes, socks, ties and a lot of other things.

FURNITURE AND FURNISHINGS: PAY FOR QUALITY

Because there's seldom anything urgent about buying or replacing furniture and furnishings, deliberate, careful shopping pays substantial dividends. A lot of people recognize this and try to approach these purchases carefully, but shady operators are out there waiting to take the unwary bargain-hunters. Phony discounts, suckers' sales, and overpriced merchandise abound; what you think is canny shopping may turn out to have been a rooking. A common-sense approach will guarantee you your money's worth—and maybe more.

■ Furniture is one item most economically bought if you stick to top quality. Many of the other things we buy today wear out, break down or go out of style within a fairly short time. Cheap furniture does; good furniture does not. Look at all the pieces made in the 18th Century that are still eminently serviceable. You'll pay more initially for quality merchandise, but the long service you can expect from it makes the higher price worthwhile.

Text continues on page 64

WHEN THE SALES ARE

JANUARY

For those whose wallets survived Christmas, there are January sales of men's suits and other winter clothing, as well as "white sales" on linens and mark-downs on appliances and other housewares. Such disparate items as furniture and lingerie are also available at a cut rate.

FEBRUARY

February's bargains include big reductions on china, glass and silver. Mattresses and bedding sales are also traditional in February. It is a good time to buy men's shirts, especially at specialty shops in smaller communities. Then too, there may be bargains from the very bottom of the Christmas barrel.

MAY

May is the time for spring cleaning, and many stores have specials on the waxes, mops and scrapers you will need to do it. Rugs and carpets are often on sale this month, too. Merchants also rush the season by offering bargains in summer sportswear for women. May sees occasional white sales as well.

JUNE

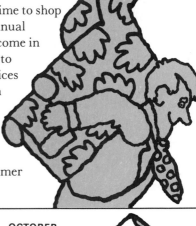

June is an excellent time to shop for furniture. Semiannual models are about to come in and merchants want to move older items. Prices also are cut on frozen foods, which are expensive for grocery stores to refrigerate in hot weather, and on summer clothes and fabrics.

SEPTEMBER

If you can wait until the end of September to buy back-to-school clothing for your children, you can save substantially, although you may not be able to get exactly what you want in all sizes. September, like May, is a good month to buy rugs and carpets, this time because the peak season is approaching and stores try to stimulate customer interest.

OCTOBER

If you are an angler, you know October marks the end of the fishing season—and with utter predictability sporting goods outlets offer bargains in rods and reels. October is also a good time to steal a march on Christmas—stores offer discounts on china, glass and silver to lure early holiday shoppers.

Picking the months to get bargains

MARCH

In March watch local papers for special sales and pre-season promotions of spring clothing for both men and women. Now, too, is the time for ski equipment and skates.

APRIL

Just as sales follow Christmas, so they come with a rush after Easter. Before you hang up your Easter finery, the local merchants slash prices on all the new outfits you and your neighbors did not buy. Men's and boys' suits, women's dresses and hats, all go for low prices in late April.

JULY

Stores begin to liquidate unsold summer merchandise in July to make room for fall goods, so this is a good month for bargains on air conditioners, garden supplies, summer sports equipment and sportswear, and men's summer suits. July is also the traditional month for sales on toilet waters and colognes.

AUGUST

Need a car? August is clearance time on current models. All summer equipment not marked down in July goes on sale now, too, so look for excellent deals on summer furniture, lawnmowers, sprinklers, yard tools, barbecue sets and camping equipment. It's also a traditional time for white sales and pre-season fur sales.

NOVEMBER

November sees excellent sales, surprisingly, of women's winter coats as clothing store owners try to cut down their inventory before second shipments arrive. This goes for women's woolen dresses and men's suits and overcoats in many stores as well. This is also the month for manufacturers' closeouts of men's shirts.

DECEMBER

Sales before Christmas are rare. But after Santa has left, there are bargains aplenty in such things as expensive lingerie and party dresses. The pre-Christmas exception is cars. Winter weather and gift-shopping keep auto showrooms almost empty and salesmen lean over backwards for a sale.

Everybody loves a bargain. But few householders realize that watching for sales can mean savings on virtually everything the family needs, from an automobile to frozen foods. The trick is to know when to expect the sale on each kind of item. The calendar above, indicating the months during which various sorts of goods almost always go on sale, contains a number of surprises. Most housewives, for instance, know that towels and sheets traditionally are on sale in January, but few realize that both men's and women's overcoats can be bought at reduced prices in November. Merchants, predictably, cut prices after a rush season like Christmas, but they sometimes also offer bargains at the height of a season as a way of stimulating additional business.

■ You find quality furniture mostly in well-established, reputable furniture and department stores. They have their seasonal clearance sales, too. By figuring out your furniture needs in advance and shopping these stores to determine normal prices, you can watch for the genuine sales and save 15 to 30 per cent.

■ Because markups on furniture are relatively high and furniture generally sells slowly, it's often possible to bargain your way to a lower price, even in the best stores. If you have done your shopping and can honestly say, "I can get that item for $50 less on the other side of town if I wait six weeks for delivery," you'll be surprised how often the lower price will be met, even in the snootiest of stores.

■ A whole class of furniture dealers specializes in "discount cards" that supposedly entitle the bearer to come in the back door, so to speak, and get near-wholesale prices. Treat such offers with extreme wariness—discount cards are passed out indiscriminately and rarely convey any special privilege. There are, however, furniture dealers whose unprepossessing offices are not just fronts. They spend no money on advertising and display hardly anything in their showrooms since they get most of their business selling office furniture to purchasing agents of large companies. They sell at genuine cut-rate prices because of their low overhead. If you know your company purchasing agent well enough to get a telephone introduction to such a dealer, you may have found the door to bargainsville. But you'd still better do your comparison shopping to make sure you are offered the same low prices that your purchasing agent gets.

■ Know prices and quality before you look for any bargains at "distress sales." There are stores that specialize in such sales. The merchandise may be genuinely distressed—bankruptcies being liquidated, most frequently. This fact is exploited so well by the merchandiser that he can sometimes jam the store with people who'll fight to buy items at their normal price . . . or a higher one.

■ Don't shrug off used furniture. That's what you're getting, after all, when you pay fancy prices at an antique shop. You can get the best quality of furniture at a fraction of its original price by attending the sales of the better auction houses. Or, if there's a handyman in the house, you can pick up serviceable furniture for next to nothing in used furniture stores and junk shops. Many a do-it-yourselfer has spent $5 for a table that, stripped of its four coats of green paint and refinished, turns out to be a handsome walnut dropleaf similar to the one offered by the antique shop down the street for $100. The best buys in secondhand furniture, though, are high-quality pieces, a few years old; they are just old enough to be out of style but not yet

Except in mild climates, heating requires the third largest housing outlay, surpassed only by mortgage payments and taxes. Yet in most households, a fair amount of money goes up in smoke unnecessarily.

scarce enough to intrigue avant-garde decorators, and they go for a small fraction of the new price.

■ Newspaper classified ads frequently lead you to householders' sales of good furniture at prices much lower than you find in a store. Again, be wary. There are people who make a living—quite a good one, some of them—by filling their apartment or house with used furniture during the week and disposing of it through the Sunday want ads, posing as a family that's ready to move to Pittsburgh.

■ For possibly no other item do you have to be a better-informed, warier and more defensive shopper than carpeting. Genuine sales are fairly rare, since styles do not change radically and there is no particular season for buying. Quality department and furniture stores have sales, from time to time, to dispose of odd lengths or ghastly colors they haven't been able to sell. But stores that specialize in carpeting tend to run ads every couple of weeks, insisting that they're offering you a once-in-a-lifetime opportunity. Be extremely skeptical. Genuinely good buys are occasionally to be found at the places that specialize in cleaning (not selling) rugs and carpets. For some reason, large numbers of people who send carpets out for cleaning never get around to claiming them. The big cleaning establishments run ads occasionally, listing unclaimed items, but you don't have to wait for the ads. Just phone and ask what they have for sale.

■ "White sales" are such an institution that it's surprising housewives ever buy linens at regular prices. The white-sale months are August and January, the latter month usually offering the bigger variety and better prices. Figure on replenishing stocks of bedding, towels and table linens then and you'll profit by planned spending.

DEPARTMENT OF BUILDING AND GROUNDS

High on the list of budget-bending day-to-day expenses are those required for the house itself. Just to stay comfortable you spend a great deal for heating and cooling. And to keep your property presentable you plow dollars into grass, trees, flowers and shrubbery. This doesn't include the 1½ per cent of the value of your home that you spend annually on essential maintenance and repairs; many a handy couple have been able to keep this cost item under control by joining the army of do-it-yourselfers, as discussed in Chapter 7. But any homeowner who keeps track of expenses can testify that the amount spent in addition to maintenance is a major item. It is one that can be cut if given attention.

Heating is an example. Except for those living in mild climates, heating requires the third largest housing outlay, surpassed only by

mortgage payments and taxes. Yet in most households—up to 80 or 90 per cent according to some estimates—there's a fair amount of money going up in smoke unnecessarily. If your house is old and you're harboring an ancient furnace in the basement, the only cure may be replacement and this is expensive. It will take many years of lower heat bills to pay for a new furnace. But relatively simple adjustment sometimes solves the problem. It is perfectly possible to lose 20 per cent of a heating system's efficiency just from faulty combustion.

If you use gas as a fuel, there is only one major adjustment but it is crucial. The efficiency of the burner depends on the proportion of air mixed into the gas, a setting that is quickly adjusted by a furnace repairman or the utility company serviceman; some utilities readjust the control without charge.

Oil burners are more complicated. In addition to the fine tuning necessary to mix fuel and air properly, oil burners have valves and screens that need to be kept clean. Periodic maintenance by a professional is essential. Some fuel suppliers offer service contracts that provide periodic cleaning and adjustment for a fixed annual fee.

One of the commonest problems, but easily remedied, is the clogging of air filters in forced-warm-air systems. Some homeowners aren't even aware that their heating plants have filters and suffer needlessly from poor heating. If you're vague about your own system, take a look. Somewhere in the unit, usually near the base, you will find a wide slot that contains a slide filled with fiberglass or metal mesh. All of the air that goes to heat your house must pass through this filter; if it is dirty it will choke up the flow of air and prevent the system from functioning properly. The remedy: Clean it if it is cleanable or replace it with a new one from the hardware store.

The other big heating problem has nothing to do with the system itself. A perfectly functioning furnace will still leave you in chilly discomfort and cost extra dollars by the handful if the house it is trying to heat is a leaky box. There are three answers to this problem: insulation, storm sash and weather stripping.

If insulation is inadequate, there isn't much you can do about it except in the attic. Here, if the floor joists are not covered with flooring you can pour loose insulating material into the spaces between the joists. If the attic is heated and destined to become living space, staple the roll type of insulation between the ceiling rafters.

The addition of tightly fitted storm windows and doors is another way of tightening up a leaky house, as is the installation of weather stripping to stop leaks around the edges of windows and doors. These too can be investments that return their cost many times over.

Tightening up a house is even more important to economy if air conditioning is used. But the cooling equipment itself may be a bigger influence on cost, and it is one that is subject to some control, particularly in the case of room air conditioners that fit into windows. When buying such a unit many people make the expensive mistake of assuming that the bigger it is the better. Much of the effectiveness of air conditioning, in producing a more comfortable room, depends not on simply lowering the temperature but on dehumidifying the air. It's the THI you hear about in weather reports—the "temperature-humidity index"—that determines your comfort. A good window conditioner will wring from 1½ to 9 pints of water per hour out of the air. But if it's too big for the room, it pulls the temperature down quickly and must be shut off before it has reduced humidity very much. The result is a cold but clammy and uncomfortable room, and occupants will usually overwork the air conditioner in an effort to get "cool." You determine the proper size of conditioner by calculating the "heat gain" of the area you're cooling; the unit has to be big enough to remove this much heat. A good appliance dealer will calculate the heat gain for you—but if he's not all that good he may simply base his recommendation on the theory "the bigger the better" (and more expensive). If you want to do your own arithmetic, you can get a form for calculating heat gain by sending a stamped, self-addressed envelope to the Association of Home Appliance Manufacturers, 20 North Wacker Drive, Chicago, Illinois 60606.

Another major house expense over which you can exercise some control is the cost of maintaining the yard. You have to keep things up at least to the standard of the neighborhood unless you're prepared to suffer social ostracism, so most suburbanites do what seems necessary without trying to control costs or even keep track of them. One who did concluded that he'd spent so much on the yard in six years that he could have covered it with a good grade of carpeting. Yet there are things you can do to keep these costs down; here are some points to keep in mind:

■ Enough is enough; too much is too much. Many homeowners broadcast $2.30-a-pound grass seed with a heavy hand, applying far more than is recommended on the package—and watch their money go down the storm sewer with the first heavy rain. Or they lay on fertilizer the same way, and the plants are either burned by the concentrated chemicals or are forced to a spurt of such late growth that they fall prey to winter frosts. If you follow the instructions on the package (or go a bit lighter), you'll save money and have a better garden. Homeowners frequently overdo, too, in putting plants too close

Make the most of what comes free. If something grows wild in the vacant lot next door, it should grow easily in your yard.

together; if the plants have to be thinned out later, that's money wasted. About the only yard treatment you are unlikely to overdo is watering during a dry spell, particularly a lawn; here it's generally better not to water at all than to water too lightly.

■ Take advantage of nature's cycle. If you are still burning leaves, you are not only polluting the air but also watching money go up in smoke. Learn to make a compost pile and convert those leaves and grass clippings into valuable fertilizer.

■ Have your soil tested. A great deal of money and effort is wasted by trying to make things grow in unsuitable soil, or by applying conditioners and fertilizers unsuited to the soil. You can get a soil analysis at little or no cost through your local county agent, the state university or a local nurseryman. The results will tell you which varieties of grass, shrubs and trees will grow in your yard—and which won't.

■ Make the most of what comes free. If you have neighbors with mature gardens, you can save by exchanging seeds, cuttings and other giveaways. If you have access to any undeveloped land, your own or any other nearby, remember that all native plants are not necessarily weeds. In fact, native trees, vines and shrubs are likely to prove tougher, faster growing and more disease-resistant than the plants you pay a pretty penny for at the nursery. If something grows wild in the lot next door, it should grow as easily in your yard.

■ Listen to all the advice you can get. Many nurseries offer free landscaping services, and most experienced home gardeners delight in helping beginners. Good advice can help protect you against the two big wasters of garden money: (1) plants that die before their time from disease or malnutrition, and (2) plants that have to be removed because they have become too large to serve their intended purpose.

HOME APPLIANCES

Prices of both small and major home appliances vary over wide ranges, depending on the store in which they are being sold. It was principally cut-rate appliances that got the big discount houses started some years ago, but today any kind of store may—or may not—sell at discount prices. Now there is no certain way to know where the bargains are to be found. These guidelines may help:

■ You can often match "discount" prices on a given make and model of appliance in the more competitive old-line department stores and appliance shops (which may offer extra service, such as free delivery).

■ Some manufacturers try to discourage price cutting on their brands by refusing to sell to discount houses. The bigger discount houses, however, swing enough weight to get around manufacturers' disapproval

and stock some of these brands, though not always all models. It takes careful shopping to make sure that the discount house gives you exactly the same item you saw in the department store uptown.

■ There are a good many imitation discount stores where prices are low for a good reason: The merchandise consists mostly of off-brands, some of it plain junk.

■ Some discount houses provide reasonably good service on faulty appliances, while some of their more traditional competitors don't have much to be proud of in this respect. The buyer can be fairly sure of one thing: He'll get more attention to his complaints in any store if he has a charge account and his purchase is yet to be paid for.

■ The figure on the price tag isn't everything. Discounters usually charge extra for installation and delivery. Some low-price department stores do too. Be sure to find out what you do and do not get for your money before you buy at a price that seems to save you a few dollars.

Installation charges are something for the buyer to be alert to, regardless of where he buys. "Normal installation free" is the information he frequently gets. Some stores seem to consider almost any installation abnormal. An installation requiring a plumbing hookup or gas connection usually involves an extra charge. In some cases, the installation charge will vary with the model line. Shoppers in one national department-store chain found that installation was charged for on the "standard" automatic washer but provided free with the "de luxe" model; as a result the installed cost of the de luxe model was only a couple of dollars more than that of the standard.

One merchandising practice of appliance manufacturers has made it possible for the diligent shopper to get more mileage out of his appliance dollar. Because the life of most major household appliances is fairly long—11 to 15 years—manufacturers try to increase sales by adopting the auto makers' scheme of "built-in obsolescence" through design changes. The ads may insist that the new model is so much more desirable that life will be bleak and barren without it. But the improvements may be confined to new colors, changed shapes and perhaps the addition of some gadgetry. If you don't feel compelled to own the latest model but just want an efficient machine, you can save a lot by getting one of the leftovers at the closeout sales, usually scheduled for January or February.

One question about buying appliances has no pat answer: Should you invest in a service contract when buying an expensive appliance? The contract is usually priced low for the first year, appealing to many buyers as inexpensive insurance. The price is low because major appliances today are reasonably trouble-free in their youth. If you

want to renew the policy for the second year, when the odds on your needing service go up a little, so does the price of the contract. By the time you've carried the protection long enough to begin collecting on free service, you'll have spent so much on the contract that you could have financed your own service arrangements for less money—if you're average. If you were unlucky enough to buy a lemon, a service policy will be a joy and a comfort indeed.

Guarantees and warranties are supposed to protect you against unsatisfactory performance and major service problems, but all too often the legalese in a guarantee spells out the manufacturer's limits of liability instead of defining the buyer's protection. If you're buying an expensive appliance, read the terms carefully.

ENTERTAINMENT AND OTHER MISCELLANY

The major categories of household expense discussed above involve the most money and biggest potential for savings. But many little expenses often cause trouble out of proportion to their real importance. Part of the problem is that they are so hard to control because they are small and therefore often unplanned and unnoted.

Newspapers and magazines, for one example, can add up to quite an item (around $45 a year just for a daily paper). Where do they go —under entertainment, education, self-improvement or something else? The people at the office regularly put the arm on you for wedding presents, flowers for the sick, gifts for the old hands who retire. Are these to be considered personal expenses or miscellaneous? What about postage stamps, bottle stoppers, Scotch tape, luggage, wrist watch repairs, ads for lost dogs?

It's a real trick to get all of this cash flow under some sort of control so you know what the score is. On the one hand, you can't have so many categories that everyone in the family becomes a full-time bookkeeper. That's where so many old-fashioned budgets broke down. What categories do you really need, and what goes into them? Let's see if only three—entertainment, personal expenses, and contributions and gifts—will do the job.

Entertainment

Entertainment is a problem category. It's easy to agree that it should cover movies, plays, cabarets, parties, ball games. But what about Father's golf? Is it fair to charge off to the family's entertainment allowance his new golf clubs, caddie fees and lost balls? Where do country club dues go? Is watching television entertainment, or is it using a household appliance? Is reading a book entertainment, even if you

It's only after a season of trying it that Tom and Kim conclude they'll never be skiers, they don't care for it, in fact they heartily dislike it. By now they have spent $200 or $300 on clothing and gear.

are working on a classic? Where do you allow for beer, wine and spirits —under entertainment or food and beverages?

One of the reasons why "entertainment" as an expense category so frequently gets out of hand is that it can, if you let it, cover almost any of the luxuries, indulgences and personal pleasures of life. If we start counting all of the things entertainment might cover, some expenses that are personally important seem frivolous when put down in cold black-and-white figures on paper. How much does Father's passion for golf cost if you really start counting? Probably so much that he doesn't want to see the sum staring at him. Mother might respond with a look that says, "Well! And who's been complaining about my spending so much on clothes?" It's a great way to start a family fight. And yet Father has been paying for his golf all this time and the family isn't quite bankrupt.

One way out of this psychological dilemma is to redefine entertainment, shifting to individual members of the family the responsibility for spending decisions having to do with the pursuit of personal pleasure. This calls for a new category of spending, personal expenses. Then if somebody in the family digs Bach and develops an overpowering yearning for a record of one of the partitas, it is a personal expense, not entertainment requiring family approval.

It's more practical to define "entertainment" as the entertaining of guests (in the home and outside), plus such communal leisure-time activities as theatergoing, sports or family outings. Expenditures then become more manageable. Taking a family vote becomes entirely workable: There's only enough of the month's entertainment money left to take the family to the movies tonight, or to the circus next weekend, but not to do both.

Even managed this way, entertainment can use up a disproportionate share of dollars. One reason is that choices are frequently made on very thin research. Tom and Kim decide, for example, that they've just got to start skiing because everybody in their circle skis. It's only after a season of trying it that they both conclude they'll never be skiers, they don't really care for it, in fact they heartily dislike it. By now they have spent $200 or $300 on clothing and gear. They could have avoided the loss by doing advance research—in this case, simply a trial period using rented or borrowed equipment.

Personal expenses

Removing personal indulgences from the area of family debate calls for increasing the types of spending that personal expenses must cover. Many people allot "personal allowances," which are usually

intended to be small amounts for frivolity, and then add on extra dollars for the hygienic-sounding "personal care." There's a good case to be made for putting both of these categories and a number of others under the umbrella of personal expenses. This avoids the heavy restrictions on an individual's freedom to make his own spending choices that can create a feeling of institutionalized poverty. And there can be that feeling, even if the institution has lovely furnishings. The broader allotment also works better because each individual member of the family has to make important decisions. If the system is so tight that no one has a larger decision to make than whether to buy a stick of gum today or tomorrow, no one feels any particular responsibility for making the system work.

You might consider, then, a comprehensive personal-expense allotment for each member of the family, adults and children alike, limited only by the maturity and judgment needed to make a wide range of decisions. (Children's allowances are discussed in Chapter 9.) This walking-around money can cover most of the cash the individual spends on himself, for himself, reflecting personal choices and decisions. Some of these might traditionally be considered "entertainment"; others would cover personal sports, hobbies, recreation, even expenditures sometimes labeled "advancement" or "self-improvement." Certainly what's generally under "personal care" should be included—money for hairdressers and barbershops, cosmetics and shaving supplies, shoeshines, manicures and pedicures.

It's possible, of course, to dump too many things into such a comprehensive personal-expense allotment. Clothing purchases, while items of personal choice, shouldn't be made out of walking-around money. They should be carefully planned, not made on impulse, so it's well to keep that money in a separate category. Furthermore, you can overwhelm an individual's decision-making capacity by giving him so many possible choices that his computer can't handle all the input. One of the key principles of planned spending is to segregate the myriad choices into manageably small categories, where the options become clear and it is possible to weigh and select. That's as true of the personal-expense allotment as of any other.

What is desirable is for each individual to have latitude to select and reject, but with the range of choices narrow enough for him to be able to recognize that he can have A or B or C, and not all three.

Contributions and gifts

A final category in traditional budgets is "contributions and gifts." Contributions are seldom a problem, and since there's frequently a

tax consideration involved, you'll find contributions discussed in Chapter 10. Gifts, in some families, do get to be troublesome. The keeping-up-with-the-Joneses syndrome, or something akin to it, is usually responsible. It can happen within a family, where at Christmastime and birthdays a competition slyly develops and the magnificence of the presents escalates from one occasion to another. Or it can occur within a social circle where "the girls" chip in on something for whoever's moving away—and the same kind of escalation in two or three years raises the level from a couple of nice hankies to a set of matched luggage. This is a difficult thing to stop, once it's underway; Orientals aren't the only ones who have strong feelings about losing face, and nobody wants to be the first to look chintzy. The best time to stop it is before it gets started.

Many imaginative and creative people need only the cost of materials to make gifts that provide the recipients more pleasure and carry a stronger personal message than any they could buy in stores. Almost everyone, for that matter, can find some kind of do-it-yourself homecrafted item that will be a welcome gift on most occasions.

One way to keep the cost of gifts under control is to arrange for them to be financed out of each individual's personal-expense fund. They tend to escalate in value much more slowly; the higher the price tag, the more personal expenditures have to give somewhere else.

THE MECHANICS: YOUR BANK CAN HELP

Planned and controlled spending, no matter how well conceived, can't work as effectively as you want it to unless the mechanics of the system make for smooth, well-oiled running. Generally, the simpler the better. One family got along fine with a formula that went, "I allocate, and she pays the bills." Still, what does "allocate" mean?

What's essential is to isolate the money assigned to each broad category so that it is earmarked, set aside and available when needed —not all mixed up in one barrel that is dipped into so long as anything is left. That makes a certain amount of record-keeping unavoidable. You need a master control sheet on which, each month, all the family-purse money is divided in advance into the accounts that cover the various kinds of expenditures made in your particular family. Try to keep this from getting too elaborate—but at the same time make it realistically detailed. Merely dividing a jumble into three or four smaller jumbles isn't going to improve things much.

One way to mechanize your system is to take advantage of the bill-paying service that many banks are beginning to offer to checking-account customers. When you provide your bank with written autho-

JOHN and MARY BRENNAN   09/30/69   ACCT 160-002   DOWNTOWN BRANCH #1

ACCT	DESCRIPTION	****** THIS MONTH ******			****** YEAR TO DATE ******		
		# ITEMS	$ AMOUNT	$ %	# ITEMS	$ AMOUNT	$ %
	EXPENSE ITEMS						
1	HOUSE PAYMENT	1	167.75	11.4	8	1,706.50	18.6
3	HOME IMPROVEMENTS	1	64.95	4.4	1	184.95	2.0
8	MISC HOUSE REPAIRS	1	71.60	4.9	2	114.10	1.3
10	HEAT	1	44.72	3.0	3	141.56	1.5
11	ELECTRICITY	1	31.94	2.2	4	265.95	2.9
12	TELEPHONE	1	44.68	3.1	3	194.60	2.1
13	WATER	1	20.70	1.4	6	65.95	.7
20	FOOD	6	180.00	12.2	32	1,397.00	15.2
30	CLOTHING	4	73.47	5.0	16	991.41	10.8
31	CLEANING & LAUNDRY	1	10.75	.7	3	81.50	.9
40	PRESCRIPTIONS	1	88.32	6.0	3	367.09	4.0
41	HOSPITAL INSURANCE	1	17.50	1.2	2	22.10	.3
42	HOSPITAL						
43	DENTIST	1	36.40	2.5	3	318.40	3.5
44	DOCTOR						
50	LIFE INSURANCE				5	403.00	4.4
60	CONTRIBUTIONS-CHURCH	1	150.00	10.1	3	440.00	4.8
70	ALLOWANCES-CHILDREN	4	25.00	1.7	25	190.75	2.4
74	VACATION	2	110.00	7.5	7	402.70	4.3
75	RECREATION				3	30.50	.3
77	ENTERTAINING	3	17.31	1.2	16	152.25	1.7
80	EDUCATION	1	100.00	6.8	4	173.99	1.9
99	SAVINGS	1	200.00	13.6	9	1,400.00	15.3
110	MISCELLANEOUS				1	11.00	.1
248	MONEY MINDER FEE	1	7.31	.5	6	51.49	.6
249	BANK SV. CHG.	3	9.00	.6	16	71.78	.7
------A------	TOTAL GENERAL EXPENSES	37	1,471.40	100.0	181	9,178.57	100.0
	INCOME ITEMS						
501	SALARY	2	1,200.00	77.2	16	10,800.00	95.5
502	DIVIDENDS-STOCK	3	46.50	3.0	6	511.28	4.5
503	INTEREST-SAVINGS	1	65.00	4.2			
506	DIVIDENDS-INSURANCE						
511	TRUST INCOME	1	100.00	6.5			
516	TAX REFUNDS	1	142.00	9.1			
------D------	TOTAL GENERAL INCOME	8	1,553.50	100.0	22	11,311.28	100.0

MONEY MINDER FEE**   5.42

UNITED STATES NATIONAL BANK OF OREGON

Computerizing a family financial plan

In some cities you can now get your bank's computer to keep track of your expenditures and send you a monthly report like the one above, listing just how much went for what. The Money Minder system, originated by the United States National Bank of Oregon in Portland, breaks expenditures down into categories you select—food, dentist, recreation—and also shows each category's percentage of total expenditure and how the figures for the year add up. This way you see how actual expenses in each category compare to allotments for them. To make the system work, you just write a code number on each check to indicate the category.

rization for paying a recurring obligation, the bank will automatically, each month, debit your account and dispatch a check. The service may cover mortgage payments and insurance payments, for example, and may also provide for utility bills and such to be sent directly to the bank for automatic payment. Inquire at your bank about this; it's often available even though not widely publicized.

Almost any bank will automatically transfer, each month, a stipulated amount from your checking account to your savings account. This is an effective way of isolating money to cover expenses you know will occur but can't predict precisely—medical and dental bills, for example, or house repairs and maintenance. Even though the bank labels this a "savings account" you shouldn't think of it as savings. It's money earmarked for spending in the not-too-distant future; it is no different from the balance that shows in your checkbook representing money that isn't spent yet but soon will be. Use a separate savings account for the funds that are set aside to realize long-term goals.

In the avant-garde of family-finance services that larger banks are beginning to offer is a detailed monthly analysis of your expenditures, making use of coded checks. Your code might, for example, use "03" on a check to indicate that it went for groceries, "04" to identify car repairs, "05" for insurance premiums, etc. The bank's computer sorts out all these codes each month and prints out a statement that lists each of your payments in its proper category, totals up what you've spent for each item, and gives you a percentage figure to show what part of your outgo the various categories accounted for. And that's added up each month to give you a running total for the year. Another benefit is that you can code checks to indicate which expenses are tax-deductible; this helps insure that you don't miss any during the year and provides a neat list all printed up to lighten the burden of preparing tax returns. At present at least, the fee charged for this service is fairly high, so it is suitable mainly for households with rather elaborate financial operations. You could code your own checks at little or no cost, of course, by simply taking advantage of the many different colors checks come in.

Your checkbook can be a help or a hindrance in the mechanics of your system. Relying on the stub balance in the checkbook as a guide to how your spending plans are working out can give dangerously misleading readings. You look at the balance and it tells you that you're doing pretty well this month, so you buy the new chair you've been talking about all year. A few days later, the barrel is near empty; the account had to be tapped heavily for a couple of things you'd forgotten about or didn't expect.

Where you can get help

It takes a knowledgeable consumer to exercise intelligent buymanship. At the end of this volume is a list of informative books on family finance. Magazines and newspapers of almost every description publish articles describing new products, exposing the latest frauds and advising on how to get the most for your money. The following publications offer specialized help:

BIBLIOGRAPHIES

Consumer Education Bibliography. Prepared for the President's Committee on Consumer Interests by the Yonkers, New York, Public Library. Superintendent of Documents, GPO, Washington, D.C. 20402.

Free and Inexpensive Materials for Teaching Family Finance. Council for Family Financial Education, Twin Towers, 1110 Fidler Lane, Silver Spring, Maryland 20910.

A Consumer's Guide to USDA Services. U.S. Department of Agriculture Miscellaneous Publication No. 959. Superintendent of Documents, GPO, Washington, D.C. 20402.

An Open Door to Family Finance Education. Pamphlet. Education in Family Finance Workshop, University of Maryland, College Park, Maryland 20742.

A Guide to Federal Consumer Services. President's Committee on Consumer Interests. Superintendent of Documents, GPO, Washington, D.C. 20402.

Consumer Information. Price List 86. Superintendent of Documents, GPO, Washington, D.C. 20402.

PUBLICATIONS

Consumer Reports. Monthly. *The Buying Guide Issue, Consumer Reports*. Annual. Consumers Union of U.S., Inc., 256 Washington Street, Mount Vernon, New York 10550.

Consumer Bulletin. Monthly. Consumers' Research, Inc., Washington, New Jersey 07882.

Money Management Library. Booklets. Money Management Institute, Household Finance Corporation, Prudential Plaza, Chicago, Illinois 60601.

Changing Times, The Kiplinger Magazine. Monthly. The Kiplinger Washington Editors, Inc., Editors Park, Maryland 20782.

USDA's Report to Consumers. Monthly newsletter. U.S. Department of Agriculture, Office of Information, Washington, D.C. 20250.

Marketing Information Guide. Monthly. Superintendent of Documents, GPO, Washington, D.C. 20402.

Your master control sheet is a more reliable guide because it anticipates and it doesn't forget. When the money is allocated to each account at the beginning of the month, you see it as earmarked for expenditure, and therefore not available—and you don't get any false readings that indicate a nonexistent prosperity.

A joint checking account works well enough in some families but in others it's a disaster. If both husband and wife write checks during the month and communication is less than perfect, neither can ever be certain of the balance remaining. The extra expense of separate accounts can be a good investment in a management system.

Most banks offer two kinds of checking accounts, "regular" and "special." The service charge for a regular account is based on "activity"—the number of checks written, deposits made, and the average or minimum balance during the month. The formulas used by banks to calculate service charges can vary considerably, and it's good economy to ask several banks in your area for the leaflet that spells out the method used to arrive at checking-account service charges. You might find that at one, for example, if you can maintain a balance that doesn't fall below $500 during the month, you'll save enough on service charges to make up for the lost interest the $500 would earn in a savings account. The "special" account typically costs you around 10 cents a check, often with a small monthly service charge in addition. Usually the family that writes a fairly large number of checks during the month and keeps the balance reasonably high will find a regular account more economical. If it's necessary in the interest of methodical control and keeping your spending money separated into neat piles, you may find that it doesn't cost much more to maintain a regular account for paying household bills and a special account on which husband and wife can draw for personal-expense money, writing a small number of checks each month.

4
Automobiles

The high cost
of mobility

Once upon a time—in 1916, to be exact—you could walk into a Ford dealer's showroom, plunk down $360, and drive away in a fully owned Model T. If anything went wrong with the faithful flivver, new parts could be had for a pittance. A brand-new fender cost $2.50; the price tag on a muffler was 25 cents. You could handle most repairs by yourself, using a ball-peen hammer, a monkey wrench and a screwdriver. Henry Ford, the genius of mass production, sold 20 million of his Model T's because he knew Americans loved a bargain. "Every time I lower the price a dollar," he said, "we gain a thousand new buyers."

Car buyers may look back on that era with misty eyes, but there is little hope of ever living in such a golden age of bargains again. The average new automobile lists for around $3,200 without accessories. Very few repairs can be done in the backyard today, but a mechanic will somewhat grudgingly fix your car at his usual rate of $9 per hour, plus the cost of parts. Repairing automobiles is a $25 billion per year industry in the U.S.—equivalent to a yearly repair bill of about $250 for each car on the road.

If you have a mechanical bent and an indifference to appearances, it is possible to pick up a battered used car for $60 to $100, sink just enough money in it to keep it running for a year or so, give it to the junk man when collapse seems imminent, then repeat the process. This is unquestionably the most frugal way to use a car. It is a rather desperate procedure, however, and most Americans are willing and able to spend more on cars than on anything except food and housing. Most people like "stylish" cars and dislike those close to the ragged edge of a breakdown. Yet few people have a precise notion of what it really costs them each year to own a set of wheels.

According to a report issued by the U.S. Department of Transportation, a typical car (standard size, one year old) costs its owner $1,467 during the year. This discouraging sum can be accounted for in the following ways: $589 for depreciation, $224 for gasoline and oil, $170 for insurance, $138 for maintenance and repairs, $199 for parking, garaging and tolls, and $147 for automotive taxes (most of which are used to pay for our roads). The total bill will of course be higher if a more expensive car is bought.

These figures are averages, however, and there is no reason why you cannot beat the numbers. With a little canniness, comparative shopping, and close attention to the various costs, you can achieve some very gratifying savings.

The prerequisite is an understanding of some little-publicized facts about cars. You need to know:

■ When it pays to trade the old car for a new one.

Where does all the money go?

Americans spend more money on their cars than on clothing. A typical car costs nearly $1,500 a year to own and operate—not counting financing charges. The figures below, for a one-year-old car driven 13,000 miles, show how that total breaks down. The largest single item (40 per cent) is depreciation—but almost $200 a year goes just for parking and tolls. As a fair rule of thumb, you can figure that, all told, you will have to spend nearly 12 cents a mile to run your car.

- How much extra a big car costs.
- When to go shopping.
- Which optional accessories are worth the money.
- Ways of outfoxing foxy salesmen.
- How to recognize the rock-bottom price on the car you want.
- Where to save safely on upkeep.
- What a second car really costs.

THE TIME TO TRADE

A shrewd car-owner saves money by knowing when to buy a new one. This is not always an easy matter because it requires a prediction of the future of the old one. To determine the most propitious time for trade-in, you must know the relationship between two costs: depreciation and maintenance.

Depreciation takes the biggest bite out of your automotive dol-

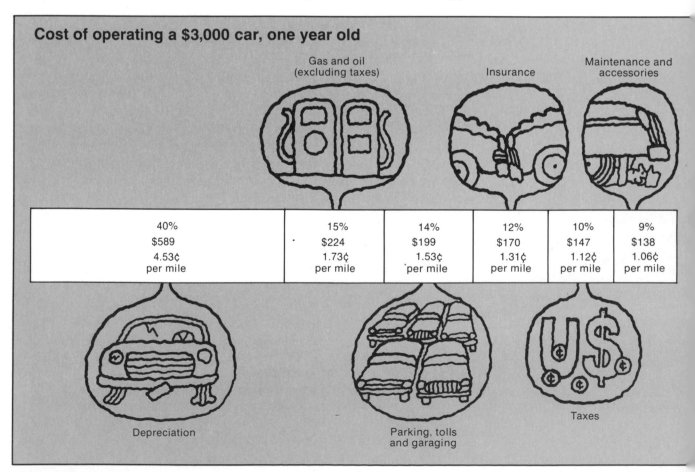

Cost of operating a $3,000 car, one year old

	Gas and oil (excluding taxes)		Insurance	Maintenance and accessories	
40% $589 4.53¢ per mile	15% $224 1.73¢ per mile	14% $199 1.53¢ per mile	12% $170 1.31¢ per mile	10% $147 1.12¢ per mile	9% $138 1.06¢ per mile
Depreciation			Parking, tolls and garaging		Taxes

lar. From the day you buy it, your car loses value the way a sieve loses water, even if you keep it in a garage just to look at and never drive it. The value of a typical car depreciates by 25 to 30 per cent the first year, 18 per cent of the original price the second year, 14 per cent the third year, 11 per cent the fourth year, 9 per cent the fifth year, 6 per cent the sixth year, and 2 per cent the seventh year. Wear and tear or high mileage will raise the depreciation rate even higher; but age is the main factor in determining a car's trade-in value.

Let's translate those percentages into cash. Suppose you buy a gleaming new Ironclad V-8 for $3,000. As soon as the next year's Ironclad model appears on the market, your car is worth $750 less. The following year, it loses another $540. The year after that its value is cut by another $420—and so on, until, at the end of 10 years, the doddering old Ironclad has only junk value. Depreciation will cost very dearly if you are in the habit of trading in your Ironclad for a new one every year. Over a period of 10 years, you will lose a total of $7,500 in depreciation alone (10 times the first-year rate).

Some makes of cars depreciate more slowly than others. Thus, there is a strong second-hand demand for Cadillacs and Volkswagens, and they retain their value relatively well. On the other hand, most imported cars (other than those favored by foreign-car buffs) depreciate more rapidly than domestic cars, due partly to the problem of parts replacement as they get older.

Since depreciation is less with each succeeding year, it would seem that the longer you keep a car, the less it will cost you. Not necessarily. In the fifth year with that Ironclad V-8, depreciation is $100 less than it was the year before. But if repair bills are $200 greater than the year before, you might decide that you would have been better off trading in the car during the fourth year of ownership.

It is hard to estimate with any degree of precision when the upkeep costs will begin to outrun depreciation, but there are some guidelines. Maintenance, like depreciation, follows a more or less standard pattern. While the car is brand-new, oddly enough, maintenance is frequent; you endure a period of numerous small repairs and adjustments. It's not that your car is a "lemon." You are in effect conducting the shakedown tests that the factory did not have time for. Once the shakedown is over and all the loose bolts are tightened, your car enters a healthy, vigorous youth. You should be able to drive at least 15,000 miles without serious incident.

Repairs at this time don't cost you anything in any case, for your new-car warranty stipulates that Detroit will pick up the tab for fixing defects over a reasonable period of time. But to keep the war-

ranty in effect you must adhere to a maintenance schedule spelled out in the owner's manual; the warranty won't cover damage due to the owner's negligence or abuse. If you fail to change the oil, replace the oil filter or check the air cleaner according to the schedule, the warranty will be voided. Don't let this happen unless you enjoy the sight of hundred-dollar bills flying out the window.

After you embark on the second 15,000 miles, you can expect steadily rising maintenance costs. Brakes may require relining or replacing, headlights should be re-aimed, and you will almost certainly have to spend $30 or so on a tune-up that includes new spark plugs, points, and adjustment of the timing and carburetor. In the third 15,000 miles, the need for a new battery, tires, and possibly other major parts may add to the maintenance pinch.

About midway through the fourth year of ownership, the cost of

When should you trade?

The cost of depreciation, very high in the first years of a car's life, drops sharply after about four years while the cost of repairs and maintenance is creeping up. If you are unwilling to squeeze the last penny out of your car by driving it until it has only junk value left (10 years or so), an economical time to trade comes when the cost of upkeep begins to outrun the cost of depreciation. In this study by the U.S. Department of Transportation, that moment falls during the car's fourth year. After that the cost of repairs rapidly begins to approach the total worth of the car.

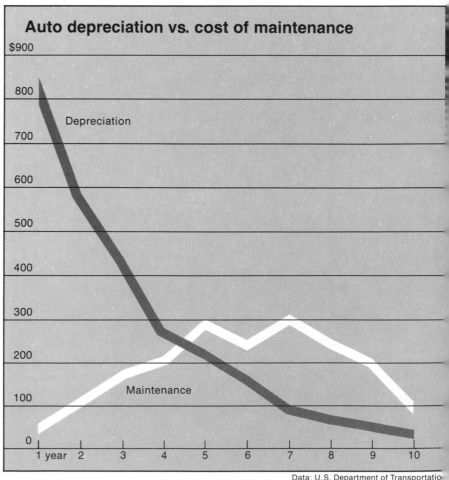

Auto depreciation vs. cost of maintenance

Data: U.S. Department of Transportation

repairs, maintenance, and replacement of tires begins to outrun the costs of depreciation, as the chart shows. It is now time to think about trading, although you'll notice that, according to the chart, average upkeep costs never seem to go over $300 a year, even when the car enters cantankerous senility. One explanation for this perplexing statistic is that a car generally gets less use in its old age. Also, people tend to let an old car slip into disrepair, figuring that they would be throwing money down the drain if they serviced it as conscientiously as a new car. Long before this you will have gotten rid of it.

No graph or formula can tell you exactly when to trade in your car. There are simply too many variables involved. Given good treatment, a car ought to go 60,000 miles (at least five years in the life of a typical automobile) before upkeep costs begin to get out of hand. Yet on the average, cars are kept only three years and ten months, not quite long enough to wring the maximum economy out of the depreciation-upkeep equation. (This explains why there are good values to be found in the used-car market.)

CHOOSING A NEW CAR

When you finally decide to take the plunge and get a new car, prepare to be a little bit shocked. The price on an average model has been creeping upward steadily at the rate of about $75 a year. There are ways to fight back, however. One is to reassess your needs in size, which more than any other factor determines car expense. The heavier a family-type car is, the more room, convenience and comfort it generally provides—also the more it costs.

With certain exceptions like sports cars, automobiles are priced more by weight than by make. A sedan in the 3,200-pound weight class costs about $2,600 new; one in the 4,100-pound class perhaps $3,300. The most popular makes offer models in several weight classes. But it's not only the first cost, it's the upkeep. Both together make the bigger car strikingly more expensive, as was shown by research conducted by Runzheimer and Company, a firm that specializes in analyzing automobile costs for corporations operating large fleets. Runzheimer studied new cars driven 10,000 miles a year and found that a standard-sized car cost half again as much per year as a small car, a luxury car nearly twice as much (*see box*).

While size affects cost immediately, two other factors exert long-term influence. One is the degree of newness in the new model. Some buyers wait for the second-year version of a radically changed model; by then the bugs will have been worked out of the "improvements." And it's always wise to look for a car that can be expected to depre-

Big car, big costs

It's expensive to "move up" to a big car, as this comparison of "sticker prices" (no accessories) and typical operating costs shows. Both initial price and operating costs increase steadily with weight—a luxury car, weighing almost twice as much as a small car, costs more than twice as much to buy and close to twice as much to run.

Class	Price	Annual cost
Small (2,600 lbs.)	$2,100	$1,100
Intermediate (3,200 lbs.)	$2,600	$1,300
Regular (3,750 lbs.)	$3,000	$1,500
Medium (4,100 lbs.)	$3,300	$1,700
Luxury (4,600 lbs.)	$5,700	$2,100

ciate slowly; check the comparative values of older models in the used-car market to see which ones hold up best.

On any make you choose, there is an opportunity for dramatic savings in the choice of optional equipment. You can knock as much as a third off the total price of a new car by simply refusing all the accessories the dealer tries to sell you. You probably won't want to go that far. But even a less puritanical approach to the frills leads to worthwhile reductions in the total price.

Be aware that the dealer wants to sell you a car that is already in his showroom, since he has money tied up in it. The car probably has some optional equipment that you don't want, and it is best to accept only a car that meets your specifications. No matter how small a salesman makes the cost of a few options seem, they can swell the bill to obese proportions. For example, one low-priced model would have cost $867 extra if you had bought it with automatic transmission, power steering, power brakes, AM radio, vinyl roof and air conditioning. Three less common accessories—special gearing for extra

How the extras boost the ante

The car you want, equipped as you want it, may cost lots more than the basic price the dealer quotes. An air conditioner, for instance, represents some 375 extra dollars, and 45 per cent of all new cars have one. Pictured below, along with a representative set of price tags, are the six most popular accessories. The man who chooses them all boosts the price of his new car by 25 per cent.

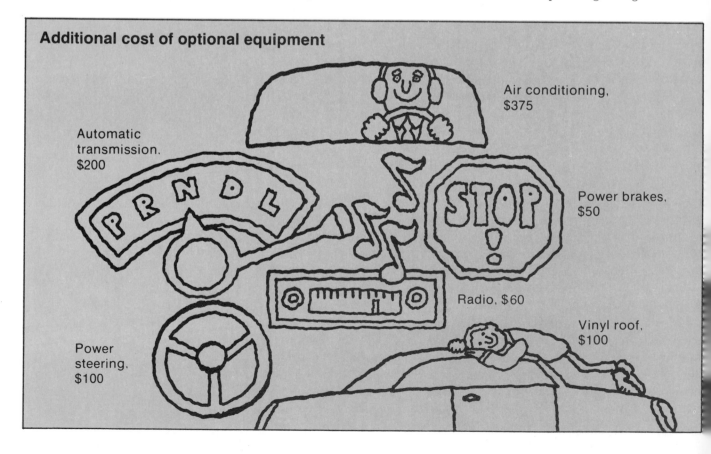

Additional cost of optional equipment

Air conditioning, $375

Automatic transmission, $200

Power brakes, $50

Radio, $60

Vinyl roof, $100

Power steering, $100

traction, power-adjusted seats, and power-operated windows—would have added another $250 to the price tag.

Optional equipment has a way of costing dollars throughout the life of the car. For example, an automatic transmission is about 12 per cent less efficient at delivering power to the wheels than a standard transmission; the efficiency drain adds perhaps $35 a year to fuel costs. With a standard transmission, you can take your foot off the accelerator and the car will be slowed down by engine retardation —thus saving wear and tear on the brakes. Automatic transmissions cannot do this as effectively, and as a result you get 20 per cent less mileage between brake relinings.

You can reap significant savings by choosing a six-cylinder engine over a V-8. The six-cylinder engine costs from $100 to $250 less than the eight. It saves about $35 per year in fuel bills, and costs less to repair. For all except large cars, the six delivers sufficient horsepower for ordinary driving, particularly in town. In fact, you can buy eights that have less horsepower than some sixes.

A new air conditioner costs about $375. At a conservative estimate, it adds $20 a year to fuel costs—although it pays back some of this outlay with higher resale value at trade-in time. Dealers may try to sell you a powerful, premium-gas V-8 to handle the extra load of the air conditioner, but the standard, regular-fuel V-8 will do the job.

Despite the expense of optional accessories, many people find them worth the money. About 90 per cent of new cars are bought with automatic transmissions and V-8 engines, about 45 per cent with air conditioners. If you drive in the mountains or like to have a surge of passing-power in reserve, a V-8 is a good investment even in intermediate-sized cars—around 3,200 pounds. If your roads are often muddy or covered with snow, a "limited-slip" differential that helps keep wheels from spinning is well worth the $40 to $50 price. Air conditioners are a boon in the South, and automatic transmissions are balm to the temper when parking or driving in traffic. Power brakes are desirable in cars that weigh more than 4,000 pounds, and power steering makes parking easier in any car of intermediate size or larger, though it causes a loss of sensitivity in handling the car.

When you set out to buy a new car, it helps to anticipate your needs in advance. The car market is a maze with an almost infinite number of paths. There are about 350 American-made models and 200 foreign models to choose from, each offering an array of attractive accessories. You can save money by not paying for a prestigious nameplate. Identical accessories usually cost less at the top of a manufacturer's low-priced line than at the bottom of his medium-priced

line. Keep a skeptical eye peeled for such disguised price factors, for you are about to enter a world where informed buymanship can mean savings of hundreds of dollars.

How to deal with a dealer

"You're practically buying at cost, believe me."

"I'm going to make you a deal you can't turn down."

"Shop around and we'll still save you $100 on the best offer."

"We've got a sale on and there's very little water in the deal."

Such blatant high-pressure pitches are becoming rarer, but you may still run into them—or slicker versions of them. If you can penetrate the razzmatazz and keep a cool wit you can save hundreds of dollars on a new car. But you need to know something about the dealer's end of the transaction if you are going to bargain on somewhat equal terms.

Not that you'll ever be truly equal. The car salesman is more adept at selling than you are at buying. He knows what to expect from every kind of customer. He knows to the dollar what his costs and profit margins are, and how much your old clunker is really worth. Some are not above using any gimmick in the bag of tricks to divert your attention or move you closer to signing on the dotted line.

You have one great weapon: the certain knowledge that he has to sell cars to stay in business, but you can buy from anyone you choose. This worries him, although he won't show it.

At the early stages, when you're looking cars over and picking up literature and asking questions and taking test runs, it's wise for husbands and wives to shop separately. You cover more ground that way, and each can plead the absence of the other in avoiding rash moves. Sooner or later—and probably sooner if you have new-car fever —the moment of action will be at hand. Every car will have a suggested price, the "sticker price," but don't take it too seriously. Federal law requires the manufacturer to attach a sticker to the window of a new car, giving the suggested retail price of the car and its particular equipment and accessories. Thanks to competition, dealers almost always sell the car for less. The rare person who pays the sticker price for a car is known as a "barefoot pilgrim" in the jargon of the trade, and he is an unfrugal fellow indeed.

Dealers offer discounts in three ways: they reduce the sticker price, inflate the value of your trade-in, or both. This can involve some bewildering sleight of hand. To see through such flummery a shrewd buyer will try to figure out in advance the lowest net price —car price minus trade-in offer—that he can expect to pay for the model of his choice. The first step is to learn how much the new car

cost the dealer. This is a lot easier to find out than you might expect.

There are several books available[1] that will tell you down to the last dollar what a dealer pays a manufacturer for any current make and model. They also list standard equipment and the dealer's cost on optional accessories that are available.

If you cannot get the exact costs, don't despair. There is a short cut. Reduce the sticker price by a percentage that will approximate the dealer's markup. For the car without accessories, deduct 17 per cent if it is a small car. If it is intermediate sized, deduct 20 per cent. If it is a regular full-sized car, deduct 22 per cent. If it is a luxury model, deduct 25 per cent. The markup on optional extras and accessories is about the same; deduct the same per cent on these. The answer you get will be a conservative figure, but it will give you an idea of what the dealer is paying. That's the first part of the equation; the trade-in on your old car is the second part.

Often the new-car discount is hidden in an abnormally high trade-in offer. But what is "abnormally high"? To answer that question, you must determine what your old car would be worth at a used-car auction. This, too, is not as difficult as it sounds. One excellent source for the information is a publication named the *Red Book, Official Used Car Market Values*. The figures in the *Red Book* are based on average prices paid for all types of used cars at wholesale auctions around the country. You can order it from National Market Reports, Inc., 900 S. Wabash Avenue, Chicago, Illinois 60605. The price, $3.18 per issue; a new issue is published every 45 days. Your banker also has a copy, and he may be willing to let you have a look at it.

If your car is in very good condition and you think it is worth more than the *Red Book* price, you may want to sell it yourself instead of trading it. Drive it into several used-car dealers and see what they bid. If the car is less than three years old and has been well cared for (a "cream puff" in the jargon of the dealers), your chances of selling it at a price above the wholesale value are reasonably good. You simply advertise it in a local newspaper and hope for the best. To help promote a sale it's worth spending some time and effort sprucing up the appearance of the car, but don't invest in major repairs.

Most people prefer the convenience of trading the car in. Once you know the true wholesale value of your trade-in and the actual

---

[1] Auto Dealer Costs. *Box 708, Dept. 94, Liberty, N.Y. 12754.*

Price Buying Directory, *Consumers Digest, 6316 North Lincoln Avenue, Chicago, Ill. 60645.*

Car Fax, *Fax Publications Inc., 220 Madison Avenue, New York 10016.*

cost of the new car to the dealer, you can estimate the amount of money you will eventually have to hand over—the difference between the trade-in allowance and the full price of the new car.

Don't forget that the dealer has his own expenses: rent, overhead, at least $25 to prepare a car for delivery, and $25 to $50 to the salesman in commissions. And he has to make a profit. As a minimum, you must add $200 to $250 to the dealer's cost to find the lowest net price he can accept and still remain in business.

Not every dealer will sell at this price. In smaller towns, discounting may be an exception to the rule. But most dealers measure success in volume and will sell a car at almost any price that promises a profit. Take your cue from the dealer. If he appears uninterested in bargaining, head for the next showroom to begin negotiations.

You can try offering a very low figure if you're an aggressive type. Chances are the salesman will first display disbelief, then annoyance. When you have assured him that you couldn't be more serious, ask him how close he can come to your figure. Such an exchange will often result in a good price.

If you don't feel up to such haggling, your best bet is to play several dealers against each other. Using the lowest price quoted by one of them, ask the others if they can beat it. This approach may squeeze out a substantial discount for you.

One other factor that will influence the bargaining is the time of year you choose to buy a new car. If you simply want a new car for the least possible money, late summer is usually your best bet. Dealers are awaiting new models and are anxious to get rid of the old. The manufacturers offer dealers special rebates, so they can cut prices even lower than usual. Discounts of $500 or $600 on medium-priced cars are common at such times.

But is it wise to buy so late in the model year? Remember that your purchase will suffer a 25 to 30 per cent depreciation the minute the new models arrive on the market. If you plan to trade every two or three years, this early loss in value will cost you at least as much as you have saved. On the other hand, if you plan to drive the car for more than three years, end-of-model-year savings are worth making.

There are other periods when bargaining is good. These come when sales fall off and dealers are anxious. One of these buyers' markets usually arrives in December when most people have their attention focused on the holidays. Another comes in late February; few people shop for a new automobile if bad weather makes it a chore. When traffic through the automobile showrooms is light, every prospective customer that comes in is treated with an extra measure of respect.

The games salesmen play

You will need every advantage you can bring to the bargaining table. The automobile salesman is an experienced adversary, and in some corners of the industry, petty trickery is not unknown. You aren't so likely to be trapped if you know what's going on, so be alert to the games that salesmen play. The most common of the ploys you might encounter goes something like this:

"Yes sir, Mr. Bryant, I guess we both know that old Ironclad of yours has seen better days. I'm determined to see you drive out of here in our power-packed Anteater 8. That means I've got to offer you the best deal in town and that's exactly what I'm going to do. What would you say if I offered you $1,500 for your Ironclad?"

Mr. Bryant, who has been praying for a thousand-dollar allowance on his car and is only normally avaricious, is staggered by the largesse being thrust upon him. He knows the old heap isn't worth $1,500. But he figures the appraiser has goofed or that this is some kind of a special discount, and he's anxious to close the deal.

Actually, Mr. Bryant has just been pitched what is, in the trade, a "highball." This is an extravagant trade-in offer, so high that no other dealer is likely to match it, and high enough to urge the prospect on to an immediate purchase. As Bryant rises to the bait, the mechanics of the sale proceed. Forms are filled out, colors and options are decided, a delivery date discussed. Psychologically, Bryant already owns this beautiful new Anteater 8—and then it happens.

The salesman finds out that he made a "mistake" on the trade-in price, or that the appraiser gave him the wrong figure, or even that the whole thing was a misunderstanding. For whatever reason, Bryant is told, sorrowfully, that they just can't allow him any more than $1,000 on his Ironclad, no matter what. His initial reaction is anger, followed by sorrow and ending in resignation. By now, he wants that car, and he consoles himself with the thought that he probably couldn't have done any better elsewhere.

A companion maneuver is a "lowball," and is used on the man who has no car to trade. In this case, the price of the new car itself is understated by a substantial amount. Again, the buyer is allowed to sell himself on getting behind the wheel of that new car immediately. Then, at the crucial moment, the low offer is withdrawn and a higher one substituted by the salesman.

A variation of these forms of trickery is the "unauthorized offer." In this case, the salesman either boosts the trade-in allowance as in the highball routine, or cuts the new car price as in lowball. When all seems set, the contract is taken to the sales manager for his

approval. He refuses to approve the deal and berates the salesman for having suggested it. Then an attempt is made to chivy the customer into paying more money than he had intended.

There is only one good way to beat these games: get all offers down in writing and have a member of the management countersign the agreement. If you are going to make a deposit, have the purchase order written so that it will be null and void if the car is not delivered at the price and terms specified.

In some showrooms, questionable practices go so far as having the waiting office bugged, so the salesman can listen to husband and wife discuss "privately" what they think of the latest offer.

In reality, though, far more customers entrap themselves than are coerced by such tactics. Many a man walks into a showroom convinced that he wants a two-door sedan, black, with six cylinders and no chrome, but drives away in a vinyl-roofed magenta hardtop with power everything, emitting the throaty roar of 440 cubes.

SHOPPING FOR A USED CAR

You have to keep your wits about you when you shop the new-car showrooms, but by comparison the used-car market can be a jungle. All of the earlier cautions apply, doubled in spades.

Yet a lot of people venture into the second-hand lots. Twice as many used cars are sold each year as new cars. The average price is about $1,000, although that low average somewhat reflects the number of cheap, battered old cars that change hands frequently.

Do used cars go to people who just can't handle the financing of a new car? Not at all. Many an astute money manager looks at the large depreciation in the first and second year of a car's life—and decides to let someone else take that rap. Affluence may make a station car desirable, and a used car fills the bill. Or little brother reaches the age of licensing and wants a car of his own to tinker with.

There is no magic key to used-car bargains, but there are some things that you should watch out for.

Be suspicious of the dealer whose lot is surrounded by signs saying, "We Undersell Everybody," "Fantastic Discounts," or other high-pressure come-ons. If you are drawn by an advertisement of some astonishingly low-priced car, expect to be told that the give-away in question has just been sold—but look at the other bargains on hand.

Usually it is wise to shop the used-car lot of an established dealer. He has the mechanics and shop facilities to put a used car in shape, and he will be around to stand behind his warranty. He has probably unloaded the worst trade-in lemons at the wholesale mar-

ket. You are likely to pay a premium for these plus-values, but it is well worth it.

The used-car warranty is generally for 30 days (though sometimes for only 24 hours), with the cost of any repairs to be split 50-50 with the buyer. If the repairs must be made in the dealer's shop, this can be small consolation when you see how they are priced. Any warranty, of course, should be in writing; oral promises are worthless. If the manufacturer's new-car warranty has been kept in effect, it can sometimes be transferred for a fee to a second owner.

Before you commit yourself to the purchase of a used car, you should hunt for signs of abnormal wear or damage. If you have access to "diagnostic clinics," where mechanics specialize in applying claborate tests to locate automotive defects, it would be worthwhile to pay the $5 to $20 fee for a trouble-shooting analysis. Even without the clinic's fancy apparatus, a good mechanic can put the car on a lift and look for tell-tale welds and frame-straightening that reveal a major accident in its past. Any car that has had such major surgery should be scrupulously avoided.

Text continues on page 94

Some cars seem to run forever
Despite the best efforts of Detroit to put a brand-new car in every garage every year, Americans insist on cherishing old ones. Almost half of all cars on the road in 1968 were five years old or older, and nearly 13 per cent had already passed the 10-year mark of old age—but the biggest single group, 24 per cent, were relatively new, two to four years old.

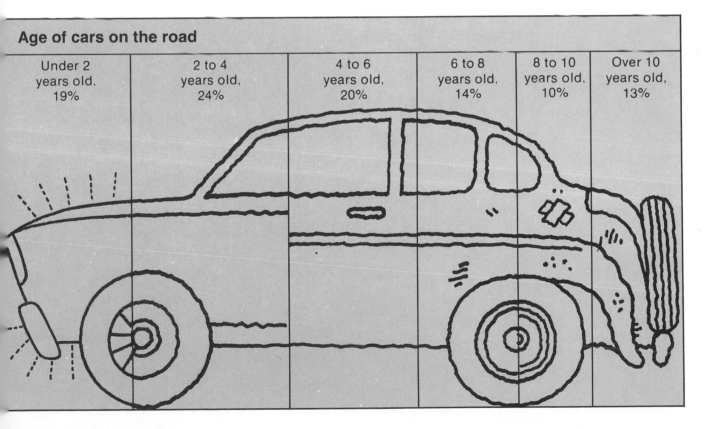

Age of cars on the road

| Under 2 years old. 19% | 2 to 4 years old, 24% | 4 to 6 years old, 20% | 6 to 8 years old, 14% | 8 to 10 years old, 10% | Over 10 years old, 13% |

On-the-lot inspection

Every dealer tries to make his cars look good; you'll have to play Sherlock Holmes to outfox him. Look first for evidence of a crash. Once you've eliminated the dogs, try to discover whether a car needs more than modest repairs (almost all cars need something). Here's an amateur's check list to help.

1 Be suspicious of new paint. What does it hide? Rippled areas or grainy patches suggest an accident.

2 Check for rust spots around body edges, behind bumpers and inside the trunk. Probe with a finger to see if the rust is only on the surface or is working through from beneath. Shun cars that are excessively rusty.

6 Hop up and down on a bumper, then jump off. If the body oscillates more than once, you can bet the car will need new shock absorbers soon.

7 Operate all switches and controls. Try door handles, window cranks, vents and seat adjustments. Such minor items can be costly to repair.

8 Check for signs of wear on "rubbing points"—seats, floormats, pedals. Wear is a better clue to mileage than the odometer, a most untrustworthy gauge.

9 Press the brake pedal down hard. If it continues to sink instead of stopping, there is a leak—most likely in the master cylinder, possibly in wheel cylinders or lines.

On-the-road testing

About one out of three used-car buyers commits himself even before driving the car. This can be a grievous error, for no inspection is thorough without a road test. If the dealer won't let you try the car out, go elsewhere. And don't buy from him if he insists on a down payment first. On the road, make these checks:

1 Again, listen for odd noises. For comparison's sake, drive a well-tuned car and listen carefully.

2 Go forward and backward several times from a full stop to make sure transmission works smoothly.

3 Accelerate rapidly from 20 to 60 mph. If the car gains speed smoothly without sputtering, you can be fairly confident that the engine is in fair shape.

Look to see how well the rear wheels line up with the front ones. Better still, have the salesman drive the car slowly away from you. If it seems to move crabwise, that means a bent frame—and a car to be skipped.

Few dealers leave tires untouched, but it is easy to spot recaps: the tread is new while the sidewalls are slightly crazed.

Grab a front wheel at the top and give it a good shake. If you hear clunking noises or discover unexpected looseness, the wheel bearings and ball joints may need replacement.

10 Start the engine with the hood up and listen for unusual hissing, squealing, grinding or grating noises. Don't be fooled by a new-looking engine; most dealers steam-clean the engine, some even repaint it. Check for leaks in the radiator and connecting hoses.

11 Race the engine and have a friend check the exhaust. Blue smoke means burning oil. (Make sure there is oil to burn; to avoid smoking, some unscrupulous dealers have been known to drain the crankcase dry, then give a very fast engine demonstration.)

At 50 mph, brake hard. Brakes should hold equally on all four wheels, without grabbing and without causing the car to pull to one side or the other.

Drive at medium speed over a rough stretch of road to check for any looseness in the steering mechanism. Also check for the bounce and sway that reveal worn shock absorbers.

6 Take the car to a diagnostic center or garage for an impartial appraisal. The professional check-up should include the engine (for cylinder compression), brake linings, frame, cooling system, exhaust system and front end (for alignment). If you can persuade the mechanic to test-drive the car for a professional analysis of its transmission and drive shaft, you will have done as much as you can.

Other points to check: Look for a well-equipped used car; most extra accessories are a bonus, for only air conditioning, power steering and good tires are enough in demand to raise the price. A used car of a make that eschews extreme styling changes is desirable, and you can save money by accepting an unpopular color. A sedan is likely to cost less than a hardtop of the same model—and give you less body trouble. You generally get more miles of trouble-free driving from a smaller, newer used car than an older, more luxurious car at the same price. Don't trust the odometer to indicate the actual mileage the car has been driven; it is usually a simple matter to turn the "clock" back, and owners themselves sometimes adjust the odometer before coming in to trade. When you are selecting a model to shop for, it pays to check the library's stacks of old automotive magazines to see how various models were rated by car analysts when they were new. To help you find the cream puffs among the dogs on the used-car lot, there is an illustrated check list on the preceding pages.

RENTING AND LEASING

If you want to avoid the hazards of buying a used car and have ruled out buying a new car for one reason or another, there is a third means available for acquiring private transportation. You can rent (short term) or lease (long term) from one of the hundreds of companies offering such services.

Renting is an obvious answer for a city family that has only occasional need for private transportation. It makes especially good sense in areas where the cost of garaging is astronomical and street storage unsafe. Garaging a car is highly advisable in Manhattan, for instance, but it may cost upwards of $55 a month. This is one reason there are 11 pages of automobile rental agency listings in the Manhattan classified telephone directory.

Renting is not always a bargain. The typical rate of a large city rental agency is $14 a day and 14 cents a mile, fuel included, but may be half that for a small car without fuel. There are almost as many rate schedules and types of deals as there are rental agencies, and assiduous comparison shopping pays off.

Leasing is hardly cheaper than owning your own car (the company has to make a profit), but may be worthwhile if you don't want to be bothered with buying, insuring and maintaining it. There are some good points. You tie up less capital by leasing a car instead of purchasing it. You have a clear idea of your costs in advance. In many cases your budget won't be reduced to a shambles by unforeseen repair bills because the leasing company will pick up the tab. Bu

consider the drawbacks: you must lease on a long-term basis—usually a minimum of 12 months—and may not be able to cancel the lease even if you discover that it is uneconomic. Also, at the end of the lease period, you have nothing. Some agencies give you the option of buying the car when the lease is over, but in most instances you would have been better off financially purchasing a car to begin with.

SAVING MONEY ON THE MONEY FOR A CAR

Often the buyer of a car, new or used, will turn in his old car as the down payment and sign an installment agreement with the dealer for the balance; no cash at all changes hands. Chances are, the salesman who sells you a car will have a purchase contract in one hand and financing papers in the other. Well he should. Some dealers make more profit on the financing than on the sale itself, for they usually sell the installment contract to a credit company for cash. Although the great majority of installment buyers finance their cars through dealers, it can be an extravagance. Some sign installment contracts that more than double the price of the car.

When you buy a car on time, you are simply borrowing money, and the amount you pay for this privilege can vary tremendously. You should shop for credit as carefully as you do for the car itself.

Take a three-year, $3,000 loan, for example. If you finance the car through the dealer, the interest on the loan may amount to $700 or more. Your local bank may charge you only $500 or $600 interest for the same loan. Dealers usually charge interest rates that are about three quarters of a percentage point above those of commercial banks. While a bank loan is cheaper than the dealer's installment contract, you may get a better deal yet if you belong to a credit union.

The least expensive way to buy a car is to pay cash. If you can steel yourself to bank the monthly payment for three years and then pay cash, the interest your money has earned will allow for some attractive extras. Between 30 and 40 per cent of car buyers manage to pay cash. But if you must borrow, borrow only as much as you really need and do so on the best terms you can find (*Chapter 2*).

THE HIGH COST OF INSURANCE

Insurance is the fastest rising expense in the whole array of car costs, and you can easily see why. Traffic—and hence accidents—continues to increase. Garage labor costs are up, medical fees are up, vandalism and car thefts are up. For stylistic reasons, today's cars are dazzling but fragile; even the bumper must be made of delicate-gauge steel in order to be so beautifully sculpted.

It pays to shop for financing

You can save more than $300 on a $3,000, three-year auto loan by going to the right place for money. Credit unions provide the best bargains, but you have to be a member. Commercial banks come next. Often the most expensive loans are ones you directly negotiate with your auto dealer.

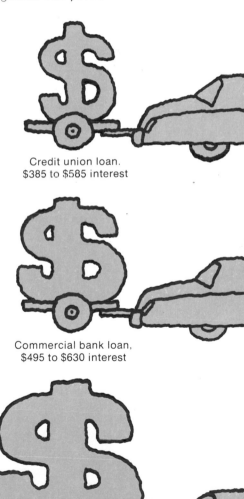

Credit union loan.
$385 to $585 interest

Commercial bank loan,
$495 to $630 interest

Dealer financing,
$585 to $720 interest

You may moan when you pay for your insurance—but don't skimp. A good case can be made for the idea that the insurance covering your car is more important than that on your house. Your house probably cost 10 times what you spent on your car. But your house can't come around a curve and plow into another vehicle, injuring four passengers. No man can afford the awesome judgments that can result when a collision kills or maims several persons.

There are three basic kinds of insurance coverage that are available for cars and their drivers:

■ Liability coverage, by far the most important, protects others against the harm you can do to them with your car.

■ Collision coverage pays for repairs to your own car if it is damaged by another or collides with an object like a wall or a telephone pole.

■ Comprehensive coverage reimburses you for losses from such hazards as theft, fire, wind damage and vandalism.

Your auto policy can also include some lesser coverages:

■ Uninsured motorist coverage to pay for injury or damages to you caused by another driver whose own insurance is insufficient, or by a hit-and-run driver who is not apprehended.

■ Medical payments coverage to pay for medical treatment for yourself or your passengers for injuries sustained in an automobile accident, no matter who is at fault.

■ Towing and road service coverage to make things a bit easier when you are forced to call for such help.

The importance of the first of these coverages—liability—cannot be overemphasized. It is truly essential for any thoughtful man, and some liability coverage is compulsory in most states. An automobile driven at today's high speeds can wreak fantastic damage when it goes out of control. Liability is usually bought in a three-part series designated by its face amounts. A policy referred to as a "50/100/10" means the insurer's liability is limited to $50,000 for injury to one person, $100,000 maximum for two or more persons injured in one accident, and $10,000 for property damage.

A 10/20/5 policy—or a $25,000 single-unit policy—should be regarded as the barest minimum under today's highway conditions. Coverage of $100,000 and $300,000 for personal injuries or deaths is commonplace, and many men with extensive assets to protect from damage suits carry million-dollar policies.

Fortunately, additional coverage is not proportionately more expensive. The chart, using figures that apply to an over-25-year-old driver in Boston in 1969, shows how a fairly small increase in the insurance premium gains a very large increase in liability coverage.

One warning is in order. If you buy insurance from the dealer who sells you a car, check carefully to see if you have liability coverage. Sometimes a motorist thinks the dealer is selling him full coverage when in fact the insurance covers only the merchandise itself —the vehicle in which the finance company still has an interest. If you check the cost of liability coverage bought from a dealer, you will find in almost every case that it is more expensive than similar insurance bought from a regular insurance agent.

Where to save on insurance

You should never pinch pennies on liability coverage, but you can save on collision coverage without gambling too much. As a car depreciates in value, you should question the necessity of collision

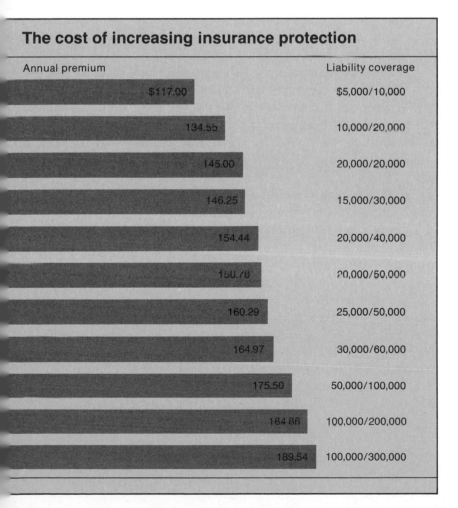

The cost of increasing insurance protection

Annual premium	Liability coverage
$117.00	$5,000/10,000
134.55	10,000/20,000
145.00	20,000/20,000
146.25	15,000/30,000
154.44	20,000/40,000
156.78	20,000/50,000
160.29	25,000/50,000
164.97	30,000/60,000
175.50	50,000/100,000
184.86	100,000/200,000
189.54	100,000/300,000

An auto insurance bargain

In a day when heavy auto insurance protection is not only prudent but something of a bargain, you can increase your personal liability protection roughly 30 times while the premium you have to pay less than doubles. The rates in the graph at left, supplied by the Liberty Mutual Insurance Company, apply to an over-25-year-old driver in Boston in 1969. Minimum coverage ($5,000 for injury to one person, $10,000 for two or more in a single accident) cost $117 a year. Increasing the protection to $100,000 for one injury and $300,000 for multiple injuries (*bottom bar*) raised the premium to $189.50—30 times the protection at less than twice the price.

Saving on collision premiums

The cost of insuring against damage to your own car can be cut in half if you agree to pay more of the repair bill out of your own pocket. For a Boston driver, over 25, with a new "standard-size" car, the premium for collision insurance drops from $161 if the company pays all but $50 to $75 for "250 deductible."

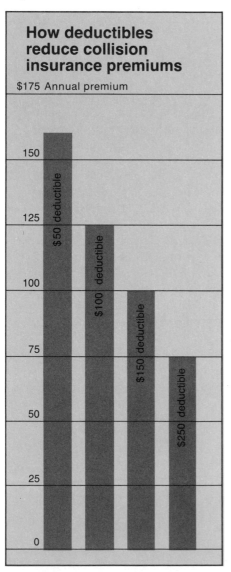

How deductibles reduce collision insurance premiums

$175 Annual premium

150

125

100

75

50

25

0

$50 deductible

$100 deductible

$150 deductible

$250 deductible

insurance; with an old car, worth less than $400, you can probably do without it. If you have a newer car, you can save money on the premium by assuming a larger part of the risk yourself. Most collision coverage includes a deductible clause. On a $50-deductible policy, for example, you pay the first $50 for repairs of collision damage and the insurance company pays the rest. You can also sign up for $100- to $250-deductible policies. The $100-deductible policy is a good buy. By permitting the insurance company to avoid the costly paperwork of frequent small claims, you save substantially on the premium rate. The chart on this page shows how much the premium rate goes down as the deductible amount rises.

Comprehensive coverage—protecting against vandalism, theft, earthquake, fire and other natural or unnatural disasters—can be similarly manipulated. You will save money on the premium by writing a deductible clause into the comprehensive coverage policy. And you may want to do without it entirely if your car is more than five years old, for an old car is less likely to be stolen.

There are ways to cut insurance costs without diminishing coverage at all; try for as many special discounts as fit your circumstances.
■ Compact car discount. If you drive a compact or small car, you may get as much as 10 per cent off on liability premiums.
■ Multiple car discount. Two (or more) cars owned by the same family are not cheaper to insure than one, but coverage bought for both together can be cheaper than for two separately.
■ Good driver discount. Some companies will give you a discount if you avoid accidents over a specified period of time.
■ Limited teen-age use discount. If any driver of your car is younger than 25, the cost of insurance will rise dramatically, as you can see from the charts on the following pages. You can hold that rise to a minimum by trying for a limited-use discount, based on the percentage of car use that will be attributed to the young driver. This is especially practical if the youngster is away at school for nine months of the year —and doesn't take the car with him.
■ Driver-training discount. Another saving possible for a family with a young driver is the reduced premium sometimes offered if that young driver has completed an approved driver-training program.
■ Good-student discount. Some companies even give a discount if a young driver is a superior scholar, presumably on the theory that if he is studying long hours, he is not out driving around town.

All these discounts and special arrangements vary from company to company, and you may have to ask around to find the combination that suits you best. But there is another way the company you choose

influences what you pay. Anyone who applies for insurance answers a lot of questions about his car: how far it is driven and where, who drives it and the like. From the answers, the insurer develops a "score" for each applicant. The score decides whether the company will insure you and at what rate. Since not all companies score alike, premium differences develop here, and that makes it worth your while to do some comparison shopping.

But suppose you can't get insurance?

Of course your score could turn out disastrously bad. Suddenly you discover that you are considered to be "uninsurable" by the insurance company of your choice.

This can happen when you apply for a policy (as it does to many under-25 males), but it can also happen during the first 60 days of a new policy's life. After this initial period, capricious cancellation is becoming a thing of the past. Most policies stipulate that cancellation after 60 days can be made only (1) for nonpayment of premium, or (2) for suspension of the car registration or driver's license. In one encouraging development, some companies now guarantee not to cancel for five years, but this does not assure you that your premium rate won't go up after you have filed a claim.

A more common hazard is a refusal to renew your policy when it is due to expire. Each company determines its own policies on renewals, but you may find one that will promise automatic renewal unless you exceed the national average for auto accidents (about one every seven years). In many states, an insurance company must give 30 to 60 days' advance notice if it does not intend to renew. This allows you time to shop around for a more lenient company that will not take such a dim view of your accumulated accident record. If you believe that you are receiving unfair or arbitrary treatment, complain to your state insurance department.

If your accident record is really bad and you fail to find a company willing to issue you a policy, you can demand that you be put in the Assigned Risk Pool. This is an arrangement to give bad risks some protection; every insurer licensed by a state must accept a share of the business. The pool is a last resort; it ordinarily offers only the coverage defined by the state as "minimum." This usually is only $5,000/$10,000 on personal injury liability. As we have seen, this coverage is grossly inadequate, but it is better than nothing.

Your only other recourse is to seek out a company specializing in high-risk insurance. These companies are usually small and often precariously run. If you must locate a high-risk insurer, do so through

an established insurance broker. He will have access to authoritative reports that rate firms according to reliability.

KEEPING UPKEEP DOWN

When you buy a car you are buying transportation. It is small consolation to have the shiniest chrome, the largest taillights and the most luxurious upholstery if your car won't run. To keep those wheels rolling you need to pay attention to maintenance.

There are two kinds. The first, "preventive," includes such things as changing oil, and cleaning or replacing air, oil and gas filters. The second, "corrective," includes fixing what has gotten out of whack and replacing what has been broken or worn out. You buy the first, of course, in order to avoid the second.

In a sense, even filling the gas tank is preventive maintenance, since it prevents the engine from quitting for lack of fuel. A lot of nonsense has been written and talked about saving money on gas. Some

Those costly young drivers
In an era when a set of car keys initiates a teenager into adulthood, auto-insurance rates reflect the fact that freewheeling young boys are notoriously accident prone. A 17-year-old boy owning his first car must pay more than three times as much as his father pays for the same coverage. The risk and the premiums decrease if the boy does not have a car all to himself —and when marriage adds to his responsibility. Girls pay less for insurance; they are involved in fewer accidents, not necessarily because they drive more cautiously but probably because they drive less, especially during dangerous late hours.

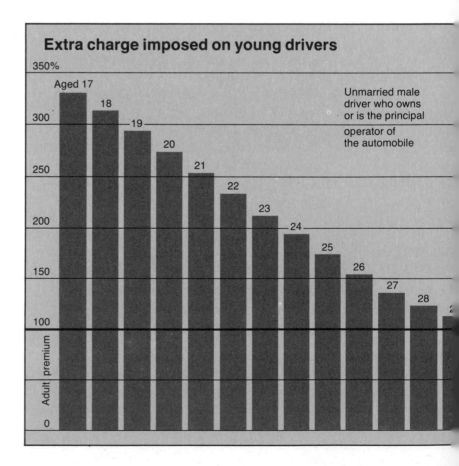

Extra charge imposed on young drivers

Unmarried male driver who owns or is the principal operator of the automobile

arithmetic shows why it's nonsense. The average motorist burns about 700 gallons of gas a year. If he drives across town to do business with a cut-rate station, thereby saving 1½ cents a gallon, after a full year he will have saved the grand total of $10.50, which he might have spent on the drive across town. You can do somewhat better if you improve the mileage you get by driving conservatively and keeping the motor tuned; an improvement from 15 to 17 miles per gallon, for example, will cut your gas bill by more than 10 per cent. Good driving habits will do wonders for your mileage. Quick starts are exhilarating, but cost you a veritable torrent of gasoline. Don't slam the accelerator to the floor when starting up; instead feed the gas to the engine slowly and evenly as you pick up speed. Try to anticipate the rhythm of the traffic to keep stops to a minimum. Drive at even speeds. Anything over 50 miles per hour will use up extra gas—and will cause greater wear on the tires, engine and other parts.

If your engine is specifically designed to burn premium fuel, don't

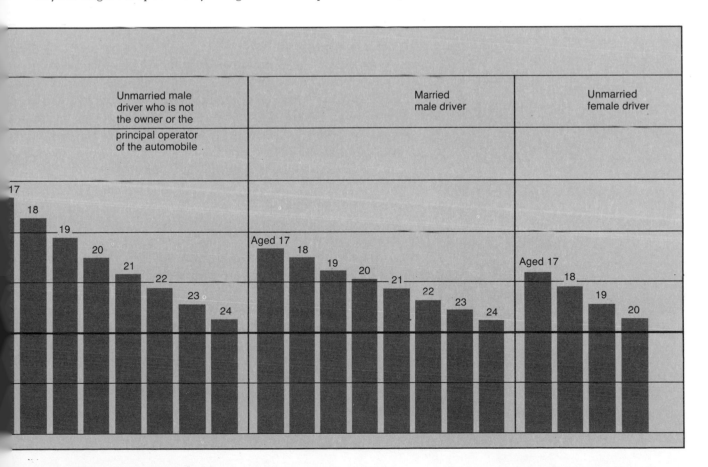

The bigger the car, the more it costs to keep up

"It's not the cost but the upkeep" is a cliché that is usually true. As a rule of thumb the heavier and more costly cars are more expensive to repair and maintain. However, complexity of design is a surer measure of expense than size of car. For body repairs, cost estimates from a garage mechanic's manual for three 1968 models were:

	$2,175 Ford Falcon (2,850 pounds)	$3,000 Dodge Polara (3,800 pounds)	$6,300 Cadillac Eldorado (4,700 pounds)
Replace door	$142	$161	$207
Replace windshield	$134	$178	$147
Replace radiator grill	$ 22	$100	$152
Replace fender	$108	$136	$203

On maintenance jobs, the cost of the mechanic's time is often as great a factor as the cost of the materials used, but again this varies radically when the design complicates a job. For the three models, labor ranged from $15 to $20 for replacing shock absorbers, from $6 to $20 for relining brakes, from $20 to $30 for an engine tune-up.

try to get away with regular, for you could cause damage. However, engines can be re-tuned to burn regular instead of premium gas. Don't waste money on premium gas if your car is designed for regular.

Next to buying gas, the most frequent maintenance chore is changing oil. Car manufacturers suggest generously long intervals. General Motors, for example, says every four months or 6,000 miles; Ford says every six months or 6,000 miles. These frequencies are required to keep new-car warranties in effect. If you make a lot of short trips, it is best to change the oil every three months or 3,000 miles, whichever comes first. This will cost a few extra dollars every year, but it may save hundreds of dollars in repairs as the car gets older.

Because front tires wear faster, many drivers rotate tires every 5,000 miles to equalize the wear. This makes sense only if you do the job yourself. A mechanic might charge you $2 per tire per rotation, and it just isn't worth it. Tire companies are beginning to sell specialized tires for the front and rear wheels—and these certainly should not be rotated. Make sure, however, that you switch from snow tires to regular treads as soon as the winter is over.

All things considered, the owner's manual is probably the best guide to knowing what to do when. Manuals tend to overdo a good thing by assuming the shortest possible interval between filter cleanings and the like, but you have to follow the manual anyway to keep your new-car warranty in effect. Manufacturers are well aware that a car serviced on a tight schedule is far less likely to give the owner any cause to file a warranty claim. It has been estimated that following their schedules costs the owner about $125 a year.

Treasure a good mechanic

Not many people run into trouble getting the oil changed. Anything more complex is another matter. One difficulty is the shortage of mechanics. In 1950, there was one mechanic for every 73 cars; by 1975, there will be one mechanic for an estimated 154 cars. Maintenance costs can go nowhere but up. Treasure a good mechanic as you would a good doctor, and let him know that you will be a regular customer.

You can't escape the problem even with a new car, for repair work covered by the warranty may cause the most frustration. Car dealers say that manufacturers allow them insufficient compensation for their warranty work, permitting only a 25 per cent profit on parts, compared to the 40 per cent profit that they make on nonwarranty work. As a result, they save the better men for work done at the full rate and give the "money-losing" warranty jobs to their least skilled mechanics—if they do it at all. During a Senate investigation of au-

tomobile repair work, one witness spoke of the "wall job." You drive your car into the dealer's garage for warranty repairs—and he parks it beside a wall and ignores it. Another witness testified that he repeatedly took his Cadillac back to a dealer to have a brake defect fixed; over and over again, the dealer insisted the brakes were fine, but when the impatient Cadillac owner went to another shop, the trouble was immediately spotted and soon repaired.

You have some protection against shoddy warranty service. If a dealer rejects a warranty claim, send him a registered letter demanding that the repair be made. If this gets no action, notify the nearest office of the manufacturer and ask that a factory representative step in. He will find the dealer, the factory or you liable, or he may find you partly at fault and offer to split the bill.

When the warranty ends you're on your own in what may prove a wicked world. Thousands of garages victimize car owners by overcharging them, performing unneeded repairs, or simply doing poor work. When an expert mechanic in Denver inspected 7,000 cars that had been "fixed" in service shops in his area, he found that only 1 per cent of them had been repaired properly—and some had not even been touched.

Dishonest shops frequently charge for tune-ups that are not needed. Many a car is given a "bargain" brake job that leaves it worse off than before. Shock absorbers are often replaced long before they need be. Sometimes a mechanic shows a car owner metal filings that he took from the bottom of the automatic transmission case. Neglecting to mention that such metal particles may come from the normal meshing of gears, the mechanic suggests a $200 overhaul—which may actually consist of a simple change of transmission fluid.

One way to avoid banditry at the garage lies in the auto diagnostic clinics that have sprung up around the country. For a fee, you can have your car put through a series of tests that indicate its weaknesses. Some clinics limit their work to diagnosis; you get the fixing done elsewhere. But many also have repair departments—and they may find more work to do than really needs to be done.

THE DISMAL ECONOMICS OF A SECOND CAR

The sneakiest thing about a second car is that at first it doesn't seem an extravagance. Frequently, the family doesn't "buy" a second car at all, but simply keeps one it owns instead of trading it in. This way, it seems as though it came free.

Even if the second car is purchased, the cost can seem reasonable enough. Second cars tend to be less than pretentious. As for operating expense, the question is often passed off as irrelevant. After all, with

two cars, each will be used only half as much as when the family had one. Operating and maintenance expense for two, then, needn't be any higher than for one, right?

Wrong. To see where this logic falls apart, let's see what happens to Harriet and Tom when they decide that any family with a two-car garage ought to have two cars to put into it:

■ Purchase. Tom's three-year-old sedan was worth $1,000 as a trade-in on the $3,500 station wagon he bought. Since he and Harriet kept the sedan instead of trading it in as a down payment on the new car they had to take $1,000 out of a savings account paying 5 per cent interest. Not only were they out $1,000, they lost the $50-plus a year it had been earning in a savings account.

■ Insurance. Tom managed to cut the $107 annual premium on the old sedan by taking a larger deductible amount on collision coverage. Even so, by the time he added coverage for the new car his insurance costs had nearly doubled.

■ Maintenance and repairs. Tom and Harriet discovered an eternal truth: The family that owns two cars just naturally drives more than the same family with one. They had been averaging 11,000 miles a year in one car; they totaled 15,000 when they acquired the second. The older car was now burning a quart of oil with every second tank of gas. Furthermore, they faced an ever-increasing round of repairs on the older car at the same time their budget was burdened with new-car payments and other expenses.

■ Licenses. It costs $16 a year to license a car in the state where they live. Not a great drain, but another expense doubled.

A nation on wheels

"Two cars in every garage" may not yet be an accurate description of the United States, but it's getting closer. By 1968 nearly half of all families in the $10,000-to-$15,000-income range had acquired a second car, and in the over-$15,000 bracket, 62 per cent had two or more cars. As for one car, even among the terribly poor —income below $1,000—more than one fourth of the families had managed to acquire an automobile.

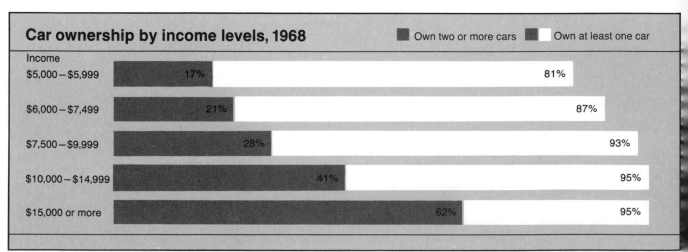

Car ownership by income levels, 1968   ■ Own two or more cars   ■ Own at least one car

Income	Own two or more cars	Own at least one car
$5,000–$5,999	17%	81%
$6,000–$7,499	21%	87%
$7,500–$9,999	28%	93%
$10,000–$14,999	41%	95%
$15,000 or more	62%	95%

Data: Survey Research Center, University of Michigan

So they are now spending about $2,000 a year on transportation, compared with about $1,200 a year when they owned just one car. This is about 20 per cent of their after-tax income. It may be worthwhile to them, but it's more likely that they never computed this cost and would be appalled if they did. They do know that now there never seems to be enough money to buy new furniture, take a nice vacation or set aside some retirement income.

A tremendous amount of our national wealth is expended on automobiles. Some droll statisticians love to point out that there are more cars than bathtubs in America. Every year, about four million cars are added to the horde that is already on the road. Even if we left all of the nation's trucks and buses in the parking lot, the entire population of the country could ride at the same time in our automobiles. In fact, we could all ride in front without being squeezed a bit.

Car-owning, then, is not just a matter of practical necessity. We enjoy driving cars. We use them to ease emotional tensions. They fill us with a sense of freedom, power, speed and general well-being. They affect our jobs, our recreation, our love-lives, our social status and the economy. They constitute a social force of roughly the same magnitude as the American Revolution or the invention of gunpowder. Throughout the lives of most of us, one car follows another like floats in a Rose Bowl parade. Models may differ with our circumstances —sports cars when we're young, station wagons in the family years and sedate sedans in old age. But the question is never whether to buy, it is only what and when. Henry Ford knew what he was up to when he envisioned an entire nation on wheels. Hopefully this excursion into the economics of car ownership will help you see more clearly just what you are up against each time you sign on the dotted line to make his dream come true.

5
Life insurance

Savings for the knowing buyer

The first person to buy a life-insurance policy was one William Gybbons of London, a purveyor of salt, who in 1583 paid a combine of merchants a premium to insure his life for one year. Before the year ran out he died, setting a standard in the astute use of life insurance few policyholders since have been able to match. The rueful merchants went to court in an attempt to contest the Gybbons claim on a technicality, but they lost. Despite this inauspicious beginning for the underwriters, the insurance industry has grown enormously over the years until today it is the No. 1 financial giant of the U.S. The combined assets of the two largest companies exceed those of General Motors, Ford, Standard Oil of New Jersey, General Electric and Chrysler—the five largest industrial corporations—all put together.

Such growth is understandable. Insurance fills a vital need in the life of almost everyone by providing protection against the economic consequences of ruinous disasters—the burning down of a house; a whopping damage suit; the death of the family breadwinner. When a man died in the old days his widow and children went to the poorhouse. Today continued family income can be guaranteed by life insurance, which is basically society's way of saying: "Let's all chip in a dollar or two a week. When one of us dies, his family can be paid something to live on from the common fund. Meanwhile the rest of us will keep on chipping in our dollars until *we* die." Insurance is simply a means of sharing the risk of individual disasters among a great many people, so the payments any one man has to make are small enough from year to year that he can afford to pay them.

There is no question about the value of insurance. The important thing is to understand what the different kinds of insurance are, and to make sure that you are buying the right kinds in the right amounts. Particularly in the case of insurance that protects you and your family directly—life insurance and medical insurance—you may have a hard time deciding what sort of protection you need, and how much. On the matter of insuring your automobile (*Chapter 4*) or your house and valuables (*Chapter 7*), many decisions are guided by measurable quantities like replacement costs. But your needs for personal insurance are more complex to calculate.

Life insurance, for example, is essential to family economic security. But nobody has any idea of how long he will live. Therefore nobody knows when his family will need the money from his life insurance. And he doesn't know how much they will need either. Will there be a good balance in the savings account by the time he dies? A portfolio of stocks? Will the children be through college or will they still need tuition? How much money will you need if you

live past retirement and into a ripe old age? On the other hand, where would your family be if you died tomorrow? The human mind possesses some wonderful protective devices and one of the best is the veil it throws over thoughts of age and death. No one (until perhaps age 80 or thereabouts) thinks that someday he will be "old." Yet the only alternative to growing old is to die young, and most people are even less able to imagine that next year or next month they may be among the departed. Dying is an abstraction; it happens to somebody else. Yet by the statistical tables insurance companies use, if you're 35 years old you can line up 400 of your peers and see the face of someone who will die within the year. As for which one it will be, Old Man Statistics couldn't care less. Somebody down the line, the person next to you . . . or you. So you need insurance, and not next year but now. And yet you've got to look well into the future, too, at all the imponderables of savings and tuitions and retirement income.

THE TWO BASIC KINDS OF LIFE INSURANCE

You'll never know exactly when you will die. But you can calculate how much life insurance you need, and what kind. There are fundamentally only two types. They come under many names and have many frills, complications and purposes, but they all offer only two basic alternatives. These are:

■ Term insurance. A term insurance policy insures your life—and that is all it does—for a certain set "term" of years—five years, perhaps —and then it must be renewed.

■ Cash-value insurance. This is insurance that remains in effect, not for a certain term of years, but until you discontinue it or its benefits are paid. In addition, part of the premium is set aside for you in what amounts to a savings account; this money belongs to you whether you keep the policy in force or not. The many common varieties of life insurance—ordinary life (also called whole life or straight life) policies, endowment policies, retirement policies—are simply forms of cash-value insurance: basic insurance plus savings accounts.

To understand the differences between these kinds of insurance, what they offer and what is best for you, you need to know something of the way life insurance works.

Suppose that a company insures the lives of a thousand 25-year-old men for $1,000 each. Eventually, when all these men have died, the company will have paid out $1,000 per man to the persons they designated as their beneficiaries, a total of a million dollars in benefits. Therefore, the company will have had to collect a million dollars

from these men—plus some more for itself to cover operating expenses, sales commissions, reserves and profit.

However, since all these men are not going to die immediately, the insurance company does not need its million right away. In fact, it can stretch collecting its million over a long period of years. To figure out how much it must collect and when, it uses a device known as a mortality table—a typical one is shown on this page—which tells how many of those 25-year-olds will die each year.

Mortality tables are based on statistics gathered from among huge numbers of people. It is easy to see from the one shown here that the insurance company is going to need to collect from its thousand 25-year-old men during the first year that they are insured only $1.93 each, plus whatever is necessary to cover running expenses and profit and to build up reserves against the unlikely, but still possible, chance that three or four men might die that first year instead of less than two. In actual practice, that $1.93 figure will more than double; for example, one company charges $4.82 per $1,000 for one of the least expensive types of insurance.

Theoretically, the initial premium paid by John Jones, aged 30, would be dirt cheap. But if he continues to live, he will be paying off on the others in the pool who die each year and in consequence his payments must go up. If he renews every five years, he will have to pay, by the time he is 40, $8.19 per $1,000, and when he is 65 he will be assessed $46.04 for that same protection.

Now, $46.04 is a lot of money to pay yearly per $1,000 worth of insurance and might be especially burdensome to a man reaching retirement age. So obviously it is to Jones's advantage to find a system whereby he pays the *same* amount each year. Taking what Jones would pay into the common fund if he lived an average length of time (the mortality table comes into play again here), the mathematicians come up with a "level premium"—a set sum that Jones will pay each year for the term of the policy. One typical company charges a level premium of $11.47 for $1,000 worth of insurance that will cover a man of 30 until he is 65. These uniform payments, though bigger at the beginning, are much smaller than they would otherwise be at the end, and they have the further advantage of enabling Jones to know long in advance just what his insurance expense is going to be.

First things first: pure protection

The example we have just given is an instance of term insurance. John Jones, 30, has undertaken to insure his life until age 65, a term of 35 years, not for his entire life. He could have done it for 10 years,

The odds on deaths

Statisticians can predict with uncanny accuracy the number of people in any age group who will die during a given year. Mortality tables like the one below tell life-insurance companies what the chances are that they will have to pay off on a policy, and form the basis for calculating premium rates. (This table, based on past records, does not reflect current death rates in the U.S.)

Age	Average deaths per thousand people
25	1.93
30	2.13
35	2.51
40	3.53
45	5.35
50	8.32
55	13.00
60	20.34
65	31.75

or 20, or, like William Gybbons of London, for only one. The total premiums paid for the shorter terms would be smaller, but otherwise the insurance would be just the same. John would have his life covered for $1,000 at all times the policy was in effect. At the end of the specified term he would have nothing.

Term insurance is pure insurance; it protects Jones's dependents against the loss of his income, just as fire insurance protects Jones against the loss of his house in case of fire. And that is the primary purpose of life insurance—to see that dependents are not left in want in the event of the death of the chief provider. All else is secondary. Thus, term is the simplest form of life insurance. It is also the cheapest. Therefore, is it not the best? Yes, except for one awkward point: What does John Jones do if he still wants to be insured

What your insurance dollars buy

The basic decision in buying life insurance is the choice between two types with radically different costs. An "ordinary life" policy includes an emergency savings fund and provides insurance protection indefinitely at a fixed, moderately high premium —$751 a year in the example charted here. A "term" policy includes no savings and must be renewed at successively higher premiums every few years. A young man, aged 30, could get $50,000 worth of insurance protection with a term policy for one-third the premium charged for an equivalent ordinary-life policy; the situation would change sharply as he grew older—if he still needed this much coverage at age 60 he would pay twice as much for term as for the ordinary-life policy.

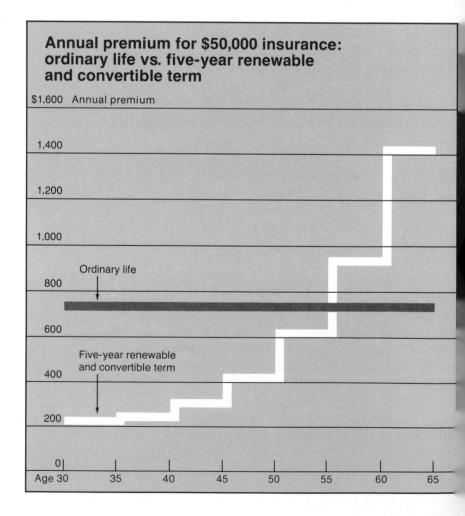

Annual premium for $50,000 insurance: ordinary life vs. five-year renewable and convertible term

when he reaches 65 and his term insurance runs out? He may have little in the way of savings and be worried about how his wife would get along if he should die suddenly at 66. So he goes back to the insurance company to take out another policy, this time for 10 years, expecting that before he is 75 he may well have passed on. Unfortunately for him, he has figured his chances pretty accurately. The mortality tables say that indeed he probably will die before he is 75. Ten-year term insurance taken out at that advanced age would be prohibitively expensive, and Jones would have to search long and hard to find an insurance firm willing to sell it to him.

It appears that this won't work. So back to the company again with 30-year-old John. The company has long since anticipated John's dilemma, and its agent stands prepared to explain that it will insure John for his entire life, no matter how long he lives. What's more, this other kind of insurance, the agent is ready to assure him, has all sorts of other benefits that, despite the higher premiums involved, will save John money in the long run. In fact, so many variations, clauses and options can be included that Jones can emerge with a "family policy" so perfectly tailored to his needs that he need never worry again. And it is precisely here that the complexities of life insurance multiply like vines in a tropical rain forest. But let's listen to the dialogue between Jones and his agent.

Enter the second player: cash value

"You don't want term insurance, Mr. Jones," says the salesman.

"I don't? I thought it was the cheapest kind," Jones replies.

"Well, it is, and it isn't."

"How much would the yearly premium be for $50,000 worth of term that will cover me until I'm 65?" Jones asks.

"Let's see, you're 30 now, so you *could* get such a policy for—ah, $192.50 a year to start. Of course, it will go up each time you renew. By age 60, you'll be paying $1,350 each and every year—seven times what it costs you to begin with."

"How much would it be for the insurance you want to sell me?"

"Well, at your present age, $50,000 worth of what I like to call permanent insurance would cost you $751 a year."

"That's a lot more than $192.50."

"On the face of it, Mr. Jones, but only on the face of it. It doesn't end when you're 65 years old and need it most. It's permanent. And you're forgetting cash value. Now, the policy I have in mind works this way. You pay us $751 a year, but a lot of this money in effect remains yours. The policy gains in cash value as the years go by—this

What price insurance?

The extra amount you will have to pay if you want life insurance to extend for long periods of time—and particularly if you want the policy to include cash savings as well as protection—is shown in these tables. The figures show the cost of six different types of policies expressed in terms of both premium charge per $1,000 (*upper table*) and how much coverage $100 will buy (*lower table*). In each chart, the first three policies listed provide pure protection—the policies have no cash value and end at age 65. The 5- and 10-year must be renewed at progressively higher premiums but can be converted into other types of policies. The other three policies provide savings accounts as well as protection, and the faster the savings grow, the more expensive the policy is. The savings grow so fast on 20-payment life that no premiums need be paid after the 20th year, while the policy continues in effect. Even faster-growing savings on the endowment policy provide a payment of the face value of the insurance after 20 years, while the policy holder is still living.

Annual premiums for $1,000 life insurance

Type of policy	Age purchased	25	35	45
Five-year renewable and convertible term (premium for first five years)		$ 3.49	$ 4.45	$ 9.10
Ten-year renewable and convertible term (premium for first 10 years)		$ 3.65	$ 5.05	$10.20
Level premium term to age 65		$ 7.30	$10.60	$15.99
Ordinary life		$12.64	$18.09	$27.58
20-payment life		$21.48	$27.83	$36.59
20-year endowment		$41.27	$42.14	$45.54

Life insurance provided by $100 in annual premiums

Type of policy	Age purchased	25	35	45
Five-year renewable and convertible term (premium for first five years)		$30,000	$22,000	$11,000
Ten-year renewable and convertible term (premium for first 10 years)		$30,000	$20,000	$10,000
Level premium term to age 65		$13,000	$10,000	$ 6,000
Ordinary life		$ 8,000	$ 5,500	$ 4,000
20-payment life		$ 5,000	$ 4,000	$ 3,000
20-year endowment		$ 2,500	$ 2,500	$ 2,000

Data: *The Unique Manual,* 1969 (The Travelers Insurance Co. non-participating figures)

is money you can withdraw at any time for a financial emergency. After 20 years' time the cash value of this $50,000 policy will be $14,150. Now, in those 20 years you will have paid $15,020 in premiums. Subtract $14,150 from $15,020 and you'll see that you will actually have spent only $870 for life insurance over that whole 20-year span. The rest of what you have paid us—the cash value—is still yours."

Jones, following the figures on the scratch pad, can only nod.

"By contrast," the salesman continues, "for the same amount of term insurance over the same 20 years, you would spend $5,625 in premiums and have *no* cash value at the end of that time to show for it. So, it's obvious that permanent insurance is what you need."

"Well, it sounds pretty convincing," says Jones. But Jones

being a careful man, decides to think it over, and we will do the same.

What the salesman has been proposing is the second basic type of life insurance, cash-value insurance in the form variously called ordinary life, whole life or straight life. It is, as the salesman says, "permanent," in the sense that it protects you not for a certain term of years but until you die or discontinue it. And it does accrue cash value. It does this by a very simple expedient: John Jones is asked to pay larger premiums than would be needed simply to insure his life. The extra that he pays accumulates on the side in what amounts to a savings account in Jones's name. That is, the premium is determined so as to cover the cost of pure insurance and an additional amount that will pile up on deposit, as in a bank, at a stipulated rate of interest.

Insurance salesmen, like the one talking with Jones, love to stress the virtues of cash value. But there are a couple of features of cash value that they may not stress and these are worth a look.

Cash value's elusive cash

The money represented by cash value belongs to you. But it is so closely bound up with the insurance part of the policy that making use of it poses problems. It is not as easy to get at as money socked away in a savings account or invested somewhere.

Cash value is sometimes, and more properly, called "cash surrender value"—you get the money free and clear only if you give up the insurance policy. If a time comes when you need the cash that has been set aside, you just inform the insurance company and it will send the money—but only on receipt of the policy. "All right," they'll say, "we've been using part one of your premiums to give you protection all these years, and part two of your premium has been in savings, accumulating at interest. If you surrender your policy, we'll give you the savings." This is important. To put your hands on the cash value, you must discontinue the policy—and the protection stops.

You might expect the cash value to materialize when the policyholder dies and the policy is paid out. It does—but not as a separate extra sum. Suppose our man Jones dies at 50, after paying premiums on an ordinary-life policy for 20 years and accumulating a cash value of $14,150. Widow Jones gets a check for the face amount of the policy, $50,000, not for $50,000 plus John's $14,150 in savings. The cash value is applied toward paying the death benefit. Jones's account consists of pure insurance that *decreases* as the savings account increases (otherwise premiums would be higher); at any given time the two total $50,000. Widow Jones gets the proceeds from $35,850 worth of insurance and $14,150 of savings in her check for $50,000.

So there is a fairly large "if" involved when a salesman counts cash value to show the net cost of ordinary-life insurance over a 20-year period. Such figures have meaning only if you intend to carry the policy 20 years and then surrender it. But the salesman has been urging permanent, lifetime insurance. If you keep the policy till the day you die, the cash value is a meaningless figure; it doesn't represent money that your beneficiaries will ever receive. There is, in fact, only one way you can have your cake and eat it too. If Jones, after 20 years, had cashed in his ordinary-life policy for its $14,150 cash value, and the same day taken out a new policy for $50,000 (assuming he was still insurable) and then died the next day, he could have left to Mrs. Jones both the amount of his insurance coverage and his accumulated savings. One conclusion is inescapable—you cannot plausibly argue cash value and permanence in the same breath. You get either one or the other: you can't have both.

The cash in cash value is never totally beyond reach, of course. There are times when it is advisable to surrender a policy and take the accumulated savings. You can also borrow against cash value without relinquishing the policy; your insurance protection is then reduced by the amount of the loan until the loan is paid back. Money for a down payment on a house or a car or just cash for thronging bills can be charged against your account (so to speak) with the insurance company. The company will charge interest—usually about 5 per cent —but this is far less than the bank rate. How much you can borrow

Tapping insurance for cash

Among the biggest bargains in loans is the one you can get on a cash-value insurance policy. The interest rate is very low, generally around 5 per cent. How much you can borrow varies, as the chart at right shows, with the type of policy —the more expensive types permit correspondingly larger loans—and the length of time you have been paying premiums on it. If you do borrow on your insurance policy, however, remember that its protection is reduced by the amount of the loan plus interest; whatever you don't pay back your heirs will, out of the death benefits.

Cash value of $1,000 life insurance

Type of policy	Age purchased	25	35	45
Ordinary life				
At end of 10 years		$ 95	$ 142	$ 199
At end of 20 years		$ 240	$ 329	$ 432
At age 65		$ 576	$ 522	$ 432
20-payment life				
At end of 10 years		$ 187	$ 241	$ 295
At end of 20 years		$ 465	$ 579	$ 696
At age 65		$ 696	$ 696	$ 696
20-year endowment				
At end of 10 years		$ 408	$ 409	$ 406
At end of 20 years		$1,000	$1,000	$1,000

Data: *The Unique Manual* (The Travelers Insurance Co. non-participating figures)

depends on how long the insurance has been in effect, for cash value usually does not begin to accumulate right away. That extra money you pay for cash-value insurance in the first year usually goes for the insurance company's expenses—it costs money to get your policy on the books. But after that it accumulates regularly.

Cash value as a savings account

Everybody needs a last-ditch emergency reserve like an ordinary-life policy's cash value (*see Chapter 11 on savings*). And it should bring in a return while it waits on your distress call, as cash value does. The interest earned by the cash set aside for you by the insurance company, however, is usually in the neighborhood of 2½ per cent a year, compounded annually. This is not very good. Interest rates offered by savings banks have not been that low since 1954 and in recent years have run about 5 per cent. So, it's obvious that if John Jones takes the money he would pay the insurance company to save for him and puts it instead into a savings account, he will be better off. As a matter of fact, if Jones has any kind of a head on his shoulders he will find prudent ways to place extra cash at more than 5 per cent. Numerous issues of high-quality bonds have been offering yields of 7 per cent or more in recent years. Jones might also invest in some blue-chip common stocks and do even better, what with dividends and long-term growth averaging above 9 per cent since 1926. But to stay with a conservative return and assured safety, let's have Jones put his difference in premiums into a savings account paying 5 per cent.

Jones has calculated that he needs $50,000 worth of insurance. He gets rates from half a dozen companies for an ordinary-life type of policy, and finds that, at his "insurance age" of 30, most quote around $15 a thousand. At one company's premium of $15.02, a $50,000 ordinary-life policy would cost him $751 a year.

Next he investigates term insurance. After a good deal of work with pencil and paper he concludes that his best buy is the type known as "five-year renewable and convertible." Such a policy can be converted in later years from term to ordinary life, and it is also guaranteed to be renewable at the end of each five-year period, until the policyholder is 65 (most companies) or 70. Thus Jones is assured of being able to continue his insurance coverage to retirement age or past, regardless of what may happen to his health and insurability.

He finds he has to do some pretty intensive shopping. Not all companies sell term policies that are both renewable and convertible. Premiums vary from more than $8 a thousand down to $3.85 per thousand at his age, or $192.50 for the $50,000 policy he wants.

Every insurance man Jones talks to gives him a stern lecture about the undesirable features of term insurance. He understands that each time he renews—every five years, that is—the premium will increase. Not so much at first, but by the time he is 60, the cost of the $50,000 policy he is considering will have shot up to around $1,350 a year—about twice as much as the premium on the ordinary-life policy. Furthermore, once he is 65 the insurance protection will cease. This term policy cannot be renewed again at that age, so if he lives a long life, he will be left without insurance after his retirement. And his term policy would not have a loan value that he could draw on in case of emergency. Nevertheless, Jones takes out $50,000 of term insurance with the company that quoted $3.85 a thousand.

His yearly premium, $192.50, represents a saving of $558.50 in comparison to the $751 an ordinary-life policy would cost. So at the time Jones pays his first premium he sends the company its $192.50 and puts the difference in a savings account, where his $558.50 will earn 5 per cent interest, compounded quarterly. Every year, during the first term of five years, he does the same. When renewal time rolls around he has $3,249.42 in the savings account—which he has earmarked as his insurance account, not to be dipped into under any circumstances. Having this much cash put away means that Jones doesn't need the full $50,000 worth of insurance when he renews, because he has more than $3,000 worth of protection in the bank. He's doing, in fact, just what an insurance company would do if it had issued Jones a cash-value type of policy. As the cash value builds up, it's there to be applied toward paying the death benefit if Jones should die. If the cash value is $3,000, the company must provide only $47,000 of death-benefit coverage out of its reserves. Jones does the same thing for himself. He renews only $47,000 worth of his term insurance.

This holds his annual cost down, even though the renewal premium has increased to $4.29 a thousand. For the next five years he sends the company a check for $201.82 each year. The difference between this amount and what he would have to pay for ordinary life —his saving of $549.18—goes into the untouchable bank account. It adds up, during this second term of five years, to $3,195.19.

Meanwhile, the sum initially saved has been on deposit for five years, and with accumulated interest has grown to $4,165.88. When this is added to the $3,195.19 more recently saved, his "insurance account" shows a balance of $7,361.07. So, at age 40, Jones needs only $43,000 of term insurance when he renews. He continues in this fashion for the next 25 years, building up his self-insurance account and whittling down the amount of his policy accordingly at each renewal:

Age	Value of policies in effect	Yearly premium	Amounts for savings account	5 years' accumulated savings	Prior savings plus earned interest	Total in cash savings
40-45	$43,000	$239.79	$511.21	$2,974.28	$ 9,437.16	$12,411.44
45-50	38,000	298.19	452.81	2,634.50	15,911.93	18,546.43
50-55	31,000	358.70	392.30	2,282.45	23,777.21	26,059.66
55-60	24,000	420.66	330.34	1,921.96	33,409.45	35,331.41
60-65	15,000	394.58	356.42	2,073.69	45,296.17	47,369.87

By age 65 Jones has accumulated his own "death benefit" of nearly $50,000, and when the insurance company regretfully notifies him that he can no longer renew his term policy, it's no skin off Jones's insurance program. He has his $50,000 worth of insurance—in cash in the bank—and he no longer has to pay any premiums. If he had bought ordinary life, back there at age 30, he would also have $50,000 in insurance but he would have to continue to pay a $751 premium on it. If he now stopped paying that premium on ordinary life, giving up his policy in return for its cash surrender value, he would receive $27,300—the cash value of his $50,000 policy after 35 years.

Jones has come out at least $20,000 ahead by paying only for "pure" insurance—term—and putting the surplus into his own savings account instead of letting an insurance company accumulate the surplus for him as cash value, in a "sort-of" savings account. And this is the main argument of the critics of cash-value insurance; it's known as "buy term and invest the difference." It tends to annoy people in the insurance business. They point out that it is highly unlikely that John will count out his savings each time he pays a premium on his term insurance and proceed forthwith to invest it.

Which should you buy?

The basic choice in life insurance lies between term and the cash-value types. A prudent man should consider buying some of each, because each serves different ends.

Term insurance's great attraction is economy. Over the 35 years between age 30 and age 65, our Mr. Jones saved $15,750 in premiums by buying a decreasing amount of term insurance and banking the difference. Such savings may be decisive when heavy protection is needed for a specific number of years, as it usually is.

Cash-value insurance can offer two separate advantages: permanence and savings. The savings feature is valuable—despite its

Text continues on page 120

VARIATIONS ON THE INSURANCE THEME

The principal purpose of life insurance is to provide income for family support if the breadwinner dies. But insurance men have devised many other ways the insurance idea can be put to use, and they have developed policies in bewildering variety. Each serves its own special purpose but most are basically forms of cash-value insurance.

Endowment policies

These policies accrue cash value fast and pay it out at the end of a fixed period, usually 20 years. The best way to understand how they work is to compare them with the $50,000 ordinary-life policy John Jones was first considering. That policy was going to cost John $751 a year, and at the end of 20 years its cash value was going to be $14,150. With 20-year endowment, John would pay a much larger annual premium—about $2,088. But at the end of 20 years the policy would have a cash surrender value of $50,000. The company then sends John a check for this amount and says "Been nice knowing you." Or, with some companies, he can take a guaranteed life income. But there is no longer any insurance on John's life; the policy has served its purpose. An endowment is therefore primarily a savings account, with insurance on the saver's life while he struggles toward the goal of amassing $50,000 in one bundle. If he becomes a statistic before he makes it, his beneficiaries get the $50,000, thanks to the insurance provided on the side.

Retirement-income policies

These are also endowment policies. The endowment matures at some selected retirement age, generally 65. Then the insurance company, instead of sending you a lump sum of, say, $50,000, begins sending "retirement income" checks, usually monthly. These continue to come until you die—or, if the policy is written that way, until a beneficiary such as your wife dies. The advantage here, of course, is with the policyholder who lives to a thumping old age; he will collect substantially more than the $50,000 he would have gotten if he had taken the lump sum. Note: Retirement-income policies (along with annuities, a form of savings account also sold by insurance companies) are discussed more fully in Chapter 14.

College-tuition policies

These are simply endowment policies made payable to children when they reach college age, providing money for educational expenses whether Father is around to write the checks or not.

Decreasing-term policies

The face value of this kind of policy gets smaller each year, falling to zero at the end of the term. Because the value declines as the risk of death rises with age, premiums are relatively low. This low cost and the fact that the coverage is heaviest at ages when the need for protection is great make decreasing-term policies attractive to young family men.

Mortgage insurance

A specialized kind of decreasing-term policy, it pays off a home mortgage if the owner dies before the mortgage runs out. As mortgage indebtedness decreases, so does the amount of insurance coverage. Many people buy it because it costs relatively little and, for survivors, eliminates at least part of a major family living expense.

Group insurance

A form of term insurance, it is issued only to those having some common bond—employees of a company, members of a fraternal organization or club, even college alumni. Many employers, especially large firms, offer group insurance as a fringe benefit either free or for a small charge. As a general rule, if group insurance is offered, take it—the rates are usually low. There can be drawbacks, however, for the premiums are seldom guaranteed and may go up if lots of deaths occur in the group. (The greatest group insurance is the GI insurance of World War I, World War II and the Korean War. If you have it, keep it.)

Limited-payment life

In the form of "20-pay life," the less common "30-pay life," life paid up at 65 or life paid up at 85, all offer an opportunity to pay for your life insurance faster than you ordinarily would and get it over with. Like ordinary life they "mature" at age 100. The only difference is that the premiums calculated to age 100 are bunched into a shorter period of time. The annual premium is accordingly higher. John Jones, for example, instead of paying $751 a year for $50,000 worth of ordinary life would pay $1,230 for "20-pay life." If he started at age 30, he would have paid all the premiums by age 50—no more payments and the insurance would continue in effect until his death. If Jones decided he did not need to pay quite that quickly, but thought he might find it convenient to stop paying premiums when he reached retirement age, he could opt for a paid-up-at-65 policy.

Family-income policies

These usually consist of a cash-value policy with an extra portion of decreasing-term insurance tacked on to provide additional family income for limited periods of time. With many (but not all) of these policies the widow gets the death benefit from the cash-value part in a lump sum as usual; then she gets monthly checks from the term insurance until a certain set period of time has passed. This is one of the aspects of family-income policies—they are not written for a given length of time but *until* a certain time. Suppose our Mr. Jones buys a 15-year family-income policy providing $50,000 plus $300 a month, and then dies a year later. His family will get $50,000 immediately and then receive $300 a month for 14 years. If he dies 14 years from now, however, his family will get the $300 for only the one remaining year. This sort of policy is designed for the man whose thoughts run like this: "For the next 15 years things will be tight; the children will be in school and then going on to college and we'll be paying off the mortgage. After that it won't be so bad, but for 15 years the family *has* to be guaranteed an income." Once past the 15-year mark the insurance lapses—but then presumably it isn't needed any more.

There are dozens of kinds of "family policies." By combining term insurance and cash value in various ways and amounts, insurance companies can provide something for everybody in the family but the cat. (It is possible to buy life insurance on pets, but not from companies that insure people.)

Insurance plus mutual funds

A combination plan that provides life insurance together with investment in mutual fund shares is a relatively new wrinkle. It is intended to counteract a serious defect that erodes all insurance, but limited-payment, endowment and retirement policies most of all. Their real value is inexorably eroded by inflation, since you pay most of their cost in today's dollars but collect their benefits in tomorrow's dollars—which may be worth only half as much.

A favored hedge against inflation is, of course, investment in stocks, either directly or through a mutual fund. Stocks have a history of increasing in value faster than inflation reduces the worth of a dollar, and insurance companies, quick to sniff a change in the wind, have been moving into the mutual fund area.

Beginning about 1967, larger firms began either acquiring mutual funds or forming affiliations with them. Depending on state regulations, the chances are that soon any insurance salesman you meet will offer you an application form for both life insurance and mutual fund shares. It is a good parlay. Caution, though, is called for. You had better be acquainted with the criteria for picking a good mutual fund, described in Chapter 12 on investments.

drawbacks of low return, inflationary attrition and restricted availability—because it forces saving. Many people cannot discipline themselves to make regular deposits in bank accounts or investments in mutual funds, and even those who set money aside regularly often give in to the temptation of drawing on their nest eggs. But few people willingly miss their insurance payments, and because cash value is not easy to get hold of, fewer still draw out the cash value and cancel their policies. So for many people, savings in the form of life insurance are safe in more than one way.

When the emergency reserve of cash-value insurance is no longer needed, its permanence is. Almost everybody needs some insurance that will deliver the face amount of the policy whenever death comes, at whatever age. How much this face amount should be depends on at least two considerations, death expenses and the costs and delays that can be expected in settling the estate. There is always a need for immediate cash when a member of a family dies. Large medical bills may have been incurred; how much should be allowed for this depends on health-insurance coverage. Funeral expense can be a big item. And living expenses may be needed for weeks and even months if there are delays in securing a widow's pension. Insurance providing an immediate $10,000 should be considered minimal.

Settling an estate also entails expenses that should be covered by insurance unless other assets can provide ready cash. Those expenses include payment of debts and taxes, legal fees, administrator's or executor's fees and court costs. These can often go as high as 10 per cent of the estate. Extra insurance comes in very handy if a family's assets are tied up in real estate or other items that cannot be quickly liquidated. Otherwise a widow may have to sell a house or some other asset so hurriedly that she will not be able to get a good price.

The lure of "dividends"
As if selecting among the many varieties of term and cash-value policies were not confusing enough, you must face still another choice in the kind of company you will deal with. There are "stock companies," which are corporations organized for profit no less than coal-mining firms or shoelace manufacturers, and "mutual insurance companies," which, in theory at least, are nonprofit cooperative organizations owned by their policyholders. The difference may or may not be important to you, since policy terms and costs vary more between individual companies than between types of companies. But the choice is complicated by the fact that all U.S. mutual companies, but not all stock companies, pay "dividends"—rebates on the premiums charged

for the cash-value type of policy. (Premiums on ordinary-life policies cited thus far have been based on non-dividend paying policies.)

Dividends are simply money that you get back at the end of the year from the insurance company. Originally, they were issued only by mutual insurance companies, never by stock companies.

The basis for the mutual company dividends was this: If fewer policyholders died than had been predicted and not all the money earmarked for death benefits was needed, the policyholders were entitled, as owners of their company, to receive refunds. Somewhere along the line the sensible words "refund" and "rebate" fell by the wayside. Americans apparently invented the misnomer "dividend"; the British did even worse—they called it a "bonus."

Then the stock companies got into the act. They began issuing policies that paid dividends and called them participating policies. Easy enough to do: they increased the premiums and then returned part of them at the end of the year. They could not, after all, really offer participating policies; since stock companies are supposed to make a profit, any extra cash they accumulate goes to the stockholders. Nonetheless, most stockholder-owned insurance companies now sell both participating and nonparticipating policies, known in the insurance industry as "par" and "nonpar."

It would seem reasonable to suppose, though, that the mutual companies' dividends would truly save you money. After all, a mutual company doesn't have to make a profit; any good fortune it enjoys should result in rebates to its policyholders. So there has to be a difference between mutual companies' dividends and those offered by stock companies. Well, there isn't. Why there isn't is impossible to explain in the space allotted here. For that matter, serious students of the insurance industry find it hard to fathom. The fact remains that there seems to be little if any advantage in getting insurance from a mutual company rather than from a stock company. The net costs of the policies offered by both kinds of companies vary astonishingly.

Is there, in fact, any advantage in buying participating insurance? Again insurance experts are stumped. Consumers Union spent a great deal of time and money collecting data on par and nonpar insurance and feeding it into a computer—a necessity because of the vast number of variables involved. It finally gave up the task as hopeless. But perhaps one fairly reliable key is offered by the U.S. Internal Revenue Service. The IRS misses few opportunities to collect a tax on income. And the IRS says that insurance dividends are not subject to tax because they are not income but simply a return of an overpayment. As far as the tax people are concerned, they are no different from a re-

fund you'd get on your lawnmower if the hardware store where you bought it discovered it had overcharged you.

Nevertheless many insurance agents are eager to sell participating policies. They always stress "net cost" in their arguments. Standard procedure is to use a "20-year summary" of premiums and past dividends, breaking the cost down to the "average annual net premium." It's not as formidable as it sounds. One of the major companies offers ordinary life, participating, at an age-35 premium of $21.97 per thousand. A summary shows:

20 years' premiums	$439.40
20 years' dividends	108.93
20 years' net	$330.47
Average annual net premium	$ 16.52

The same company offers nonpar ordinary life insurance for $15.06 per thousand if purchased at age 35.

Every insurance buyer should understand that any average annual net premium quoted on a participating policy is only an estimate. No company guarantees any specific amount of dividends in the future. The 20-year summary is based on dividends paid during the past 20 years. Studies of various companies comparing what was quoted 20 years ago as estimated dividends and what has actually been paid show that some companies paid more than estimated, some less.

The only firm conclusion anybody has come to is that for people who live a long time, participating policies can be advantageous. The reason is that insurance companies are flexible about how they parcel out dividends. Most companies pay small dividends during a policy's early years, loading them on later. Thus, if you don't live to a ripe old age, or if you let a policy lapse, you're likely to get shorted on your share of dividends. The companies know that a certain number of policies lapse long before they're in force 20 years—so they pick up quite a bit in dividends they never have to pay.

How much insurance—when?

Now comes the question of the amount of insurance you need. This it turns out, is bound up not only with the kinds of insurance you buy but also with your own family calendar. You don't have to think about it long to realize that insurance needs change as a family progresses from one stage of life to another. A young mother who is widowed will need a great deal of money to see her through the years until the children finish college. The family with teen-age children

REQUEST FOR
STATEMENT
OF EARNINGS

SOCIAL
SECURITY
NUMBER ➜

DATE OF
BIRTH ➜

MONTH	DAY	YEAR

Please send a statement of the amount of earnings recorded in my social security account to:

NAME { MISS / MRS. / MR. } _____

STREET & NUMBER _____

CITY & STATE _____ ZIP CODE _____

Print
Name
and
Address
In Ink
Or Use
Type-
writer

SIGN YOUR NAME AS
YOU USUALLY WRITE IT _____

Sign your own name only. Under the law, information in your social security record is
confidential and anyone who signs someone else's name can be prosecuted.
If your name has been changed from that shown on your social security account number
card, please copy your name below exactly as it appears on that card.

What is your Social Security?

The size of your Social Security benefits, which helps determine total insurance needs, depends on the amount of your yearly salary. To ensure that the Social Security Administration is crediting you with the right amount, fill out and send in a postcard form, OAR-7004 *(left)*, which you can pick up at a local office. If the government accounting of your last three years' earnings does not jibe with your records, write to the Social Security Administration, Baltimore, Maryland 21235. With a completed earnings record, your local Social Security office can tell how much your survivors would receive if you died now, what disability payments you are entitled to, and what your old-age pension will be.

needs correspondingly less to cover the fewer years of support. Once the family's children have finished school and left the nest, insurance needs will diminish considerably. From this time on it is difficult to justify carrying a substantial amount of insurance for protection alone. What is protected in the case of the young father is his earning power over the years, his ability to provide for his children and from there on to provide for his wife. To be realistic about it, there is little or no earning power to protect after the breadwinner reaches age 65, or whenever retirement occurs. The primary need from this point is for income. Take the Nicholsons, a fictitious name in a true case history:

Mr. Nicholson was in his late sixties, retired from the job he'd held with a leather goods manufacturer. He was the type of man that the term "solid citizen" was coined to describe. He had started at the company in his youth and ended his career there, having risen to a position in management. It was a small, conservative company, not given to such things as profit sharing, and most of Mr. Nicholson's working life antedated widespread pension funds. He took a gold watch with him when he left, and not much else to increase his assets.

As a conscientious provider, Mr. Nicholson had begun buying insurance in his twenties, and he had added to it when he could. He had acquired, in all, about $42,000 worth of ordinary life. Its cash value, building up over 30 years and more, totaled nearly $29,000. That, plus the home they owned and some modest savings in the bank,

constituted the Nicholsons' assets when he retired. But Mr. Nicholson didn't feel improvident; he never missed an insurance premium, and so he felt he was putting aside a substantial sum for his wife.

The Nicholsons were only a few months into retirement when it dawned on them that they were in severe straits. Their sole income then was $207 a month from Social Security—his $138 and her allotment of one-half that amount as a dependent. Out of this Mr. Nicholson struggled to pay the premiums on his five policies—about $600 a year. That left $157 a month—not enough for them to live on.

Soon Mrs. Nicholson went to their minister to confide her fears: she suspected that her husband might be going to "do away with himself," as she put it, for the sake of the insurance money that would come to her. The clergyman quickly called a friend, the trust officer at the local bank, and arranged for the Nicholsons to visit him.

Mr. Nicholson assented readily to what the trust officer explained had to be done. All the insurance policies were to be surrendered for cash value except one that was converted to paid-up insurance with a death benefit of $5,000. The cash value of the remaining policies, about $24,000, was invested to yield about 7 per cent, an income of $168 a month. In addition, the elimination of $600 in annual insurance premiums was an effective increase of $50 a month. They would now have $375 a month to live on instead of $157.

The Nicholsons' case has something to say about a couple of matters. As an illustration of how the need for insurance-as-protection changes drastically when a couple reaches the retirement years, it suggests that the argument for "permanent" or life-long insurance is not quite as simple as insurance agents usually make out. The $37,000 worth of protection Mr. Nicholson had was too much at age 65; at age 30, it might have been too little. Some might better have been term rather than cash value. And he should have had his heaviest coverage early rather than late in his lifetime.

Any realistic insurance program begins with one premise. It assumes that the family income might be eliminated right now. If the breadwinner were to die tomorrow, what would be the family's minimum need for income in the years ahead? The answer to this question, oddly enough, must be arrived at only after a calculation is made of what income would still remain to support the family.

An insurance foundation: Social Security

Almost every American family with young children is guaranteed some financial support if the head of the family dies. It comes from Social Security, which provides life-insurance protection as well as old

age pensions. These payments are so basic that any family insurance program must be blocked out around them. To determine benefits for your family, get *The Social Security Handbook* (about $2) from your local Social Security office or the Government Printing Office, Washington, D.C. 20402. (The amounts change from time to time; the Social Security law was amended in 1968 to increase benefits; the figures used here are those of 1969.)

It is important to know just what your family can count on at the time you plan an insurance program because the payments depend on a number of factors: the age of the surviving spouse, the number and ages of children, and even on how long the children stay in school. This means that the amounts that could be paid your family will change radically as the years go by; they may be high for a while, drop off a bit, then stop entirely, only to begin again later. Knowing how they will go up and down in your case enables you to determine how much additional insurance you will need at what times.

Take the example of Mrs. Brown. If she were left a widow at age 35 with two children to care for, Tom, 9, and Susan, 7, Mrs. Brown would at first receive Social Security checks for $395.60 a month. This income would continue until Tom reached 18 (or 22 if he went to college full time). Then Mrs. Brown would get $285 a month, the benefits due a widow and one child, for another two years, assuming Susan attended college full time until she reached 22.

At this point Mrs. Brown's income from Social Security stops. She has been receiving it for 15 years, and is now 50 years old. There is then a "widow's gap" until she reaches age 60, when she could claim partial old-age benefits, or until she is 62 if she waits until she is entitled to full benefits, providing a monthly income of $156.70. This old-age pension will then continue as long as she lives.

In this way the changes in Social Security benefits set three periods of need for supplementary income:
◄ The years when Mrs. Brown is getting survivor's income payments.
◄ The middle years of the widow's gap.
◄ The years after she reaches 62 and collects old-age benefits.

The Browns might decide that, since their home mortgage would be paid off by mortgage insurance, $500 a month could cover living expenses while the children are growing up. Social Security provides 395.60, so $100 of supplemental income is called for.

During the 12-year widow's gap Mrs. Brown probably would find employment. It's not a safe assumption, but one that's commonly made. With much of her housing expense covered, $150 a month to supplement her earnings might be the income goal during this period.

Text continues on page 128

Q. How should life insurance be paid?

A. The four standard settlement options:

1. The entire face amount is paid in cash as a lump sum.

2. The proceeds are paid in installments over a certain period of years. (A $10,000 policy, for example, will pay $100 a month for 9 years and 3 months, or $92 a month for 10 years, not counting dividends.)

3. The proceeds are paid as an annuity, to provide lifetime income. (A $10,000 policy will pay $73 a month for life to a woman 65 years old.)

4. The proceeds are left with the insurance company to earn interest, and the interest is paid to the beneficiary. (At 2½ per cent, interest will be $250 a year on a $10,000 policy.)

For death expenses and immediate cash, one recent policy of moderate size should provide for lump-sum payments. Older policies are better for installment or annuity settlement; written when mortality tables indicated a shorter life expectancy, they provide larger income payments.

Limited installments—the second option—can leave a widow without income if she outlives the payment term. This option is suitable where the duration of the need for income is known and limited—for example, the time during which children are growing up and finishing college.

The third option has two possibilities. One is "life income only." If the beneficiary lives to old age, she (or he) will probably realize a good return; otherwise substantial benefits are lost. The other possibility is "life income with installments certain." Life income is guaranteed for the primary beneficiary, but if he dies before the end of a stipulated period—5, 10, 15 or 20 years—payments continue to someone else designated.

Proceeds left with the company at interest—the fourth option—do not provide optimum income for survivors because the interest rates are low.

Q. Are insurance proceeds taxable?

A. Contrary to popular belief, there is little tax advantage in insurance proceeds for the average estate. Lump-sum settlements are usually not subject to income tax, but neither are other assets. Insurance proceeds are subject to estate taxes, like other assets of an estate, unless policies have been irrevocably assigned to or are owned by the beneficiary. Proceeds paid in installments can be subject to income tax, but with liberal exclusions.

Q. Can you borrow against insurance without sacrificing protection?

A. Yes, if you borrow against a dividend-paying policy. To do so, elect the "fifth dividend option" many companies now offer. Your dividends are automatically used to buy, each year, a one-year term policy up to an amount equal to the current cash value of your basic policy. The company buys the term insurance for you at "net cost," making it one of your better insurance buys. Thus you'll continue to have, until you repay the loan, the full protection of your policy's face value.

If you don't have a dividend-paying policy, you can accomplish the same purpose by simply buying a "term-insurance rider" in the amount of your loan—adding extra insurance equal to the loan debt.

Q. What are the advantages of the various dividend options?

A. The usual choice is:

1. Take your dividends in cash.
2. Let them accumulate at interest.
3. Apply them toward payment of the next premium.
4. Let the company use them to buy additional paid-up insurance.

The last option can be useful if you are underinsured and have become uninsurable. Even if you're at death's door you can buy additional coverage by electing this option. However, it is expensive coverage: $400 to $500 for $1,000 worth.

When you leave your dividends with the company to accumulate at interest (option 2) you are in effect putting money into a savings account that pays an interest rate of $2\frac{1}{2}$ to $3\frac{1}{2}$ per cent. Banks offer more.

Ordinarily you make best use of your dividend money by taking the dividends in cash (option 1) and banking the money, or by applying it on the next premium (option 3).

Q. What are the arguments for paying premiums annually?

A. They're all financial, and very persuasive. Suppose you're told that paying semiannually costs 3 per cent extra. Fair enough, you think, you can do better than that with your money in the bank. Or can you? You'd have only half the premium in the bank for six months; that half would have to earn $3 per $100 of premiums in half a year —more than 12 per cent annually—just to come out even.

You can avoid both the extra charge for semiannual payments and the inconvenience of one whopping annual payment by staggering the anniversary dates of a number of separate policies—giving yourself, in effect, interest-free quarterly or even bimonthly payments.

Q. Should insurance be carried on a wife and children?

A. If the wife is the family breadwinner, the same rules apply as for insurance on a husband breadwinner. But it's rare for the wife to support the family, and it's difficult to justify insurance on the life of a housewife. The primary purpose of insurance is protection of survivors against loss of income. It is sometimes argued that a mother's death, when there are children, would burden the father with the expenses of a housekeeper. The rebuttal is that it nearly always costs less to hire a housekeeper than to keep a wife. The same principles apply on insurance on children's lives.

Q. Is flight insurance a good buy?

A. If you have basic needs covered, why do you need additional protection just because you're getting on an airplane? If you feel an urge to visit the insurance machine when you hit an airport, better take a look at your whole insurance program.

Q. Is double indemnity a good thing to have?

A. The cost is low, usually $1 and change per $1,000 worth of insurance. But the family's insurance needs aren't related to how you die. After you have your basic needs covered, paying for a double-indemnity rider is making a gambler's book that you might leave your family something extra. Better use the money for more basic coverage or for savings.

During the after-62 period, when Mrs. Brown can no longer count on earned income, $200 a month to supplement Social Security might be considered sufficient to meet minimum needs.

To determine how much insurance is called for to provide these sums, income needs can be translated into face amounts, approximately if not precisely, with the following table. It assumes that the death benefit of the insurance is invested by the insurance company and the widow is given both interest and part of the principal to make up her income during the three periods.

If $100 a month is required for:	The amount of insurance needed to provide this income is:
10 years	$10,000
15	13,600
20	16,600
30	21,200
40	24,200

Mrs. Brown is going to need $100 in extra income above her Social Security benefits for about 15 years while the children are growing up, from the time she is 35 until she is 50. This, the chart tells us, could be provided by $13,600 worth of insurance.

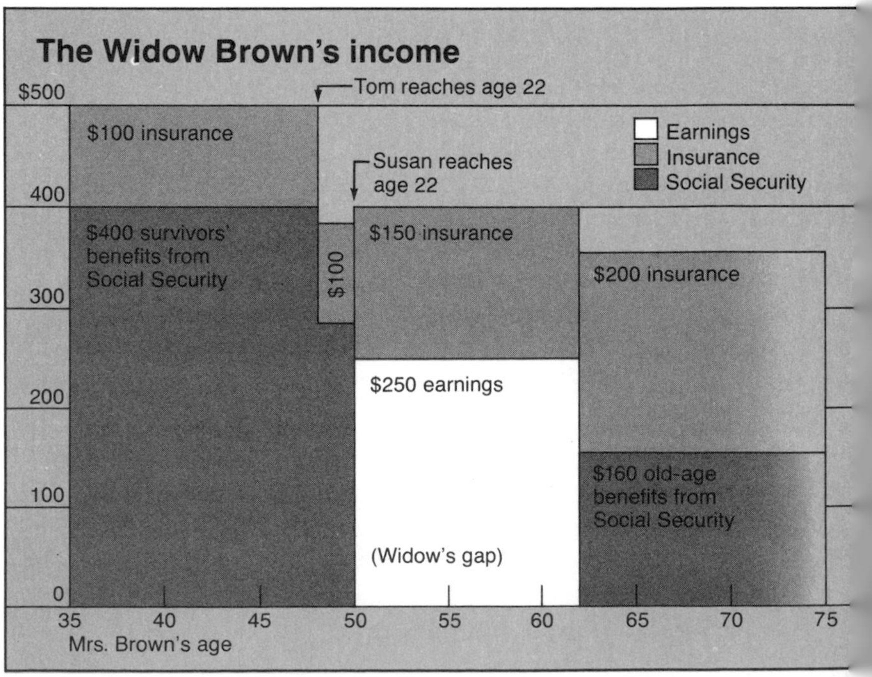

The three stages of widowhood
How a flexible, no-frills life-insurance program guarantees sufficient income for Mrs. Brown, left a widow at age 35 with two children to care for —Tom, 9, and Susan, 7—is shown in the chart at right. She receives Social Security benefits during the stages of her life when she is least able to earn income, the maximum monthly benefits coming while the children are growing up and lesser amounts after she's 62; in between, during the "widow's gap," she is most able to work. Varying amounts of supplementary monthly income for each stage are provided by insurance.

The Widow Brown's income

- Earnings
- Insurance
- Social Security

$100 insurance

$400 survivors' benefits from Social Security

Tom reaches age 22

Susan reaches age 22

$150 insurance

$100

$250 earnings

(Widow's gap)

$200 insurance

$160 old-age benefits from Social Security

Mrs. Brown's age

Then she is going to need $150 a month during the 12-year widow's gap between 50 and 62 as a supplement to what she might earn. This comes out to around $16,000 in insurance.

After that she is going to need $200 a month to add to her own Social Security. Let's assume Mrs. Brown lives to 92 and therefore needs $200 a month for 30 years. That's another $42,400.

Putting all these figures together, it appears that *right now* the Browns need $72,000 worth of income-producing insurance just for living expenses. And that huge sum does not include the mortgage insurance, which was counted on to reduce housing costs; the Browns needed $18,000 worth. Nor does it include an allowance for college for Tom and Susan. The average college education costs about $10,000, but this sum can be cut if necessary (*Chapter 9*) and the children can be expected to earn part of it themselves; Mr. Brown figured he should set aside $5,000 each to see them through.

That's $100,000 worth in all! It seems pretty formidable, at least at first glance. How can an average man with an average income possibly afford it? But it's not as discouraging as it looks. In the first place, that much insurance—if you make it pure protection with no frills can be had for a good deal less money than you probably imagine. Second, Mr. Brown need not keep this much protection for very long.

Many insurance agents will help you work out an insurance program in this fashion; some will even have the use of a computer to speed things along. Or you could figure out your own by looking again at the case of the Browns and drawing up a simple balance sheet for your family. The key questions that you must consider are all there. How old are you—that is, how many years of income would your widow need if you died tomorrow? How many children are there and how old are they? Could your widow work after the children are grown, or even while they're in school? House? Mortgage? Above all, what benefits would Social Security provide, and therefore how much insurance would produce the *additional* income needed?

Not everyone needs the heavy protection the Browns do now. It makes sense, for example, for a just-married couple to take out only a small amount of ordinary life to be kept permanently. If the husband dies young, the widow has enough for funeral and other expenses; if he lives to old age this same policy, kept up, would serve the same purpose later. In between, it is a last-ditch emergency reserve of cash.

Suppose Mr. Brown lives 15 years, until the children are through with college. He can then drop the college tuition insurance and also those policies that were designed to give Mrs. Brown those 15 years of $100 a month extra income: $24,000 of insurance in all can now lapse.

Protection can therefore be provided by decreasing term insurance, or by five-year renewable term policies of $10,000 each, which can be dropped as insurance needs diminish. By using one of the least expensive types of insurance, 35-year-old Brown can get his $100,000 worth for premiums of only about $500 a year for the first five years. It may cost him even less if part of his coverage is ordinary-life and inexpensive group insurance he already has.

Allowing for the contingencies

Whatever insurance plan you devise, try to keep it flexible. Needs change as unanticipated events alter the family situation. If serious illness or accident disables the breadwinner, income may be interrupted and life insurance wiped out; at the least they may make it difficult to continue needed insurance.

Some of these hazards can be allowed for with a wise choice of policies (not all can, so don't make yourself insurance-poor trying).

Suppose you bought three five-year term policies for $10,000 each, figuring that you could drop one of them in five years and renew the other two. Then suppose you had a mild heart attack. You'd want to keep all three policies for extra protection, right? But the insurance company might not be enthusiastic, and if the policies did not guarantee your right to renew them, the company could well refuse to do so. As one report on the subject delicately put it, chronic ailments like heart disease "tend to infect insurance companies with hypercaution." So be sure to read the fine print. See that your policies have a statement *guaranteeing* you the right to renew for full face value, up to age 65 or 70, regardless of your health. Likewise, if you buy decreasing term insurance, which declines in value each year, make sure it can be converted into steady-value ordinary life.

But suppose the heart attack is worse. You are laid up for many months on sick-pay or no-pay and you can't continue to pay your insurance premiums. Unless you have allowed for this contingency, your big term policies vanish as though they never existed and the cash-value policies shrink to a fraction of their former value.

The clause that can prevent such a catastrophe is the "disability waiver." It relieves you of paying premiums when you are permanently disabled and unable to work. "Permanently" is usually defined as a minimum of six months; that is, after you're disabled six months, you pay no more premiums until you're able to go back to work. This waiver is generally an addition to the policy, a "rider" put on at an extra cost that depends on your age. Rates vary considerably. At 25, for example, the extra cost for a disability rider on ordinary life and five-year

term is usually around 40 cents a year per thousand, but some companies charge half again as much and a few include the waiver at no charge. Some policies have disability riders that waive the premium and in addition pay the policyholder an income as long as he is disabled —commonly only until age 60, however.

Total disability of the family breadwinner is indeed a financial disaster, but Social Security benefits afford fairly good protection in this event. A young disabled worker, with earnings that entitle him to maximum benefits, receives disability income of $204 a month (rising to $218 by 1985). To get this amount of income protection with a disability policy would cost $70 to $80 a year. In a de luxe insurance program, the added protection would be desirable, but the head of a young family may be better off putting his dollars into life insurance.

Money for medical bills

Extra clauses in life-insurance policies will not allow for one of the most serious financial hazards: the staggering cost of hospitals and doctors. For that you need health insurance. Most people acquire it by joining the group health-insurance plans sponsored by their employers, usually Blue Cross and Blue Shield, which pay most hospital and many doctor bills. They are usually worth their cost.

Blue Cross and Blue Shield may not be enough, however, if illness is prolonged. Their benefits run out. To cover the risk of truly catastrophic medical costs, many employers supplement the basic protection with "major medical" plans. These generally provide for payment of 75 per cent of medical expenses not covered by other insurance. If your bill comes to $1,000 and Blue Cross covers half of this, major medical will pick up 75 per cent of the remaining $500. You then pay only $125 out of that whole $1,000. Major medical is rather expensive. But, if available, it is usually a wise protection.

What you do *not* need, many experts advise, is what the insurance industry calls first-dollar health insurance. It covers the first dollar of your medical expenses—and the last. If your hospital bill is $200, then the insurance company pays $200. It sounds great until you look at the premiums. They are so high that in most cases you will be better off ponying up the "first dollar" yourself and buying insurance that pays most, but not all, of your medical bills.

How it fits together

So you have health insurance, provided by you if not by the place where you work. Then there's mortgage insurance if you own a house that's not paid for yet. Then some ordinary life for some inescapable needs.

Finally, sufficient term to provide income as needed. This is an insurance plan, but it is only part of a family's overall plan for financial security. The insurance must be combined with two other elements: a savings system *(Chapter 11)*, which will provide cash for emergencies and for large purchases, and an investment program *(Chapter 12)*, which will build into a nest egg to underwrite the retirement years. Here is what the Browns did:

They decided they could set aside $150 a month for their financial plan. About $45 of this went for premiums on that $100,000 worth of life insurance, and another $35 or so went for health-insurance policies. That left $70. For a few years all of it was consigned to the bank, to build up the cash reserve. But once this was established, the savings deposits were reduced to an amount sufficient to match withdrawals. The difference was now plowed into investments—mainly mutual funds

Security for $115 a month

The sum of $100,000 seems a grandiose one for a young man to leave behind. But 35-year-old Brown guarantees that much to supplement Social Security benefits for his family. He does it by combining regular mutual fund investments with life insurance—for only $115 a month (health insurance would be extra). The life insurance is mainly flexible, low-cost term policies that end when they are no longer essential: the mortgage policy when the mortgage is paid off, the college-tuition policies when the children graduate, other policies when Mrs. Brown passes the "widow's gap" that temporarily cuts off her Social Security benefits. Meanwhile the stock fund—begun after a few years of concentrating extra money in a savings account—grows steadily, if it follows the trend of recent decades. Then, if Brown dies at any time after age 35, insurance plus investments will total $100,000, with something to spare to allow for stock market fluctuations.

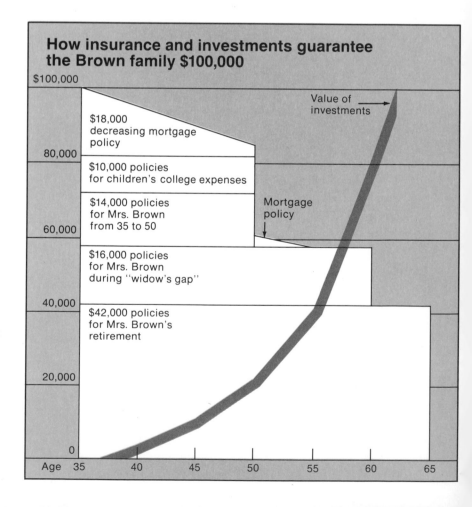

How insurance and investments guarantee the Brown family $100,000

$100,000

$18,000 decreasing mortgage policy

80,000

$10,000 policies for children's college expenses

$14,000 policies for Mrs. Brown from 35 to 50

60,000

$16,000 policies for Mrs. Brown during "widow's gap"

40,000

$42,000 policies for Mrs. Brown's retirement

20,000

0

Age   35   40   45   50   55   60   65

Value of investments

Mortgage policy

—that would provide protection against inflation erosion and pay a higher return than the savings bank. As the years went by and unneeded life-insurance policies were dropped, insurance protection decreased but the growth of investments more than made up for that, as the chart shows.

By setting aside $150 a month, Brown very handsomely provided for his family—and himself, too. He established, at age 35, an estate that should stay at a fairly steady $100,000 from the present into the foreseeable future. If he dies young, there is $100,000 in life insurance to give his family the income they need to add to Social Security benefits. If he dies in middle age, his widow will get less from his insurance but will come into a substantial legacy. And if, best of all, he lives to a ripe old age, he and his wife can enjoy their autumn years on the earnings they will receive from their investments.

To most people, an estate of $100,000 seems the mark of a well-to-do man. But, as the example of the Browns demonstrates, it is within reach of those who never consider themselves wealthy.

6
Second incomes
When it pays to make money on the side

Fred Hodges, coming home after a full day's work on the job, pulls into the driveway. His dinner is at this minute being put on the table by his two daughters, 11-year-old Valerie and nine-year-old Penny. Experience has taught Fred that whatever they have whipped up won't be too good. But it will be something he can eat quickly—and that's important. He has only 45 minutes to shave, eat dinner and drive to the community college, where he teaches adult-education classes in merchandising techniques five nights a week. If he is lucky, he may pass his wife, Joanne, coming in the door as he goes out. She will be getting home from her weekday selling stint in the dress shop at the shopping center. Between them, Fred and Joanne hold down three jobs, work 82 hours a week and earn about $19,000 a year.

Exaggerated? Not really. There is such a family, although the name isn't Hodges; they have been following this routine for several years. To them it is worth it. Even after allowing for additional income taxes, the cost of a second car and all of the other extra costs involved in their busy lives, they figure they still net almost $4,000 more than Fred's daytime job alone brings in. To them, that means the difference between squeaking by and living in relative comfort.

Not many couples hold down three jobs, but two jobs per family is today becoming the rule rather than the exception. In half the nation's families, two or more members earn paychecks—this usually means a working wife plus a working husband. In addition, according to an informed estimate, more than one out of 10 men "moonlight" —that is, take on extra work in addition to their full-time jobs.

Many of these people take on extra work because they want to. Women are apt to look forward to the opportunity of escaping household routine for the challenges of new people and tasks. Men may enjoy a change to work quite different from their 9-to-5 duties. But the most common incentive for increasing the number of paychecks coming in is simply the need—or desire—for more money.

Young men, just starting their careers, are likely to be poorly paid as they learn their jobs and wait for advancement—just when they have the greatest need for extra money to furnish and equip a home from scratch. A couple of decades later, when children approach college age, the tuition crunch sets in as the family has visions of outflow increasing by thousands of dollars. At any time, the desire to enjoy the good things so temptingly displayed in a prosperous land impels many people to get the money for a higher standard of living.

Extra income is not hard to find in a time when there is more work to be done—for pay—than there are people to do it. Making the most of these opportunities, however, requires carefully weighed de-

cisions. What kind of work should be sought? How should you go about finding it? Is it better to take a job or do something in your home —in effect start a little business of your own? Who should go after that extra income? Mother? Father? Will the added money compensate for the drain on energies and the time lost from family life?

Every family answers those questions a little differently, but there is a consensus on one point. If a family wants or needs money, Mother most commonly brings it in. The working wife is five times as common as the two-job husband. It is she who usually makes the big difference in the family economy. In fact, it is the income earned by working wives that is primarily responsible for tripling the number of families with incomes of $10,000 or more between 1950 and 1970. Of the 20 million families now in that upper-income bracket, close to half the wives are working wives.

THE WORKING WIFE

The old stigma that used to attach to a family in which the wife worked has pretty well faded away. No longer does a working wife reflect upon the abilities and earning capacity of her husband. No longer

A modern army of working wives

Two statistics document the reason behind the radical changes in family finances during recent decades: 15 million married women have jobs; one fifth of the nation's labor force is female and married. To the second incomes that these wives bring home is owed much of the country's affluence. No longer is it true that the working wife is an impoverished woman who must take any job she can get. Today she comes from a more affluent level of our society, works because she wants to, and holds a job requiring education and training.

There are five times as many working wives as there are husbands with two jobs

More than half the women who work are married

is it considered reprehensible for a mother to leave home and children to return to work, especially after the children are old enough to go to school. There are now more than 30 million American women at work, and more than half of them are married. Most work full time. Most live in the suburbs. More than one out of three women who work have children; these working mothers make up one third of all the mothers in the nation. Behind these figures is one of the most radical peaceful revolutions in history, for the involvement of women in the working world has changed completely in only a few decades:

■ Back in the '20s most women who worked were single and under 30; now most are married and over 40. Millions are over 50.

■ In the '40s most women worked in factories. Now most do clerical work of one type or another, but since the mid-'50s, the number of female professional and technical workers has doubled.

■ Most women today marry shortly after they turn 20 and have their last child before they are 26. They stay home an average of 10 years with their first child but only two or three years with each later child. The rate at which they return to work almost doubles when the youngest child reaches school age. Thus, since there is also a tendency to

More than
one third of
all working wives
are mothers...
and they make
up one third
of all the mothers
in the U.S.

Most working
wives live in
the suburbs

Increasingly the
working wives
are women whose
husbands have
above-average
incomes

have fewer children, the typical wife is able to go back to work shortly after she reaches 30.

The job opportunities may be waiting, the excitement of returning to the workaday world electrifying, the prospect of another paycheck alluring—but is it really worth it? Before a mother takes on a job she should take a cold look at all the facts. The first consideration is this: Of all that extra cash coming in, how much can actually be kept?

Does it pay to work?

For the wife who is trying to decide whether or not to seek a job, the biggest discouragement is financial. She quickly discovers she cannot add as much to family funds as it might seem. First of all, there is still that old double standard—not so much in hiring practice any more but in wages paid. All the missionary work that has been done, all the equal-rights-for-women provisions of the Fair Labor Standards Act and the Civil Rights Act, have failed to eliminate dual wage scales that offer women unequal pay for equal work. "Nowhere," reported TIME magazine in an article about working women, "are women paid at the same rate as men, even when they perform the same

The more schooling a wife has, the more likely she is to work

A majority of working women are married and past 40

Most working women do some sort of clerical work

tasks." Employers apparently reason that a man needs money to support his family but a woman doesn't, and they pay the woman less, overlooking the fact that a working wife generally makes job-related outlays her husband avoids.

Many of these costs of working arise in unexpected ways, and some seem minor. How quickly they add up, however, can be seen from the hard fact that most wives who work net only about one dollar for every three that they earn. Here is why:

■ Child care. The cost of this varies, of course, with the age of the children, the availability of relatives to help, and the mother's feelings about how carefully children should be supervised at various ages. Often there is an obliging grandmother or aunt nearby. Or there may be a nonworking mother in the neighborhood who earns extra money herself by caring for the children of working mothers during the day. Some young families pool resources, with mothers at home sharing the care of a friend's children by day in exchange for babysitting stints at night or on weekends. Many communities are opening day-care centers with professional attendants. But if the working mother must hire a babysitter at the going rates, this expense will take a big

The number of professional and technical job-holders among working wives has doubled since the mid-'50s

The rate of return to work among mothers doubles when the youngest child reaches school age

The number of families with incomes over $10,000 has tripled in the last 30 years, and the major credit for bringing in that extra bread goes to working wives

The tax bite on working wives

The federal income-tax laws treat a wife's paycheck harshly—a wife grossing $2,500 a year has only $1,615 left after taxes when her husband's income is $25,000. The government exacts so much because her income is the extra that goes on top of her husband's, into the upper tax brackets. If they file joint returns, all of her earnings are taxed at the high rates that are applied to only a small part of her husband's earnings.

How taxes reduce a working wife's income

Wife's income	$15,000	$20,000	$25,000	Husband's income
$2,500	1,825	1,730	1,615	
5,000	3,618	3,390	3,125	
7,500	5,348	5,005	4,599	Net gain from wife's income after federal income taxes, joint return
10,000	7,008	6,515	6,027	
12,500	8,623	7,989	7,385	
15,000	10,133	9,417	8,710	

slice of her earnings. Although the expense is large, and a legitimate business expense in every sense of the term—it makes work possible for Mother—it is rarely a deductible business expense to the tax men. Only if the tax return shows the "joint adjusted gross income" of Father and Mother to be quite low (below about $7,000) can child-minding costs be listed as a deduction.

■ Household help. Older children can be dragooned into helping with housekeeping chores. But in many cases a once- or twice-a-week cleaning woman or even a full-time domestic may be necessary. How much this will cost varies with the community, but the federal minimum wage of $1.60 an hour is a useful guide in anticipating costs, even though domestics are not covered by this law at present. Hired help is covered by Social Security, though, and that costs money. If a household employee earns $50 or more in a calendar quarter, the employer must pay 4.8 per cent of the wages as her share in building up the employee's Social Security fund (many women feel obliged to pay the employee's share of the Social Security tax as well, which means a total of almost 10 per cent added to the expense for a domestic).

■ Taxes. The government takes several bites from the paycheck of a working wife. Largest of these is that taken by the federal income tax. Unless a working wife receives a high income, there will continue to be an advantage in filing a joint return with her husband (Chapter 10). But this means that all of her income will be taxed at the level of the highest bracket his income falls into; some of her income may even slip into the next highest bracket. If a husband earns $15,000, a wife's extra $5,000 will be nicked for something like $1,000 in federal income tax. It can come as a rude shock to discover the large amount of

income tax due on a relatively modest contribution to the family coffers, particularly since the amount withheld from the wife's paycheck is computed on the basis of her small salary without counting her husband's larger income. The only way to foresee the true size of the tax bite is to do some careful advance calculations—listing all of the husband's income, plus all family income from interest, dividends and other sources, then adding the wife's anticipated income and figuring the joint-return tax on the total. The same calculations should be made on any state and local income taxes that will be imposed.[1]

■ Clothing. When a wife works, the suit she used to wear once a month for a few hours will be getting a full day's workout once a week. That means it will have to be cleaned more often and it will wear out faster. She will also need more clothes for variety. It is estimated that a woman's clothes budget jumps 25 per cent when she goes to work. The cost of hose alone triples. Laundry may have to be sent out for finished work, which is expensive. And spare time seldom allows for all the mending and altering that should be done; more clothes have to be written off sooner as outworn.

Grooming. Greater demands on both appearance and time are likely to send a working wife to the hairdresser more often than before, and her cosmetic costs will increase.

■ Food. If she is anything like typical, the working wife spends 10 to 15 per cent more on food and household supplies than her nonworking counterpart. This is largely because she is no longer able to be the bargain-hunter and comparison-shopper she once was and because she relies more frequently on prepared foods that may cost a bit more but take less time to cook. At work she may have to buy lunch in a restaurant every day and allow for distressingly frequent special occasions—expensive lunches when a colleague leaves or has a birthday. In addition, there will be those days when she phones her husband to say, "Honey, I'm bushed. Could we eat out tonight? Nothing fancy." Such meals cost at least four times as much as dinner at home.

■ Transportation. If a working wife is lucky with hours and location, her husband can drop her at her job in the morning and pick her up on his way home. But the logistics are rarely that smooth. If they are not, she'll have to count on extra fares or on all the heavy expenses

---

[1]*Some husbands joke that they can't afford to let their wives go to work because the added income would put them into higher tax brackets and they would actually lose money. It may seem that way at income-tax time, but it isn't quite true, as you quickly discover when you figure it out. The additional tax due is always less than the extra money earned, no matter what tax bracket you're in.*

that go along with owning and operating a second car *(Chapter 4)*.
■ Miscellaneous. A working wife may find herself "investing" in extra labor-saving devices—a freezer to save trips to the supermarket, a dishwasher to save time—and amortizing them at high finance charges. She may find that her income is important enough to the security of her family so that she should carry life insurance to protect it—another extra cost. She may have to pay dues to a union or professional society. And with all the stresses and hard work of the job, and with that extra income on hand, an occasional weekend away or a self-indulgent vacation is easy to justify.

To compensate for at least some of the costs that erode a paycheck, there are a few fringe benefits besides the spendable money that remains. The overall financial strength of a family is bolstered if the job provides a wife with her own life insurance, a pension plan, an occasional bonus, a profit-sharing program or special educational opportunities. On almost any job, she adds to the Social Security benefits she will collect in later years. Far from the least of a job's recompenses are paid vacations. A working mother may have trouble synchronizing her vacations with those of her husband and children, but after years of unsalaried housework being paid for not working can seem pretty special.

It is spendable money, however, that most working wives are after. Sometimes the extra outgo seems to cancel the extra income. The only way to tell how it really comes out is to add everything up. Here is how a second income worked for Harry and Charlotte.

Charlotte takes a job

Harry, a chemist at a plastics plant, earned $12,000 a year. When the youngest child entered second grade, the whole family talked over the idea of Charlotte's going back to work. She wanted to, the children agreed to cooperate, and Harry went along.

Charlotte had been a secretary for two years before her marriage. Now she enrolled in a brush-up course in typing and shorthand offered by the high school's adult-education program. Six months later she was working full time as secretary to an officer of one of the local banks. Her salary: $4,940 a year.

When Charlotte got her weekly paycheck, she found that withholding taxes, Social Security and other payroll deductions totaled $23.91, leaving $71.09 in weekly take-home pay *(see tabulation on these pages)*. After a few weeks of keeping track of her expenses, she was able to determine that transportation, lunches, someone to be home with the children and do some housework in the afternoons, clothing

grooming and added food costs were taking a further bite of $38.42 out of her paycheck. That left her with a weekly net of $32.67, or $1,698.84 a year instead of $4,940. Still not too bad a sum—if all of it were spendable income.

Then along came income-tax time the following spring, and a rude shock. When Harry and Charlotte made out their joint return, they discovered that because all of Charlotte's income was being taxed at rates equal to or higher than the highest bracket reached by Harry's income, they still owed $352.60 in federal and state income taxes. Deducting that from Charlotte's income left her with $1,346.24 to show for a year's work—$25.89 a week, substantially less than one third of the $95 a week that was nominally her salary.

Charlotte's earnings shrank so drastically partly because she is a mother with small children working full time. She is away from home so much of the day that she incurs a number of extra household costs; the most expensive of these is child care. On a relatively low salary like $95 a week, these costs constitute a very high percentage of what she earns. An alternative is part-time work.

Let's see how the balance sheet changes if Charlotte takes a half-day job at $2,496 a year while the children are small. She could then eliminate her domestic help and child care (all the children are in school from 8:30 to 3). This in turn would eliminate the Social Security taxes for hired help. She could save by eating her lunches at home. And of course her own payroll deductions, based on her lower salary, would be less. Her net after taxes and extra expenses is then $1,747.20—actually more than if she worked full time—and she is keeping 70 per cent of what she earns.

Part-time work is a compromise, and one that can be hard on the mother. She holds down a job, but at the same time she may be expected to continue with all the duties of a full-time housewife —cleaning, child care, economy-minded shopping and cooking. This arrangement does suit many young mothers, however. As the years pass, an outside job—even a full-time job—becomes easier and much more attractive financially.

Let's take a look at Charlotte and Harry seven years later. The youngest child has now reached high-school age, so Charlotte is free to leave her home untended all day. There are no more child-care costs (Charlotte makes herself available by phone, since teenagers need attention, too), and the youngsters are old enough to take over the laundry, much of the cleaning and some cooking. At this stage in family life, Charlotte can take a full-time job without incurring heavy extra household costs. Her income is again $4,940, and her net after

Text continues on page 146

Charlotte's paycheck: an analysis of three cases

The three balance sheets at right show what happens to the paycheck of Charlotte, a working mother, in three situations: (1) She works full time while the children are still young. (2) She works part time during that same period. (3) She works full time when the children are old enough to look after themselves. The examples demonstrate two things: First, working full time while the children are young may have no financial advantage over working part time; in fact, she may net less. Second, Charlotte doesn't add much to her husband's $12,000-a-year salary until the children are grown; only then can she earn and keep a substantial sum.

THE THREE SITUATIONS

Charlotte works full time while children are small

Expenses—particularly for child care—make Charlotte's solid $95 a week melt rapidly. She pays someone $1.60 an hour ($20 a week) to clean the house and be home with her children in the afternoons; she also pays all of her employee's Social Security tax. She needs more clothing and grooming aids, spends more for food and cleaning than stay-at-home wives, and gets stuck for extra income tax on the increased family income.

Charlotte works part time while children are small

Astonishingly, Charlotte's net take from a week of part-time work is more than it was for full time, even though her gross salary is only $48. The main reason is obvious—she doesn't need hired help at home for the children during the afternoons. Her deductions and other expenses are smaller or nonexistent. She is ineligible for group life and health insurance. The income-tax bite is smaller; she goes home for lunch; she can trim other expenses.

Charlotte works full time after children are grown

Charlotte keeps the most money for her efforts if she takes a full-time job after the children have reached high-school age. Although taxes and other extra expenses are unaffected by this change in her family situation, the savings on hired help to care for the children make the big difference. Her net spendable income in these circumstances still would not impress Croesus, but it is a bit more than half of her gross pay.

THE DEDUCTIONS

Federal income tax	$15.00
State income tax	2.20
State disability insurance	.30
Social Security	4.56
Group life insurance	.35
Group health insurance	1.50
Total deductions	$23.91

Gross pay	— Deductions
$95.00	**—$23.91**

Federal income tax	$4.50
State income tax	.30
State disability insurance	.15
Social Security	2.30
Group life insurance	none
Group health insurance	none
Total deductions	$7.25

Gross pay	— Deductions
$48.00	**—$7.25**

Federal income tax	$15.00
State income tax	2.20
State disability insurance	.30
Social Security	4.56
Group life insurance	.35
Group health insurance	1.50
Total deductions	$23.91

Gross pay	— Deductions
$95.00	**—$23.9**

THE EXPENSES

		THE EXTRA TAXES	
Transportation	$2.50	Weekly tax on	
Lunches	6.25	husband's income	$31.98
Part-time child care		Weekly tax on	
and household help	20.00	both incomes	55.96
Social Security tax		Increases due to	
on household help	1.92	Charlotte's salary	23.98
Clothing and grooming	3.50	Tax deducted from	
Extra household costs	4.00	Charlotte's salary	17.20
Miscellaneous	.25	Net added weekly tax	$ 6.78
Total extra expenses	$38.42		

− Expenses	− Extra taxes	= Net income
− $38.42	− $6.78	= $25.89

Transportation	$2.50	Weekly tax on	
Lunches	none	husband's income	$31.98
Part-time child care		Weekly tax on	
and household help	none	both incomes	43.59
Social Security tax		Increases due to	
on household help	none	Charlotte's salary	11.61
Clothing and grooming	2.50	Tax deducted from	
Extra household costs	2.00	Charlotte's salary	4.80
Miscellaneous	.15	Net added weekly tax	$ 6.81
Total extra expenses	$7.15		

− Expenses	− Extra taxes	= Net income
− $7.15	− $6.81	= $26.79

Transportation	$ 2.50	Weekly tax on	
Lunches	6.25	husband's income	$31.98
Part-time child care		Weekly tax on	
and household help	none	both incomes	55.96
Clothing and grooming	3.50	Increase due to	
Extra household costs	4.00	Charlotte's salary	23.98
Miscellaneous	.25	Tax deducted from	
Total extra expenses	$16.50	Charlotte's salary	17.20
		Net added weekly tax	$ 6.78

− Expenses	Extra taxes	= Net income
− $16.50	− $6.78	= $47.81

taxes and expenses is $2,486.12, so she is keeping just over half of what she earns.

Charlotte might well have decided to go to work under any of these circumstances—millions of women do. There can be situations that make any additional income better than none. The point is that a woman considering a job must be realistic about the costs of working and not count on more affluence than outside earnings can provide. Only if the net return compensates for the demands of a job is it worthwhile even to begin looking for one.

How to find a job

The first rule for a woman about to begin job hunting is: Aim high. She should seek a job that will enable her to make the most of her talents, abilities and experience—because that's where both the most money and the most satisfaction lie. Self evident? Not necessarily. When a woman tries to assess her aptitudes and skills, the greatest danger is not that she will overrate herself but that she will sell herself short. Many feel diffident and unsure of their qualifications, and will settle for a job below their abilities. In the late 1960s almost 20 per cent of all women college graduates who worked did so in unskilled or semiskilled jobs; even more startling is the fact that 8 per cent of working women with five years of college held similar low-level jobs.

So a hard self-appraisal is in order. List all qualifications and skills. Then look around at friends and neighbors to see what kinds of jobs women of similar backgrounds have found—and look for an opening at the top level. But make sure the job suits. If dealing with strangers is a trial, a woman is not likely to feel comfortable in retail selling, interviewing or politics. If she finds routine boring, a job indexing books or wiring switches in an assembly plant could drive her up the wall. Hard and fast preconceptions are a mistake, of course; most women check to see what openings are available and try to imagine how they will fit in.

The places to start looking are where you would expect—the newspaper classified ads and the employment agencies. Too many classifieds leave a lot to the imagination, so an exploratory phone call may be in order. Employers often refuse to go into details—particularly about salary—on the phone, but they are anxious to avoid nonproductive interviews and will usually explain the job requirements better than the ad did. Many classifieds are actually placed by agencies; sometimes the ad says so and sometimes it does not but merely lists a cryptic address or telephone number. Phoning an agency is seldom productive because the agency can perform its function properly only

if the job-seeker is interviewed and fills out an application form.

A good agency helps save effort for both employer and employee. It brings together in one place information about a variety of job openings. And it attracts a variety of people for the employer to choose from. When efficiently run, it matches prospect to job—and vice versa. An inexperienced housewife is not sent to fill an opening for a legal secretary, and a department-store buyer does not waste her time discovering that the job listed is really for a sales clerk.

There are two main kinds of employment agencies. The state employment service is government-operated and charges no fee. In large cities this agency may have separate branches for different kinds of jobs (one in New York specializes in apparel industries, while Chicago has one for hotel placement). But most state agency listings are likely to be jobs at the lower end of the pay scale. The other kind of agency is private; many of these, too, specialize in filling jobs in specific fields. Most charge a fee. The fees generally vary from 1 per cent to 5 per cent of the first year's salary. In many cases, employers pay part or all of the agency fee.

Whether a job-seeker uses an agency or follows up the classifieds, she often finds herself filling out lengthy application forms, waiting interminable stretches in reception rooms and undergoing the cross-examination of interviews only to discover that the expedition was a wild-goose chase after all. This has to be expected.

The job interview can be a trying experience. No matter how well the job-seeker has prepared herself for this moment, she is going to feel inadequate and vulnerable. Nearly all job applicants are nervous and show it. Interviewers expect this and make allowances for it. But the applicant should, too, and plan her strategy in advance. Like a hitter aiming for a home run, she should not try too hard. She should avoid exaggerating past experience or minimizing the time she has been out of the job market. There is one thing worse than not getting the job, and that is getting it and failing miserably. The applicant should be perfectly candid about her capabilities, explaining what she has done to brush up on rusty skills and making out as good a case as possible for activities that have a bearing on the job, including volunteer work.

A common mistake is talking too much about reasons for wanting to go back to work. They aren't likely to be either pertinent or unique. Nor should the applicant give the impression that she is merely dallying with the idea of working, or that she really doesn't have to work. Employers want her to be serious about the job, and in order to do it well, she has to be. Nor should she emphasize the arrangements

she has made for care of home and family. An employer assumes she has such matters under control.

The applicant should listen closely to the description of the job, weigh her own qualifications to fill it, ask questions and consider the answers carefully. Overeagerness to get started can easily tempt her to accept the wrong job, one that she cannot handle or one that she will find unrewarding. This is more than demoralizing; it leads to the spotty kind of job record that labels her a job-hopper and makes it increasingly difficult to find any kind of employment.

A job-seeker who has a special skill to sell or an unusual record of achievement in past jobs would do well to prepare a résumé of information about herself. It should include the basic facts—name, address, telephone number, age, family status, education, job experience. But it can convey more information than a formal application form, including not merely the names of companies and individuals worked for, but explicit details about training, the kind of work done, the rate of advancement, and any special achievements that might qualify the applicant for a better-than-average position. The résumé should be simple and brief enough, if possible, to fit on a single neatly typed page. There are special service agencies that for a fee will help a job candidate prepare a good résumé and duplicate it; they usually can be found under "Job Résumé Service" in the Yellow Pages of the telephone directory.

Better than a résumé of past achievements, though, are (1) special preparation for entering the job market—particularly training that meets today's requirements, and (2) a knowledge of the new fields that have opened up a variety of stimulating jobs never before available to women.

Catching up with the world

The professional or skilled worker planning to reenter the job market will find the way easier if she makes some effort to catch up on the new knowledge and techniques in her field. A secretary will discover that a great many offices, even small ones, are packed with machinery she never used before—dictating machines, electric typewriters, reproducing machines; a nurse must learn a whole new armamentarium of drugs. At the very least a skilled worker should pore over back issues of the journals in her field, take advantage of lectures and seminars and maintain memberships in professional societies.

But even better is adding to past education. There are 157 universities, 1,490 four-year colleges, 890 community colleges and many university extension departments scattered throughout the land. Vir-

tually every one of them has the red carpet out for adults who want to extend and update their education and stretch their minds. Many of these institutions offer special counseling and flexible schedules geared to a housewife's free daytime hours; residence requirements or entrance exams are seldom required.

A list of these schools, with the names and addresses of specific people to write to in each state, is included in a pamphlet, "Continuing Education Programs and Services for Women" (Pamphlet 10), issued by the Women's Bureau of the U.S. Department of Labor. You can order the pamphlet for less than a dollar from the Superintendent of Documents, GPO, Washington, D.C. 20402.

Many communities offer refresher courses for married women who want to return to work. Some of the courses, like those given at the Career Clinic for Mature Women in Minneapolis, Minnesota, are specific, with titles like "Typing and Office Practice." Others, like one run by the public schools in Arlington, Virginia, try to forestall general back-to-work problems and include everything from tips on household management to group discussions with local employers.

A number of colleges and universities offer correspondence courses. For a list of these, send 50 cents to the National University Extension Association, 122 Social Science Building, University of Minnesota, Minneapolis, Minnesota 55455. The National Home Study Council, 1601 18th Street N.W., Washington, D.C. 20009, lists more than 100 privately operated correspondence schools that meet its standards. Some correspondence courses are particularly useful in vocational preparation for licensing; about 20 per cent of all certified public accountants, for example, used correspondence courses to study for their qualifying examinations. Some schools offering job-oriented courses, by correspondence or in classes, promise more than they can deliver, and a few are frauds. Investigate in advance as you would for any major investment—and read the fine print before you sign.

A college degree helps win any job and usually brings a premium salary. It may be easier to get, even late in life, than you think.

Many women have never obtained a degree but have acquired the equivalent of many years of higher education from experience, reading and informal study. Now they can gain formal credit for their self-education through a series of tests called CLEP, for College-Level Examination Program.

The tests are given once a month during the school year at 60 centers throughout the United States for modest fees. They include a five-part general exam and additional exams in individual subjects. By passing the tests you get official credit for the subjects, just as if you

had taken them in a regular college. You cannot quite win a degree through CLEP, for the tests are not designed to be a substitute for college—the maximum number of credits that can be earned are those of a junior. Rather, they provide a realistic way for mature, informally educated people to come within shooting distance of getting a degree. The additional formal study then might be a worthwhile investment for anyone planning a working career. For further information, including the locations of testing centers, write the College Entrance Examination Board, Box 592, Princeton, New Jersey 08540.

New pastures, and greener old pastures

Going to school, aside from being intellectually satisfying in itself, serves as a useful bridge to the routine of a job, a warm-up period that may be as valuable as the information gathered or the degree earned. It also reveals new opportunities. Most women returning to work go back to the kind of work they did before; this is usually a good idea since their experience and skills are valuable assets that should not lightly be discarded. But today there are well-paid careers that did not exist a few years back, or existed on a much smaller scale, or were simply not open to women at all. Here are a few:

■ Computer technology. Electronic data processing is the fastest growing of all industries. Jobs range from keypunch and machine operations, which are similar to typing and fairly simple to learn, to systems analysis, which usually requires a degree in engineering or science. In between lies programming—the process of defining a problem, analyzing it, breaking it down into manageable, logical steps, then converting those steps into instructions that enable a computer to reach a solution. It is in this area of programming that large numbers of women, some with college degrees, some without, are finding rewarding careers. Opportunities exist within corporations that manufacture data-processing equipment as well as in the government offices, businesses and industries that use the equipment in a growing number of ways—to prepare payrolls, issue bills, control inventories, process checks, issue insurance policies, forecast weather, analyze medical information and design machinery. A mathematics background helps but is not essential for a job as a programmer. Applicants are usually given aptitude tests designed to reveal that special kind of analytical mind that is more of a requirement for success in programming than specific experience or education.

■ Travel services. With the spread of affluence, travel has become the third largest industry in the United States. Women fill more than 50 per cent of all travel agency jobs and own more than 20 per cent of all

travel bureaus belonging to the American Society of Travel Agents (ASTA). In addition, there are increasing opportunities in other sections of the travel complex—in transportation (bus companies, airlines, steamship lines), hotels, restaurants and sightseeing services. Travel agency jobs, like most that seem glamorous, offer low pay at the bottom, and training for higher levels until recently was largely by the apprentice method. But now ASTA offers a correspondence course to employees of member agencies as well as to a limited number of nonmembers. Some state chapters of ASTA also offer classroom courses. For information, write ASTA Education and Training Department, 360 Lexington Avenue, New York, New York 10017.

■ Personnel work, counseling and guidance. This rapidly expanding field attracts many women. A college degree is usually required for personnel work and for some vocational counseling, such as that done in state employment service offices. School counseling and rehabilitation work usually demand more advanced training, but this can be obtained at colleges and universities in many parts of the country, often through part-time study. For information about programs, write the American Personnel and Guidance Association, 1605 New Hampshire Avenue N.W., Washington, D.C. 20009; the National Defense Education Act Counseling and Guidance Institutes Office, U.S. Office of Education, Washington, D.C. 20201; and the Vocational Rehabilitation Administration, U.S. Department of Health, Education and Welfare, Washington, D.C. 20201.

■ Banking. Once a stuffy male monopoly, banking has in the past generation opened the doors wide to women employees. Now, two thirds of all bank employees and 10 per cent of all bank officers are women, and the numbers are growing. Maturity is considered an asset. Specialized business education is not needed, for the banking industry operates the world's most extensive on-the-job training system. Almost all large banks have their own officer training programs, and evening courses in many phases of banking are given by the 371 chapters of the American Institute of Banking at little or no cost.

■ Real estate and insurance. These two fields were also once hostile to women employees but now welcome them. Both are especially appealing because of their adaptability to part-time work and flexible hours. As in banking, training is readily available. Many local real-estate boards offer courses in real-estate law, financing and related topics, as do more than 200 colleges and universities. Insurance courses are offered by the companies themselves and by agents' associations and the American Society of Chartered Life Underwriters. Both insurance and real-estate firms provide on-the-job training.

■ Advertising and publishing. These two old fields of work are also newly congenial to women—but still tough for anyone to break into and tough, too, to work in. Because the jobs often involve heavy personal pressure and erratic hours, they are not ideal for mothers of small children. But if a woman's family life can withstand the buffetings of deadlines, she will find more openings than ever before available to her as an editor or reporter or copywriter or account executive.

■ Health. The always urgent need for nurses and technicians has increased even further in recent years. Many opportunities are available in the field of mental health; write the National Association for Mental Health, 10 Columbus Circle, New York, New York 10009.

■ Education. "Being a teacher" describes a wide range of jobs these days, from assisting a teacher, to running a play school, to lecturing in adult-education programs, to giving courses to the elderly at civic centers. Some public schools actively recruit mothers to serve as assistants. The eagerness of mothers to return to work has spurred the creation of countless nursery schools. There is plenty of room for helpers. Anyone with a solid background in education plus a good amount of administrative ability might operate a nursery school.

■ Home economics. Opportunities in this field range through industry, education, government and international affairs. Demand runs five times ahead of supply. One specific need is for college-trained food-management specialists to help in the nation's largest food service —the school lunch program. But many other kinds of jobs are available; information can be provided by the Office of Information, U.S. Department of Agriculture, Washington, D.C. 20250.

■ Retailing. Burgeoning shopping centers are creating dozens of new selling jobs across the land. With selling jobs also go jobs in purchasing, administration and data processing.

■ Library work. The media explosion means that a librarian now deals not only with books but with art reproductions, phonograph records, movies, microfilms, tapes, discussion groups, readings and exhibits. And librarians work not only in the classical old building down on Main Street but in bookmobiles, in hospitals and museums, in newspaper offices, research institutions, businesses and industries.

Part-time work for women

Among the most useful of the new opportunities for working wives are those offered by the proliferation of part-time jobs. Working only part of a day is a good way for a woman to ease into the business world. It keeps to a minimum disruption of family life and serves as a transition before a full-time job is undertaken. It may be especially at-

tractive to an older woman who wishes to avoid the strain of a full day's stint day after day.

Industries, stores, restaurants and hospitals all hire part-timers to ease the pressure during peak-load hours and holidays. Real-estate and insurance companies use part-time workers on weekends and evenings. There are many 9-to-1 and 9-to-3 jobs as employers adjust their needs to the hours when young mothers are free.

There are several drawbacks to part-time work, aside from the obvious one of less income. The most important is that it almost always deprives the worker of fringe benefits—no paid vacations, no health insurance, no bonuses. Another is a neither-here-nor-there feeling, a sense of not really being accepted into the close-knit group that spends a full day on the job. Finally, if the job involves accomplishing a certain amount of work rather than merely being on hand for a certain number of hours, a part-time worker may find that what has to be done spills into unscheduled hours, and she winds up doing close to a full day's work for part-time pay.

One of the most convenient ways to work part-time is to sign up with a temporary-help firm, many of which, like Manpower, Kelly Services and Olsten, have offices in cities across the country. A development of the past 20 years, these companies recruit, test and often train a roster of workers—all kinds from typists to models—whom they then bond, insure and "lease" to other companies on a cost-plus basis for work during emergency rush periods, overloads, illnesses and vacations. Under this system you may work in one place for a while, then put in a few days someplace else. Your employer is not your boss, whoever that happens to be, but the temporary-help service, and it sends you your paycheck. The big advantage of such an arrangement is the flexibility it permits. You can specify that you will work only a day, a week or a few months—or even only Tuesday mornings or Friday afternoons. If an assignment is offered when you'd rather not work, you can decline. Among the disadvantages: a generally low pay scale, and, for some women, the uncertainty involved in being on call for assignments among strangers.

With so many opportunities for wives to add to the family income it is no wonder that large numbers of them do—and enjoy themselves at the same time. But the strains that a job places on a woman and her family should not be underestimated. It is the better part of avarice to assess personal limits before undertaking any job. If this is true of women workers, full-time or part-time, it is even more true of the second means of bolstering family income, a second job for the man of the family.

MOONLIGHTING HUSBANDS

Moonlighting as a source of additional income is more closely tied to need than to desire. Most people won't take a second job on top of a full day's work unless they truly believe they have to. Statistics bear this out. Of the nearly four million Americans who are known to hold down two jobs, there are three times as many men as women, and twice as many married men as single. The highest incidence is among married men 25 to 44, the peak period for acquiring and equipping a home and for adjusting to the increased costs of raising a family. The average moonlighter puts in approximately 13 hours a week on the second job. A shorter work week on the main job without a cutback in earnings does not by itself lead to an increase in moonlighting.

Frequently the extra work is temporary—something to take care of a large tax bite or a hospital bill or the down payment on a house. But the tendency is for these short stints to stretch out into steady routines as new needs replace the old.

Some labor economists think the figure of four million moonlighters—close to one out of every 20 employed Americans—is far too low. They are convinced the number is actually twice that high, that

The prevalence of moonlighters

At least three million U.S. men earn second incomes by working at second jobs. Moonlighters are far less numerous than working wives and most are young. But a harsh need for the necessities of life is not always the incentive for a second job. Increasingly moonlighters are professional men or technicians: 18 per cent of such men hold second jobs. They work not only for the money but also for other opportunities outside employment can bring.

A majority of the men with second jobs work in two unrelated fields

One third of all men with second jobs are self-employed

18 per cent of all professional men and technicians hold second jobs

BUY SMITH (I'M SMITH)

at least half of all moonlighting goes unreported because the worker wants to avoid paying taxes on the extra income or because his main employer frowns on outside work.

Among the millions of moonlighters are an increasing number of successful executives and professionals who increase their incomes —and sometimes, more important, their opportunities for advancement—with work on the side. Company lawyers serve private clients. Accountants prepare personal tax returns for friends and small businessmen. Officials of businesses and public organizations are associated with other businesses, banks, law firms. Editors edit or write articles and books on their own time. College professors write books and articles or serve as consultants—to industry, to government, to publishers. These men are moonlighting, but they do not often hold second jobs. Rather they are in business for themselves, generally providing some service and working at home. This seems like a fine distinction, but it's no small matter at tax time. Because of the income-tax rules, you usually get to keep more of money you earn on your own than of money you earn on someone else's payroll.

But there are decided drawbacks to moonlighting on a job or at

15 per cent of all second jobs are in technical or professional fields

One half of the self-employed moonlighters are farmers

20 per cent of all self-employed moonlighters are professional men who use existing skills on outside work

home. There is physical wear and tear. In factory work, for instance, accident rates rise when moonlighters are involved because, as one concerned official put it, "they come to work tired." This doesn't apply only to men who do physical work. Pressure, tension, frustration and difficult commuting can feed fatigue too.

Moonlighting can also seriously erode family life. Lonely wives, neglected children, lost friends—all are a high price to pay for a bit more financial security. Years race by that can never be recouped.

As we saw in the case of the working wife, there are financial leaks that must be calculated. First, there will be that added income-tax bite on the extra income, usually at a rate higher than on regular income. Food costs can add up substantially if dinner is not eaten at home. There may be extra out-of-pocket expenses for added fuel or fare, special equipment, special clothes, extra cleaning. It may be necessary to join a union. The extra income will almost certainly be substantially less than it would seem to be from the amount earned.

But if a man feels he really must take on an extra job, the most likely areas, comprising more than 40 per cent of all part-time employment, are (1) selling or shop-tending at peak hours of trade or during hours when regular help is least available (which, happily for the moonlighter, is often during evenings and weekends), and (2) performing a service of almost any kind.

Most of these jobs don't demand much, and they don't pay much, either. But the man who has a special skill—who can time an engine, balance a set of books, guide a hunting party, give knowledgeable advice about ski equipment—will find that extra know-how means extra money in the bank. Making the most of extra work, therefore—just as of full-time work—means finding a job where talents, abilities and experience can be put to the greatest possible use.

One answer is to find a second job that uses the skills sharpened in day-to-day work. Many a carpenter or tile-setter or bricklayer has taken on small remodeling projects on the side. Accountants find opportunities to give a hand to operators of small businesses. Salesmen pinch-hit in real estate or insurance.

It is often desirable, however, to do something completely different during moonlighting hours. Here, an inventory of talents is in order. There are part-time jobs available for tennis teachers, parachute riggers, landscape gardeners, sailors, typesetters, paperhangers and photographers, to list a few at random. Many men have had some experience, often through hobbies, that enables them to tackle a job few others can do. If a man can paint a sign, upholster a chair, play an organ or repair a typewriter, there is a job waiting for him somewhere

Most such possibilities turn up in the want-ad columns of the newspaper. Oddly enough, part-time employment opportunities are often listed with full-time openings. Classifieds being what they are, it's often hard to tell what is being offered. Here is an example:

PROOFREADERS. Med. pubs. Accuracy
essential. $7,000 plus all fringe.
Also pt. time. LA4-4598

Only a call to LA4-4598 would reveal whether this is a part-time job that could be handled nights and on weekends. This particular employer, as it happened, was willing to let part-time proofreaders work at home, paying by the page for work completed.

In fact, a good many phone calls are in order. A man should be more particular about a second job than a first. Location is one problem. It may make sense to commute 90 minutes each day to and from a primary job, but the same does not hold true for part-time work. Pay rates are often vague in ads, so they must be checked. Sometimes it is tough to pin down the exact nature of a part-time job, partly because the employer himself may not be sure of exactly what he is looking for. Only careful investigation can provide the answers.

A man with unusual talents who doesn't find anything suitable advertised may have to take the initiative. Don did, in an unexpected way. As a youngster, he had bred tropical fish for a hobby. But he hadn't looked at a fish for years until his oldest son, Bobby, attracted by a window display, lured him to the local pet shop. The shop was closed on each of the two weekday evenings they stopped by; when they found the shop open on Saturday Don asked about the hours.

"How does a widower with two teen-age kids keep a shop open evenings and a family together at the same time?" the shop owner asked. "Twice I hired part-time help, but it didn't work out. One was a woman who didn't know anything about pets, and the other was a young fellow who couldn't have sold dollar bills at a discount. Where do you find good help willing to work only evenings?"

A week later Don was embarked on a job that he held for more than two years, to the mutual benefit of himself and the owner.

What happened with Don was largely luck, but when he saw the plum, he reached for it, which is a point to remember. Don's story makes another point, which is that in this period of near-full employment, with so many services in demand and relatively few people inclined to provide them, there are probably more people wanting help than the other way around.

A particularly good field to plow is any place that sells a product that requires periodic servicing. A friend of Don's, Jack, inspired by

Don's experience, came up with an idea of his own. Back in the spring, when he brought his lawn mower in for its annual tune-up at the hardware store where he'd been taking it every year, he was told that the store had lost its repairman and couldn't offer service anymore. Annoyed at having to go eight miles to the other side of town for the only service available, Jack decided to write to the mower manufacturer for a service manual and tune up the contraption himself.

The chore turned out to be a pleasure. Jack worked in a brokerage firm, mostly at paperwork, and he savored the satisfaction of fixing something with his hands. Two days after Don started work at the pet shop, Jack stopped in at the hardware store and asked the manager if he would pass any service and repair customers on to him. He now puts in two nights a week, four in spring and summer, in his basement workshop fixing not only mowers but also other equipment.

There are many such opportunities waiting. If one doesn't come like a bolt from the blue, the way to search them out is to make a list of all your interests and capabilities, past, present and potential. Then follow these up with all the places you can think of where they could be put to use (*see illustration on opposite page*). It's a little like taking a financial inventory of your personal worth, including the gold in your teeth: You don't know how much you've got till you start counting.

A BUSINESS AT HOME

In many ways the best source of extra income is work you do on your own, with your home as a base. This self-employment can range all the way from breeding poodles to making jam for sale to gourmet shops to serving as a consultant in your special field. Jack the broker who fixes lawn mowers in his basement is self-employed. So are the corporation lawyer who handles a few extra cases on the side and the college professor who writes textbooks. Such an enterprise can involve Father alone, or Mother too as his assistant. Or it can involve Mother alone, or both of them the other way around, with Mother making hand-stitched wall decorations, and Father in charge of packaging them and delivering them to retail outlets.

There are no clear figures on how many part-time businesses are run out of homes. About a third of all moonlighters are self-employed, but half of these get their second income from farms. About one family in 10 owns and operates some type of small business. There is a tremendous risk involved—about 1,000 new businesses are started each day, many on a part-time basis, and about 930 are discontinued.

Home manufacturing enterprises are the riskiest, for they often turn out to be little more than expensive hobbies. One advertising ex-

MAKING HIDDEN TALENTS PAY

Everybody has skills that can be put to work producing a second income—but how numerous and how varied they are won't become clear until you inventory them. Their money-making potential may surprise you, as it did this couple when they began matching their backgrounds and talents against opportunities:

He: Radio mechanic in the Air Force during the Korean War
Opportunities in local appliance shops selling or repairing.

She: Know German
Opportunities in local businesses that have correspondence abroad. Or in private tutoring.

She: Love dogs, have four poodles at home
Opportunities in breeding dogs and selling the puppies. Or in dog-sitting for people on vacation.

He: Good skier
Opportunities at nearby ski resorts on weekends and in equipment shops. Might also run ski expeditions for local youngsters.

He: Handle tax-accounting problems at the office
Opportunities doing tax returns for neighbors and, through ads in the paper, other puzzled citizens.

He: Experienced in photography, including developing and enlarging
Opportunities taking pictures of birthdays and wedding parties, or in working part time in a processing lab, or in clerking Saturdays in the camera store.

She: Good swimmer
Opportunities at the Y and also nearby motels and hotels that have pools.

She: A flair for words
Opportunities writing ads for local merchants, demonstrating products in a department store, selling over the telephone.

ecutive equipped his basement with woodworking tools and set about making TV snack tables. They were well made, handsomely varnished and functional. But they didn't sell. They cost seven times as much as a sheet-metal table sold for the same purpose, and instead of folding easily, the wooden table had to be dismantled for storage. The ad-man had gotten himself involved in manufacturing something that he liked to make, not something that would sell.

Services are a different story. Cities are filled with people who need help on their income-tax returns, gardeners who can't find any place to get a pruning saw sharpened, poodles that need grooming, clothes that need altering, lawns that need tending, manuscripts that need editing and heating systems that need cleaning. Otherwise perfectly good toasters, waffle irons and coffeemakers are consigned to the junk heap because there's no one around to insert a new heating element. Any of these needs, plus dozens more, can form the basis for a service operation that could yield a good secondary income.

Beware

When you explore any kind of home activity, you'll get a lot of information, a lot of advice—and a lot of tempting suggestions that may cost you money. People interested in part-time projects are considered easy marks for fraudulent schemes. Unscrupulous franchise operators thrive on many a life's savings lost to the lure of business opportunity ads reading "A PART-TIME BUSINESS OF YOUR OWN. HUGE PROFITS. BE YOUR OWN BOSS!" Other swindlers have pulled in hundreds of thousands of dollars—in one case, six *million* dollars—from innocent readers with classified ads offering earn-money-at-home schemes that bait you bit by bit. Here's a classic sequence: A help-wanted ad reads, "LADIES—MAKE MONEY in the quiet of your home. Large earnings assured, market for all you produce. Experience unnecessary. Send $1 for information." The "information" tells you of an instruction booklet, available at a price, and materials and patterns, at an additional price, to make aprons. Not only is the price of the materials and patterns six times what it would be at a yard-goods counter, but when the women who respond send their finished work in, it is always returned as "not up to standard." This is an inherent part of the scheme. None of the aprons are ever quite "up to standard."

Getting started

It is beyond the scope of this book to analyze the hazards and rewards of starting a business of your own. But a simple example is in

structive. Let's assume that Charlotte, instead of taking that secretarial job at the bank, has decided to start a party-counseling service at home, planning activities, menus, even decorations for parties to be given for children. Harry pitches in too, working evenings on the bookkeeping, helping write the sales letters, standing by ready to make emergency ice-cream deliveries.

Charlotte and Harry make the same hardheaded self-analysis of this venture as they did of Charlotte's job. They do it before they buy the first postage stamp; doing it afterward can be a very costly exercise. The factors that will make the party-planning service succeed or fail are the same as those that make any business succeed or fail. Among the questions they ask themselves are:

■ Did they pick the right business? To answer this, they examine Charlotte's skill as a party planner, the extent of the competition, the local demand for such a service, and the convenience of their location.

■ Can either Charlotte or Harry sell? If they have never tried, they will soon learn that it is a rare product or service that sells itself. They will have to face up to long hours spent peddling their wares.

■ Do they have enough capital or credit to launch the business? Almost any venture loses money at first, and sometimes losses continue for a painfully long time. Supplies have to be purchased. Equipment —even if only a double-entry journal for bookkeeping— will be needed.

■ Do they have any business experience? If Charlotte and Harry are unable to keep good records, figuring profit-and-loss closely and continuously, calculating their costs down to the last penny, they will soon be out of business because they are likely to lose money rapidly without realizing it.

■ Are they tough enough and strong enough? Tough enough, because many customers never seem ready to pay a bill, and collecting from neighbors and friends takes will power. Strong enough, because even a simple business like party-counseling can easily take many, many more hours than Charlotte would put in as a secretary at the bank.

The Small Business Administration offers guidance even on such part-time home ventures as Charlotte and Harry's. Look up the nearest office in the telephone directory, listed under "U.S. Government."

If Charlotte and Harry decide to launch their home-based counseling service, there are a number of steps to take first:

■ They must check with the local zoning board to see if such an enterprise is permitted in the neighborhood where they live. Many areas are zoned as "strictly residential." If this is the case, there will almost certainly be a neighbor ready to protest the increased traffic or the danger that a home-based business will depreciate property values.

Text continues on page 164

SHOULD YOU START A BUSINESS OF YOUR OWN?

The odds against achieving success in a small business are great, but they can be leveled off somewhat by a cautious self-analysis before the first step is taken. The check list on these pages, adapted from one prepared by the government's Small Business Administration, is designed to help the user foresee some of the hazards and weigh his qualifications for such an enterprise.

1 Are you the right type to run a successful small business? Study yourself honestly; have you rated your personal traits such as leadership, organizing ability, perseverance and physical energy? Have you considered getting an associate whose strong points will balance your weak traits?

4 What sort of facilities will you need? Do you know how much space your business would require, what type of building would be needed? Do you know of any special features you require in lighting, heating, ventilating, air conditioning or parking facilities? Have you listed the tools and equipment you would need room for? Are there local ordinances governing safety that would apply to the space you plan to use? If you use space in your own home, how much can you charge off against rental or mortgage payments when filing your income-tax report? Do the income-tax advantages warrant using space in your home rather than other space outside it? Would the operation of a business in your home interfere seriously with family activities—or vice versa?

5 How should you organize your business? Have you checked the advantages and disadvantages of individual proprietorship, incorporation and, if you plan to take in a partner or two, partnership? Do you need a partner who can give you financial assistance?

8 How will you go about selling your product or service? Have you studied the sales promotional methods used by competitors? Do you know what makes customers buy your product—service, price, quality, styling? Will you have to spend money on promotion? Or can you rely on personal contacts and word-of-mouth? Will you advertise in newspapers, by direct mail, on handbills, on posters?

9 Will you need help? Will you be able to hire satisfactory employees locally? Do you know what skills they will need? Have you checked prevailing wage scales?

10 Have you a plan for keeping up with new developments in your line of business? Is there someone you can go to for expert advice in solving new problems?

What, really, are your chances for success? Have you had any actual experience running a business? Do you have any special technical skills? Have you analyzed recent business trends, especially in the city and neighborhood where you plan to locate? Have you analyzed conditions in the sort of business you are thinking of starting? Have you figured out how much time it will take for your income to equal your expenses? Have you planned what net profit you should make? Have you figured out what rate of return on your investment such a profit would give you?

3 How much capital will you need? Have you worked out how much money you would have to invest to get the business you envision off the ground? Do you have, or could you borrow, the needed amount, plus a reserve for unforeseen costs? Have you made a forecast of expenses including a regular salary for yourself? Have you compared this with what you could make working for someone else? Are you willing to risk irregular income? Have you discussed your plans with a banker? Is he favorably impressed? Do you have a reserve for unexpected needs—assets you could sell or on which you could borrow?

Are you qualified to market your product and to buy needed supplies? This can offer a complex series of problems: Do you have a fairly accurate notion of just how many customers you might expect? Should you buy supplies in bulk, getting them cheaper but using up storage space? Or should you buy in small but probably more expensive lots? Should you give a discount on large orders? Have you worked out a plan to control the flow of supplies, so there will always be enough, but never too much, on hand? Do you know the suppliers with whom you will deal?

7 Do you know how to go about pricing your product or service? Have you determined what prices you will have to charge in order to cover your costs and still earn a profit? How do these prices that you have figured on compare with those of competitors?

What laws do you have to take into account? Will you need a license? Will you have to meet health regulations? Are there local or state laws regulating this kind of business? Is there a chance you might have trouble with zoning laws? Do you have a lawyer to give you advice?

What records will you have to keep? Do you have a suitable bookkeeping system for checking on costs and sales? Will you need a professional accountant, at least occasionally? What kind of system will you establish to regulate the flow of supplies and merchandise? Do you know what sorts of ratios between costs, sales, profits and so on are common in businesses similar to yours?

13 What other headaches will you face? How about taxes and a system for handling them? Have you thought about: insurance? having enough capital to keep going if people don't pay their bills on time? whether you will sell on credit? what to do about returned goods? how to assign work to others? Do you have a sound work plan for yourself that your family will approve?

■ If they live in a rented house or apartment, they may have to get written consent from their landlord.

■ If the business has a name other than their own, they must file a trade-name certificate with the county clerk.

■ They must check with their insurance broker to see if any changes are needed in fire and liability protection; they may find that their rates increase when the business gets under way.

■ Charlotte must pay Social Security tax as a self-employed person (about 7 per cent of the first $7,800 she earns).

■ They must determine what local business taxes apply to them.

Once their home-based business is under way Charlotte and Harry soon find that being self-employed has some advantages over working for hire. From a financial point of view, the greatest help comes from the income-tax laws. They still have to pay taxes on what the business earns, of course. But they can subtract from earnings all business expenses. Because their business headquarters is in their house, a portion of all their housing costs counts as a business expense. They can deduct part of what they pay for home insurance, heat, light, repairs and maintenance, real-estate taxes and the like. Even depreciation—a deduction not available to most homeowners —could be taken on that portion of the house used for business. The "business share" of the house depends on either the number of rooms or the number of square feet used for business. If they use, say, 200 square feet for business and the house contains a total of 1,600 square feet, their deductible "business rent" would be 200/1,600—one eighth —of their total housing expenses.

The general rule is that you can deduct whatever expenses you incur in order to make taxable income. This means that advertising expenses, postage and even part of the phone bill are deductible. In fact, should the business grow to the point where one of the children could be employed to help, his wages (assuming they are reasonable) would also be deductible as a business expense. Should the business show a loss rather than a taxable profit, this loss can sometimes be used to reduce the amount of tax owed on other taxable income.

Of course, Harry and Charlotte have to be prepared to prove all this. For tax purposes, it is essential to keep careful and documented records of all expenses (receipted bills, not just canceled checks). In addition, it is wise to keep a record of mail addressed to the home business and a list of business visitors to the home. The Internal Revenue Service keeps a sharp eye on home-business expenses and is often skeptical of such items as wages paid to children. The burden of proof is on the taxpayer.

If Harry and Charlotte compare working at home with a job at the bank, they find other financial advantages. Charlotte can eliminate child-care expenses unless the business grows quite large. She also saves the costs of transportation to and from work, eating lunches out and housekeeping help. And she limits the extra costs of clothing, laundry, cosmetics and the like that go with a 9-to-5 office job.

How much extra

Not only does working at home let you keep more of what you make than other means of earning extra income, it also beats any other means in convenience. You can regulate the hours you work to meet the demands of your family life. You are not separated from your family. You can be on hand for emergencies. And as much as anyone can be free and independent these days, you're your own boss. A home sideline can also be a trial run for what could turn out to be a full-scale, full-time business. But even the best arrangement for augmenting family income leaves a major question: How much moonlighting, how much wife-working, how much family-enterprising should you do? There is no doubt that the more you do the more you can do—up to a point. Consider the drawbacks of added activities as objectively as possible before undertaking the tempting opportunities for getting extra income today. Some couples build a living pattern so based on a second income that the whole picture would be shattered if the second income were ever dropped. The place they live in, the cars they drive, the clothes they wear, the food they eat, the entertainment they enjoy, the people they see, the schools their children attend—all would have to be changed. It is difficult to avoid the upward spiral; affluence is easy to get used to. Part of the price for a higher standard of living is the loss of freedom to change that way of living.

You *could* get to the point reached by one family we know who built a weekend cottage overlooking a bay. "Where do you live in the city?" we asked, imagining an enclosed life amid urban towers. "Oh, we have a house just like this outside of town; it overlooks the water, too," the mother said. "Then why this one here?" we asked. "Well," she said, "we're all so busy all the time, with jobs and projects and whatnot, that we never see each other. We thought that maybe here we could say hello."

7
Your house
The biggest outlay

So you are going to buy a house. How much should you spend? Where should you look? What kind of house? New? Old? Almost new? Should you consider custom-building? How should the house be financed? Above all, when you finally choose a house, will you make a wise choice, or will you base your decision—possibly involving the biggest purchase you have ever made—on considerations that are irrelevant, perhaps frivolous, certainly costly?

According to the most comprehensive study ever made of how people buy houses, and why—a survey commissioned by the National Association of Home Builders—the typical decision is made in such haste that it verges on impulse buying. In the following pages we'll try to answer your questions and help you guard against the most common pitfalls—expensive in money, expensive in family happiness.

First things first: know thyself
When a family decides to buy a house, it should begin not by looking at houses but by looking at itself.

A home must suit its owners—in design, cost, appearance, size, type. If seclusion is your ideal, don't waste time considering the built-up suburbs. If your house is always a meeting place for friends, the important considerations are a large kitchen, ample dining space and perhaps a separate recreation room. If your children lead individualistic lives—one listening to records, another studying, another turning in early—separate rooms for each may be crucial. The way you like to live should determine the kind of house you choose to live in. A young couple we know, Phil and Helen, learned this the hard way. They had been apartment dwellers during their five years of marriage. Now their son Mark was four, Phil was doing well in his job, and they had enough saved for a down payment on a house. They began thinking of moving to the suburbs for the usual reasons: good schools for Mark, the need for roots in a community, more space—a yard for Mark, and maybe a dog, to romp in—more privacy, security, a settled feeling of permanence.

First they considered new houses, but luxury tracts such as Hickory Hills were too expensive, and developments in their own price range turned out to be rows of boxlike ranches they did not like. So they settled on Greenville, a suburb of mature houses set well back on streets lined with tall maples, oaks and elms.

"You get more for your money in the old ones," they agreed, as they stood looking at a two-and-a-half-story Victorian Gothic. It sat on a corner half-acre and had a generous sloping front yard that dropped off sharply two or three feet to the sidewalk—a pleasing bit

of old-fashioned charm, they thought (and a curse to mow, as Phil subsequently learned). They walked around the house counting the trees: 17 of them, including an enormous maple that must have been a sapling when the land belonged to the Indians.

They looked inside and began the "Well, what do you think?" exchange that is the prelude to buying. There was a lot of work to be done, they admitted, but that was why the place was a bargain. Once in, they could transform it into the kind of house they had always wanted, stylish outside, gracious inside. They bought it.

The first year most of Phil's free time and all the money they could spare went into repairs and urgent maintenance: installing new flashing around the chimney, replacing rotted window sills, digging up a sewer line that had been invaded by the majestic maple (with its majestic roots that reached out 30 feet), dealing with a basement wall that leaked in heavy rain, and endless minor fixing. It all had to be done, but none of it added style or graciousness.

Come spring, Phil tackled the lawn. A disgrace to the neighborhood, it had been made into a turfbuilder's nightmare by the 17 trees, which cast too much shade and exhausted the soil. He tilled, sowed, mulched, fertilized, fought crabgrass, dug out ancient, gnarled shrubbery—and learned that one can spend an appalling amount of money on the effort to grow grass. His resentment rose as he watched his neighbors loading up for golf on Saturday mornings. He also began to have the uncomfortable feeling that he was neglecting his job.

"I'm nothing but a slave to this damned house!" he finally snapped one evening at dinner. Sadly, Helen admitted she felt the same way. There was so little time for any fun. "If we had $2,500 or $3,000 to spend on the house and yard, we could get everything done and have it over with," she said. But they did not have that kind of money. And it wouldn't have mattered if a fairy godmother had waved her hand and transformed the house instantly, free of charge.

For they had finally realized that the trouble really wasn't with the house. The real problem was that the house and its occupants simply weren't suited to each other. Phil was handy enough with tools, but he didn't *like* doing the work. And Helen, too, found all the gardening a chore instead of a delight. They were, they knew now, essentially urban types. Where they belonged was back in an apartment or a condominium—a modern efficient place that made minimum demands. "And the hell with character," said Phil. "Amen," said Helen, "and you can throw in a couple of rose bushes."

So they decided to put the house up for sale, swallow the loss they would have to take and start again.

The cost of the mistake

It was an expensive education for Phil and Helen. The sale brought $500 more than they had paid—but against this "profit" they had to count the following expenditures:

- Closing costs on purchase of house, $500.
- Maintenance, repair and improvement, $1,900.
- Broker's commission on sale, $1,230.
- Moving costs back to the city, $350.

They charged off their mortgage payments as rent, and the income-tax deductions for interest and real-estate taxes softened the blow a bit. Even so, they were out almost $4,000 as a result of the episode, not to speak of the emotional toll. They cut the loss a little more when they sold their second car—which they had bought in the first place only because they needed it to live in Greenville.

The moral of this tale is not, of course, that there is anything intrinsically wrong with old houses or with living in the suburbs. Millions of families live happily in both, and would find sterile and unsatisfying the kind of efficient dwelling place Phil and Helen needed. The moral is that when looking for a place to live, a family should do what an architect does before he begins to design a house: It should take a good hard look at its living patterns, its interests, its likes and dislikes, its needs and its capabilities. You can't match them all, of course, but you can force yourself to decide what is important to your life and what is not. Only when these questions have been honestly faced can the next stage of exploration safely begin.

The first step in finding a house to suit your family is one that, oddly enough, requires you to ignore the house itself. At this point, it's not the building that matters but the location.

It's natural for people in the mood to buy a house to want to look at houses. That's the mistake Jack and Ginny made. Reading the Sunday classifieds, Jack says, "Gee, this sounds good! 'Sacrifice —builder forced to sell below cost—spacious three-bedroom, sunken living room, built-in aviary, many other desirable features; low, low down payment. Make reasonable offer.' " Ginny: "Where is it?" Jack: "Maple Acres." Ginny: "Where's that?" Jack: "The ad tells how to get there. Want to take a run out?" Ginny: "Sure, why not?"

This is not the way to do it. Before you know it you may find yourself backing into a house. When you see one you like, the tendency is to keep on liking it. And once you get as far as saying "This is a possibility," you will have "taken mental possession," to use the salesman's phrase, and any subsequent appraisal of its location is likely to be superficial, to say the least.

Even house-hunters less impetuous than Jack and Ginny go astray. Their friends Harold and Priscilla are circumspect enough to consider location. They know they want something northwest of the city because there's a good commuter train that will bring Harold within a four-minute walk of his office, so they start scouting the area on weekends. Eventually, to get some notion of what's on the market and how it's priced they pull into a broker's parking lot and walk in. The next thing they know they are being conducted on a tour of houses. A particular one catches their fancy. The immediate surroundings look fine, and it isn't long before they slide from the stage of "just looking" to a decision to buy, with only a cursory investigation of the community and neighborhood. This, too, is not the way to do it. All experts on houses agree: Don't look at houses when you set out to buy a house. First look at locations.

LOCATION: THE GATEWAY TO A HOUSE

No doubt there are some ivory-tower types for whom external surroundings mean little. As long as the house they have is dandy, they don't care where it is. But such people are rare. For most families, location quickly acquires major importance—in pleasure, convenience and pure cost accounting. It would seem to make sense then to give location your first consideration after you've studied yourself.

But this procedure is rarely followed. When asked to name the most important factors in the selection of a house, the largest percentage of the families queried in the National Association of Home Builders survey—63 per cent—listed adequate heating. Location rated 19th, turning up in only 9 per cent of the answers—below adequate wiring, good insulation, low taxes and 14 other items. When you consider that insufficient heat can usually be remedied but where you live cannot unless you move, this seems a little odd.

To most people the word location means position on a map. It means that to housing experts, too, but much more as well. It includes the character of the neighborhood—not just the houses you can see from your house, but the economic and social atmosphere of the nearby area. It also includes the character of the community, its shops and schools, local government and local taxes. But beyond that, location means just about anything that bears on the desirability, marketability and price of a property except the character and condition of its buildings and grounds. When housing experts talk about location, they combine a lot of widely assorted factors:

■ Geographic position—county, township, municipality, neighborhood, and place on a particular block.

■ Time and mileage from distant points such as your office, your mother-in-law's house, a ski area or vacation cottage, or anything else you might like to have as near (or as far away) as possible.

■ Time and mileage from local necessities and conveniences such as schools, shopping facilities, houses of worship and commuter stops.

■ Distance from points neither necessary nor desirable to have nearby, such as dumps, football fields, airports, truck routes, artillery ranges.

■ Social position—is it a luxury community, average, or a place in which you wouldn't want to be caught dead or, even worse, alive?

■ Socio-geographic position within the community—is the house near the golf and country club or two blocks from the Happy Time Bowling Lanes and Cocktail Lounge?

■ Any number of other considerations that are only indirectly dependent on location, such as zoning ordinances, building codes, the availability of utilities, the presence or absence of trees and winding streets, recent trends in neighborhood values, and the possibility that one of the neighbors plays the trombone.

Zoning and codes: location insurance

One among the odd assortment of factors that enter into location deserves special attention. That is the existence of strict—and strictly enforced—zoning ordinances and building codes, which stabilize all the factors making up location. Only with the protection of these codes and ordinances can you be confident that the location you have so deliberately sought will be a reasonably permanent characteristic.

A house's position on a map may never change, but almost everything else that contributes to location can. Everyone who has lived some years in a suburb remembers tree-lined streets of fine old houses that now are parking-lot-lined concentrations of supermarkets. Jammed in among the commercial buildings may still be a few of those once-envied homes, but you wouldn't want to live in one now. Their location has changed as drastically as if they had been jacked up and hauled away to new sites.

Change is essential, of course, as community needs evolve. Nearly all neighborhoods go through a fairly predictable life cycle. Like people, they age. Some do it slowly and gracefully, while others begin to look decrepit in their teens. In almost all cases, it's zoning laws and building codes that make the difference.

Zoning stabilizes the use of property in a neighborhood. If you choose a place in the middle of a section zoned for single-family residences you have some assurance that other uses will be forbidden; you won't wake up some morning to find your own home suddenly

Pitfalls in the path of the house-hunter

■ Wrong house for the family.

■ Good house, wrong neighborhood.

■ Too much house, too little income.

■ Undependable builder.

■ Falling in love with a gimmick instead of "heading at once for the basement" to examine quality.

■ Making too large—or too small—a down payment.

■ Putting anything in writing without the advice of a competent lawyer.

less desirable because the house next door is being converted into apartments or the empty lot across the street is being excavated for a gas station. Building codes stabilize an area by guaranteeing that construction in it meets certain standards of quality; you don't want your block disgraced, for example, by one new house so inadequately supported that its walls take on a new angle of tilt after every winter freeze. Zones vary not only from town to town but also from neighborhood to neighborhood within a single community. There may be four or five zones for single-family residences, each regulating land use but in different ways. You should make certain you understand which one applies to your chosen location.

And the existence of zoning and building codes on paper is not enough. There's always someone looking for a variance, and the people who try for one are frequently capable of exerting considerable political pressure. Whether or not codes are rigidly enforced depends on the local political administration and, ultimately, on a strong community spirit that makes itself felt on the enforcement level.

It's almost impossible to exaggerate the importance of these laws —and their effect on every type of community. An area of new homes all in the same general price range, for example, is generally thought to provide the most stable balance of location factors and therefore to offer the highest probability of sustained property value over the longest period of time. (We're not talking here of personal tastes or personal values—just property value in dollars and cents.) But this holds true only if controls are stringent. Give that same area weak zoning, and it can succumb to instant decay.

It is zoning that helps keep the balance in communities of older houses, or of houses of diverse sizes, types and ages. If properly protected by codes they retain their quality and value just as well as uniform new developments do—some of the country's most desirable communities contain houses of many styles and periods.

Where diversity includes racial diversity—a development that is occurring all over the country as more and more communities become integrated under the Fair Housing Law of 1968—strong zoning is especially helpful in maintaining price stability. In the past, where zoning was weak, unscrupulous real-estate manipulators often moved into areas in the process of integration and frightened owners into panic selling by preying on racial prejudice, fear and economic anxiety. Their ugly (and now illegal) tactics enabled some manipulators to make a killing by buying up good houses at radically depreciated prices, and carving them into jerry-built apartments or rooms. This has not happened in areas where high zoning standards exist.

Where to fit into the price structure

A community where prices are markedly diverse presents special problems that strong zoning can solve only partially. There is an old economic law that says: Where property values vary widely, prices tend to fall to the lowest levels. Once again, other values have every right to override economic maxims. But if money is your chief consideration, it is wise to obey the maxim "Don't come in at the top" —that is, don't buy the most expensive house on the block. Say you're looking for a certain house that sells for $25,000 or $26,000. You may find exactly the house you want at what seems to be a bargain. It is flanked by $18,000 houses on smaller lots, and its price is $750 below that of an identical house in an area where all the homes are in the $24,-000 to $28,000 range. Will you buy the first house to save $750? You'd be exercising poor financial judgment if you did.

Be wary of coming in at the bottom, too. If you can find a $21,000 house nestled in a colony of new $28,000 houses, that's one thing. But don't buy next door to some big, old, expensive and uneconomic place in an area where the zoning laws are so lax that it might be turned into a rooming house or nursing home.

How these ingredients that make up location must be juggled to arrive at a good location for you, only you can tell. As part of your know-thyself examination, you will by now have determined whether your family needs lots of privacy and space, with only the hootie owls for neighbors and snowshoes in the corner for getting into town when you need a loaf of bread, or whether you'll put up with some traffic noise and close neighbors in exchange for the convenience of being able to get a pizza delivered in 10 minutes.

The best approach to a final decision on location is to zero in. Start by narrowing down possible communities to the two or three most suitable for your family. Within those communities, scrutinize the most promising neighborhoods. Only within the neighborhoods that meet your requirements and standards should you then begin looking at houses. This zeroing-in technique is used by professional appraisers when they assemble data on the value of a house. It's a technique that will give you the best chance of producing a house well suited for your family—if you go at it methodically. Some sort of notes are almost essential, and a checklist like the one that follows will make it easy to measure each location against your needs.

How much should you spend?

Location may be the most important thing to consider when you're buying a house, but it's not the only thing. At some point your choice

Text continues on page 180

LOCATION CHECK LIST

General impressions—they're important

Probably the most important factor to consider when you buy a house is the nature of its surroundings—its location. Location will large determine how long you stay in the house and how much you'll get for it when you sell. Some elements of a location will be more vital to you than others. Here is a list of points to consider:

1 Does the community look clean and well kept? Drive through the shopping areas. Are the curb clean? Trees and grass trimmed?

2 Are roads and sidewalks well maintained, or are there potholes? Are crosswalks well marked

6 Are there a good number of families with school-age children? Such families give stability to an area. They have probably already expanded into as large a house as they'll need, and are likely to remain in the community until the children finish school. They have a long-term stake in their neighborhood, and this results in a continuity of community interest.

Always keep zoning in mind

7 Are there big old houses in the neighborhood, and if so are they in good shape? Dilapidated ones spell trouble —trouble that can often be traced to zoning laws. When laws call for single-family dwellings and are enforced, large houses can still draw high prices and look well kept. Where zoning laws are lax, big houses are often cut up into apartments and, deteriorating further, end up as seedy rooming houses.

8 Do the smaller houses show any signs o neglect or carelessness? If so, this often indicates that they are lived in by tenan rather than their owners. This, in turn, can indicate that the neighborhood is ir transition—downward.

10 What are the zoning laws? Drive over to the town hall and ask the town clerk. If the building code allows industrial development in the next block, watch out!

11 Are new highways contemplated? After you see the clerk, hunt up the town engineer and ask if any heavy-traffic routes are being planned for the area.

12 If you are planning to build, are there local restrictions governing the kind of house you have in mind? Ask at the building inspector's office. Some communities prohibit contemporary designs, some veto all or certain kinds of prefabricated houses, some specify the kinds of building materials that can be used, some will not let you add to the structure once it has been built.

3 Are the streets well lighted? Take time to tour around at night. Besides lights, you'll see what sort of night crawlers, if any, there are.

4 Are houses and grounds well kept? Elaborateness may or may not be your cup of tea, but neatness counts as a way of measuring if people care about where they live.

5 Do the residents seem congenial? All towns have moods and personalities. Much of your scouting will be on weekends, so you're bound to see enough activity to get an idea of what the natives are like. Stop and ask questions. If you get gruff answers, that will tell you something too.

Are there, in fact, any rooming houses or boarding houses around? You can usually spot them by the number of cars in the driveway. Such multiple dwellings are usually a definite sign of a decaying neighborhood. Not always, however. Values can be both high and stable in some areas where rooming houses are numerous—in college communities, for example. "It is the type of occupant, not the fact that he is a tenant, that largely determines the character of the property and the area," says a guide published for the Society of Real Estate Appraisers. The proprietress of a rooming house in one Midwestern university neighborhood is one of the most imposing and aristocratic *grandes dames* in town.

Do the zoning laws prohibit certain special features you were planning to have? Some areas, for example, prohibit a basement workshop from being used for the making of anything for sale.

14 Are zoning laws well enforced? Ask the local civic association. Or look through current and back issues of the local newspaper for reports of variances, disputes, possible changes and so on. You can find copies of the paper at the library, of course, or at the newspaper office itself.

15 Are there rumors of apartment developments or industry coming in? Ask the local shopkeepers.

The schools—How far? How good?

16 Where would your children's school be? Even if you see a school building right in the area you are considering, it could be in a different school district with the one your kids would attend a mile away.

17 What hazards would your children encounter getting to school? Make a trip to the school to find out for yourself. Also, ask at the school if there is bus service. If so, does the school system expect children to walk farther than you consider desirable?

20 Is there a large playground? A well-equipped gym? A well-stocked library? What is the cafeteria like? Are there any audio-visual tools, and if so, are they used as substitutes for personal attention or to free the teacher to give *more* personal attention?

21 Is the school now, or soon likely to be, on double session? Don't be shy about asking the principal such questions. Ask how large classes are—they should not have more than 25 pupils, preferably fewer. Are there specialist teachers in music, art, shop, math, foreign languages, science?

22 Is there a staff nurse? A psychiatrist or psychologist? A guidance counselor?

23 How much money does the school budget allot per pupil? What is the teachers' salary range? How do these figures compare with other schools in the county the state? High salaries in themselves do not guarante good teaching; nevertheless a town with a higher sala schedule than others nearby can be more selective in hiring personnel. These facts are all part of the public record. If the principal seems reluctant to give you the information, go to the school system's superintendent

Rate the fire and police protection

28 You can find out how good the fire department is by going to the mayor's office (or, if the town has no mayor, to the office of the top administrative officer) and asking to see the fire department rating. The American Insurance Association rates the fire departments of 470 large U.S. cities. Elsewhere state insurance-rating bureaus do the job. Both the Association and the state bureaus use a scale of 1 to 10, 1 being the top rating and 10 the lowest. Large cities tend to earn the better ratings, with an average of about 4. Smaller communities average about 5. The best way to judge the fire department in the community you're considering is to compare its rating with those of a half-dozen neighboring towns. If the neighboring towns average 6 and your town rates 5, you can figure on better-than-average protection for your part of the country.

3 How good is the school? Ask the principal for permission to look around. Your senses will tell you things you'd never learn any other way. Arrange to visit a class in your child's grade and watch for enthusiasm and spontaneity on the part of the pupils—signs of creative teaching that cannot be contrived for visitors. Does the teacher simply lecture and demand rote answers, or are independent thinking and discussion encouraged? Notice also how much individual attention each pupil gets.

19 Are the classrooms bright, cheerful, clean, well lighted and airy? Are the seats and desks comfortable? Is the general atmosphere happy?

Does the community support its schools where it counts—with money? Find out how the town has voted on school-budget requests. Consistent defeats would indicate where the community does *not* put its priorities. Then there is the other side of the coin: sometimes a town will vote against school bond issues to show dissatisfaction with the superintendent and the school board. The people may feel the superintendent and board are expanding the physical plant at the expense of the teaching staff, or that their educational philosophy is too radical. The local League of Women Voters can usually fill you in on this. Also check the system's "capital-and-debt-service ratio." This tells what part of the budget goes to improve the physical plant, and whether the system is saddled with debt.

25 Is there an active PTA? If so, talk to a member or two. They may not be objective about the school system, but they'll help round out the picture.

26 Does a local civic association take a lively interest in the school? This is another source of information.

27 How do the schools compare with the one your children have been attending? Compare all the figures you've gathered from the area you are considering with those of the district you live in now.

Is the police department on the job? Again you can find out, although there are no official ratings for police as there are for fire departments. One way is by comparing theft-insurance rates in the area with those of nearby areas. You can also compute the ratio of policemen to population and compare that figure with those for neighboring towns. In addition, ask a few property owners if police protection is adequate. If the answers run along the lines of "I don't know—all right, I guess," be reassured; if there are complaints, you'll almost certainly hear about them.

Other services you should check

30 What sort of water and sewerage systems does the community have? Ask for the results of the most recent test of the water supply. You should note its bacterial count and its hardness. Hardness above 500 parts of dissolved mineral salts per million gallons of water produces heavy scale inside hot-water pipes; concentrations of iron salts above three parts per million may stain laundry. The bacteria count should react "negative."

31 Is there free garbage collection? If not, how much does private service cost? Where are the town's present disposal areas? Are there provisions for the future?

32 Are there good libraries, museums, parks and other recreational facilities? Invest tim. in examining them and comparing them v others you know. Good ones contribute to the stability of a community and bring hig returns in property value as well as a richer life for your whole family.

Taxes—the whole truth

34 Ask at the town hall about *all* local taxes and assessments, and compare them with those of similar communities nearby. Make sure you inquire about special assessments and not just real-estate taxes. This is especially necessary in newly developed areas where you could find yourself assessed extra to pay for the new streets, curbs, sidewalks and sewers that are still being put in. But keep in mind that relatively high taxes are not necessarily bad. Good schools, good police and fire departments, well-tended parks—all these cost money. When comparing tax schedules, you can't fault town X for having a park-district tax and a fine park system when town Y has neither the tax nor the parks. The trick is to determine, by comparisons and the right questions, whether local officials are using taxes efficiently and responsibly.

Distances from here to there

35 How will you get from this new home you thinking about to all the places you will need to go? Can you easily drive to a goo market, for example? And can you park when you get there? Test the routes. Find out how heavy traffic is in rush hours.

37 Can you commute by public transportati If so, how long is the *total* trip, door to door? How much does monthly commutation cost? Perhaps most important, can you get to the railroad station or the bus depot on the town bus or will you have to make this part of the trip by car? If by car, will you need a second automobile in the family? This, a parking at the station, can be expensive. Lastly, is there decent rail or bus service after rush hours in case you're delayed in the morning or at night?

38 If the car breaks down, can your wife get to the market on local transportation?

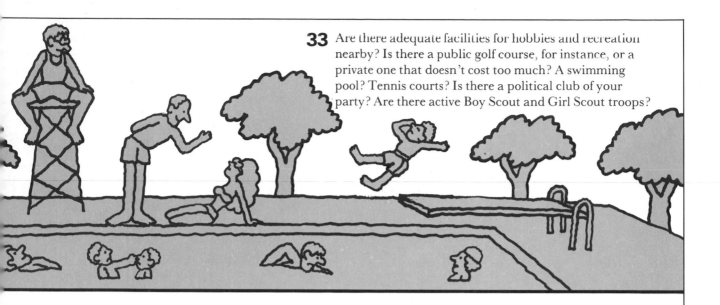

33 Are there adequate facilities for hobbies and recreation nearby? Is there a public golf course, for instance, or a private one that doesn't cost too much? A swimming pool? Tennis courts? Is there a political club of your party? Are there active Boy Scout and Girl Scout troops?

Will you have to commute by car to your job? If so, you'd better find out how long the trip takes in rush hour, door to door. Or will your working hours enable you to avoid peak traffic? How much will tolls, if any, cost? Is there a place to keep your car at work? Is there a parking fee? Are new highways planned? The local planning commission can give you information about this.

Where's the nearest place to shop? If you forget to buy milk or bread at the supermarket, can you get it at a delicatessen down the block?

40 Are other services nearby, such as a post-office branch, a bank? Is there a hospital nearby in case of an emergency? How close will you be to a church of your denomination? Is there a playground near enough for the children to get to on foot? Is there a neighborhood movie they can attend?

of location is going to be narrowed by the answers to two basic questions: How much can you afford to spend? Are you going to buy a new house or would you prefer an older one?

Whether you'll find happiness in something old or something new, the price range should be decided on first. It is determined by your income—present and anticipated—measured against the mortgage terms available at the time of purchase, present and expected taxes, expected running costs and repairs, and your own evaluation of what things are most important to you.

If you buy too high, you'll wind up in a lovely house without the means to do much living in it. (Perhaps you're willing to be house-poor for a while; a lovely house may be worth a squeeze on other things.) If you buy too little house now, you may soon be faced with the need for a better one, with all the additional costs an extra move entails. (But maybe you're the type who'll never care a whit about the walls around you as long as you can go to Aruba every year.)

There used to be rules of thumb—"purchase price should not exceed two and a half times annual income," "monthly payments should approximate weekly income"—but they never really were substitutes for the hard arithmetic of personal values. Today inflation, low down payments and the financial latitude permitted by affluence have made them less valid than they ever were.

Just try to settle on a reasonable mean. Don't strap yourself too much, for you may find that you're not willing to sacrifice other things as much as you thought, and there are always those unexpected expenses that come out of nowhere. But don't penny-pinch too much; Aruba may not quite make up for the other 50 weeks of the year.

The search for bargains

Almost all house-hunters nourish the secret hope that they will find bargains everybody else missed, especially among older houses. There aren't many. The old economic law of supply and demand works pretty well in relating price to value. If a buyer pays less initially, he'll most likely make up the difference through higher maintenance costs or declining resale price as the house ages further.

But the value of a given house may be quite different to you than to most people. When you find a house that *you* rate high it can be a bargain. Most are priced well above or well below the average. At the lower end of the price scale numerous opportunities await the amateur with building-trade skills to rehabilitate a distressed house either as a family home or as an investment.

A professor of history who left the Midwest to take a post at a Cal-

ifornia university bought a structurally sound but badly run-down house for $8,000 and devoted his spare time to refurbishing it inside and out. He enjoyed the work so much he made it a business. He sold his first house for a profit of more than 50 per cent, repeated the performance even more successfully with a second house, then retired from teaching to devote full time to hunting down houses that needed cosmetic treatment. Within two years his income surpassed that of the president of the university.

As an example from the other end of the bargain table, there is an impressive old house on an acre of hillside in northern New Jersey that a local real-estate broker can never pass without a choleric rise in blood pressure. Several years ago the house was for sale at $49,000. Prospects at that price being in short supply at the time, the house had been on the market for six months when an executive transferred to the area agreed to look at it. "Make the owner an offer of $20,000," he said. The broker indignantly refused. "All right," said the prospect affably. "Then will you release the house so I can make my offer directly to the owner?" The broker testily agreed to waive his exclusive right to handle the sale of the house—and a week later the house on the hill was sold to the executive for $25,000.

Almost any real-estate man can tell similar stories of incredibly low prices being paid for big houses with a limited market. Sales at half the asking price don't occur every day, but there's sometimes a surprising amount of give in the price of seemingly expensive older houses. If you feel equipped to handle a house of that sort (it can be costly to maintain), take a deep breath and make your offer.

SOMETHING OLD OR SOMETHING NEW?

Bargains are rare among average houses. If you want what most people want you must pay what most people pay. Having faced that fact, you must still decide whether you are going to buy a new house or an "older home." Terminology gets a bit foggy here. From the buyer's point of view, an almost-new house—two or three years old, say—and a never-lived-in one are usually lumped together, while a house that's unmistakably not new, in fact is distinguished by a certain maturity, is in a category of its own.

Real-estate brokers and people who turn out housing statistics, however, look at it differently. A house is either brand, spanking new, never occupied by anyone, or it's an "existing home"—which means that it may be anywhere from a month to a couple of centuries old and have had one or a hundred owners.

As we saw with Phil and Helen, young couples buying their first

Housing's inflated price tags

Consider inflation when you think about selling your house. You may get more than you paid for it, but you'll have to pay more to replace it. The typical new one-family home you could have bought for $20,000 in 1963 cost $23,580 only five years later—a rise of almost 18 per cent.

A house designed just for you . . .

There is great appeal in the idea of having an architect design a house that will exactly suit your taste, and be tailored to fit the plot of land you've bought as well. But it can be expensive. The architect's fee and the extra expense of getting a custom builder to construct a one-of-a-kind house may add 20 per cent over the cost of equivalent living quarters ready made. But it can all be worth it in long-term satisfaction.

house may not have any clear-cut predilection; they're often willing to settle for whatever fits their purse. Of the roughly 68 million single-family houses of all types and ages in the country today, at least 40 million are 20 years or more old. The typical buyer has the means to make a choice between one of these and a new house.

The people who opt for older houses generally do so partly from personal taste but principally in the widely held belief that an older house will give them more for their money—that dollar for dollar you get more space, more solid construction and a more generous use of materials, because they just don't build 'em like that anymore.

An opposing view is expressed by Robert W. Murray Jr. of the Federal Housing Administration in his book, *How to Buy the Right House at the Right Price* (Collier Books, New York, 1965). "New houses are much better built than old houses were, even when once new," writes Mr. Murray. "New houses are often located in better-planned neighborhoods, even though they don't look so well-landscaped when new. As for spaciousness, larger old homes are not as good bargains as they sometimes seem. The spacious rooms may be poorly located in a bad floor plan."

A new house offers utter freshness, its materials have their full life span ahead of them, and there's sometimes an opportunity to modify design. An older house, on the other hand, gives you mellowness and, to some extent, the benefit of hindsight: It enables you to see what it has become rather than simply guess at what it will be (though there's still room for guessing what it will be after what it has become). It shows you the neighbors and neighborhood as they are. Settlement cracks, damp basements and other structural flaws have had a chance to reveal themselves. And lawn and trees are established.

The average price of new houses has risen at a sharper rate with inflation than the average price of existing homes, so comparisons have to be studied carefully for actual value given. From a strictly economic point of view—taking nothing else into consideration—the best buy in a single-family dwelling today is generally a new or almost-new house in a group of similar houses.

SHOPPING FOR A NEW HOUSE

A majority of people who buy new houses pick one from one of the tracts of similar houses put up by merchant builders, whose houses make up 60 per cent of the new-house market. A builder acquires a parcel of land, subdivides it, constructs houses to a few standard designs, and merchandises house and lot as a package, usually displaying one as a model. The best merchant builders lay out well-planned, at-

tractive communities, save as many trees as possible and use good design for maximum efficiency and living comfort. By taking advantage of new materials, time-saving techniques and quantity production economies, they produce good houses at relatively low cost. In terms of strict economic value, a good development house gives you more living space and equipment per dollar than other kinds.

Merchant builders make ready-to-wear houses. If you want something a bit different you have to be willing to spend more. If you must have the ultimate in individualized design, you can commission a custom-built house, one that is uniquely conceived and designed by an architect to suit your needs, wants and even whims. The land is of your choosing, perhaps in consultation with the architect, and construction will be contracted for with a custom builder, who must be qualified by more than ordinary skill, experience and ingenuity since he may find himself having to devise ways of doing something never done before. Many builders, even very good ones, will have nothing to do with custom building because of the unusual, the unforeseeable, the delays as problems are solved, and the need for maintaining crews of exceptional workmen. They find standardized mass production more profitable and less ulcerogenic. So do most buyers. A custom-built house usually costs about 20 per cent more than a development house of similar size and materials—though the range may be as great as from 10 per cent less to 100 per cent more.

A more modest approach to custom building—sometimes called personalized building—is possible if you use an architect to modify an existing basic design, such as one you choose from books of stock plans available through lumber dealers or one you purchase from a magazine. Most architects charge a percentage of construction costs —usually 10 to 15 per cent—and therefore prefer to devote their talents to costly homes or commercial construction. But some just enjoy solving the living-space problems of a family, and you may find one willing to give you half a hand with your house, working on an hourly fee basis. Such fees run $15 to $25 an hour.

The merchant builder, too, can personalize one of his tract houses somewhat to meet some special tastes. Many builders give the buyer considerable latitude within which to alter the room arrangement and interior treatment of a basic design. This kind of customizing may run 5 to 20 per cent or more above the cost of the basic design bought "off the shelf"—that is, already finished by the builder—depending on how much free rein you allow your imagination.

In recent years a completely different—and economical—kind of new house has become widely available. This is the prefabricated, or

. . . or a house ready made

There are advantages, too, in buying a house ready made by a merchant builder. You usually get a bigger house and a better one—in terms of materials—for the same money you would spend on a house designed especially for you. The merchant builder typically buys a large tract of land, subdivides it and then, using a few standard designs, builds a number of houses at once. This saves expense for him—and for you.

manufactured, house. Producers of these instant houses would like to forget the postwar years, when rinky-dink prefabs sold for $7,500, and town fathers everywhere were kept busy rewriting building codes to keep them out. Times have changed. Today you can spend $40,000 and more for a so-called prefabricated house—though most are far less costly—and live in it as pridefully as if a hometown carpenter had nailed the boards together one by one.

The extra value of manufactured homes comes from the economies of carload purchasing, lower-cost labor and assembly-line techniques. The packages for some prefabricated houses are virtually all inclusive, with pre-cut floor beams notched and marked, pre-cut floor stock bundled together, and all other material down to the decorative moldings packaged and trucked to the buyer's site for assembly. A local builder usually acts as contractor for the assembly of the house.

The larger producers offer several basic designs, with modular lengths of wall, floor and roof sections making it possible for the buyer to add, for example, 4, 8 or 12 feet to the standard living room. The buyer can also choose from a variety of exteriors, so that two side-by-side houses from one manufacturer may never be recognized as having come off the same, or any, assembly line.

Land and loans for customs and prefabs

A prefab or custom home presents more financing problems than a completed merchant-built house. To start with, you need a lot. How much to spend for it is an important consideration. To keep the proper ratio between land cost and house cost, and avoid overbuilding or underbuilding, the land should run 20 to 25 per cent of the total value of completed house plus lot. If you contemplate building a $37,500 custom house, for example, the land itself should cost between $10,000 and $12,500. Cheap land is often false economy, especially in sparsely settled areas. You're likely to become surrounded by cheap houses.

Once you've bought the land and paid for it, you can often use the paid-for land as security for a mortgage loan that will cover the cost of building the house. The money will be turned over to you in installments so that you can pay the builder as various stages of construction are completed. If you're fortunate, you may find a lender willing to make a mortgage commitment for 65 per cent of the appraised value of the completed property (house and lot). Typically, you'd need at least $17,500 of your own money (including your paid-for lot) to finance $37,500 in construction costs for the house. An equivalent house in a development might cost you $40,000 to $45,000 instead of $50,000, with a down payment of 30 to 35 per cent.

Judging a builder and his work

If you buy a new house of any kind, ready made, custom built or pre-fab, you deal with a builder. There are good builders—and, unfortunately, there are others. The industry has its share of not-so-goods, incompetents and fast-buck artists, with a fringe of dishonest operators. You run about the same risk of taking a shellacking in buying a new house as you do of picking a lemon in the garden of older homes. Check out thoroughly the builders of any houses you're considering (*see box at right*) and don't allow yourself to be lax about it. Only then look at the houses and check them out from head to footing (*see New-House Check List*). It's surprising how much you can discover about a man's honesty and competence if you know what questions to ask and what to look for in his work.

Above all else, do business only with men of unimpeachable honesty. Borderline operators can not only cheat you out of your money, they can make you liable for debts they run up. See if the builder has both a business and a home phone listed in the local directory. Some fly-by-nights will be doing business under another name, in another location, when a buyer comes around to see about the rest of the landscaping that was supposed to be done, or to complain that the tiles are coming off in the bathroom and half the doors have warped so much they won't close. If the builder lives near any houses he's building, that's usually a good sign. It means he's not afraid to be accessible to his customers. But even if he is locally based, find out if he's built under other corporate names, and check those out too.

There are a number of semi-official agencies that can give you a line on builders. The Better Business Bureau is one. The National Association of Home Builders has 450 chapters, and the local secretary may tell you about builder Blank; any favorable answer is likely to be fluff but you may get some surprisingly candid information. Most producers of manufactured homes belong to the Home Manufacturers Association (1701 Eighteenth Street, N.W., Washington, D.C. 20009), which issues a yearbook of members, types of houses and areas covered (cost: $2); the manufacturer can direct you to builders near you who handle his work. You can also look up a builder in Dun & Bradstreet's *Middle Market Directory* or *Million Dollar Directory*, which are in the reference sections of many libraries. An explanation of the listings at the beginning of the volumes shows where to look for two key pieces of information about your man: His annual sales tell how substantial his operation is, and the "proportion of worth represented by assets not used in the business" indicates the solidity of his finances.

But the best clues to responsibility come from a bank—the build-

Text continues on page 189

Rating the builder

Buying a new house is such a large investment that investigation of the builder's credentials is worth the effort. Here are a few simple ways to check up on his reputation.

■ Ask at the local office of the National Association of Home Builders about your builder.

■ Call the Better Business Bureau and ask if they have had any complaints about your man.

■ Ask the builder the name of his bank—he'll consider this a routine question. Visit the bank and talk with one of the commercial officers about the builder, carefully explaining the reason for your inquiry.

■ Look in the telephone book and see if your builder has a local home number as well as his business number. If he does, that means he's probably in permanent business locally and not a fly-by-night. Also, see if he lives near any of the houses he has built. If he does, it should mean that he's not worried about being accessible.

■ Ask the builder for the names of a few people he has built houses for. Call on a couple of these people and see what you—and they—think of the quality of the construction.

CHECK LIST FOR A NEW HOUSE

You can judge the quality of a new house pretty accurately if you look around carefully, prying and poking in all the corners. Of course, some parts of a house —the wiring, for example—are always partly hidden. To judge these parts, get the builder's specifications. You should check the builder's reputation, too. Here is a list of specific things to look for.

The bathroom

1 Flush the toilet and watch the water. If it runs straight down the sides of the bowl, the fixture is probably an economy model. If you can see separate streams, it is of a better grade. If the streams swirl, it is a quality bowl.

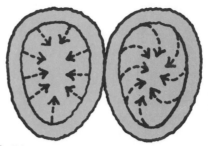

2 Listen as the tank refills. If it's noisy, somebody has saved from $2.50 to $4 on the flush mechanism; that's about the extra cost of a quiet type.

3 Look for a trademark on the fixtures. If there is none, it ma be an indication that the fixtures are second-line. They may have been made by a top manufacturer, but since they are his cheaper goods, he decided to leave his name off.

4 Measure the top of the wash bowl. It should be at least 20 inches by 24. This is the smallest bowl used by good builders. Smaller bowls—15 17 inches or 18 by 20—indica a builder has really cut corne in an effort to save about $4.

The basement or utility area

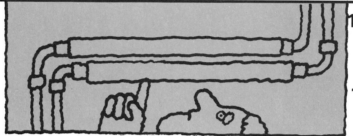

9 Check the heating system carefully. If it's a warm-air system, look for a pulley-driven air blower, a 10-year guarantee on the heater, duct outlets at the base of outside walls. In a hot-water system, the boiler should be cast iron, have at least a 20-year guarantee and bear the IBR seal of the Institute of Boiler and Radiator Manufacturers and the H of the American Society of Mechanical Engineers. On gas-fired burners, look for the AGA of the American Gas Association. If the home is all-electric, check installation with the local utility office.

10 Hot-water pipes should be copper; cold-water, copper o plastic. Long hot-water pipes should be insulated.

11 Examine the hot-water heater It should have a 40-to-50-gallon capacity if it is gas, 80 gallons if electric.

12 Look at the plate or placard on the electricity switchbox. I should show 240 volts and 100 amps, or, preferably, 150 am Count the circuits; eight is th minimum for a small house, 12 for a large.

17 Give all the windows a similar test. Make sure there is weather stripping between the movable sash and the frames. If the sashes are made of metal, look for plastic slide tracks. They make windows easier to open.

18 Check the way the frames of all windows and doors fit into the exterior wall of the house. Any gaps or cracks at the edges are infallible signs of inferior workmanship.

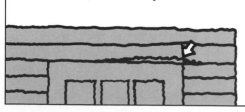

Masonry and floors

19 Examine brick or concrete blocks to be sure they're laid in even rows, an even spread of mortar between them

20 Be sure hardwood floors are tightly fitted, with no high edges or gaps between boards. The longer each board the better. As you walk listen for creaks. There should be none.

21 Look for high-grade flooring. Oak or maple tongue-and-groove boards remain a hallmark of quality, but the lack of them does not indicate a substandard house. Many people prefer one of the newer materials.

Notice the faucet handles. The simple four-spoke ones are the least expensive, indicating low quality.

Turn on the hot-water faucet. If you get hot water at once, the plumbing probably circulates on an "upfeed and gravity return" system, the best and an indication of good construction.

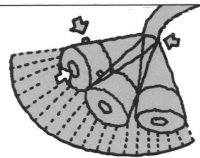

7 Examine the shower head. It should swivel on a ball joint; all but the cheapest do. It should also have a lever for adjusting the spray. In addition, the plate that creates the spray should be made of plastic to reduce clogging from minerals.

8 Check for shut-off valves on the pipes under the washbowl and the flush tank. Their absence means that the builder saved $3 or $4 at the cost of almost certain inconvenience.

The kitchen

13 Turn on the hot-water faucet to see if you get hot water almost at once.

14 Look under the sink for shut-off valves, as in the bathroom.

15 Pull out a kitchen drawer. If it is on rollers, that's one more touch of quality you can give the builder credit for.

Windows and doors

16 Grasp the knobs of all outside doors and try to rattle them. Doors should fit snugly and also have weather stripping that closes the gaps between edges and frames.

Visible fundamentals

Check even the parts of a house you can't see by using the builder's specifications. Make sure, for example, that the foundation has a poured concrete footing that lies below the frost line. This will prevent settling. Most building codes specify proper footing depth.

23 For quiet rooms interior walls should be made of wallboard ½ inch thick, not the ⅜-inch grade.

24 See that the roof shingles, if of asphalt composition, are windproof and of at least 235-pound weight. Some people prefer wood shingles.

25 Be sure the insulation is of the blanket, batt or foil type. Thicknesses needed for a cold climate (like that of the upper Mississippi Valley): roof, 6 inches; walls, 3 inches.

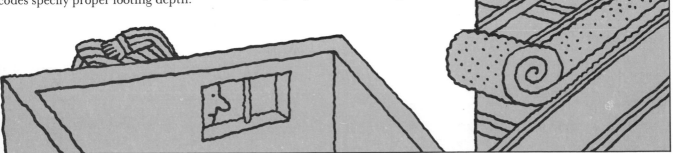

Evaluating the floor plan

A well-thought-out floor plan gives a house more than just step-saving convenience and comfort. It adds a feeling of space and provides privacy for each member of the family when wanted, two things that make a house a satisfying place in which to live. A bad floor plan is also a bad investment, for it downgrades the resale value of the house. Appraisers have a sharp eye for poor layout. They also tend to distrust unusual floor plans, even if they are actually quite efficient. This is something to remember if you ask the builder to incorporate design idiosyncrasies you happen to prefer. It may be well worth it to you, but you should be prepared for the fact that these unusual touches could cost you money if you sold the house. Here are some simple things to check when examining a house's interior design.

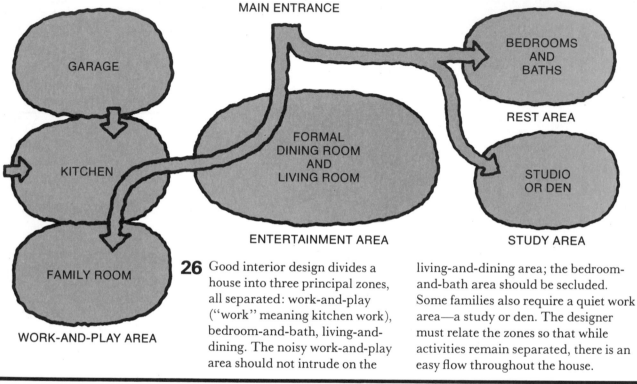

26 Good interior design divides a house into three principal zones, all separated: work-and-play ("work" meaning kitchen work), bedroom-and-bath, living-and-dining. The noisy work-and-play area should not intrude on the living-and-dining area; the bedroom-and-bath area should be secluded. Some families also require a quiet work area—a study or den. The designer must relate the zones so that while activities remain separated, there is an easy flow throughout the house.

27 Time-and-motion studies have shown that the best kitchen arrangement is the "kitchen triangle," shown here. This step-saving design places the three major appliances —refrigerator, range and sink —on two legs of a triangle. The total of the sides of the triangle should be 23 to 26 feet. Serving space should be outside the triangle of working space.

28 The family room should, modern designers say, be on the same level as the kitchen, rather than down a flight of stairs in the basement, the popular spot two decades ago.

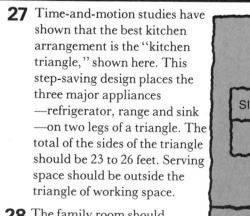
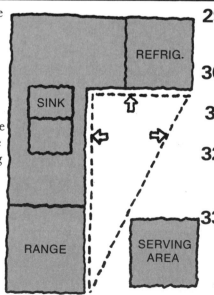

29 There should be at least three bedrooms, each with a minimum of four feet of closet per person.

30 Two bathrooms are now a minimum; one should adjoin the master bedroom.

31 The laundry area should have at least 3½ feet of space in front of appliances.

32 General storage—not counting closets, kitchen cabinets and so on—should provide about 800 cubic feet of space.

33 Finally, don't ignore an instinctive feeling that somehow a house is just not right. It may meet all measurable requirements and still make you edgy. Conversely, don't buy a house just because you "love" it.

er's bank. The only way to get the name of his bank is to come right out and ask him for it. If the builder is a good businessman, he has asked the same question of others repeatedly; it's about as routine as giving someone a business card. Pay a visit to the bank, ask to speak to one of the officers in the commercial department, tell him you are considering buying a house from Mr. Blank and ask him what he knows about Mr. Blank. You'll get some useful information and, if the bank officer is on his toes, he will then introduce you to a mortgage loan officer or solicit your business himself; it's a good time to begin collecting information about available terms.

Once you're satisfied you're dealing with an honest man, you'll want some assurance that he knows his business. Ask him for the names and addresses of a half-dozen or so previous customers, and visit a few. It's a good idea to telephone first rather than walk in cold, but don't hesitate to make this first-hand check. Most people love to talk about their houses. If their experience with the builder was good, this reflects well on their acumen and they'll boast. ("Look at this marvelous little extra closet he got in for me," or "He's not imaginative but he's sound.") If their experience was bad, they will probably still be fuming and will be more than eager to sound off. ("That damn shower rod is still hanging loose!")

Sometimes, of course, criticism is just carping and praise a cover-up for the buyer's poor judgment. One easily put-upon couple pointed to an enormous exposed wooden beam running across their living-room ceiling. How clever their builder had been to install such a rustic touch, they said. Clever in what sense, they were asked. Well, they said, the builder put it in after the building inspector refused to issue a certificate of occupancy. The room, it turned out, had been built too wide for its original supports.

Ask to look around the house, including the basement. Even if the house you're visiting is quite different from the one you're planning for yourself, the quality of the masonry and electrical work of the one you're inspecting will be a good indication of the builder's general quality. Builders are often curiously consistent: once shoddy, most likely always so; once quality, most likely always so too. If you're investigating a merchant builder, a visit to his earlier buyers offers the feel of the basic house he's building.

Judging the house

You may have your heart set on a low-lying house that looks just like one you saw on Cape Cod last summer; or you may want your new home to be tall and impressive as befits your improving status. To

you and your family personally, style will be as important as the grade of lumber in the siding, but it matters little in economic terms. Quality matters a lot—quality in materials and workmanship but also in design for convenience and comfort. The house on which the builder has cut corners so that he can trim his price by a few hundred dollars is a poor bargain. The difference between "economy" materials and the best, and between a well-planned, well-built house and one that's slapped together, is 10 per cent at most. Yet studies have shown that the "economy" house costs the householder at least $250 to $300 a year more—in operating costs and maintenance—than the house built to high standards. And the cost in frustration generated by ill-conceived floor plans cannot be estimated.

How, you say, can you judge the quality of design and construction when you can't tell a ball-peen hammer from an adze? You can't for sure without an expert—an impartial builder, appraiser, architect or engineer. If there's any room for serious doubt, spend the money—it will cost $50 to $100—to hire one.

Actually you need to know next to nothing about materials, design and methods of construction to determine, fairly quickly and easily, whether the builder of a house has skimped or given full measure of quality. The first step is simply to ask about some key elements. Like the thickness of the plasterboard applied to interior walls: 1/2" plasterboard instead of 3/8" makes rooms quieter. Or the grade of roofing shingles: 235-pound shingles cost only a little more than 210-pound and last much longer. Certain minimum standards are specified for houses built with FHA mortgages; your bank can give you information about them.

An even easier way to get a line on quality is to look yourself for certain telltale features that indicate the builder's concern for value. This method makes use of a kind of sampling technique, similar to that of the political pollsters—an assumption that if a builder has used quality materials and construction for a number of visible and easily examined features, the whole house has been built with the same good workmanship and attention to quality where it counts but can't be seen. This is not an infallible method, and should never be relied on to the extent of not getting a professional appraisal where that's desirable, but it should give you a fairly good indication of where the house stands in the general range of quality.

For the inspect-it-yourself check on quality, the demands on you are minimal—like being able to flush a toilet, or knowing how to recognize a circuit breaker. You simply tour the house looking for specific details in a few significant areas. The bathroom is one; there you can

quickly tell if the builder has spent a few dollars extra to give you a shower head with a side-mounted spray-adjusting lever (then you won't get splashed every time you readjust). The kitchen is another place where care shows—a handy door simplifies carrying the groceries in (and the garbage out). Exactly where to look and what to look for are spelled out in the check list that follows.

SHOPPING FOR AN OLDER HOME
Shopping for an older home is different from delving into the new-house market. The intermediaries between you and the house are different. The things you have to check out in the house are different. The financing of the house is different.

To start with, you deal not with a builder or his salesman, but with the owner or his broker. Try both. You can turn up possibilities by watching the classified ads (not only in the big-city daily but in the local weekly too) and by spotting "For Sale" signs. But more likely than not, your best bets will come from a broker.

There are more than 800,000 real-estate brokers and salesmen in the country, and they sell three fourths of all the existing homes that change hands each year. Each broker is licensed by his state, and in most states each must pass an examination. Of the brokers, approximately 89,000 are Realtors, a trademarked term denoting members of the National Association of Real Estate Boards.

A good broker can save you money
Most brokers conscientiously try to serve the interests of buyer as well as seller. But not all. So ask any brokers you're thinking of using how long they've been operating in the community, then check them out at the local Better Business Bureau and the civic association. If you find a first-rate broker, you have experience and knowledge on your side. He knows what is for sale in and around his community. (He may have a cooperative arrangement with other brokers to share listings, either informally or through a multiple listing service.) He can tick off the virtues and faults of a house as he walks through and then estimate what it should sell for—not will, but should—and seldom miss by more than a handful of $10 bills. He can help fit a house to your family, particularly if you have given him the personal information he needs. He may even be helpful in bargaining the price of your choice down to a figure that will make you beam with pleasure, but don't count on him to do this.

This is somewhat paradoxical. The broker, after all, represents the seller, being entrusted with the task of finding a purchaser in re-

Text continues on page 194

CHECK LIST FOR AN OLDER HOUSE

The fundamental difference between judging an old house and judging a new one is that the quality of workmanship and materials originally put into the old house is no longer your primary concern. The question is how well they have withstood the test of time.

1 Go straight to the basement to learn the worst, spending only enough time in the living area to get a general impression. If the impression is favorable, head downstairs fast—before any infatuation with the house or with the charm of its setting blinds you to signs of decay that may lie below ground. That's where structural defects are most likely to show up. If they're extensive, repairs can greatly increase the cost of the house.

2 Tour the foundation walls looking for cracks, crumbling mortar or oth evidence of deterioration—or fresh patches indicating a recent cover-u

3 Look over the walls for a "high-wa mark." This is often visible if a basement has been flooded. Look also for any signs of leaks or seepag on the walls and floor.

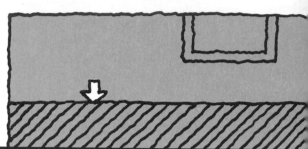

6 Check any exposed structural beams —especially the timbers called joists that support the floor above. Water seeping down from the kitchen and bathrooms above can rot them.

7 See if the joists have been notched for pipes so deeply as to weaken them. One third of the depth is the maximum for safe notching. Joists pulled away from supporting masonry indicate wall movement.

8 If joists are shored up by intermediate jackposts or timbers, ask an expert why.

9 Get an expert to inspect foundation walls inside and out for signs of termites at work. Termites travel up foundation walls to get to the woodwork above, using mud tunnels that look like ordinary dirt streaks. Termites are now found in all parts of the U.S. and they are so destructive that the Federal Housing Administration and Veterans Administration frequently require a "no-termite certification" before they will approve mortgage loans on old houses. Brokers often urge sellers to get certification as an added selling point; if this has not been done, it's worth paying for yourself. Make sure the inspection is made by a recognized pest-control operator, most of whom are member of the National Pest Control Association or a state pest-control association.

14 To do a thorough job, make your next stop the roof (or send up a professional roofer). Look for broken or missing shingles, or—in a roof that is surfaced with layers of gravel and asphalt—for bubbles or peeling or broken patches.

15 Look at the flashing—the bootlike coverings that prevent leaks around chimneys and vent pipes. It should be intact and watertight, of nonrusting copper, aluminum or plastic.

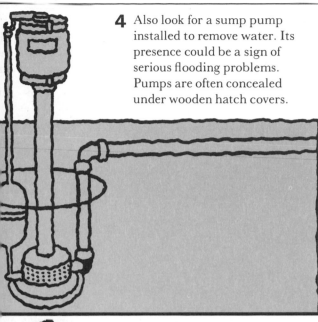

4 Also look for a sump pump installed to remove water. Its presence could be a sign of serious flooding problems. Pumps are often concealed under wooden hatch covers.

5 Even if there are no signs of water having entered, sniff around for a dank odor. This is a danger signal. Call in an expert before you go further.

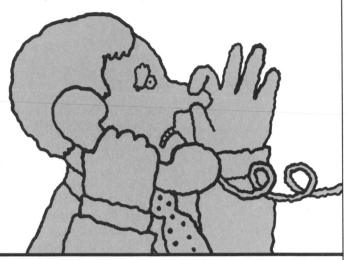

10 Before returning to the living area, walk around outside. See if the chimney has separated from the house. Look for missing mortar and broken bricks.

11 If there are stone or brick walls, look for mortar-joint cracks in a stairstep pattern —evidence of a major separation. An extra-wide mortar joint in this pattern may be a sign that such a crack has been repaired.

12 On your rounds, examine window sills and frames, where deterioration often begins. Are they freshly painted—with no fresh paint on the rest of the house? The paint may be covering rot. Get the opinion of an expert.

13 Look at the gutters. Are there any signs of breaks or leaks? Downspouts should lead directly to underground drainage at least three feet away from the house or to storm sewers.

16 If you can get into the attic or crawl space, check underneath the roof with a flashlight, looking for telltale water stains that signal leaks.

17 Now it's time to go back into the house. Use the check list for new houses as a general guide, but keep in mind that components have changed, and age will have to be taken into account. And once again, don't ignore your personal reaction: You're going to have to live in that house if you buy it.

turn for a commission paid by the seller, usually 6 per cent. Nevertheless, a house that an owner himself is selling is more likely to be overpriced than one being handled by a broker.

Most owners have an exaggerated idea of what their houses are worth. Sneevely bought his split-level for a certain price, he's put so much into it and prices have gone up 20 per cent, so he's going to make a handsome profit when he sells. Besides, it's *his* house, so naturally it's worth more than the other houses on the block. An experienced broker, on the other hand, will decide what it will sell for and won't waste time trying to sell it for more.

The broker is in a position to be both objective and practical. He wants to make a sale because that's his livelihood, and he wants the price to be as high as possible in order to get as high a commission as possible, but he'd rather sell at a lower price than not at all.

Can you save the broker's fee?

The 6 per cent broker's fee has to go somewhere, and many people think they save at least some of it if they buy directly from the owner. In theory, that's true and logical. But it presupposes that the price would be the same with or without a broker, which isn't necessarily so. As we saw with Sneevely, unless a broker has put a realistic price tag on the house, the owner is likely to have it overpriced, and so even if he concedes you the commission, the figure may still be high. And if you are first shown the house by a broker but don't buy it until much later—perhaps as much as six months later—that broker is still entitled by contract to his commission whether you buy it through another broker, directly from the owner, or however.

Judging an older house

The advantages and cost of using a broker when you are buying a house should be filed away in your memory against the time when you have a house to sell. That is the other side of the coin. But even on this side of the coin, remember that, however good and reputable and useful your broker may be, his business is selling houses—to you, the buyer. When he shows you houses, watch for the pitfalls.

Judging an older house is different from evaluating a new house in one fundamental respect: The quality of the original materials and workmanship are academic now. They've been put to the test by time —and the question is how well they've survived its ravages.

Many people tend to think of a house as something indestructible. It doesn't have any moving parts, and there are a few houses dating back to Colonial days that are still livable. Yet houses wear out.

For one thing the earth is not as stable a foundation as we would like it to be. It moves, and with it houses shift their weight to some extent, creating stresses and strains. Houses also expand and contract with heat and cold (they do have moving parts), they are under constant attack by wind and water, and wood and mortar have more enemies than friends. Equipment inside the house is even more prone to wear, breakdown and obsolescence. The Internal Revenue Service isn't just being nice to the landlords of rented houses when it permits a depreciation allowance based on the assumption that a building will be worn out in 40 years. It's being factual.

If you are planning to finance the house with a mortgage insured by the Federal Housing Administration, you can protect yourself somewhat by making your "offer to purchase" conditional upon the FHA appraisal being not less than the offered price. But an FHA appraisal is not a guarantee against defects, even major ones, and it probably won't give you as good an idea of the assets and problems of a house as a private evaluation. The fee for an appraisal by an impartial builder, architect, engineer or appraiser runs from $50 to $100.

But before you engage an appraiser, you need to evaluate the house yourself to decide whether it's even worth professional examination. One professional who is often called on for expert testimony in court cases has a system that has helped many house-hunters. He advises: When you first look at a house, spend only enough time in the living area to get an impression—"I like it" or "I don't like it." If it appeals to you, head at once for the basement.

The reason for so quickly ducking out of the living area is psychological. Typically, a couple with a favorable first impression will wander around taking in the kitchen, the bedrooms, the bathrooms —"Hey, look at that! Real ceramic tile!"—exposing themselves to the most attractive features of the house. "Look, darling, a built-in dishwasher." "Yes, and built-in hi-fi speakers in the family room." In the basement, termites gnawing away at the main beams could be waving a sign, "Termites at work," but the happy couple would never notice. They'd walk through the basement wearing the blinders that lovers wear. The idea is to look at the seamy side first, while you still can see. And it's in the basement that you will most likely find structural defects *(see Old-House Check List)*.

The art of bargaining

If you have settled on a new house, you can't expect to gain much by haggling over the price. But if it's an existing house, you must expect to take part in a hallowed ritual of bargaining. A broker can often elim-

inate the opening extremes of negotiation by getting the owner to start off at a fairly reasonable level, and he can also often cut down on some of the intervening rocking-horse effects. But even his help will not much alter the ceremony, which goes something like this:

The owner asks $28,000. Privately you may agree, from what you've seen previously, that the house indeed is worth $28,000, or possibly $27,500. Never mind. Your first feeler is for no more than 90 per cent of the asking price. After fingering a chip in the living-room wall, or asking how much it would cost to replace those gutters, you reluctantly say you *might* consider it at $25,000. A number of things can happen next depending on the role now assumed by the owner.

The eager seller. To your surprise, after looking pained for a moment, he answers, "All right, you've bought yourself a house." Now you know that you haven't found his bottom price. And you haven't bought yourself a house, either, since all this has simply been verbal jockeying. Even if there were both verbal offer and acceptance, neither would be any more binding than an invitation to lunch.

"Twenty-five, huh?" you reply. "Well, I'll think it over." You return the following evening with the news that you've checked on the cost of new gutters, and meanwhile noticed that the chimney needs repair. "I'm afraid $24,000 is the most I can offer, under the circumstances." And you may just get it at that, or at $24,500.

This may sound farfetched, but anyone who has been in the business long knows of cases with this degree of difference between asking and selling prices. When your first counteroffer is taken up at once, it's always a sign that you've come in at just about the figure the seller really had in mind, and you haven't hit bottom yet.

The stand-patter. He lets you know in no uncertain terms that his asking price is his selling price. Chances are he has just put his house on the market. When he's had a dozen people shake their heads and walk out during the next two or three weeks, he'll begin to soften. Unless you're absolutely positive that the house is a gold-plated bargain at his asking price, go away and let him age.

The bargainer. He couldn't possibly entertain such an offer as your $25,000—but he doesn't throw you out of the house either. After reminding you of features that make the house worth at least $30,000, he admits that he's under pressure to get his family moved to the new job in Seattle, and since you are really interested, he'll make it $27,000.

You tell him, regretfully, that this is more than you're prepared to pay, but you do like the house, and if he decides to come down, to give you a call. He phones the office the next day: "I've been offered $27,000, but I don't think this fellow can swing the financing. Make

it $26,500 and it's yours." You reply that you may have to go see another house tonight (you may), which your wife might like more (she might), but if you don't work something out you'll try to come by and take another look at his house. Then, just before you're both ready to hang up, you add: "You know, we do like your location, and when we talked about the house we wondered how much it would cost to finish off the basement. Around $1,500 or $2,000, I suppose. Tell you what—would you consider $25,500?"

This will go on until you meet somewhere between $25,500 and $26,500, or until each arrives at his final offer with still a gap between. The mistake made by most buyers lies in being too hasty in agreeing to a price after the seller makes his first concession.

When you've decided that this is the house you want, admittedly it's difficult to shake your head and walk away, pretending that you've made your final offer. And it's easy to be panicked by that phantom prospect who's due to arrive in a couple of hours—and who may, let's face it, turn out to have substance after all. But if you're willing to run the risk of losing out, and can keep in mind that this really isn't the "one and only," you'll almost always buy for less by waiting; you'll sense the point at which the seller has set his teeth and absolutely isn't going to give another nickel.

This is also the point at which you have to decide whether the price really is too high for you—whether you're running the risk of being house-poor. If you do decide to go ahead, you will probably be expected to give the seller a deposit—"earnest money." Don't be too fast with your check book. Stop and think carefully about how you pay that deposit, for a wrong step here can get you into big trouble.

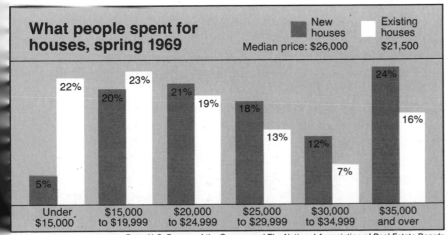

Data: U.S. Bureau of the Census and The National Association of Real Estate Boards

The high price of housing

How far the cost of the American home has climbed is indicated by the graph at left. The bulk of the houses sold fall into two distinct and fairly narrow price ranges—around $20,000 and over $35,000. Very few new houses go for less than $15,000, and the biggest percentage of new-house sales is in the over-$35,000 price class. The median price for all new houses, a modest $18,000 as recently as 1963, had jumped to $26,000 six years later.

Legal hazards and safeguards

When you are finally ready to make an offer on a house, you are standing at the brink of a Dante-esque pit filled with seething legal tangles, writhing whereases, and the tormented souls of buyers who signed a paper they shouldn't have. For example:

A St. Louis couple particularly wanted a house with an oversized, heated garage. The husband needed it for the radio and TV repairs that were his hobby. They eventually found exactly what they were looking for in a nearby suburban town. Dan gave the owner $100 as "earnest money" and noted on the check, "Deposit toward purchase of property at 640 Maple Avenue at price of $23,750."

Dan consulted a lawyer during his lunch hour next day. The attorney asked if he'd checked zoning laws in connection with the intended workshop. No, said Dan, but the owner had assured him there would be no difficulty. On the contrary, said the lawyer, he knew about a complaint made by residents of the neighborhood involving a similar use of residential property; Dan would almost certainly run into trouble. Dan went back to the owner and explained that he'd have to back out. "A deal's a deal," said the owner. "All right, my tough luck," said Dan, and went home to give his wife the news that they'd kissed $100 goodbye.

But that wasn't quite what the owner had meant. After some conversations between his lawyer and Dan's, it turned out that Dan was going to buy the house, willy-nilly. That notation on his check was as binding as a three-page contract.

Putting something in writing too soon is only one of many legal snares. Here are a few others you might not think of:

■ If a fence, driveway or even part of the house intrudes onto an adjacent lot or a street, sidewalk or alley, you may have to remove it.
■ There may be easements in the title giving other people permission to use your property at will—a utility might have the right to put poles on your land, a neighbor might have the right to drive on it. One Florida buyer found out too late that the Central and South Florida Flood Control District could flood his property to a depth of 10 feet.
■ If a fire burns the house to the ground after you've signed a contract but before you've arranged for insurance, you may be stuck with an inescapable agreement to purchase a heap of charred ruins.

You need a competent lawyer

The best way to avoid traps like those listed above is to obey one cardinal rule: Never get involved in buying or selling real estate—never put anything in writing or sign anything—unless it's been approved

by a lawyer experienced in real-estate practice who represents you.

If a check is given for a deposit, put no notations on it.

If a cash deposit is given as earnest money, take only a receipt for the amount, with no stipulations about why it was paid or for what. That way, if anything goes wrong, the worst that can happen is that you'll lose your deposit.

Agreements and contracts drawn to your attorney's satisfaction can protect you against most hazards by giving you the right to withdraw in certain instances or by providing compensation for loss or damage. The cost of a lawyer of your own should be considered an essential part of the cost of buying a house.

Now all you have to do is raise the money.

THE MORTGAGE

The basic principle of a mortgage loan is that you borrow money—cash —which you immediately hand over to buy property; simultaneously the property becomes security for the loan, which you pay off over a relatively long period of time in regular installments. Obtaining the mortgage and buying the property are two separate transactions, although both take place at the same time at a single sitting, called a closing. At the closing you receive title to the property—that is, you become the actual owner, with all of an owner's legal rights and obligations. If you fail to repay the loan, the lender can take possession of the property; he will "foreclose," sell the house, keep whatever amount is still owed him and give you the remainder, if any. Foreclosure, fortunately, has been quite rare in recent years.

One of the nice things about mortgages is that they are still the least expensive loans most ordinary men ever get. The true interest rate is comparatively low, even at $7\frac{1}{2}$ or 8 per cent, partly because you pay interest only on the balance of principal outstanding—the amount of the lender's money that you have yet to pay back.

This differs from the method used in installment loans to finance the purchase of, say, furniture or an automobile. On an installment loan, the lender charges for interest as though you had the use of the total amount borrowed for the entire period of the loan, even though you are paying back a portion of it each month. This nearly doubles the true annual interest rate, making an apparent 6 per cent charge come out close to a true 12 per cent.

While the percentage interest rate on mortgages is comparatively low, the total dollar amount of interest you pay on a house mortgage is staggering; most homeowners pay at least as much in interest as the house sold for in the first place—a $25,000 house may cost $50,000

or more before you finish paying it off. These two facts together make the signing of a mortgage one of the crucial decisions of your financial life. You have more choice among lenders and terms than you might realize, and choosing wisely may not only save you a bundle but can even provide resources to help you make a bundle.

The price—and sources—of money

Some people manage to borrow the total cost of their houses and make no down payments at all. Most, however, get mortgages covering 70 to 80 per cent of the total and pay the rest from their own assets. Both the size of the down payment and the interest rate charged depend partly on economic conditions, partly on the kind of institution that lends the money and partly on the kind of mortgage.

The usual sources of mortgage money—and generally the best —are commercial banks, mutual savings banks (in some states), mortgage banks, savings and loan associations, life-insurance companies. You'll see banks and S&L offices around you; insurance

How much house do you own?

The old saw about the bank owning your house is more truth than humor. Monthly mortgage payments do not really pay much toward a house at first; they go mainly for interest. The chart at right shows what happens to a typical 25-year, $25,000 mortgage. After five years—one fifth the mortgage's lifetime—you might expect to have paid one fifth the mortgage. But, as the chart shows, you have increased your ownership by only 8.5 per cent over the 20 per cent you bought with the down payment. Five years later you still own only 36.6 per cent of the house. After that your ownership grows progressively faster. As payments reduce the principal owed, the interest charges become smaller. This in turn allows a larger proportion of each payment to be applied to reducing the principal further. In the last five years of a typical mortgage, your payments take care of almost 30 per cent of the original total.

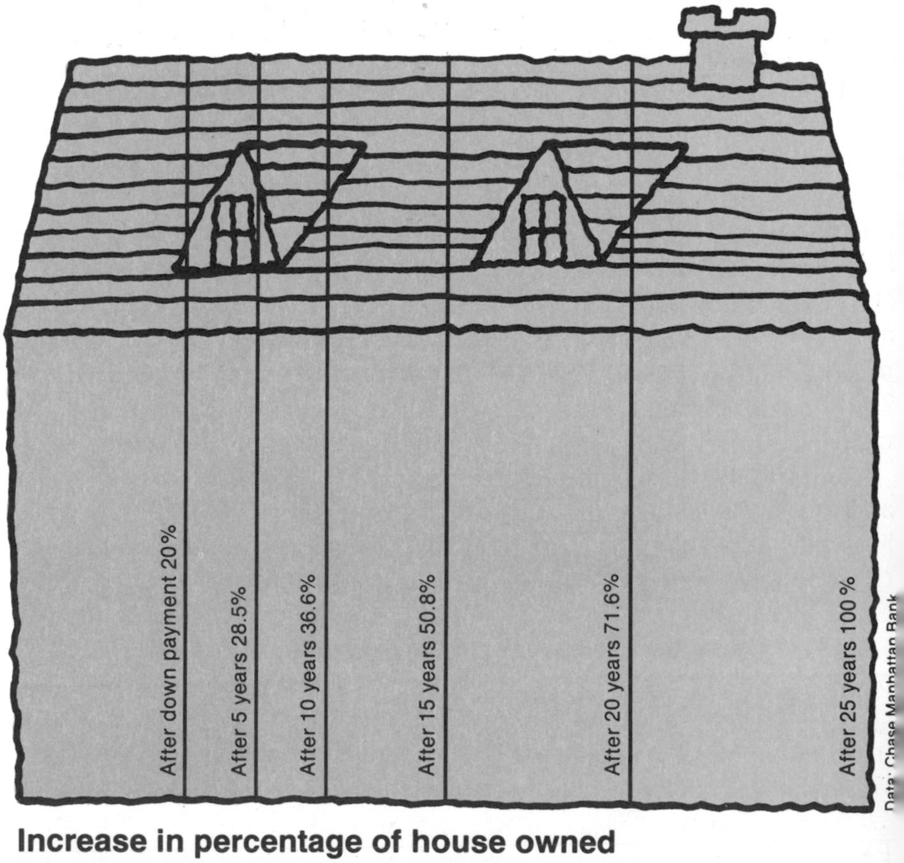

After down payment 20%
After 5 years 28.5%
After 10 years 36.6%
After 15 years 50.8%
After 20 years 71.6%
After 25 years 100 %

Data: Chase Manhattan Bank

Increase in percentage of house owned
(25-year $25,000 mortgage at 7.5 per cent, $5,000 down payment)

company mortgages are usually available through mortgage brokers (listed in the Yellow Pages of the telephone book). Depending on fluctuations in the money market, you may find that one type of lender can offer lower rates than another. Between two lenders of the same type, one may shave the rate a little because he has more money to lend than people are applying for. Even ⅛ per cent saved, especially over the term of a 25- or 30-year mortgage, can be worth some shopping around (an increase from 6 to 6⅛ per cent on a $20,000 mortgage for 30 years costs $580).

If you are dealing through a real-estate broker, he may offer to arrange financing for you. This can be a useful and time-saving service. But don't accept the arrangement without question. Make some inquiries of your own to see whether better terms are available.

All the lending institutions can, if they choose to, make any of three major types of loans: conventional, on which risk is assumed by the institution itself; FHA, on which the risk is covered by mortgage insurance issued by the Federal Housing Administration and paid for by the borrower; and VA, on which the risk is covered by the guarantee of the Veterans Administration at no cost to the borrower.

A conventional mortgage is made on terms worked out between you and the lender. Nevertheless it is subject to some government restrictions. National banks, for instance, can lend no more than 80 per cent of the appraised value of residences, for a term of not more than 25 years. Most mutual savings banks and state savings and loan associations are permitted to lend up to 90 per cent of value, but some states set an 80 per cent limit. Most conventional loans wind up at around 75 per cent of purchase price. The length of the mortgage may be 20 to 30 years for a new house (25 years is typical) and 15 to 25 for existing homes (20 to 25 years is typical). Interest rates have ranged in recent years from 6 per cent to 9 per cent.

On the whole, conventional loans require larger down payments and shorter repayment periods than FHA or VA loans. In their favor: less red tape and more speed in getting the application approved and the loan processed. And when money is tight and interest rates soar, you may find that only a conventional mortgage is available.

FHA loans are not made by the government. Private lenders make the loans, and the FHA insures the lender against loss. The chief advantage of FHA over conventional loans is that the down payment may be lower. On a $25,000 house you may be able to borrow 92 per cent of the appraised value if an FHA loan is available.

VA mortgages (also called GI loans) in some respects resemble FHA-insured loans, but are available only to present and former mem-

bers of the armed forces who meet certain requirements. They are made by private lenders and guaranteed by the Veterans Administration to protect lenders against loss. Terms are more liberal—up to 100 per cent of the VA's appraised value, which often means the veteran gets a no-money-down deal. Repayment time may be as long as 30 years. The loans are usually available only once to each veteran. One special type of VA loan is made directly by the government; it is available in limited supply to veterans in small towns or rural areas, where GI loans are generally unobtainable.

Both VA and FHA mortgages are subject to certain special fees that may not apply to conventional loans. These fees make VA and FHA mortgages about equal in actual interest rate to conventional mortgages. But their other advantages—especially lower down payment—may make them more attractive if you can take advantage of them. This has been very difficult to do in recent years, when interest rates generally have risen to levels higher than at any time in the past 100 years. FHA and VA rates also have risen during recent years, but they have consistently lagged behind the market. It is easy to guess what has happened. Put yourself in the place of a loan officer whose job is making maximum profit in the use of money. He can use it for VA or FHA loans at, say, 7½ per cent or for conventional loans at 8 per cent or more, with takers for all the money available. There is no requirement that he grant VA or FHA loans. How many does he make? Right; jolly few. The supply of money for VA and FHA loans simply dries up—or would except for something known as "points."

Points are a fee charged by the lender as a prerequisite for the granting of a mortgage loan. Each point is 1 per cent of the amount of the loan—for example, a six-point charge on a $20,000 mortgage would come to $1,200. In some money-tight periods as many as 12 points have been charged. The result is the same as an increase in interest rate; by charging points on FHA and VA mortgages, lenders bring their return on those mortgages into line with what they could receive on conventional mortgage loans.

How large a mortgage should you carry?

It seems obvious that you should always borrow money at the lowest true interest offered. Yet that may not always be prudent, for you might have to make an expensive concession to get the lower rate. A lender might, for example, offer one rate if you ask for a mortgage loan covering 90 per cent of the purchase price of the house, and a rate ¼ or ½ per cent lower if you need to borrow only two thirds of the total. Whether you should "buy" the lower rate depends on how

profitably you can invest the difference in the down payments. If you are a good money manager, it may pay to take the larger mortgage loan at the higher rate. You may be able to put that extra capital to work for you so effectively that the profits will more than make up for the higher interest on the mortgage.

This same balancing of mortgage costs against investment possibilities is called for when you decide how fast to pay off the loan. A standard piece of advice to home buyers, repeated dozens of times a year, goes: Make as big a down payment as you can, and pay off the mortgage as quickly as possible. This injunction is usually accompanied by arithmetic showing how much you can save on interest costs. It's true, you will pay less interest doing it this way. But that doesn't necessarily mean that you're managing your money well. The fact is, you may lose money if you pour all—or even much—of your reserves into paying off a mortgage.

Take the case of Alvin. A few years ago he bought a $25,000 house. He took out a 30-year, 6½ per cent, $20,000 mortgage loan, on which he will pay over the 30 years a total of $25,508.90 in interest —slightly more than the price of his house. If he had cut the term of the mortgage in half, and reduced the amount of the loan from $20,000 to $15,000 by taking $5,000 more out of his savings account for a larg-

Where people get mortgages

The towering banker below symbolizes the fact that most U.S. homes are mortgaged on regular commercial bank terms. The reason: High interest rates discourage controlled-rate VA and FHA loans. Fewer than 5 per cent of houses were purchased entirely with cash.

Conventional mortgages from banks 62%

FHA insured mortgages 20%

VA guaranteed mortgages 13%

Cash and other 5%

Data: U.S. Department of Commerce

How home purchases are financed

er down payment, he would have brought his total interest down to only $8,519.90—a savings of almost $17,000. Well, not really a net savings, because if he had left the $5,000 in his savings account at, say, 5 per cent interest compounded quarterly, it would have earned about $5,000. So the net savings would have been $11,500.

But Alvin is a fellow with considerable imagination and skill in making capital grow, and he knew he could do better than that. He decided to leave the mortgage at $20,000 and take the full 30 years to pay it off—and *also* take the $5,000 out of his savings account and invest it, conservatively, in high-grade stocks.

Obviously, there's no guarantee on what will happen to those stocks. But according to a University of Chicago study, covering a 40-year period (including the Great Depression), stocks listed on the New York Stock Exchange would have returned an average gain of 9.3 per cent a year, compounded annually. So let's grant Alvin a 9 per cent return over his 30-year mortgage period, and let's see how his decision is likely to work out, as compared with what would have happened if he'd saved on interest with a shorter, smaller mortgage:

If he had taken the 15-year, $15,000 mortgage

With the smaller, shorter mortgage, the house would have been paid for at the end of 15 years. Thereafter Alvin would have had the amount of the monthly payment, $130.67, to invest in stocks. At the end of the second 15 years, this would have grown to $47,380. In addition, during the first 15 years, Alvin gets back some of his mortgage interest payments in the form of income-tax deductions. In his 25 per cent tax bracket, the tax savings on the $8,520 total interest would average $4.75 a month. Invested regularly during the first 15 years, with additional growth during the second 15 years, this

If he had taken the 30-year, $20,000 mortgage

By choosing the long-term, low-down-payment approach, Alvin has the lump sum, $5,000, invested in stocks for the entire 30 years, during which time it grows to $66,340. Since he pays more interest on his mortgage, the average monthly tax saving on mortgage interest is bigger, coming to $17.50. In addition, the monthly mortgage payment for the 30-year loan is smaller by $4.21. Combining the interest saving and the monthly payment difference, Alvin has a total of $21.71 available for his monthly investment plan, which grows over 30 years to $28,890. Thus, by this method, he will have,

would have grown to $6,220. At the end of 30 years, he would have the house paid for, plus an accumulation of $53,600.

at the end of 30 years, the house free and clear, plus a total of $95,230. It's also worth noting that in times of inflation, the longer the mortgage, the lower the true value of the dollars used to pay it off.

The success of Alvin's method depends not only on skill (and luck) in investing but also on will power. To make it work you must defend the regular investment program against all conflicting demands —for orthodontics, say, or college tuition, or even the purchase of a new car. If you can't count on yourself to keep the investing plan inviolate, you probably would be better off with a smaller mortgage.

The prepayment safeguard
Alvin's method is based on the simple principle that says it pays to borrow money if you can make it earn more than it costs you to borrow it. But what if the return turns out not to be higher? What if the inflationary curve, instead of continuing upward as everyone expects, takes a dip, and we enter a period of extended deflation? Alvin's return on his stocks would then drop *below* the cost of the interest on his mortgage. In that unlikely event, is he stuck?

He may lose some of his capital, of course. But he is not necessarily burdened forever with high interest payments on his mortgage. The safeguard here is a prepayment clause—a stipulation in the mortgage that gives you the right to pay up at a faster rate than scheduled —making it, in other words, a shorter, smaller mortgage when it no longer pays for it to be a longer, bigger mortgage. The option usually carries with it penalties and restrictions, but it still manages to do that rare thing: It enables you, more or less, to have it both ways.

If you don't have the down payment
When you lack cash to cover a down payment, the first question to ask is, should you be making the purchase at all? The question is especially valid if liberal financing is available—80 to 90 per cent of the purchase price. Millions of families have become owners by paying less than 10 per cent down. You must decide if it's wise.

In some circumstances substitutes for some or all of the cash down payment can be justified—for example, when you buy an older home that may require a down payment as large as a third of the total price, or when tight money has caused lenders to raise all down

Text continues on page 208

TERMS OF MORTGAGES FROM FIVE SOURCES

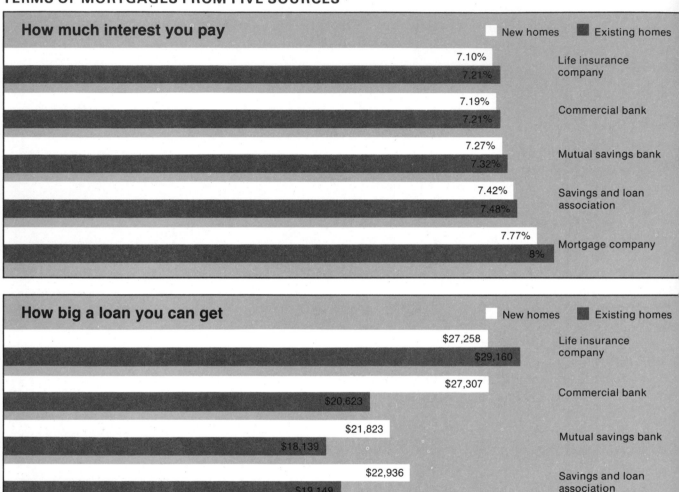

How much interest you pay

☐ New homes   ■ Existing homes

	New homes	Existing homes
Life insurance company	7.10%	7.21%
Commercial bank	7.19%	7.21%
Mutual savings bank	7.27%	7.32%
Savings and loan association	7.42%	7.48%
Mortgage company	7.77%	8%

How big a loan you can get

☐ New homes   ■ Existing homes

	New homes	Existing homes
Life insurance company	$27,258	$29,160
Commercial bank	$27,307	$20,623
Mutual savings bank	$21,823	$18,139
Savings and loan association	$22,936	$19,149
Mortgage company	$23,876	$30,599

How to find the best mortgage deal

It's not just how big a loan you can get that counts when you arrange a mortgage for a house. The interest rate, the size of down payment required, and the number of years allowed for payments all influence both the cost and the utility of the mortgage. As these four graphs show, terms vary in such a complicated way among the different lending institutions that you must compare them carefully to find the one that best suits your needs.

If you want a rather large and expensive new home and can raise a good-sized down payment, a life-insurance

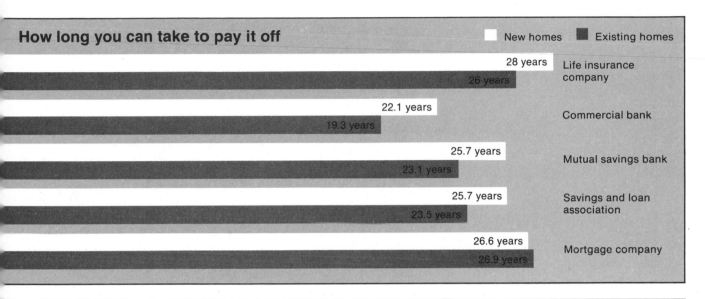

How long you can take to pay it off

☐ New homes ■ Existing homes

Life insurance company
28 years (New homes)
26 years (Existing homes)

Commercial bank
22.1 years (New homes)
19.3 years (Existing homes)

Mutual savings bank
25.7 years (New homes)
23.1 years (Existing homes)

Savings and loan association
25.7 years (New homes)
23.5 years (Existing homes)

Mortgage company
26.6 years (New homes)
26.9 years (Existing homes)

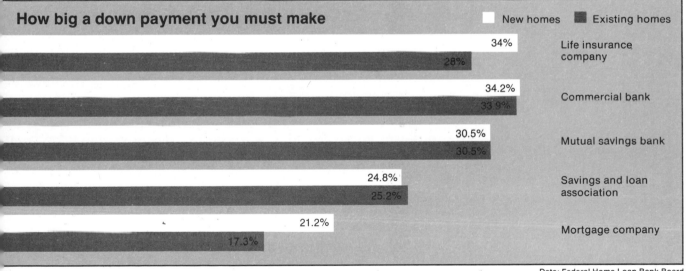

How big a down payment you must make

☐ New homes ■ Existing homes

Life insurance company
34% (New homes)
28% (Existing homes)

Commercial bank
34.2% (New homes)
33.9% (Existing homes)

Mutual savings bank
30.5% (New homes)
30.5% (Existing homes)

Savings and loan association
24.8% (New homes)
25.2% (Existing homes)

Mortgage company
21.2% (New homes)
17.3% (Existing homes)

Data: Federal Home Loan Bank Board

ompany might be the best bet. Such firms give big loans nd charge the lowest interest. But if you don't have much ash for a down payment, you might check the mortgage ompanies. These banklike firms generally charge the highest nterest rate but offer large loans on small down payments nd give a generous amount of time to pay.

After the mortgage companies, the institutions that require he smallest down payments are usually savings and loan ssociations, and their interest rates are often lower. The ize of the maximum loans they offer may be relatively small, however. The terms of commercial banks and mutual savings banks fall between these extremes. They generally offer low interest on fairly small loans and ask for high down payments.

The figures in these graphs are based on the loans for one-family homes that were made during one month in the late 1960s. The interest rates and the other requirements fluctuate according to the business climate, the availability of money and credit, and the appraisal of the property that you are negotiating to buy.

payments. But in most cases, the methods for filling the gap between the cash you have and the cash you need are not recommended.

A "second mortgage" is a common gap-filler. It is simply another mortgage, usually on costly terms, on your house. Suppose you obtain a 25-year first mortgage for $17,000 at 8 per cent. This monthly payment is $131.21. To cover your down payment, you also take on a three-year second mortgage at 9½ per cent for not very much —only $1,500. This obligates you to pay an additional $48.05 every month, or a total of $179.26 monthly for three years.

The reason second mortgages carry high interest rates and short terms is that they are high-risk investments. The burden of two sets of mortgage payments is often more than the homeowner can carry; the first mortgage takes precedence by law, and the lender of the second mortgage may never get his money back.

You may find that a builder who is eager to sell a house will take a second mortgage if you are short of the down payment by a few hundred dollars or even several thousand. But approach a second mortgage with caution; it can be the millstone that drags you under. Most private lenders will view a loan application with distrust if they know a second mortgage is involved. Under no conditions will the FHA approve a loan if the borrower is taking on a second mortgage.

In still another device, a contract sale, the buyer does not receive title until the contract is completely paid off. Usually the agreement calls for regular monthly payments, similar to mortgage payments with no down payment or only a small one. The monthly payment is consequently high. If the buyer is skating on thin financial ice, a contract sale is risky because his payments bring him no equity. If he's forced to abandon ship, he stands to lose everything. He can't bail out by selling the house because he doesn't own anything to sell. If he defaults, the owners simply takes possession, and the would-be buyer has nothing to show for what may have been years of payments.

Assuming an existing mortgage

You sometimes can buy a house without going through the usual channels by assuming a mortgage that has not been paid off. Bypassing lenders, you deal directly with the owner, paying him whatever amount represents his equity in the property and agreeing to take full responsibility for the balance of the mortgage debt.

This can be a very attractive proposition for the buyer. If the original mortgage was acquired some time ago, the interest rate is certain to be lower than any you could get on a mortgage loan today. But even if there is nothing to be gained through a lower interest rate, you

save yourself closing costs, which can amount to several hundred dollars. Buyer and seller can make this agreement without consulting the mortgage holder unless the mortgage prohibits it. This applies to FHA and VA as well as conventional loans, and the buyer need not be a veteran to assume a VA mortgage.

For the seller, however, transferring a mortgage is not so simple. He remains liable for the mortgage debt and must take responsibility for any deficiency in the event of a default unless he can get the mortgage holder to give him a written release. That means the seller must have the buyer approved by the mortgage holder. The mortgage holder is always fussy—and not only about the buyer's credit rating. Permission for transfer of a mortgage is often difficult to obtain if it means the lender is approving continuation of a 5 per cent loan when new loans are being made at 8 or 9 per cent. So if this sounded like something too good to be true, it often is.

MOMENT OF TRUTH: THE CLOSING

All the tension of selecting and financing a home is resolved in one dramatic climax, the closing. It is a solemn ritual attended by many individuals, some of whom bring checks. At one point in the proceeding you become the owner of a house and thousands of dollars in debt. The closing is always expensive and often unexpectedly so. If you can understand what is going on and what is happening to your money, it is likely that you have advanced degrees in law, accountancy and higher mathematics. You need help. Bring a lawyer.

This a fairly typical sequence of events:

After the decision makers at the lending institution approve your application for a loan, you receive from them a "letter of commitment." It tells you how much you will get and on what terms.

After you accept the loan, the lender's attorney begins an examination of title—that is, of the seller's right to claim that the property he is selling is truly his. There are title companies that specialize in this work, and the job is frequently turned over to one of them. The title, spelled out in a succession of legal documents called deeds, which over the centuries have transferred the property from one owner to another, will at some time have been traced back literally to the Indians, the conquistadors, William Penn or some other original owner. The object now is to see that there is no cloud on the title—that rights to the property are not limited by any obligation still outstanding. Records will be searched to make sure there is no lien making the property security for a debt, that there are no court judgments requiring payments from the seller or his wife, that divorced spouses have signed

quitclaim deeds giving up their rights to the property, and so forth —all to insure that no one can come along later and maintain that he or she really owns the property or has a claim against it.

The lender is so careful because the property—your property, after the closing—will secure his loan. If the loan goes bad, he has the property to console him. It would not be very consoling if an Indian turned up with an 18th Century deed on birch bark proving that he owned the property. So the experts make as certain as possible that the title is clear, free of all obligations and restrictions, and then issue title insurance just in case. If an Indian does turn up, the title insurance company is on the hook to defend the title, all the way to the Supreme Court, and pay the losses if any.

This title insurance policy, although you will probably be charged for it at the closing, might be for the protection of the lender only, guarding him against loss of the principal amount of the loan. It is conceivable that if this Indian turned up, the lender might say to you "Good luck, Jack, I'm insured—how about you?" If you want your total investment in your home protected, you should buy your own title insurance policy. Because you are taking advantage of the search the lender will have made, it doesn't cost a great deal—perhaps $50 —and it's worth having.

Meanwhile, the lender's attorney has been collecting documents, perhaps including a recent survey of the property you are buying, a certificate that there are no legal claims against the property, escrow forms certifying that money due for taxes and insurance has been set aside, and the mortgage document itself.

Some of these items are going to be charged to you. The title insurance policy for the lender's protection may cost you less than $100 or as much as $350 (depending on the complexity of the search, the price of the house and its location); the survey, $50 to $100. The lender will commonly bill you for a service charge—a flat fee of $100 or $200, or 1 per cent of the amount of the loan, or give you an itemized bill covering the time and money spent preparing the necessary papers. You may pay, in addition, a fee covering his attorney's services. There will be smaller items such as the fee for recording the deed at the county government office, the price of the tax stamps required on every property transfer, and the cost of getting a report on your credit standing. The closing statement will usually juggle some other money matters—there might be $127.62 that the seller already paid in real estate taxes, covering 63 days subsequent to the closing date, plus $19.80 for the remaining fuel oil, all of which you have to pay for.

All in all, you can expect your closing costs to total anywhere

from $200 to $1,000 or more. You should get as detailed a list of closing costs as possible when you first inquire about a loan. There is wide variation from one locality to another, and sometimes from one lender to another in the same locality. This should be part of your shopping around for the mortgage. It's sometimes possible to save $100 to $200 just by visiting two or three more lenders and getting their figures on closing costs. Shortly before the closing you will be notified of the exact amount so you can bring a certified check.

In addition to that check, count on another $150 to $300 for your own lawyer. You'll need him at the closing, but you needed him worse before you got into all this. For one thing he should be asked whether the house ought to be in the husband's name, the wife's name or both *(Chapter 14)*. If you've made any legal mistakes they'll probably show up at the closing, or there may not be any closing.

But of course, you're really a lucky fellow, so everything will go beautifully, and you'll walk out clinking a set of keys in your hand, a little numb from it all, but happy and excited. Enjoy.

INSURING YOUR HOME

Even before you actually own your home, you must get insurance; the bank insists on it. In days gone by, trying to insure real estate against the usual perils involved the collection of a confusing variety of separate policies, their coverages overlapping in some places and in others never quite fitting together for complete protection. This patchwork system has now been replaced by package plans called homeowners' policies. They can protect you against financial loss from many different causes—everything from a fire in the kitchen to a pet dog with a taste for quick-to-sue mailmen to a burglary loss. Not everyone realizes, however, that these blanket policies range from king size to crib size. Some actually cover too much while others leave you exposed where you may feel it.

Look at what happened to Harry. His thoughts were only of hot food and warm slippers as he eased his car over the icy driveway and into the garage of his Connecticut split-level one January night. But as he opened the door leading from the garage into the recreation room, he beheld a waterlogged nightmare. A pipe in the ceiling of the recreation room had frozen and burst.

It took two days to repair the pipe, replace the ceiling, and send carpet and furniture off to be cleaned and repaired. Then Harry called his insurance agent. Gently the agent explained that although Harry did have a homeowners' policy, it didn't cover that frozen plumbing.

"Plumbing is covered only in the Broad Form," he said. "You've

Choosing insurance for a home

Instead of old-fashioned fire insurance, most people now protect their homes with broader "homeowners" policies. The cheapest is Basic Form, covering damage from 11 perils. Next is Broad Form, covering five more. Then there are the more expensive Comprehensive and Special Forms. Best bet is probably Broad Form; it covers all likely perils and the cost is moderate.

got the Basic Form. When you moved in, you remember, you said it was all you could possibly afford."

Harry, like every insurance buyer, had had to balance risk against cost and decide what he could afford. Obviously it is impossible to insure against all of life's risks. So choices have to be made. Harry had decided wrong, perhaps because he had failed to analyze the choices.

How much protection you need

There are two aspects of risk to be considered: magnitude and "likelihood." Magnitude refers to the amount of your exposure. If you own a $25,000 house filled with $10,000 worth of furniture, you're ex-

Basic Form (HO-1)

- Fire or lightning

- Loss of property removed from endangered premises; for example, if a fire next door threatens your house and you flee with some belongings, some of which are then lost, stolen or damaged—they're covered.

- Windstorm or hail
- Explosion
- Riot
- Aircraft
- Vehicles
- Sudden and accidental damage from smoke

- Vandalism and malicious mischief
- Theft (except of credit cards and checks)
- Breakage of glass that is part of a building

Broad Form (HO-2) and Tenants Form (HO-4)

- Falling objects
- Weight of ice, snow, sleet
- Collapse of building

- Certain accidental damage to or from steam and water systems; for example, damage from a defective safety valve in a boiler or from a defective cut-off valve in a toilet tank.

- Certain accidents involving electrical equipment; for example, if you overload your circuits and cause a short circuit that burns out the wiring in an electric coffeemaker, the coffeemaker is covered.

Comprehensive Form (HO-5)

All perils EXCEPT: earthquake, landslide, flood, surface water, waves, tidal water or tidal wave, the backing up of sewers, seepage, war and nuclear radiation.

Special Form (HO-3)

Provides Broad Form (HO-2) coverage on personal property and Comprehensive Form (HO-5) coverage on a house.

Data: Insurance Information Insti

posed to a loss of about $30,000 if fire consumes all but the land and foundation. Few of us are in a position to withstand such a loss, so we insure against fire almost to the total amount of our property and belongings. On the other hand, a thief couldn't possibly walk out with everything we own, so the coverage for theft can be much smaller.

Likelihood refers to the odds of falling victim to a given hazard. Calculating these odds is beyond most of us, but to some degree they are obvious. The chances that your house will burn, for example, are far greater than that it will collapse beneath the weight of ice and snow. Protection against ice and snow, therefore, has a lower priority than insurance against fire. Some basic protections may be chosen for you. If your home is mortgaged, the mortgage holder will require you to insure it against such dangers as fire and lightning.

The hazards you are protected against

The magnitude of risk determines the size of the insurance policy you get. Likelihood, however, influences the kind of policy you need. There are five forms but only three basic types of homeowners' insurance (*see chart*), which differ from one another in the particular perils they protect your property against.

The minimum policy is called the Basic Form (also Homeowners 1 or Homeowners A). This costs the least money. It covers your property against damage by only the 11 most likely perils, and there are more than 11 fairly likely ones in this perilous world.

The next type is called, appropriately, the Broad Form, or Homeowners 2. This protects your property against all the perils that the Basic Form does, plus a number of others, as specified on the chart. It is widely sold, and for most people it is the best.

The third major type is the Comprehensive Form, known technically—and confusingly—as Homeowners 5 or Homeowners C. Comprehensive is just what it sounds like. It guards you from just about everything except visits from your mother-in-law. Instead of listing what it protects against, it simply lists a few exclusions and admits to being responsible for everything else. For this reason it is often referred to as an "all-risks" policy, although it really is "all-risks-except," the exceptions being cataclysms so great that even an insurance company can't cope with them.

Salesmen often sell all-risks policies on the basis that "it's so cheap, you may as well have it." Your attitude should be the reverse. If it is cheap, it is because insurers know the risk is microscopic. If the risk is microscopic, you ought to think twice or three times to see how far you want to carry protection.

If you want the extensive coverage of the Comprehensive policy for your house but feel you need only Broad Form protection for your personal property, Homeowners 3, known as the Special Form, combines the two for you. Insurers say this is the most popular of the homeowners' packages. (Number 4 is a package designed for tenants —persons who live in rented houses or apartments.)

In addition to these perils to your property, other types of perils to your pocketbook are guarded against by most homeowners' policies. These protections are usually included in all four forms—Basic, Broad, Comprehensive and Special:

■ Additional living expense. If your house burns down and you are forced to live in a motel and eat in restaurants while it is being rebuilt, this part of the policy will reimburse you for what you spend above everyday expenses, up to the limit provided by the policy.

■ Personal liability. This covers claims against you for damages from someone injured in an accident on your property. It also covers a similar accident away from your property if it is caused by you, a member of your family, or your pets—if your dog bites the postman, for example, or if your golf ball hits another player. Excluded are certain claims involving business, cars and workmen's compensation.

■ Personal medical payments. If a guest slips on your icy sidewalk and is injured, this part of the policy pays for his treatment.

■ Damage to property of others. If Johnny accidentally tosses a football through the neighbor's picture window, this is where the money will come from to pay for a replacement. (If he's under 13, you're covered even if he does it on purpose.)

The property your policy protects

While the various homeowners' policies protect your property against varying assortments of perils, the kind of property they protect is the same in all policies. Here's the list:

■ Your house. This is referred to as your "dwelling" in the policy and takes in such additions as porches, attached garages and patios. Built-in household equipment, such as the furnace, is counted as part of the house. If you so desire, the policy can be issued while the building is in the course of construction.

■ Other structures. These are auxiliary buildings, such as a detached garage, tool shed or guest house. The policy does not ordinarily cover a building used for commercial purposes or one that you rent to others unless it is used exclusively for private garaging.

■ Personal property. This means all your household contents and personal belongings. Items of high value, such as fur coats, jewels

antiques or paintings, must be specifically "scheduled" (itemized) in a special endorsement—at extra cost—if you hope to recover their full worth in case of fire, theft or other loss.

The money you get for a loss

There are two points to understand about the dollar coverages available in homeowners' policies. First, all policies provide the same standard liability protection—up to $25,000 for personal liability, up to $500 in medical payments to any one person, and up to $250 for each occurrence that damages another's property; higher limits are available at extra cost. Second, limits on coverage other than that on the house are percentages of the basic coverage on the house. Thus:

Type of policy:	Basic	Broad	Comprehensive and Special
Auxiliary buildings	10%	10%	10%
Personal property at home	50%	50%	50%
Personal property away from home	10%	10%	100%
Additional living expense	10%	20%	20%
Damage to trees, shrubs, plants (Limit $250 per item)	5%	5%	5%

To receive full payment for any partial loss, you must insure your house for at least 80 per cent of its replacement value. Inflation being what it is, that's likely to be more than you paid for it, so keep track of real-estate values in your area.

Let's assume you've had your house appraised and its value has been set at $25,000. So you insure the house for 80 per cent of this amount, $20,000, and choose the Broad Form. The insurer is then obligated to pay you up to $20,000 on the house, up to $2,000 (10 per cent of $20,000) on auxiliary buildings, up to $10,000 (50 per cent) on unscheduled personal property at home, and up to $4,000 (20 per cent) for additional living expense.

In many states you can obtain an "inflation guard" endorsement, which periodically increases coverage. This endorsement provides an automatic increase every three months, at the rate of 1 per cent of the original amount of coverage. This means that a $20,000 homeowners' policy with an inflation guard endorsement would offer protection totaling $22,400 at the end of three years.

Most homeowners' policies are sold with a variable deductible amount: You pay all losses under $50, and a gradually reduced amount

Text continues on page 218

Household and personal property inventory

Living, dining and family rooms	Living	Dining	Family	Bedrooms and study or den	Master	No. 2	No. 3	No.
Rugs and pads	$	$	$	Rugs and pads	$	$	$	$
Couch or sofa				Beds, mattresses and springs				
Chairs				Dressers, dressing tables				
Tables				Chests, night tables, chairs				
Desk and desk sets				Desks and contents				
Bookcases and books				Filing cabinets and contents				
Draperies, curtains and blinds				Bookcases and books				
Lamps				TV and radio				
Clocks				Lamps and clocks				
Pillows				Pictures, mirrors and sculpture				
Mirrors				Plants				
Pictures and sculpture				Toilet and vanity sets				
TV, radio and stereo				Perfume and cologne				
Phonograph records				Draperies, curtains and blinds				
Tape recorder and tapes				Blankets, bed linens				
Musical instruments				Air conditioners				
Fireplace fixtures								
Electric utensils								
Tablecloths and napkins								
Silver, china and glassware				**Totals**	$	$	$	$
Plants				Clothing and personal effects		Men's	Ladies'	Chil
Air conditioner				Coats		$	$	$
				Furs				
Totals	$	$	$	Suits and dresses				
Kitchen				Slacks and skirts				
Tables and chairs			$	Sweaters, jackets and gloves				
Cabinets				Shirts and blouses				
Refrigerator				Underwear and lingerie				
Range				Socks and hosiery				
Dishwasher				Shoes (all types)				
Cutlery and crockery				Neckties, belts, billfolds and scarves				
Dishes and silverware				Jewelry and watches				
Pots, pans and utensils				Rainwear and umbrellas				
Electrical appliances				Electric razors and hairdryers				
Clocks				Eyeglasses				
Freezer and contents				Dentures and orthodontic appliances				
Curtains								
Brooms, mops and other cleaning utensils								
Vacuum cleaner								
Total	$			**Totals**		$	$	$

Basement, attic and garage	Value
Washing machine	$
Dryer	
Iron and ironing board	
Trunks and luggage	
Lawn mower	
Garden tools	
Portable fans, heaters, humidifiers	
Sewing machine and equipment	
Hobby and sports equipment	
Bicycles and toys	
Cameras	
Furniture	
Garden and recreation room	
Total	$

Miscellaneous

	$
Total	$

SUMMARY OF TOTALS

Living, dining and family rooms	$
Kitchen	$
Bedrooms and study or den	$
Clothing and personal effects	$
Basement, attic and garage	$
Miscellaneous	$
Value of contents	$
Insurance in force	$
Value of home	$
Insurance in force	$

Data: Government Employees Insurance Company

How to be prepared for the insurance man

If you have to file an insurance claim for damaged property, you'll be surprised how hard it is to remember every item and its value. Be prepared. Keep an itemized list of your things like the one shown at left. When you estimate value, take depreciation into account—your insurance adjuster most certainly will. Start with the current replacement cost of each item and then depreciate that value by the following percentages for each year of use: upholstered furniture, 20 per cent; other furniture, 5 per cent; electronic appliances (a TV set), 25 per cent; electrical appliances (refrigerator), 10 per cent; current books, 20 per cent; standard authors and reference books, 3 per cent; china, glass and silverware, 2 per cent; clothing, 33 per cent; blankets and linens, 7 per cent; sports equipment, 14 per cent. In estimating value, you should also take wear and tear into account. If you have a family of four vigorous young boys, your furniture will take a worse beating than the furnishings belonging to a childless couple. But also remember that some possessions—paintings or fine antiques—increase in value as they age.

for losses between $50 and $500; when the loss exceeds $500, the insurance company pays the entire amount—subject to any specific limits in the policy. You can, however, save as much as 25 per cent in premiums if you opt to pay higher "flat" deductibles (the whole amount) of $100, $250 and $500; that is, you pay the loss up to the specified deductible amount and the insurance company pays the rest.

IMPROVING YOUR HOME

Americans never stop tinkering with their homes. They build patios, panel walls, rebuild kitchens and bathrooms, and add second stories at such a rate that they spend roughly 60 cents on altering and modernizing old homes for every dollar spent building new ones.

There are good reasons for improving the home you have rather than going out and buying another. The most common is that you may become attached to your home and neighborhood and prefer to remain where you are rather than go through the jolting experience of moving. Economy runs a close second. Even if you can find another house with all the features you want at a price that doesn't exceed what you plan to spend on remodeling, there are still auxiliary costs to be considered. Charges for a new mortgage, moving expenses, the cost of adapting or replacing carpets and draperies, and many other outlays must be taken into account.

If you do want to remodel your current home, there are two major cautions. First, be sure your neighborhood is not going downhill. If it is, you may change your mind about the desirability of keeping the home into which you've put so much money and effort. Second, try not to over-improve. Sooner or later the house will be sold, and it is difficult to get a price higher than the neighborhood average.

Improvements that pay back their cost

The basic reason for improving your home is to make it a more enjoyable place for you to live in. But the fact is that some changes can add to the monetary value of your house while others may actually reduce its value. If the improvement you make is something that other people will also want, you stand to recover much of its cost when you finally sell the house. When this happens, the cost may become less an expense than a long-range investment.

Deciding what other people will want enough to pay extra money for is not as difficult as it may seem. Mostly it's a matter of common sense coupled with an understanding of some generally accepted desires. Here are estimates of the recovery factor that is involved in the most popular home improvements:

■ An extra bedroom. Adding a well-located third bedroom to a two-bedroom house is the soundest of investments, for two-bedroom houses are difficult to sell. You should get back nearly all the money spent for a third bedroom, and some of the cost of a fourth. The recovery rate may drop very low with a fifth bedroom, however. Buyers will like the idea but will resist paying for it.

■ Added bathroom. Like three bedrooms, a second bathroom, or at least a second lavatory, has become standard in newer homes. This means that adding a second bathroom to a house with only one is an expenditure that should be recovered almost in full.

■ Remodeled kitchen. Few improvements will add more to the value of a house than an up-to-date kitchen. Builders of new houses have long understood the selling power of a gleaming work area. The chances of recovering your investment here are excellent. In fact, an attractive kitchen may prove crucial when it comes time to sell.

■ Family room. Location is the key to the recovery factor in a family room. Real-estate appraisers rarely add more than 15 or 20 per cent of family-room cost to the appraised value of the house. Rooms at grade level are generally more valuable than those carved out of basements and attics, which are less accessible.

One man's improvement, however, is another man's nuisance. Alterations that lack broad general appeal not only fail to return their cost but can even jeopardize the sale of the house. Not everybody is quite as zealous a flower grower as Henry, for example. He wanted to be able to have flowers all year round, even when the snow was high. So he added a small greenhouse to his home. Nothing pretentious —just two sides and a roof of glass set into a corner where the garage jutted out. It cost $2,000. When he put the house up for sale a few years later, he got a rude shock.

"I'm afraid you won't get much of that $2,000 back," the broker said. And he was right. Most prospects didn't show the slightest interest in the greenhouse, and some were actually repelled by the idea of owning one. Henry even heard one couple muttering how much it would cost to rip it down if they bought the place. Moral: People who build glass houses shouldn't expect to get their money back.

Where do you start?

Let's assume that you're not planning any unusual additions and that you live in a stable neighborhood containing a number of homes worth more than yours. You know what you want to accomplish and have some idea of how it might be done. You can now start looking in the Yellow Pages under "Home Improvements," but it's better to ask

friends and neighbors for recommendations. Try to choose a contractor who has been around for awhile. This is a business that has more than its share of marginal operators. There is no way to be certain you are getting a good man, but if he has been in business a reasonable time, can produce the names of satisfied customers and seems to know what he's talking about, that may be all you can ask. Visit his previous customers and inspect the work, just as you would when choosing a builder for a new home (see Builder's Check List).

If you're planning something fairly complex, you may need an architect. Some architects are willing to work by the hour on modest jobs, serving chiefly as advisers. Most will insist on following the classic arrangement in which the fee is a percentage of the contract price, usually 10 or 15 per cent, with a stipulated minimum.

Whether to seek bids on a remodeling contract is a tough question. Many of the better contractors get all the work they can handle without going through the expensive and time-consuming process of submitting bids on jobs they may never get. If you insist on bids, you may end up dealing only with builders who can't make the top rank. Also, there is the problem of what to do if you turn up a low bidder about whom you have doubts. The temptation is to accept a low bid even when you are suspicious, and this often is the prelude to trouble.

In the final analysis, your best bet is probably to put your faith in a contractor who comes very highly recommended and settle for

Shopping for remodeling loans

The three most common types of home-improvement loans are shown in the chart at right. The one with the lowest true interest rate is the short-term FHA loan, known as "Title I," but loans of this type are sometimes hard to get. The costs of the other two types vary from bank to bank; shop several before signing. Other means of financing home improvements include long-term FHA loans ("Title II") and refinancing your present mortgage. At today's inflated interest rates, refinancing only makes sense if the improvements you make are major and will substantially increase the value of your house.

Cost of a 3-year $5,000 home-improvement loan

Type of loan	Annual rate of interest	Total interest o the 3 years
FHA Title I short-term loan	9.31%	$749
Conventional bank home-improvement loan	11.18% to 13.07%	$908 to $1,071
Personal bank loan	10.24% to 13.07%	$828 to $1,071

his estimate, based on his costs plus a stated percentage (usually 10 per cent). But if you don't choose your builder very carefully, such a "cost-plus" contract could put you on the verge of bankruptcy. Beware above all of home-improvement cheats, those masters of the come-on who surely belong in one of the lowest circles of the Inferno. Never sign up for such a "deal" without investigating it thoroughly.

Home-improvement loans

Once you know what the job will cost, you are ready to consider how to pay for it. Since a remodeled kitchen may run up to several thousand dollars, this usually means borrowing money. Some contractors may urge you to let them arrange financing. You should avoid this unless you have trouble getting a loan yourself. It's not likely that a contractor can get you better terms than you can get yourself.

There are a number of types of loans available for remodeling. Most banks offer special "home-improvement loans," typically providing a maximum of $5,000 for five years at true annual interest of about 11 to 13 per cent. There are also federally insured loans—the so-called FHA Title I program—of up to $5,000 for seven years. For a typical FHA-insured remodeling loan of $1,300, repayable in 48 months, the effective annual interest rate would be 10.09 per cent.

Even the best of the special home-improvement loans costs much more than a regular house-mortgage loan. You may be able to tap

Maximum amounts and repayment periods
for each type of loan

Maximum amount: $5,000
Repayment period: 6 months to 7 years and 32 days

Maximum amount: usually $5,000 (but minimum is usually $3,500)
Repayment period: usually up to 5 years

Maximum amount varies with borrower's income and credit standing.
Repayment period: up to 3 years

this inexpensive source of funds if the principal still unpaid on your mortgage is fairly small. You simply ask the bank to refinance your house, giving you a new mortgage that covers the old balance outstanding plus the cash they are going to advance for your remodeling project. There are pitfalls here, too, naturally. Your old mortgage probably carries a lower interest rate than the new one will, so refinancing means that you will pay more interest on the outstanding balance than you otherwise would pay. This extra cost on the old money you got years ago may outweigh the potential savings on the new money you're to get now. Ask the loan officer to figure it out for you, comparing costs of refinancing with costs of other types of loans.

Those few homeowners who have what is known as an "open-end" mortgage can avail themselves of its provisions to borrow for home improvements. An open-end mortgage is one containing a clause allowing you to reborrow that part of the principal that you have already repaid. For example, suppose you took out a 25-year, 6 per cent mortgage for $20,000 some 15 years ago. Now, with 10 years to go, you have paid off $11,520 of the principal. The open-end provision allows you to reborrow this brand new amount and start all over again with a 25-year mortgage.

If the current rate for mortgages is roughly equivalent to the rate you have been paying on yours, reborrowing will be largely a formality, requiring only the payment of a fee for paperwork. If interest rates have risen, however, the lender will require you to pay the higher rate on the reborrowed money. If the difference between past and presents rates is extreme, the lender may even require that the entire mortgage be rewritten at the current rate as the price of allowing you to reborrow. If this is the case, do some figuring. It might well turn out that borrowing home-improvement money through such refinancing would be spectacularly expensive.

If you need only a relatively small sum for a short period of time, you can simply apply for a personal loan; it's quick, but the interest rate is high. Whatever kind of loan you get, just remember that the more you borrow and the longer you take to pay it off, the more interest you will pay. If it's any consolation, the interest is tax deductible.

The remodeling contract

The question of contracts for remodeling jobs is difficult. You want to be sure that you and the contractor agree on what's to be done, when it's to be completed and what materials are to be used. On the other hand, a contract that covers every eventuality can be totally unmanageable. Such a contract would demand a lot of expensive help from

a lawyer, too. Of course, if a large outlay is involved, the contract *should* be reviewed by your lawyer.

The best general advice is to let the contract suit the job. Most home-improvement work is relatively simple and should be governed by a contract to match. Here are elements it should cover:

■ A general description of the work to be done and the location.

■ A sketch of the work.

■ Specifications of the materials to be used, complete with brand names, grades, sizes and quantities.

■ An assurance that the contractor will provide workmen's compensation, property damage and general liability insurance, and will comply with local and state codes, regulations and ordinances.

■ A stipulation that the contractor will remove all debris and leave the premises "brush clean" when the job is finished.

■ The cost of the work to be done.

■ A schedule of payments to be made by you as work progresses.

■ A timetable showing when the job will be completed, specifying penalties if the work is not completed on time.

Should you do it yourself?

One look at home-improvement costs leads the least handy homeowner to consider doing the work himself. On many jobs, labor makes up 50 per cent of the price, and there are few projects that can't be mastered by a reasonably handy male with plenty of time. Over-optimism is common, however, so be realistic when you balance your skills and free time against the magnitude of the job you want to do.

Usually it is best to let professionals handle plumbing, heating, wiring and structural framing, which demand special techniques, unusual tools and speed at certain crucial steps. But many other kinds of work are more commonly done—and often better done—by the homeowners than by hired help. The easiest to manage are the finishing-up tasks, which can be accomplished as time (and money) permit after basic remodeling work is completed. When the plumbers and carpenters leave your rebuilt kitchen, you can proceed at your own pace to paint the walls and cabinets and lay the floor tile. Be more cautious about taking on tasks that must fit into hired workmen's schedules. Stapling insulation between the wall studs of a new recreation room is easy enough for teenagers to do—but it must be completed quickly as soon as the wall framing is up; otherwise the carpenters have to stand by and wait (at $8 or more an hour) until they can apply the plasterboard to finish their part of the work.

When your remodeling is complete—or even better, when it's in

midstream—be certain that you remember to add its value to your homeowners' insurance coverage. There often are extra fire and theft hazards when a major remodeling is underway.

SELLING YOUR HOUSE

Some people put so much of themselves into their house, they look upon it as a family homestead, to be passed on from eldest son to eldest son generation after generation. That just doesn't happen anymore. One day or another you are going to sell the house.

Selling is not just the reverse of buying, and it may be quite as frustrating. As a buyer you were faced with an array of houses from which to select, your choice limited only by your budget and stamina. You were free to peek into closets and count bedrooms from dawn to dusk, so long as your feet held out. You could have fallen for the first charming cottage you came to, or searched months for your dream house. As a seller you have only one house to sell. You cannot enlarge closets or alter the number of bedrooms, not now. All you can do is try to make what you have seem irresistible to those who come to look, and plan logically to attract plenty of serious buyers.

How a broker earns his fee

The first part of a logical selling plan is a decision, and not a simple one: Should you use a broker or should you try to sell the house yourself? Most brokers charge 6 per cent of the selling price as a commission. On a $25,000 home, that amounts to $1,500. It's a sum well worth saving, but if you're not cut out for the selling job, you can lose more than that on the transaction.

As a professional, a broker can muster a number of talents the layman usually lacks. The broker knows how to locate potential buyers through advertising, how to show a house to its best advantage, how to bypass a prospect's objections and how to close a sale. He'll smooth every step of a trying process, and you'll come to appreciate little services like calling ahead to tell you he has someone to bring over, which is a lot better than having strangers ring your bell unannounced because they saw a sign on the front lawn. He will also have a working familiarity with the legal and financial factors involved. Even so, you should retain a lawyer.

To list a house with a broker, you must sign a contract. It often gives the broker an exclusive right to sell your house for a specified period of time. In many areas, groups of brokers share listings. This "multiple listing service" means that the man who makes the sale splits the commission with the broker who got the original listing.

Once you have signed a contract, the broker will inspect the house, assess its strong and weak points, and prepare to show it to prospects. He can help you set a realistic price, and his counsel should be weighed, for his knowledge of houses, neighborhoods and market conditions makes him a shrewd judge. Some expert advice is often necessary at this point, for deciding on the offering price is a tricky step in the selling process.

How much to ask

Many an amateur, faced with the problem of pricing his home, will take the sum paid for it, estimate what he has spent for repairs and upkeep, throw in a few hundred for good luck and add it up. Whatever the total, that's the price. In an inflationary period he might get it. But usually the figure holds only until it becomes obvious that no one will pay it; then the owner becomes more realistic. By that time, though, he may have scared off many prospective buyers. The problem is not only how much a buyer will pay, but also how large a mortgage a bank will grant based on its appraisal of the house's value.

The best way to price a house is to hire a professional appraiser to do an objective job. His services are relatively inexpensive—usually between $50 and $100—and when he is through, you'll know exactly where you stand. He will make a written report and deliver it only to you. If you think the house will bring more, you can always pad his figure. On the other hand, since he is a disinterested party, his written, signed appraisal can be used as an effective selling tool, convincing buyers of the house's true value. Ask your bank to suggest someone.

If you try to set the price all by yourself, be unemotional. Go over your house with a cold eye and compare it honestly with similar ones advertised for sale. You are unlikely to get much more than the going price. But don't start too low; remember that most house-shoppers expect to bargain, and it's easier to come down than to go up.

How to be your own salesman

If you have decided to sell the house on your own, and have set a price and prepared the house for showing, you must attract customers. An obvious way is to put out a sign, which you should do even though it won't help much unless you live on a busy street. It's more productive to advertise in the classified sections of local newspapers.

Writing a good classified ad is an art. The aim is to attract attention, not to look like another picket in the fence. You accomplish this by concentrating on your home's best qualities. Don't ignore such details as the number of bedrooms, but try to "sell the sizzle,

not the steak." *(See samples.)* Are there trees on your lot? Say so, in a way that lets the reader feel the coolness of the shade. Is there space for two more bedrooms upstairs? Play up the economy angle for a large family. On a dead-end street? Sell the quiet of a country lane. Use the space you need; don't skimp. Run the ad for several days, preferably at the end of the week, and repeat as often as necessary.

Now, steel yourself for some disappointments. Your sign and your ads are bound to produce some "lookers." There are people with nothing better to do on Sunday afternoons than look at houses they have no intention of buying. There's not much you can do about them except waste as little time as possible.

Showing the house

"When you put a house up for sale, the first thing to do is wash the front door," advises one broker. You can take his advice both literally and figuratively. A gleaming entrance sets a positive tone for the approaching prospect. More than that, a modest investment in cleaning and repairing a house makes it easier to sell and may even increase the price you will get. Fix dripping faucets, ease balky doors, make sure all light switches work and replace cracked window glass. Clear the junk out of basement and garage, straighten closets, mow the lawn and sweep the front walk.

One couple we know has vivid memories of a disastrous house-hunting trip. Even though they'd called for an appointment, they had trouble rousing anyone—it turned out the doorbell didn't work. They found themselves taking the grand tour accompanied by the lady of

House-for-sale ads that work

An eye-catching opening phrase is one secret of success when you advertise your house for sale in a newspaper. The four successful ads below all have first lines that would stand out in a column of competing ads. But it pays to go beyond the first line and buy enough space to emphasize all the good points of the house and its site.

Seven mature oaks	**You may not have six kids**	**Private beach**	**Commuters special**
shade this pocket estate. Snug ranch w. 3 bdrms, 1½ baths, on full acre. Play space, gardens galore. Quiet street, 2 blks. to school, 5 blks. to shopping, ½ mile to town ctr. Asking $23,-900. Can assume 5½% mtg. Call for appointment now. 555-3098.	but 4 bdrms. come in handy. Cape Cod with 2 full baths, garage, rec room. Xtra wide lot, 3 blks. to new high school. Low $20s. 567-7099.	membership comes w. this stately older home nr. lake. 14x30 lvgrm., dng. rm., kitch. on 1st flr., 3 bdrms. & den above. Kitch. remod. last yr. Beaut. l'scaped. Nr. schools, shopping, trans. 524-2599.	3 blks. from Xpressway. 20 mins. to Loop. 3 bdrm. raised ranch on ½ acre. 1½ baths, sun rm., fully air cond., gas ht., dbl. gar. Nr. stores, schools. Priced to sell at $25,900. Call 565-1099.

the house and four children under six. The door to the basement stairway was stuck so tight the owner couldn't get it open; her male guest succeeded after much tugging. To climax the visit, the couple was barred from one upstairs bedroom. "Oh, I can't let you in there," the woman explained. "That's my glory-hole." A glimpse through the slightly open door confirmed her statement—the room was piled high with unironed laundry, old toys and declining furniture.

That's not the way to sell a house. Be prepared, welcome the prospects, and do what you can to make their inspection of your property easy and pleasant. But don't overdo. For people who are serious, the best thing is to let them be. Here are a few tips:

■ Try not to have many people around; otherwise the buyer may feel like an intruder and hurry through.

■ Quiet is helpful. Shut off the radio or TV.

■ Keep Fido out of the way—and Johnny, too, if possible.

■ Don't feel you have to make conversation. They haven't come for tea.

■ Don't apologize for anything. If dishes are still on the table after breakfast, that's perfectly natural—you're still living there.

■ If you're showing the house at night, have all your lights on. There's something cheery and expansive about a fully lit house.

■ Don't dog the buyers' footsteps, and don't try to push particular features. Point out the less obvious benefits of the house, such as modest heating bills, an attic fan, built-in storage or nearness to schools. If they have questions about other things, they'll ask.

Honest-to-goodness prospects are not hard to spot. They nose around a lot and ask many questions. They ask each other *sotto voce* whether "the hutch will fit in the dining room," and they'll ask you if they can come back for another look. Tell them by all means, and give them a data sheet listing the basic facts about your house.

The data sheet is necessary because practically everyone who looks at your house will have looked at other houses as well. Organized house-hunters take copious notes to prevent confusion, but others bumble along on poor memory, and your house may suffer. The more homes they see, the more confused they get. "Was it that split on Birch Street that had the built-in dishwasher?" she asks. "I don't think so," he replies. "That was the ranch on Bayberry Road. I think the split had that awful Dutch windmill in the garden."

The data sheet prevents that sort of thing from happening to you. The sheet can include not only pertinent facts but some soft-sell wording as well. Once you're satisfied with it, get 50 copies made and give one to each prospect as he leaves. It will keep him from confusing your house with others, and it will act as a silent salesman.

Some houses are sold in a day; some take six months or longer. Spring and summer used to be considered the best time to sell, but this isn't necessarily true anymore. A buyer may accept the listed price, but he is more apt to make a counteroffer. Be clear in your own mind what is the lowest price you'll accept. This is the point where people who have not retained a broker wish they had. For even a well-prepared, almost-sold prospect must be nudged into a commitment; after all, he's on the brink of spending $20,000 or $30,000 or more.

No book can pretend to tell you how to close a sale, simply because there is no one good way. One prospect is only waiting to be asked; with him you simply get a deposit and take him to your lawyer as quickly as you can. Another expects to sign, but the thought scares him; with him, perhaps a discussion of mortgage alternatives will distract him to the point where the deal is closed. A third will still have honest doubts; it's up to you to find out what those doubts are (it may not be easy), and then find a way to overcome them.

Once you have a potential buyer who has put some money down, there's little you can do but let time take its course until the closing. When that ordeal is past, you'll have a substantial check. What you do next may have serious repercussions at income-tax time.

Most people who sell their homes use the money to buy another. If they buy anew within a year (or build anew within 18 months), there's no tax due immediately on profit made on the sale of the old one. But if they don't buy or build within the stipulated time period, they must pay a tax on the profit. (There are some exceptions to this if you are over 65.) This profit will really be less than you think, especially if you compute it the way the Internal Revenue people say *(Chapter 10)*. But if it should turn out to be a substantial sum in your case you may want to reconsider your decision not to buy another house. Even if the children have all grown and moved out and you think you're ready for the simple existence of an apartment, explore the possibilities of buying a cooperative or condominium. Any money you can save on taxes will come in handy.

EASING THE PAIN OF MOVING

One American family in five changes dwellings each year. Those who have survived this unnerving experience a few times know some of the tricks that help cushion the worst shocks. One is timing. If possible, schedule your move to avoid penalty payments on leases, midsemester school changes and the worst weather periods.

Most people prefer to move in the summer, and chances are you will too. As a result, moving companies are swamped during June,

Sample data sheet

Property:	3 Geranium Court Park Ridge, N.J. (201) 555-2368	Owner: Richard Doe Price: $33,900

Description: Eight-room raised ranch on quarter-acre wooded lot. Grounds fully landscaped. Located on dead-end street. Upper floor has 15x30 living room, 12x14 dining room, 10x12 kitchen (w/ built-in oven, dishwasher and countertop range), three bedrooms, two baths and foyer. Lower floor has fourth bedroom (or den), 12x18 family room, 8x10 laundry, two walk-in closets and two-car garage deep enough to allow for storage and workshop area.

Location: One mile from town center, half mile from shopping area, elementary school six blocks away. High school one-half mile. Parochial school one-half mile. Turnpike exit 1 mile.

Construction: Vertical redwood and double-course cedar shingles. Total wall and ceiling insulation. Three-zone baseboard hot-water heat. Forty-gallon hot water heater. Pine-paneled den and family room.

Financing: Buyer can assume $6\frac{1}{2}$ per cent mortgage. Current balance: $14,000. Monthly payments: $106.95.

How to hold onto customers

If you're trying to sell your house, a data sheet like the one at left will keep its values fresh in the minds of the people who come to look. It should begin with your address, name, phone number and asking price, but it should also give a factual description of the house—with just a few soft-sell phrases ("wooded lot") salted in. Have copies made and give one to any interested prospect as he leaves. He will be grateful and you will have a hook in a live prospect.

July and August. If you move at the height of the season, get your bid in early and try not to let other conditions alter it. One family, all set for an August 1 move, was forced to put it off to allow time for a septic tank to be replaced. The postponement lost them their shipping priority. It was the third week in September before they finally got their goods on a truck. In the meantime, they'd paid two months' rent on a house in New Jersey, nearly lost the sale of their home in Illinois and put their youngsters behind in school. However, if a fall or spring move is convenient for you, the off-season will give you a wider choice among moving companies. Once you are committed to a mover, the success of the operation is largely in his hands.

There are two types of movers—local and long distance—and it's important that you understand the difference. A local mover operates solely within one state. He is usually licensed by the state in which he has his office. His charges are based on the number of men required to do the job and the number of hours they work.

Interstate moving is quite another thing. Long-distance movers are licensed by the Interstate Commerce Commission and must abide by its regulations. Their charges are based on two factors—weight and distance. The weight is determined by an actual weighing of the loaded truck; the truck's empty weight is then subtracted.

The distance is known in advance because it is based not on the truck's odometer reading but on figures published in the official *Mileage Guide*, which specifies standard route lengths between cities. Weight, however, will be known only when your furnishings are loaded in the van. Movers do, however, provide "estimates" so you'll have an idea of what the job will cost. These estimates have been a major source of misunderstanding. Since government rules fix long-distance moving rates, the price for a move will be the same no matter which company does the job. Shopping around for the best price is pointless. But many people, unaware of this, request a number of estimates under the impression they are getting true bids. Some movers have done little to discourage this impression, and have been known to make estimates deliberately and misleadingly low in the hope of "winning" the job. The sole purpose of an estimate is to give you and the mover a clear idea of the size of the job; it does not set an absolute price. ICC regulations require the mover to notify you 24 hours in advance of delivery if the price is going to be higher than the estimate by more than 10 per cent or $25, whichever is greater.

When you're getting ready to move, take stock of your belongings. Look coldly at every item in the house and ask yourself: Is this worth packing, unpacking and paying to have shipped? You may be sur-

prised how often the answer is no. It makes no sense to pay the moving costs of a swaybacked studio couch from Pittsburgh, Pennsylvania, to Pittsburg, California, only to find that it looks too shabby to be allowed in your new home. Many children's toys are not worth the expense of shipment, and neither are those boxes of odds and ends in the garage and workshop. In most metropolitan areas organizations such as the Salvation Army and Good Will Industries will pick up your unwanteds—and give you a receipt for the dollar value that you can deduct as charitable contributions on your income-tax return.

If you plan to do the packing yourself, make sure you have the materials to do it right. You'll need dozens of common cartons, plus some special ones. For lightweight items, clean undamaged cartons from the supermarket are fine; start stocking up on them early. Remember that books and magazines are very heavy, so use *small* cartons for these; otherwise they will be unmanageable and may tear under their own weight. The best way to get special containers—cartons for mattresses and box springs, and vertical wardrobes for shipping clothes on hangers—is to buy them from the moving company. Most movers will give you credit for any you return unused.

You'll need lots of newspapers for wrapping fragile items. Shredded newsprint is excellent packing material but often hard to find. Try to pack things that you'll need right away in one carton, and mark it clearly. Have it put on the van last so it can be first off.

All boxes should be marked with the contents and, if possible, the room in which they are to be put at the end of the trip.

Some appliances need special protection from moving. Most refrigerators, for example, have "hold-down" nuts on the compressor that need to be tightened before shipment. Have a local repairman show you in advance what needs to be done. Better yet, make a date with him to do the job himself when moving day comes—if he can be depended on to keep the appointment.

Besides packing, there are quite a few other things to take care of in advance of the move. They range all the way from canceling your order with the paper boy to applying for a telephone in your new home (do that in advance; there may be a waiting list). These details are very easy to forget and it's best to make up a complete check list like the one on the next page and refer to it frequently.

Insuring your shipment

You should insure your goods during shipment, and this is another area of misunderstanding. The mover is responsible for loss or damage, but for a maximum of only 60 cents a pound. This is reasonable

A CHECK LIST FOR MOVING

Moving from one town to another requires some clerical chores. As grouped together here, they can, with luck, be ticked off in a day.

1 Send change-of-address cards to: your post office; book and magazine companies you subscribe to; all your insurance companies (life, hospitalization, accident, automobile, homeowners'); the state automobile license bureau.

2 Transfer: homeowners' policy (make sure new home is covered while you travel); bank accounts.

3 Get record transcripts from: the school; your doctors (especially records of shots, special medications and eyeglass prescriptions); your church (birth, baptism, confirmation).

4 Arrange installment payments with: your car dealer if your automobile is not paid for; your furniture and appliance dealers if you are buying on the installment plan.

5 Get final bills from: the gas, electric and telephone companies. It is advisable to ask for the bills and announce the date you want service terminated by letter, keeping a copy, in case there is ever any question about whether you gave final notice. Read the gas and electric meters the day before you leave so you can check the final bills. You should also get your bill from the milkman and the newspaper delivery boy. Telephone the laundry and ask for a bill; call around at the dry cleaner's to settle your account.

6 Arrange in advance for basic services at your new home. Otherwise you may have to wait for things like a phone.

7 Leave the house keys with your real-estate broker, your landlord (if you've been renting) or a neighbor.

8 At your new home: Ask the town clerk or League of Women Voters where to register to vote. Get names of a family physician and dentist. If you have moved out of state, change your driver's license and car registration.

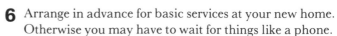

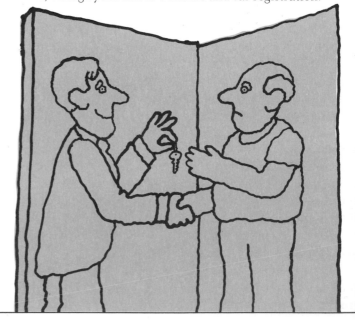

if he loses one of your trash cans, but not if the item is both light and valuable. Let's say he loses your AM-FM radio, which cost $85 but weighs only 11 pounds. He owes you $6.60 and you're out $78.40.

Getting paid at the rate of 60 cents a pound is hardly worth the trouble of filing a claim. You can improve your protection somewhat by paying an extra fee to the mover. This raises the "release value" of the shipment and extends his liability. If you have a claim, however, you must still plead your case with the mover himself, who is a participant in the argument. A more sensible arrangement is to buy true insurance on your goods from an insurance broker. This may not be a perfect solution to all claim problems, but at least an insurer is a third party in any difference of opinion, not a direct participant.

Moving day

On loading day, there is little you can do. Be around to answer questions, but otherwise stay out of the way. Each item loaded will be numbered, usually with a paste-on label, and recorded on the driver's list. (Try to take the labels off as soon after you arrive at your new place as possible. Some of them harden and stick to furniture forever.) A copy of the driver's list goes to you as a receipt for your goods. The driver will note the condition of the articles loaded; you should speak up and make a written notation if you disagree about whether an article is bent, chipped, scratched or broken.

The carrier is required by law to provide you with an estimated arrival date and with adequate notice if the load encounters unexpected delay. For your part, you (or someone designated by you) must be there to meet the van and let the men into the house or apartment. The truck is required to wait from one to three hours (depending on the distance moved); after that time the driver will put your goods in temporary storage and you'll have to pay extra to get them out.

You should be on hand yourself when your goods arrive if it's at all possible. This allows you to check the items off your list as they are unloaded and check for damage in transit. You can also help by telling the men where you want items placed.

Don't forget that you must be prepared to pay the full amount of the mover's charge at the time of unloading. This means cash, a money order or a certified check, so be prepared. It's not easy to dig up several hundred dollars on short notice in a community where you're not known, so work out some method of payment in advance.

Then buy a bunch of flowers, some paper cups and a split of champagne, and toast your new life as you begin it. If you can't find the carton your vases are packed in, put the flowers in the empty bottle.

8
Vacations

Having more fun
for less money

One woman we know remembers with great fondness a vacation she never took. "It was one my grandmother told me about when I was a little girl," she says. "I had found an old, faded picture in a trunk in her attic. It showed a group of people in front of a huge, white tent. The men wore vests and derby hats and the women had on dresses that reached the ground. Grandmother said it was her first vacation. Her family had risen at 5 a.m., packed all their things in a horse-drawn wagon and driven 21 miles to a lake, where they camped for four days. She said they took their food with them, and all they bought was milk and eggs from a nearby farm. The whole trip cost the five of them less than a dollar. It must have been idyllic."

Idyllic it may have been, but the anecdote serves chiefly to illustrate the beginnings of the vacation as a part of American life. Just how far we have come along the road from such simplicity is apparent in current statistics. We may still rise at 5 a.m. and load everything and everyone into the family wagon (station variety), but otherwise things have changed radically.

Today, a distance of 21 miles hardly gets most Americans to work, much less to a vacation site. One national survey of vacation habits showed that more than two thirds of the people questioned traveled more than 1,000 miles to go on vacation. Most of them were away for two weeks or more instead of only four days. The biggest change of all, however, is in cost. Fifty-five per cent of those queried spent more than $400 while they were on vacation. And one family in 10 counted on spending more than $1,000.

Now $1,000 is about 12 per cent of the average family income in the United States. Even if we assume that the families spending this much are above average in income, that still means they are spending more for vacationing than for medical care. In other words, the family vacation accounts for a hefty chunk of family spending. As such, the vacation should be dealt with as a major expenditure.

Still another statistic indicates the extent to which family finances control vacation patterns. Almost half of all American families —48 per cent—resolve the question of where to go on vacation by returning to a place where they have been before. Granted, it might be Palm Beach instead of Lake Kickapoo. But many families return, year after year, to a familiar place because they know what they will spend and that the amount will be one they can cope with.

If you really prefer returning to Lake Kickapoo year after year, doing the same things and seeing the same faces, fine and dandy. But if you would rather open up some fresh vistas occasionally, there are ways of doing it without going broke. No book could possibly offer a

complete catalogue of vacation possibilities and their costs, but there are more economical holidays—and more ways to find the money for them—than you might think.

How to pay the vacation piper

Paying for most vacations differs little from financing any major purchase. You either set aside enough income in advance, or you take the vacation first and pay for it later. Saving ahead of time is substantially less expensive because you are not stuck for finance charges. It's preferable for other reasons as well. It's one thing to pay for a refrigerator over a period of three years while the box stands there, humming away in the kitchen. It is quite another to spend three years paying for a vacation you can barely remember by the time the last payment is made.

But not having to pay for a trip immediately has a certain charm. It allows you to go on impulse, which is always exhilarating. If you find that Pete and Freda are going to Europe, what could be more pleasant than a spur-of-the-moment decision to join them? In addition, the disciplined repayment cycle of any go-now, pay-later arrangement is essential to some people. Without big brother to squeeze the money out of them, they'd never make it. Often the choice is between going-now-and-paying-later, or not going at all.

There are several ways to finance a go-now, pay-later trip. One is a personal loan from a bank or credit union (*Chapter 2*).

Credit cards may also be used to charge virtually all the cost of some trips. The full payment will come due in a few weeks, however, unless arrangements are made for repayment in installments over 12 months (with interest added at a rate of about 18 per cent annually).

The air fare alone can be charged through the airline itself, with payment in full within a month, or in installments over as much as 24 months. Again the interest rate will be about 18 per cent.

If you want to have the money in hand before you make the trip, there are several ways to save methodically. The best way is to rely on will power and simply make regular deposits in a savings account. You can collect interest, watch the fund grow, and even chide yourself if you miss a weekly payment. It will be more satisfying, and therefore easier, if you maintain this vacation cache as a separate account. If you need some form of crutch to help you save methodically, you can use the so-called Vacation Club plan operated by many banks. You simply sign up, make a deposit each week and at the end of 12 months receive a check for the full amount that you have deposited. Such plans have one big drawback: Few pay interest. Still another

way to save for travel is to join a communal venture called a Travel Club, described later in this chapter, which will require you to make regular payments in advance over a stipulated period. How much you have to save depends on where you want to go, of course, but it can also depend to a surprising extent on how you get there.

FLYING VS. DRIVING

Most vacation travel is done by car, and sensibly so, if it covers only a short distance. This is the most convenient and least expensive way to go for trips taking less than a day. But for longer hops the presumed economies of auto travel can be misleading.

The distance between Chicago and New York, for instance, is roughly 800 miles. Let's suppose that Fred and Irma and their daughters, aged 6 and 9, want to make the trip to visit the children's grandparents. The big question is—should they play it poor and drive, or play it rich and fly? Let's see how the costs compare.

A chart provided by a consultant on automobile operations shows that it costs about 4.5 cents per mile to operate a five-year-old car like Fred and Irma's. That's just running costs, not maintenance costs. If we included such items as insurance, registration, depreciation and the like, the figure would rise to about 12 cents (*Chapter 4*). Such standing costs go on even if the car only sits in the garage, however, so for the purposes of this example we can ignore them.

The running costs from Fred and Irma's home in Chicago to New York therefore will be 800 miles times 4.5 cents, or $36. But since the trip will be on toll roads, there are also tolls of $12.

Fred and Irma have taken long trips by car with the children before, and they know they can't drive 800 miles in one day. It would mean 18 to 20 hours of riding, and that won't do. The answer is a motel stopover somewhere near Pittsburgh, at a cost of $26 for the four of them. They will have to eat several times on the road. If they have breakfast at home before they leave and dinner at the grandparents' after they arrive, they will need four meals during the two days en route. Fred knows from experience that two lunches, one breakfast and one dinner for four will come to about $31.

That's about it for the big items of expense.

Running costs for car	$ 36
Motel	26
Four meals	31
Tolls	12
Total	$105

Sample car-rental rates

Renting a car on vacation may not be as expensive as you think —if you shop around for the best deal. Prices charged by car-rental firms vary surprisingly. In the samples given below for a week's rental in the Los Angeles area, Company A was a hefty $33.01 more than Company G.

Company A	$112.60
Company B	103.00
Company C	93.18
Company D	109.50
Company E	103.60
Company F	86.10
Company G	79.59

One rule of thumb: If you plan to drive a long way, be willing to pay a fairly stiff basic weekly fee in return for lots of "free" miles; if you need the car only for local mobility to the market and the golf course, take the car with a low basic rental even if the mileage rate is high. But make sure your bargain is as good as it seems. Sometimes low prices mean bad service and a dirty, asthmatic car.

The costs given above were for the least expensive cars offered and included 800 miles of driving. They were adjusted to compensate for variations in the rental contracts.

Now let's see what happens if Irma and Fred decide to fly. Since they are going together, they can qualify for what the airlines call the family-plan fare. This means that Fred buys one full-fare coach ticket for himself at about $48 (one way). He buys another for Irma, and gets it at a discount of 25 per cent, or for $36. The kids can fly at one-third fare, which is $16 each. Let's add up that much:

Fred's ticket	$ 48
Irma's ticket	36
Child 1	16
Child 2	16
Total	$116

Fred and Irma must get themselves and the children to and from the airports at both ends of the trip. If they go by airport limousine instead of hitching a ride with a friend, the fares will come to $14. Add that to the price of the tickets and the total is $130. But that's all. No motels, because the trip takes only 95 minutes. No meals, because airline food is included in the fare. And no tolls.

The result is that it will cost Fred and his family $25 more to fly than to drive. Even that figure may be misleading. Chances are they would have spent another $5 or $10 en route on cups of coffee, pay toilets, candy and ice cream, and all the other odds and ends that go with automobile travel. In any event, by flying they get a bonus of three extra days at Grandma's.

In weighing the merits of air travel versus the joys of the highway, you should remember that a combination of the two is often the best solution. Combining air travel for a long cross-country leg of a trip with rental-car maneuverability at the destination often saves time, money and tempers.

The possibilities of this plan have not been lost on the marketing men of either business. Special packages that include air fares and car rentals are available through most of the airlines. Typical is one that would fly a young New York family of four round trip to Los Angeles and give them a car for a week, all for less than $500.

A discount for almost everyone

One reason flying is so often economical is the special fares that airlines offer to promote business. Few people are aware of it, but domestic airlines consider that they have had a good year when they have managed to fill slightly more than half the seats on their flights. The year 1968, for example, was a good one and 56 per cent of the available seats were filled. Obviously, the jetting of empty chairs back and

forth across the country is no way to make money, so the airlines do what they can to fill the seats that would otherwise be a total loss. The result is an array of discounts of which the family plan used by Fred and Irma is only one. Here are some of the most common:

■ Youth fare. A reduced fare offered any youngster if he purchases an identification card for a few dollars. If he is willing to be a "stand-by," which means he gets a seat only after all full-fare passengers have been accommodated, he can get a bigger break on his ticket.

■ Triangle fare. A special rate offered for a route covering three (or sometimes more) cities. Usually only slightly higher than the standard fare between the two cities that are the farthest apart.

■ Excursion fare. A discount, usually 25 per cent, off the standard round-trip fare when you depart during one week and return the next. One restriction: No travel on weekends.

■ Children's fare. Children from two to 12 pay only half the standard rate. An infant under two travels free when accompanied by an adult.

■ Night coach. A discount of about 25 per cent for traveling on the red-eye special, which usually takes off after midnight and lands when respectable citizens are abed.

■ Thrift fare. Lower than economy-class fares. Offered on certain flights within the U.S. and to Puerto Rico. (Many thrift flights do not offer meals.)

This list is not complete; other discount plans exist. You have to search for them. Not all discounts are available on all airlines at all times, either. And any one of those now available may be rescinded at any time. The point to remember is that you can almost always fly for less than standard fare if you are willing to be somewhat elastic in your planning. Often as small a concession as flying at a time of day different from the one you originally planned, or returning on a Monday instead of a Sunday, can save you a substantial sum. The trick is to decide where you want to go, and when. Then call any airline and find out which lines fly that route. Then begin calling for prices, emphasizing that you're looking for the lowest possible fare and will adjust your schedule to obtain it. In almost every instance, you'll find at least one airline that offers a really good deal.

Flying overseas

Whatever can be said about bargain hunting for airline fares in the United States goes double for trips overseas. Because of the strange workings of the International Air Transport Association (IATA), which sets fares for overseas travel, rates vary widely. The IATA rules are a statistical nightmare, but most of them needn't concern

What fare will you pay?

Nowadays it takes a mathematician to keep track of the various air fares from here to there; a Philadelphia-to-Los Angeles trip can cost a couple with two small children as much as $1,096 or as little as $696. A few of the possible permutations are listed at the right. Your best bet is to decide where you want to go, stay a bit flexible on the day of departure and call various airlines serving your destination to see which will get you there and back at the lowest cost.

A variety of air fares for a family trip

PLAN	ROUND-TRIP FARE (FAMILY OF FOUR)	CONDITIONS
Domestic: Philadelphia-Los Angeles		
First class	$1,096	No restrictions.
First-class family plan	1,005	Available Mon. noon through Fri. noon, all day Sat., before noon Sun.
Economy class	876	No restrictions.
Economy-class family plan	803	Available Mon. noon through Fri. noon, all day Sat., before noon Sun.
Discover America excursion fare	696	Same as economy-class family plan except that minimum stay is 7 days, maximum 30.
Foreign: New York-Paris		
First class	2,382	No restrictions.
Economy class	1,392	Available at this fare Sept. through May.
21-day excursion fare	993	Available at this fare Sept. through May, Mon. through Thurs. Minimum stay 14 days, maximum 21.
Individual inclusive tour (ITX)	903	Available at this fare Sept. through May, Mon. through Thurs. Minimum stay 14 days, maximum 21. You must pay in advance $70 per person for land accommodations.
Group inclusive tour (GIT)	750	Same restrictions as ITX tour, but you must also fly over and back with a group of at least 15 assembled by the airline.
Bulk inclusive tour (BIT)	552	Available Nov. through March, excluding 2 weeks at Christmas. Minimum stay 14 days, maximum 21. You must pay in advance $100 per person for land accommodations. You must also fly over and back with a group of at least 40 people assembled by the airline. 10 per cent of total cost payable 3 months in advance (nonrefundable); balance due 1 month in advance.

you. The ones you really need to know about have been translated into usable information by travel agents.

For any trip outside the U.S. (and many inside it), the services of a travel agent will usually save you a great deal of effort, guarantee a more pleasant vacation and probably reduce the cost as well. His principal role is serving as a one-stop travel market; you can buy as much of your travel accommodations and services from him as you want. He can set up a small part of a trip, delivering to you only airplane tickets and a certificate good for one night's lodging in a hotel, or he can arrange and collect in advance for every last detail of a complex tour: airplane, ship, train and bus tickets, sightseeing tours, guides and interpreters, restaurant meals, hotel rooms, even—if you live that way—a chauffeured limousine to be at your beck and call in every city on the itinerary. The agent charges you nothing for his services; he makes his money on commissions paid by the people who get your business through him.

Most travel agents do a great deal of traveling themselves; they may know from personal experience which hotels in Paris are quiet and informal, where the swinging provincial cities are, and how many suitcases you really need to take. They can match a vacation to your pocketbook and your tastes, and this informed guidance is a valuable bonus to their convenient grouping of travel services.

One bargain agents use as a base for planning many overseas trips is the 21-day economy excursion fare. It's available weekdays most of the year, and on weekends for a nominal extra charge.

The cheapest rates to Europe are provided by "group" and "bulk" inclusive tours (GIT and BIT). To take advantage of them you must be a member of a group, generally of 15 to 40 persons, and pay in advance a certain sum for services in Europe. Don't let the group requirement put you off. Agents and airlines simply take the requisite number of people who are buying tickets for the same day, label them a group, and book them on the same airplane. The passengers needn't know each other, or even speak en route, but they must be on the same plane both going and returning. What they do abroad is up to them. Cheapest is the BIT (Bulk Inclusive Tour), requiring 40 people, designed to fill the huge airliners of the '70s.

The advance payment can be put toward rooms, meals, a rented car or guided tours in the countries you visit, or a combination of these. With variations, the large airlines offer round-trip passage, a room at a guesthouse for three weeks, and use of a rented car during the same period. The price for a trip from New York to one European city with these extras thrown in runs around $300, or roughly the

The passengers' choice

When vacationers head for Europe, 94 per cent take a plane, and nearly half the individuals understandably pick one or the other of the two U.S. airlines that fly the Atlantic. But surprisingly, German Lufthansa is fourth choice, with 8 per cent of the scheduled passenger traffic, twice as much as the long-established Dutch line KLM. When it comes to flying people wholesale on planes rented for charter flights, however, KLM and Irish are up near the top.

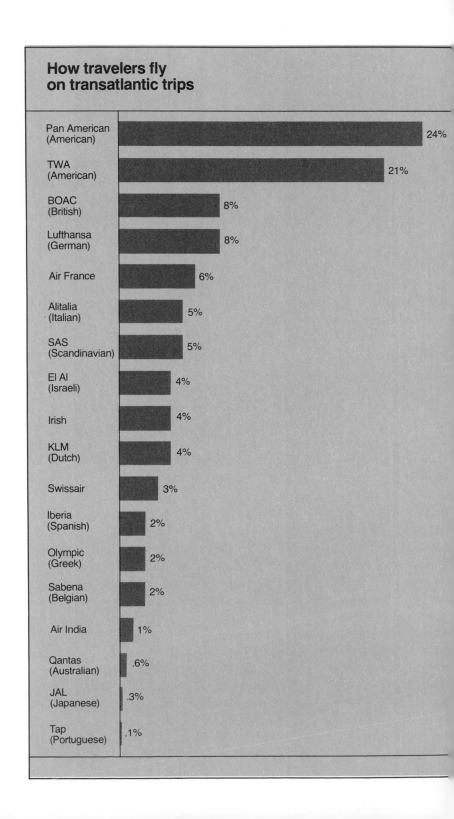

How travelers fly on transatlantic trips

Airline	Percentage
Pan American (American)	24%
TWA (American)	21%
BOAC (British)	8%
Lufthansa (German)	8%
Air France	6%
Alitalia (Italian)	5%
SAS (Scandinavian)	5%
El Al (Israeli)	4%
Irish	4%
KLM (Dutch)	4%
Swissair	3%
Iberia (Spanish)	2%
Olympic (Greek)	2%
Sabena (Belgian)	2%
Air India	1%
Qantas (Australian)	.6%
JAL (Japanese)	.3%
Tap (Portuguese)	.1%

same as a 21-day excursion fare to the same city without the extras.

Other bargain fares are based on variations of this arrangement. The ITX (Individual Inclusive Tour), for instance, resembles the GIT but does not require the 15-man group arrangement. It is often called the tour-basing fare because so many packaged tours are superimposed on it. ITX bargains come in every conceivable style. If you want to ski, eat, visit wineries, do the museums or follow the opera season, somebody is likely to have a tour that fits your whims exactly. Travel agents have all the necessary information and literature.

THE TOUR—FRIEND OR FOE?

The packaging of tours is not limited to overseas trips. It is even more important in the travel business than in the sale of detergents. In an era when secretaries spend their vacations in Mexico, the tour package that includes rooms, transportation and meals is usual.

And that's not as bad as it sounds. The idea of a prepackaged tour may seem stifling, but the packages come in such infinite variety that almost anything is possible. They range from a weekend in Las Vegas to a six-month, round-the-world cruise. They can vary from a round of bird sanctuaries to a swingers' tour of the Caribbean. Some tours are crammed so full of activity that there is hardly time to unpack. Others leave plenty of free time for personal exploration.

It is safe to say that most people will get the most for their money if they buy some sort of tour package. There are three basic types—the economy package, the escorted tour and the independent tour. Here is how they work:

■ The economy package. This can be as simple as a weekend at the nearest luxury motel, with a single price for bed, board, a pair of theater tickets and a visit to a night club. For quick regeneration at a bargain price, this is hard to beat. More frequently, the economy package includes the cost of transportation, rooms and meals for a short period at a heavily patronized resort. Honeymoon specials to Bermuda, golf or fishing weeks at American resorts, the "six heavenly nights and seven days" in Hawaii are typical economy packages. They are high-volume operations. Like any mass-produced product, they tend to be unimaginative, but they give the vacationer a lot for his money. Any travel agent can give you details.

■ The escorted tour. This is just what it sounds like, a tour conducted by a guide. You join a group of people who want to see more or less the same things you do for a well-delineated trip. Ordinarily, it is fully paid for in advance—sometimes even to tips—and includes everything a traveler wants or needs except souvenirs. Baggage, res-

Text continues on page 246

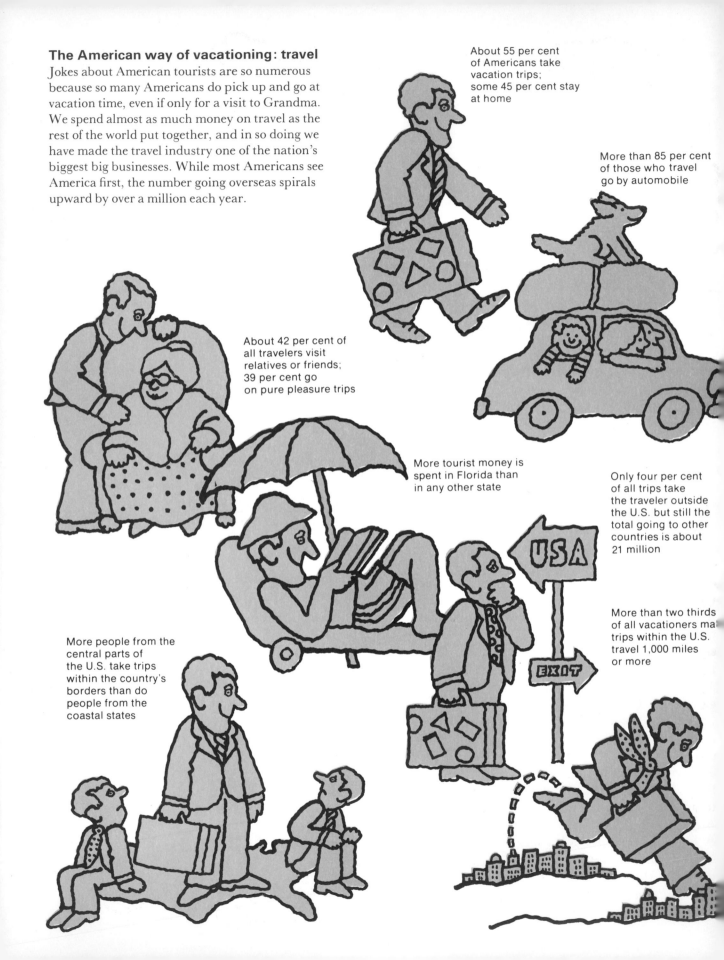

The American way of vacationing: travel

Jokes about American tourists are so numerous because so many Americans do pick up and go at vacation time, even if only for a visit to Grandma. We spend almost as much money on travel as the rest of the world put together, and in so doing we have made the travel industry one of the nation's biggest big businesses. While most Americans see America first, the number going overseas spirals upward by over a million each year.

About 55 per cent of Americans take vacation trips; some 45 per cent stay at home

More than 85 per cent of those who travel go by automobile

About 42 per cent of all travelers visit relatives or friends; 39 per cent go on pure pleasure trips

More tourist money is spent in Florida than in any other state

Only four per cent of all trips take the traveler outside the U.S. but still the total going to other countries is about 21 million

More people from the central parts of the U.S. take trips within the country's borders than do people from the coastal states

More than two thirds of all vacationers ma trips within the U.S. travel 1,000 miles or more

USA

EXIT

About 20 per cent of the trips last more than a week...but two thirds of the overseas travelers go for more than a month

Americans traveling both at home and abroad account for 45 per cent of all the money spent on travel in the entire world

Forty per cent of overseas travelers are under 30; students are the largest group after business and professional men

About a third of all Americans traveling overseas come from New York and California

The average daily expenditure of U.S. tourists overseas is $17. In Europe, they spend the most per day in Switzerland ($20) and the least in West Germany ($11)

Ninety-seven per cent of all overseas travel is by air

It is estimated that by 1980 American travel to the Far East will increase 10 times, from less than 1 million to more than 7 million

Almost twice as many Americans go to Europe as visit the Caribbean islands

ervations and transfers are handled by porters and clerks at every stop. Again, consult your travel agent, or study the advertisements in newspaper travel sections and travel magazines.

■ The independent tour. This is a do-it-yourself arrangement. You go alone and you go where you like, but you and the travel agent plan it in advance. For example, you might choose to visit five European cities in three weeks. The travel agent then plucks out for each of the five cities a package supplying as many of your needs—accommodations, meals, sightseeing trips—as you choose. He puts them together and sends you off with a pocketful of prepaid coupons good for this, that and the other. You are on your own, but your requirements have been arranged for in advance. In some cases, a local representative will meet you on arrival.

How to judge a tour

There are many reputable and experienced agencies that make up tours. Unfortunately, there are also travel agencies of dubious qualifications. The uninitiated find it difficult to tell a good tour from a poor one until it's too late. Many of the marginal operators, having no reputation to sell, rely on price to pull in customers, and their product suffers. Your best guide to any particular tour or firm is the recommendation of someone who has used it before and liked it. If you have no recommendation and you still want to deal with an agent unknown to you, be sure to read all the fine print in the contract. There are several methods used by operators to shave tour costs.

First, look to see just how many meals—and which ones—are provided. The cheapest tours may offer only breakfasts, or all meals except dinners. Since food takes up a sizable part of any vacation budget, omissions are expensive. Just as common is the tour that feeds you all three meals in some cities, but none in others. This is made to sound like an effort to free you from routine, but it leaves you paying extra for one third to one half of your meals.

Second, tour prices are almost always quoted on the basis of double rooms. For married couples, this is fine. Those traveling singly discover that they must either share a room with a complete stranger, or pay extra for a single room.

Finally, try to get some gauge of the quality of the hotels you will be booked into. This is rarely simple, but it can be done even for hotels in foreign countries. If you're offered the Hotel Platzl in Munich, for example, take a look at a German hotel directory, which can be obtained from the German National Tourist Office in New York. You will find that the Platzl has 200 beds and 100 baths and charges from

20 to 40 marks, or $5 to $8, for a night's lodging. In other words, it is a moderately good hotel. The ratio of baths to beds indicates that nearly every room has a private bath. The room prices tell you that you are in the middle range for German hotels. In the same way you can evaluate hotels in almost any major country, simply by writing to the nation's government tourist bureau in New York City for its hotel directory. Most give out brochure-sized listings free.

The club plan

The packaged tour is carried to its ultimate in an arrangement called the club plan. The name is confusing, because this "club" can easily be mixed up with the "vacation clubs" to which you make deposits in a bank and with the "travel club" in which you make regular payments until you have accumulated enough to pay for a trip. All three are different. In the club plan the member pays a modest yearly membership fee of about $10 or less. Then, when he is ready to take a trip, he makes one single payment, much as he would for any tour arranged by a travel agent. The unique feature of the plan is that his membership entitles him to stay at a "village" owned and operated by the club. The price is generally lower than that for a hotel with comparable accommodations. Two weeks in Morocco, for instance, costs around $500, including room, meals, air fare and just about everything except drinks, which the member pays for with beads that he buys like poker chips and carries strung on a necklace, popping out as needed so many beads for a drink. There is no tipping.

TRAVEL CLUBS

Among the biggest bargains in out-of-the-ordinary vacations are those of the travel clubs, which take their members on package tours, in club-owned airplanes. The idea originated in the early 1960s, when the commercial airlines adopted jets and found their hangars full of old propeller planes that were commercially useless but too good to throw away. Some imaginative entrepreneur had the brainstorm of buying one—they could be had for a mere $100,000—and of rounding up 1,000 friends, acquaintances and friends-of-friends to ante $100 apiece. With their jointly held plane, the new owners had only to hire themselves a pilot and maintenance crew, schedule a trip, and they were off.

The idea was an instantaneous hit. The first club had hardly gotten itself airborne before other clubs sprang up, and a number of cities now have them. Some operate as business ventures; you can find out about these through the usual sources of tour information—travel agencies and travel advertisements. Others are nonprofit, and the

In New England and Florida and on the West Coast you can sign up for a cruise aboard a real sailing ship. Most of the ships are former yachts from the days when rich men could afford their own, but conversion hasn't wiped out their former glory.

members own the plane and the club; you have to be invited to join one of these. Some of the commercial clubs require regular deposits made over a period of months or years until you have saved enough to buy a given trip; others operate on annual dues that quickly make you eligible to take any of several trips scheduled throughout the year, paying as you go for the trips you elect to take. Membership fees in the latter are generally high, sometimes as much as $150 for initiation and upwards of $100 a year in dues, but once you have joined, the travel offerings are genuine bargains—a weekend in Miami for the Super Bowl cost one club's members $111 from New York, including fare, lodging, food, drinks and a ticket to the game, and a quick trip to Caracas cost another group $140 each instead of the standard airline fare of $400.

Fares average about three cents a mile—half the cost of the cheapest commercial rate—and hotel charges are low since they are booked in wholesale lots.

Is it better to join a club than simply to save for your tour? This depends largely on your own temperament. It's a safe bet that many of the people who are now enjoying vacations under club sponsorship might never have made it if they had not had the discipline of a club's deposit arrangement, or the incentive of getting their money's worth out of their dues.

The biggest drawback to club membership is the same element that is its greatest strength—commitment. If the club requires you to sign up for a three-year stint of payments before you get your trip, you must complete the course or lose money. Three years is a long stretch. Much can happen that might alter hopes, plans and financial capacity. Before signing up for anything that takes so much time, you will be wise to find out what it will cost, and how difficult it will be to change your mind.

But suppose you do not feel like jetting off to Europe or the Far East this year. The possibilities for something new and different that will not exhaust the family exchequer are almost endless if you know where to look for them. A cruise on a sailing ship? A houseboat trip down the river? Some comfortable roughing it in a special camping truck? A visit to America's wilderness? All are possible, all economical —and nothing like two weeks at Lake Kickapoo.

SAILING-SHIP CRUISE

In at least three parts of the country—New England, Florida and the West Coast—you can sign up for a cruise aboard a real sailing ship. A typical voyage lasts a week or 10 days and costs from $180 to $300

a person, all meals included—considerably less than a similar vacation in a resort hotel. The ship is likely to be schooner-rigged, from 70 to 200 feet long, fitted for 25 to 65 passengers. Cabins will be small and modestly furnished, and the food will be plain but plentiful. Passengers are encouraged to lend a hand in the sailing of the ship, and almost total informality is the rule.

Most of the ships in service are former yachts dating from the days when rich men could afford their own, and conversion hasn't wiped out all vestiges of their former glory. Some of the ships formerly carried cargo in coastal trade. A very few are new, built for the use to which they are currently put.

Ships based in Florida commonly cruise the Bahamas. They sail every month of the year, but are most heavily booked in the winter. The usual plan is to sail at night and anchor at a new island port each day. Swimming, sightseeing, parties and shopping ashore are part of the planned routine.

New England skippers generally cruise the coast of Maine, and only in the summer months. The sailing area is often Penobscot Bay, one of the most beautiful cruising grounds in the world. In contrast to the Florida ships, those in New England sail by day and anchor at night; but like the others they take time for swimming, beachcombing, sightseeing and picnics ashore.

The West Coast skippers sail down the Mexican coast, stopping at islands, fishing villages and some of the more exotic ports. Mazatlán, Puerto Vallarta and Acapulco are usually on the itinerary.

Sailing vacations are not for everyone, but they are a great treat for those to whom they appeal. If you are among them, you can find out about ships and their schedules by consulting a travel agent or the Sunday travel section of your newspaper.

AT HOME ON A HOUSEBOAT

If the water appeals but roughing it on a sailboat does not, and if you've ever envied Huckleberry Finn's fascinating voyage downriver on that raft, you may be a candidate for houseboating, a form of vacation that combines the comfort of a lakeside cottage with the romance of yachting. Houseboats ply all the major bodies of water from the St. Lawrence Seaway to the Bahamas and can be rented for $245 to $450 a week or about what you might have to spend for a cottage on the seashore. They are usually powered by a pair of heavy-duty outboard engines, and they present few problems in handling that can't be managed easily after an hour's instruction.

To the true yachtsman, a houseboat may lack much of the dig-

Mr. and Mrs. Walker and their two sons travel 300 miles a day, stopping at motels. They spend $64.50 a day; cramming all four in one room would reduce the total only $6. No matter how you slice it, the 10-day trip sets the Walkers back $600.

nity and grace of most other craft, but the vacationer will find she more than makes up for it in other virtues. One is her shallow draft, which means you can nose into spots that are inaccessible to yachts and sailboats, explore inviting coves and picnic off the beaten track. Or you can dock at a city wharf where you will find some of the country's finest seafood restaurants, and you won't have to dress for dinner.

The modern houseboat is a carpeted and picture-windowed floating home with a kitchen, one or more baths, and bedrooms. Both bow and stern usually have open space for lounging and fishing, and the cabin roof can be used as a sun deck. Utensils, linen and equipment usually come with the boat, so that all the renter needs to supply are food and gas. If you want to try houseboating, you can get a *Houseboat Rental Directory* for less than a dollar by writing to *Family Houseboating* magazine, Box 2081, Toluca Lake, California 91602.

THE GREAT OUTDOORS

If you always thought camping meant sleeping on the ground in an old Army blanket, you should take a look at the way people do it now. Modern tents, trailers, stoves and sleeping bags have made roughing it simple and comfortable. And for economy it is unsurpassed.

Camping can't cut transportation costs, but it keeps the food bill low and almost eliminates the expense of shelter. You can see the difference this makes by comparing the costs of two 10-day trips.

Mr. and Mrs. Walker and their two sons set out on a cross-country trip. They travel 300 miles a day, stopping at motels and eating their meals in restaurants for 10 days. If they are average vacationers, they spend $64.50 a day, according to an American Automobile Association survey. Of this total, $26 goes for lodging (one room for the parents, another for the kids), $25 for three restaurant meals, $8.50 for gas and oil, and $5 for such miscellany as soda, candy, tips and the like. The AAA found that even cramming all four in one room would reduce the total by only $6 a day. No matter how you slice it, the 10-day trip sets the Walkers back $600.

Mr. and Mrs. Maxon travel the same distance in the same 10 days, but they sleep in a tent that they carry with them and fix most of their own meals in camp. They spend the same $8.50 for gas (or perhaps a trifle more, since their car also carries their camping gear, and the extra weight requires more gas) and they may even spend $5 for miscellany. But the cost of their lodging for the night will be the $2.50 fee typical for tenting in a campground. The food bill for picnic-style meals needn't cost more than $10 a day, maybe $12 if they splurge on steak and lobster. Their total cost per day, then, will run

from $26 to $28. The 10-day trip will set them back $260 to $280. Their vacation, in other words, will cost less than half what it would if they stayed in motels and ate in restaurants.

This assumes that the family owns its camping equipment. If not, the cost of buying an outfit is enough to wipe out much of the first-year savings. Mr. and Mrs. Maxon would need to allow $100 for a tent, $70 for four sleeping bags, $20 for a gasoline or propane stove, and $15 for a gasoline lantern. Pots and dishes from home would suffice, but there's at least another $25 for miscellany (ground sheet, flashlight, ice chest, first-aid kit).

Purchasing camping equipment makes sense only if you are sure you will use it over again through a number of seasons. If you're not sure, you can rent an outfit. Camping gear is usually rented by sporting goods stores, rather than general rental agencies. An outfit similar to the one described above will cost $35 to $40 for a week, or about $50 for a 10-day trip.

One note of caution: Camping is not just motel living with a canvas roof. Setting up and breaking camp takes more time and effort than checking in and out of a motel. Preparation of meals also takes time. And if it rains a great deal, you will be uncomfortable. A combination of insects, dampness and faulty plumbing has soured more than one family's outing. But you will have the satisfaction of seeing some of the great outdoors of this country—and as testament to its pleasures, half of all renters of camping equipment later buy their own. The National Park Service has thousands of camping grounds, situated in forests, on seashores and by historic monuments. For further information on federal campsites, write to the Superintendent of Documents, U.S. Government Printing Office, Washington, D.C. 20402, for the publications "Camping in the National Park System," "National Forest Vacations" and "Vacationing with the Indians." There is a small charge, but a dollar covers the cost of all three. State governments operate their own campgrounds; you can get information from state tourist offices. Books you might find useful are *The Handbook of Auto Camping and Motorist's Guide to Public Campgrounds* (Harper & Row), *Rand McNally Guidebook to Campgrounds* (Barcam Publishing Co.) and *National Parks, A Guide to the National Parks and Monuments of the United States* (Golden Press).

THE ROLLING HOME

For those who like physical comfort as well as a chance to see the sights, the "motor home" provides an ideal answer. The motor home is a fully powered, self-contained unit, a sort of house that is built

Hundreds of bona fide farmers rent their rooms to guests. Depending on the type of farm you choose, you could find yourself helping to round up cattle or showing a prize sheep at a county fair.

into a bus and can be driven anywhere there's a road and parked in any spot big enough to hold two cars—though it is wise to look for a campsite. For touring in rugged country, you might prefer a camper, a small cabin that fits into the loadbed of a pickup truck.

Motor homes are made by several manufacturers, and rented by franchised agents, usually auto dealers, for $100 to $250 per week —less than a family would spend for motel rooms—plus mileage. They come in several sizes and accommodate from four to eight persons. They have full-sized beds with foam mattresses, showers and toilets, heat and air conditioning, small kitchens, and tanks of water and gas. Some even include a stereo sound system and television. The unit is perfect for touring, since unlike camping it requires no daily making and breaking. The unit is also good for an indefinite stay in any location that has sufficient appeal to the family. While parked, it serves your needs for food and lodging, right at the site of your choice.

FARMS AND RANCHES

Another way to enjoy the comforts of home while on vacation is to visit a farm or ranch as a paying guest. Hundreds of bona fide farmers rent their extra rooms to guests. These family-owned farms range in size from a few acres to 10,000 acres. You will be treated as one of the household and will eat with the family. Depending on the type of farm you choose and the region where it is located, you could find yourself helping to round up cattle, showing a prize sheep at a county fair, panning for gold, or attending a corn boil.

The costs of a holiday on a farm or ranch are reasonable compared to resort hotel charges, ranging from $50 to $150 a week, meals included, for an adult (approximately half for a child). For detailed information on accommodations, consult the *Farm and Ranch Vacation Guide*, 36 East 57th Street, New York, New York 10022.

HOME SWAPPING

If you are willing to swap your home for somebody else's, you can have a comfortable holiday at a faraway place without paying any motel charges at all. This is an idea of such startling simplicity that you may find it hard to believe it can work, but it does. It's simply an agreement between two families, living at some distance from each other, usually in different kinds of places, to exchange homes temporarily. A New York CPA might trade his Brooklyn Heights apartment for a Phoenix salesman's suburban house. While the CPA and his family are marveling at life on the edge of the desert, complete with giant cacti and a swimming pool, the salesman's wife is hap-

pily shopping on Fifth Avenue and the whole family is looking forward to an evening of ballet.

The best way to find a house to swap is to write to distant relatives and friends, asking which of *their* friends would like to vacation where you live. Or you can pick an area you would like to stay in and place an ad in the local newspaper. For a fee, you can list your house in directories published by such organizations as Vacation Exchange Club, 550 Fifth Avenue, New York, New York 10036, or Home Interchange, Ltd., 19 Bolton Street, Piccadilly, London W.1, England. An exchange of letters, often with pictures of the homes involved, is the next step. The final decision is left to the participants; usually the only cost is that of the listing, plus the family's transportation.

THE CASE FOR VACATION HOMES

For many people the ideal way to spend a vacation is in a cottage of their own; for most it is still an extravagance. Real estate prices are high and going higher. The cost of materials, especially lumber, has been rising rapidly. Maintenance of established property is an added expense, and sometimes a continuing headache. And above all, our ideas of what constitutes comfortable surroundings, even on vacation, are now so high that the place we stay must have such expensive elements as heat, hot and cold running water and electricity. Today a summer cottage is a second home. More modest than the original, perhaps, but a full-fledged house nevertheless.

Yet if a vacation home can be put to year-round use, a good case can be made for owning one, particularly if it is located within a reasonable distance, allowing the family to spend weekends there. The case becomes much stronger if you can rent your vacation home to others when you are not using it yourself. Not only will you receive income from it, but at the same time, a portion of the cost becomes tax-deductible as a business expense. You might discover that a vacation home can almost pay for itself.

There is no absolute way to establish in advance the profit/loss potential of a vacation house. You can, however, come up with a good estimate by investigating the demand for holiday quarters and the rents being charged for them in the area you are considering. Often prospective owners of vacation properties rent in the same area first, anyway. That's what convinces them they'd like to have a place of their own there.

Tom and Leslie had dreamed of owning a summer place on a small lake about 60 miles from their year-round home in Minneapolis. They knew all about rents at the lake because they'd rented a place

themselves for two years in succession and paid $175 a week for it. The house they rented had only two bedrooms, but it had a screened porch that could be used for sleeping. It also had an adequate kitchen and bath, a view of the lake and access to a private beach.

The place they rented had been built six years before. Now the same builder was about to erect another colony at the other end of the lake. Tom and Leslie already had one mortgage. Could they afford another? One evening they tried outlining on paper what they hoped to do and how they could manage it.

The houses were priced at $18,000. Tom and Leslie knew that their savings account would yield the necessary down payment of $3,000, and the developer was offering a $15,000 mortgage to cover the rest. The mortgage was for 20 years, at an interest rate of $7\frac{1}{2}$ per cent.

This meant a monthly payment of $121. A call to the township assessor's office informed Tom that taxes and insurance would cost $420 per year. He guessed that $200 a year would cover maintenance, at least at the outset.

Tom also figured that he and Leslie, with their two kids, normally spent about $750 on their annual three-week vacation. If they were using their own place, they would save all the rent, or $525. He also decided that in the summer vacation months and the fall hunting season, he could reasonably expect to rent his place to others for 10 weeks a year at $175 per week. Balancing the cost against the income, he would have:

Annual expense

12 months' mortgage payments at $121	$1,452
Taxes and insurance	420
Maintenance	200
Total	$2,072

Annual income

10 weeks' rent at $175	$1,750
Savings on vacation	525
Total	$2,275

This looked pretty good, but Tom reminded himself that the $1,750 he hoped to get in rent was taxable income. In his tax bracket this meant he'd owe some 25 per cent of that income to Uncle Sam come April. He would, that is, except for the fact that he could claim deductions to offset some of it.

If the place was to be rented for 10 weeks, then for one fifth o

the year it could be treated as a business property. Thus one fifth of all the expenses—mortgage payments, taxes, insurance, maintenance and even depreciation—could be applied to reduce his taxable income. He computed this amount to be $464, leaving $1,286 as taxable income. He estimated that this would increase his present tax bill by about $420.

So, if Tom and Leslie bought the place, their annual expense would be:

Direct expense of vacation house	$2,072
Tax on added income	464
Total	$2,536
To offset this, they'd have:	
Rental income	$1,750
Vacation savings	525
Total	$2,275

In other words, their vacation house would cost them $261 a year more than they were currently spending. Of course, to be realistic, they would also have to accept the loss of some $150 in interest that their $3,000 down payment would earn if they left it in the savings bank. But Tom pointed out that this would be partly offset by the added equity in the house resulting from their payments on the mortgage principal.

On paper Tom's plan to finance the summer place looks good. And it may well be. But before you run off to follow suit, better take a look at the possible pitfalls. The biggest would be the possibility that the place might not rent for the full 10 weeks annually; some years it might stand empty. Yet the costs would continue. Also, taxes could rise, and maintenance costs could jump if tenants proved to be hard on the place. Attracting tenants might be more of a chore than expected, too. If so, the job might have to be turned over to an agent, and his fee (15 to 20 per cent of the rental) would add to your expense. After thinking it over carefully, you may decide you'd rather leave the way open to vacationing in a different place every year, a place for which you have no continuing responsibilities, and one you don't *have* to return to—be it the Riviera or Lake Kickapoo.

9
The younger generation
Allowances, earnings, tuition

Bob has just returned home after visiting his wife and his brand-new baby son at the hospital. He's trying to calm his nerves with a drink when the telephone rings. It's a friendly insurance man, full of hearty congratulations—and some immediate hard-sell advice. "I'll bet he's a smart little guy," says the agent. Bob mumbles that he seems pretty normal so far. "And you're going to want to give him the very best education you can, right?"

"Well, yeah. I suppose so."

"Right now is the time to start!" the agent presses. "You're going to need at least $10,000 to see him through four years of college, you know. And costs are going up. But I've got an endowment plan that would be just the thing for you. I'll come right over."

Bob puts the agent off somehow. Glancing at the evening newspaper, he notices an ad for a savings bank. "Are you planning for HIM?" the ad demands, over a picture of a bright-eyed boy in cap and gown. He still hasn't had time to buy a box of cigars to pass out, and here they are, worrying him about what's going to happen to the kid 18 years from now.

Eighteen years from now the problem will be real. The average cost of four years of college is estimated to be around $10,000 and climbing. But the college crunch is merely the climax to a series of financial demands that begin soon after baby is born.

In the early years children form attitudes toward money and habits of handling it that will do much to determine whether they grow up to be responsible members of the family, considerate of its needs and competently managing their own finances, or extravagant and always in need of a bit extra. In the beginning, when a child's sense of time is too limited for anything beyond now, the main idea to get across is what money really is—a medium of exchange—and how it is properly used. The foundations for this understanding come from other, more basic concepts that do not seem to relate directly to money.

First comes sharing. Children quickly learn to share Mother's attention, to share family chores, to share toys, to share in buying gifts and then to share family income. As they grow they learn to share with broader and broader communities—the school and church by performing volunteer work, the state by paying taxes. The second concept that children learn early is trading—the barter that is a primitive form of a money transaction. They learn much about values by swapping treasures (a moose's tooth for a ball) or items from school lunches. Such experiences emphasize the usefulness of money as a medium of exchange (rather than as a desirable entity in itself), but they can mislead children into looking upon money only as a medium for the ex-

change of things. That money can also be exchanged for intangibles —protection (insurance), new friends (memberships in clubs), even preferential treatment (the exclusive right to be the town's Ford dealer) —is a much broader idea grasped more slowly.

One idea about money that nearly all parents try to inculcate in very young children is the importance of saving. The effort is frequently wasted, perhaps because so many people go about it in the wrong way. Too often saving is not presented in its true light, as a practical method of satisfying needs and desires, but as a vague ideal, a Good Thing symbolized by the ubiquitous piggy bank. Junior is bound to have acquired one or more, maybe the day he first drew breath. Savings banks give them away. Every dime store and department store has its shelf-full. All of which is proper because the piggy bank teaches Junior to save. Or does it?

Saving can be either a negative action—a self-denial—or a positive action leading to some desired goal. For most of us, saving must be positive: The desire for some future good has to be stronger than that for an immediate satisfaction. In academic jargon this is the deferred-satisfaction principle. "Buy a big car or build up retirement funds?" "Would you rather have costly clothes now or a college education later?" "Go out for hamburgers today or have a real dinner out next week?" As the deferred value draws closer and becomes more attractive, a point is reached at which we all will choose it over an immediate satisfaction. At that point we save. But the reward must always be both attainable and attractive. If it is not, we will not save, and neither will Junior.

Against this backdrop, let's try to imagine what goes on in Junior's mind vis à vis his piggy bank. From time to time, when Daddy is in a good mood or when Mother is feeling flush because she's saved $2.18 by buying a $19.95 hat for $17.77, Junior is given pennies. He is instructed to "put them in Piggy." This is accompanied by smiles and a general air of "we're doing a good thing." It seems to be a game that adults enjoy playing, possibly because of the interesting noise the pennies make when Piggy is shaken. It is also an interesting kind of magic, because the pennies do a disappearing act. You never see them again. In fact, Junior is admonished that you never take money out of Piggy. That money is being *saved*.

It is not clear what Junior is learning from all this, unless what the parents have in mind is training him to be a miser. It certainly is not teaching him that a deferred use of money can be more satisfying than a present one. If Junior is very young, it may even be futile to try to teach saving, since the very idea of "deferred" has to grow on

child. But grow it does, and after a few years children become eager savers—for the school picnic, for a gift for Mother, for a contribution to the cancer fund, though seldom for Piggy.

ALLOWANCES: LEARNING BY SPENDING

A child's first awareness of the use of money generally comes as he accompanies Mother on her rounds of shopping. As soon as he has a grasp of numbers—the difference, say, between one and three—it's not amiss to give him a coin occasionally and let him pay for his candy or a small toy. He will soon discover that some things cost more than others: "I can't get that one for one nickel; it costs two."

At this point it is tempting to push him to the next big step: a decision. He has two nickels to spend, so you explain: "You can buy either *one* toy—it costs two nickels—or *two* pieces of candy, because they're a nickel apiece." But don't move too fast. A child is apt to be able to understand this intellectually before he is emotionally able to make such a difficult choice. You can also be misled by the fact that children can name the various coins and count to 10 much earlier than they can understand how to relate money to the price of something. It's usually not until the fourth grade that children develop a grasp of the mechanics of exchanging money.

An irregular allowance

Most students of child behavior agree that you can begin giving an allowance at five or six, depending on the child. There is still no such thing as tomorrow at this age, so the allowance must be tuned to opportunities for using it—enough to buy candy when he goes shopping with Mother or a cone when the ice-cream wagon comes by. If the money has been spent or lost when the wagon arrives, the child will ask for more. This is when you explain that he has used up his money. Do this very matter-of-factly. Don't scold; avoid even a tone that suggests he has done something wrong. A small child is incapable of being foresighted, but he can begin to grasp the fact that when his money for the day is gone, he gets no more to use.

Don't make the mistake of telling him, "You can't have another nickel because there isn't any more." He knows better. He sees you buying things, and he knows that if you stop for a Coke later you won't refuse him one just because he has spent his allowance. Always level with him. If he cannot have another nickel, explain that he has had all the nickels he is entitled to at this time.

Up to age eight or nine you can't expect a child to be judicious. He's likely to blow his money on things that strike you as outrageous.

A child settles into money habits surprisingly early, and sensible attitudes can be instilled even before he goes to kindergarten or learns to count.

First steps for the preschool toddler

The supermarket is a good place to start basic lessons in money management for a three-year-old. Give him a nickel to spend and explain that it will buy a piece of candy, or a toy, but not both. Money management involves choices.

Through second grade

An allowance is the best way to give a child experience in handling money, but until third grade it should be doled out when it can be used; he's still too young to plan. He can learn, however, that gum in the morning means no money for ice cream in the afternoon.

Piggy banks frustrate young children, who can't understand that the money inside is still theirs. Wait until age seven or eight to teach that money saved is piling up to buy something he wants.

Third or fourth grade and older

When the time comes for a weekly allowance, ask your child to work out what he needs for movies, carfare, lunch and so on, and base the allowance on the figures he comes up with.

An allowance based on a child's estimate may need revisions; ask him to show you where the money really went over the first few weeks.

Allowances should be kept on a businesslike basis; once you agree to give the child a set amount, give it to him even if he misbehaves. Withholding an allowance as a disciplinary measure suggests to him that money is used to buy good behavior.

Allowances should also be removed from any connection with normal household chores. Raking leaves, making beds are jobs a child should take on without pay. But he should be paid for doing unusual jobs.

He's acting like a child because he is a child. Being critical or trying to "correct" him is at best ineffective and at worst an impediment to learning. You can offer suggestions when a child is confronted with a buying decision, but let it finally be his own decision and accept it without criticism. If the toy quits working 30 minutes later and Junior complains, it is tempting to say, "I told you so," but you will want to be more comforting. You might say, "Sometimes these little toys aren't very well made, are they?" Little by little, children do learn, with help, sympathy and lots of patience.

A real allowance

Authorities disagree about when a child is truly capable of learning how to handle money, but this time usually comes in the third and fourth grades. The typical third-grader is beginning to think in terms of tomorrow, and has developed some concept of saving money for future use, but his follow-through can be erratic. The fourth-grader lives in a world of plans and projects, and his capacity for making decisions marks his arrival at a new level of development. Somewhere in this phase, the child is usually ready for a weekly allowance.

The agonizing question is always "How much?" If you listen to Junior and Suzy, all their friends get enormous allowances and want for nothing. Basing the decision on "what the other kids get," even if you have reliable data, contributes little to a child's education in managing personal finances. Everyone will benefit more if the figure is worked out on a rational basis that takes into account the family's means and the individual children. An active boy, for example, may need less money than a boy who gets his pleasure from acquiring books or records. For you to stipulate an allowance based upon this distinction, however, wouldn't be fair—and you can be sure it would not be long before you were told so. Indeed, why should it seem that self-sufficiency is being penalized?

A better tack to take when you sit down with a child to work out an allowance is to let *him* do most of the proposing. Most children are inclined to be reasonable in their estimates of their money needs. Let Junior point out some of his needs—money for a movie once a week, two trips to the skating rink, an occasional treat at the soda fountain. He will then have a greater stake in making the allotments work out.

What should be covered?

What do you include in the allowance? As many of the items on which a child spends money, or on which the parents have been spending money for him, as you can include without requiring him to make

decisions that are too much for him. Let him take as much responsibility as he can handle. Up to age nine, for example, the list will start with regular necessary expenses: school carfare and lunch money, music lessons, church contributions, regular savings and any other fixed and recurrent outlays. He'll want money for amusements and recreation—which should be specified. Hobbies, magazines, toys and other week-to-week items are easy to estimate and control, particularly if you and the child together can distinguish between what he ought to have and what he might like to have. There should also be a contingency fund for such things as gifts or bicycle repairs. Children cannot live on rigid allowances any more than adults succeed in living on rigid budgets. A contingency fund allows for greater precision on specific items and entitles you to expect reasonably close adherence to the overall plan. It also demands occasional sacrifices of wants.

During the next three years the list of expenses to be covered will expand—and should—to include social activities that increasingly involve a child. High-school years aren't far away, a time that tests a youngster's financial control and responsibility.

The first few weeks of an allowance will necessarily be based on estimates. A child will accept that idea and come up with good ideas for needed revisions. With such an approach you can get him to cooperate in keeping a record of expenditures over the first three or four weeks—again, with the understanding that he's not being permanently saddled with accounting for every nickel spent. This will not only help to produce a realistic allowance that he can accept but should also give him a concrete view of what he's doing with his money, and how this world of planned and controlled spending works.

When the spending is planned and controlled, you'll probably hand out less than if Junior runs to Mother or Daddy every time he feels he needs some money. It's better to give Junior a weekly allowance of $5 that he handles on his own than 75 cents a week that he blows while you keep buying for him all the things he needs.

Crime and punishment

It is fairly common for parents to use an allowance as a disciplinary tool. When Junior misbehaves he's told, "Okay, no allowance this week." It is an easy out because it doesn't require positive action that might provoke rebellion. All it requires is a lack of action, and there isn't much Junior can do about that, not at the moment, at least, or overtly, although he might get back at you in devious ways.

What's wrong with using the allowance as a disciplinary club is that you're defeating one of its purposes, which is to help Junior

learn how to manage money responsibly. When you give him an allowance, you're saying in effect: "Here are some things that have to be paid for every week. And here is some money to pay for them with. We want you to learn how to manage the money so it will be there when it's needed." When you take the allowance away, you're saying: "We were only kidding about making this a businesslike arrangement. This money is really a love gift that you'll get when you're good but not when you're bad." So to Junior money becomes not something to manage in a businesslike way but something to buy love with—a conclusion that can have some pretty mixed-up emotional connotations. Use other methods of discipline when they are called for. People say business and pleasure do not mix. In this case, neither do business and displeasure.

"The laborer is worthy of his hire"

Nor should an allowance get involved in family chores. Parents who need help with the dishes or the lawn, and know that Junior and Suzy have to be paid allowances in any case, often cannily play off one against the other: Suzy gets so much a week for cleaning up after dinner and Junior gets so much for mowing the lawn.

This confuses two entirely separate aspects of family life: the businesslike arrangement of the allowance, aimed primarily at teaching Junior and Suzy how to manage money, and the responsibilities of each member of a family in the functioning of the family. Keep the two things separate. If Junior refuses to mow the lawn, hang him up by his thumbs in the attic for a couple of weeks. He'll come around.

A common-sense rule to follow is: Don't pay for chores if they're the kind of work that members of the family normally take upon themselves to keep the household running. They are duties that must be performed and have no connection with money, allowances or outright payments. Other kinds of work beyond routine chores should be treated differently. If it's a job that you would ordinarily call in paid help for —such as digging up a sewer line to repair a leak—and Junior is capable of doing it in his spare time, then it's proper to pay him for it. It's not a chore; neither is it compensated for by his allowance. When he's working as a laborer, whether for you or for somebody across town, he is worthy of his hire—in addition to his allowance.

Some ingenious refinements

The theory is fine: You teach children how to manage their money simply by turning the responsibility—and some of the money—over to them. As any parent who has tried this knows, the idea seldom works

very smoothly at first. Here are a couple of ingenious refinements that can help allowances fulfill their objectives:

A Memphis father was faced with a brood of teenagers who just could not seem to make their allowances cover their expenses. They frittered away their money without knowing where it went or why. And so, borrowing a leaf from the profession of banking—which depends on the keeping of accurate records of the inflow and outflow of cash—the father went into the family banking business.

He provided each of the children with homemade checkbooks. At the beginning of every month he gave each child a deposit receipt (such as you get from a bank when you deposit by mail) in the amount of that child's monthly allowance. The child entered the allowance in his checkbook, and whenever he needed a dollar or so he made out a check to cash and presented it to Dad, who, in his role of teller, paid out the money in legal tender. At the end of the month, Daddy-the-banker gave each of the children a statement showing deposits, checks drawn and balance in each account. It was up to the children to reconcile these statements and figure out exactly what they'd spent their money for during the month. The statements also provided a visible record of how much money had been used up, and before long the children were trying hard to control their expenditures in order to balance their accounts at the end of each month. Elaborate though it was, the family bank worked so well that the neighbors were soon asking for a supply of forms to try out the system themselves, and before long requests began coming in from total strangers.

Another parent who managed to cope with the problem was a lady stockbroker in Washington, D.C. Like all mothers of teenagers, she'd been financing all sorts of last-minute "necessities" over and above the normally accepted items in the children's budget. These raids on the family exchequer became so insistent that she feared the children were developing undisciplined financial habits and warped senses of value. She decided, in the spirit of classic capitalism, to appeal to their economic self-interest.

The method she came up with was twofold. She continued the children's monthly allowances—which they were expected to manage themselves to cover all reasonable needs. And she made additional money available for nonessential items, but with a twist. Each child was given a share of stock at Christmas and another on his birthday. He was free to sell stock whenever he felt it necessary to finance something not provided for in his regular allowance.

Watching the price of a stock climb from 20 to 23 to 28 and 30 —and calculating profits as the stock rose—the children soon changed

their perspective. Sell some shares in United Conglomerate in order to buy a psychedelic light composer? Nosireee. End of raids on the family treasury. (There is no record so far of what happened when the stock fell. Presumably Mother was prepared to use the situation as a lesson in the uncertainties attending any financial decision.)

THE COLLEGE CRUNCH

By the time young people finish high school they usually exercise considerable independence in money matters. Many own and keep up their own cars. They buy their own clothes, restaurant meals, haircuts and cosmetics, records, books, jewelry, movie tickets, sports equipment and so much else that the "youth market" is a bonanza for businessmen. Much of this money comes not from Dad but from jobs. The total income of people under 19 is estimated at more than $18 billion per year. They do not spend all of it; almost three quarters of these youngsters have bank accounts.

Not only does Junior probably know how to use money when he enters college, he should also be able to chip in part of what he needs. Seldom, however, can he provide all. Most must come from his family.

How badly even upper-middle-income families neglect plans for college costs—and the rude awakening in store for them—was revealed in a study, *How Affluent Families Plan to Pay for College,* recently published by the College Entrance Examination Board, the organization that tests applicants for most of the nation's great universities. The families surveyed had incomes ($14,000 average) and children (average age, nine) that indicated expenditures for higher education within a few years. And yet:

■ Only two out of five families had any savings plan at all.

■ The average amount actually saved in the year of the survey was about $100 per child.

■ The families surveyed had "a dangerous overestimate of the outside financial aid available to people of their economic level."

This last revelation seems to explain much of the lack of concern. Somehow the idea has got around that scholarships are there for the taking, and that financial aid falls like manna from heaven. About a fourth of these parents expected their children to receive scholarships. They believed that nearly a third of all students received financial aid, and that the aid covered almost half of their expenses (the average guess was 42 per cent). Almost half the parents—41 per cent —thought financial aid covered half of a student's total costs.

As the College Board study pointed out, this just isn't so. In more than 1,200 colleges and universities surveyed, only one student

in five received any form of outside financial aid, and the average award was only $553 a year. What's more, a moderately affluent family cannot expect even a one-in-five chance that its children will qualify for financial aid. Guidelines suggested by the national College Scholarship Service specify the amount, per school year, that a family should contribute from its own funds before children will be considered for aid. The shares listed for a family with two children were:

Family income	Amount to be contributed by family each year
$10,000	$1,620
12,000	2,100
14,000	2,670

Said the College Board study: "The average income of parents whose children are receiving aid at even the most expensive colleges today is probably well below $10,000."

As much as parents overestimate the help they can expect from outside sources of college money, they underestimate the total cost of four years of higher education. "We never imagined it would be so much" is a plaint familiar to financial-aid officers. The figure of $10,000 mentioned earlier is an overall average—it can be much lower and much higher—but it is steadily rising.

In the decade between 1957 and 1967, the average cost of tuition alone in private colleges and universities jumped from $700 a year to more than $1,200. And at the end of the period, the total of all expenses for four years ranged to more than $15,000 at the University of Chicago. In some 40 per cent of 105 universities surveyed, the total figure was $12,000 or more; in 20 per cent, the cost was $14,000 or more. These figures are conservative since they allowed only $500 a year for all necessary expenses and foolishness, over and above tuition and fees and room and board. They are based on nonresident fees in state universities, however. One professional estimate of four-year costs in a typical public institution is $8,000. One size shoe obviously won't fit everybody's feet, but many estimates indicate that the average current cost of a college education is around $10,000.

The ceiling has not yet been reached. For one thing, the number of students is increasing and this is forcing many institutions to expand their facilities to make room for the influx. The U.S. Census Bureau estimates that by 1985 college enrollments will be more than double the 1965 figure—an addition of some six million students. As the student body grows, so does the faculty. And as the cost of living

rises, so do faculty salaries. There is also another factor. Many of the nation's private colleges are trying to remain more or less at their present size in order to maintain the intimate nature of their classes and the high quality of their education. This places the burden of expansion on state and city universities—which means that educational bargains once available to residents are disappearing.

Meeting the challenge

In the best of worlds, every family would set up a long-range plan for gradually accumulating college money for each child. Few families can stick with it. And it doesn't always work as you might expect. There are three traditional ways to build funds for college. One is to do it through insurance, generally with an endowment policy that guarantees Junior a certain amount of money when he reaches college age. Another is to buy U.S. Savings Bonds. Still another is to put money away in a savings account so that it will be there when Junior is ready to enroll. Unfortunately, none of these methods by itself

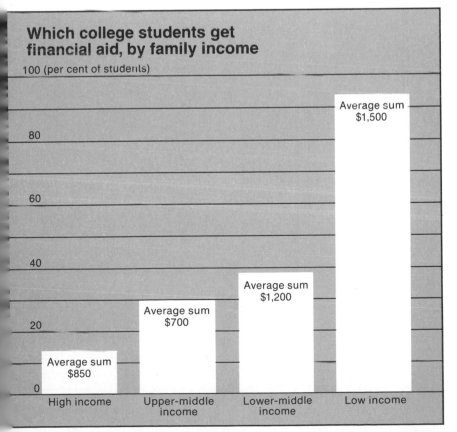

Which college students get financial aid, by family income

100 (per cent of students)

- High income — Average sum $850
- Upper-middle income — Average sum $700
- Lower-middle income — Average sum $1,200
- Low income — Average sum $1,500

Who gets money for college

Financial aid for undergraduates is far less common than most people think, and really liberal grants are scarce. Of the 20 per cent of all U.S. college students who receive help, most are from families with incomes under $10,000. Both colleges and the government, the two main sources of grants, reserve most of their scholarships and low-interest loans for those in real need. About 94 per cent of students from families with low incomes (below $4,000 annually) receive some assistance, and the grants are fairly high, averaging close to $1,500. But only about 40 per cent of the students in the lower-middle-income group (mean income, $6,795) receive aid, and the proportion drops to 29 per cent for students in the upper-middle-income group (mean income, $9,647). Among students from high-income families (over $15,000) fewer than 15 per cent get financial assistance.

is a complete or adequate solution in today's economic climate.

■ The endowment. If you take out a $10,000 endowment-insurance policy on your life—naming Junior as your beneficiary—the nice thing is that it guarantees Junior $10,000 for college whether you are around to see him off or not. That's the insurance part of the policy. The endowment part is a method of forced savings that builds up a total of $10,000 over the period the policy is in force. It is a rather expensive way to save money because of the low interest rate. The premium for a man 25 years old would be something more than $400 annually if the policy is taken out when Junior is first born. You are going to have to put in a total of between $7,000 and $8,000, depending on dividends, in order to have $10,000 on hand 18 years later.

■ Savings Bonds. As pointed out in Chapter 11 on savings, one big appeal of U.S. Savings Bonds is that you can have them paid for automatically on a payroll checkoff or bond-a-month plan. Like the endowment policy, then, they are a method of forced savings, a big advantage. Unlike the endowment policy, they include no insurance—if you should die when Junior is two years old, there's only two years' worth of savings in the college fund. The yield on U.S. Savings Bonds has lagged behind the open market rates on regular savings accounts. To build up $10,000 in Savings Bonds over 18 years would require a total outlay of about $8,000.

■ Savings account. Among the three traditional ways of putting money aside for college, sticking it into a savings account is the best in terms of return. If the rate were 5 per cent compounded annually, you would have to deposit a little more than $300 a year—a total of close to $6,000—to end up with that $10,000 after 18 years. But there is no life insurance to protect against premature death, and no simple way to force yourself to keep up the deposits.

The trouble that plagues all three of these methods is inflation. You are arranging to have $10,000, in dollars, delivered to you 18 years from now. But over the 18 years, as the dollar cost of education itself is going up, inflation will be eating away at the value of those dollars and the total worth of your money will be declining.

To see what can happen, take the case of Roger, who was destined to go to Harvard from the very day in 1948 on which he was born. The tuition at Harvard in 1948 was $400 per year—as it had been for 20 years previously. But by 1968, twenty years later, the yearly tuition had shot up because of expansion and increased costs to $2,000 per year. Even if Roger's father had begun to set aside enough money in 1948 to provide the lad, say, $5,000 during his Harvard years, by 1968 he would have needed three or four times as much.

The standard prescription for keeping up with inflation is to put savings not into investments that buy dollars for future delivery but into investments that buy a share in property—usually common stocks (*Chapter 12*). Over a long period of time the value of sound stocks usually increases enough to stay even with inflation (or even get ahead of it). It would take only about $180 a year invested in a mutual fund returning 12 per cent per year to provide the $10,000 in 18 years.

Forestalling the tax bite

But it isn't only inflation that will be nibbling away at college funds. Even if you put your money into stock investments as a hedge against inflation, as soon as the market starts to give you some growth the tax man will come along and want his share. You are automatically protected against at least part of this erosion by the tax break built into stock ownership. Interest on savings accounts and other fixed-income investments is taxed as ordinary income, and you pay the full rate. But when you invest in common stocks or mutual fund shares, part of each year's income from dividends is tax-free, and long-term increases in value, which provide most of the return from stock ownership, are taxed at a lower rate than ordinary income (*Chapter 12*).

You can do even better than that to protect your educational savings from taxes if you turn the investments over to Junior ahead of time and let the income accrue to him. This would not be necessary in the case of an endowment insurance policy, for it is essentially tax-free until the money is actually delivered to him. But such a device would be useful with Savings Bonds, savings accounts, mutual fund shares or stock certificates. You simply open a custodial account registering the investments in Junior's name and making yourself custodian. You control the investments but they belong legally to Junior, and income derived from them is now taxable to Junior. Since Junior, as a minor, is not required even to report income less than $900 per year, his college fund profits probably escape taxation altogether; if he is taxed, he will pay at a rate lower than you would. The only thing to worry about here as far as your taxes are concerned is the possibility that the sums you put into Junior's name each year will exceed $3,000 in that year ($6,000 in the case of a joint return). That's not likely, but if they do, you, as the donor, are obligated to pay a gift tax.

Indian giving: a special kind of trust

There is one very special device that could be used as a tax shelter by a family that has been thrifty enough to accumulate a large surplus early in life—or is lucky enough to have a rich uncle or a generous

Keeping up with college costs

The steady inflation of the past two decades has sent college tuitions spiraling upward in step with the stock market. The cost of a year at Harvard, as the graph (*right*) shows, increased sixfold from $400 to $2,400, its climb almost exactly paralleled by the rise in the Dow-Jones Industrial average of stock prices. A man who invested $400 for his son's education by purchasing the blue chips of the DJI in 1948 would have had the money on hand to pay the inflated tuition 20 years later.

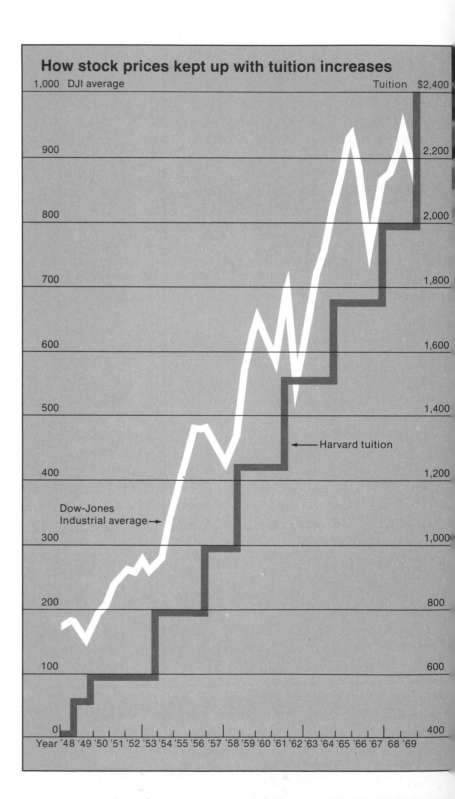

How stock prices kept up with tuition increases

grandfather. Known as the Crestol-Schneider trust (after the New York lawyer and certified public accountant who thought it up), it provides about as much protection against taxes for college money as it is possible to get anywhere.

It consists of two separate accounts registered in Junior's name but controlled by a trustee and a custodian, who must be two different people but can be any combination of you, your wife, a rich uncle or generous grandfather. The first is a short-term trust to which the donor gives certain income-producing assets (stock certificates, mutual fund shares, cash) for a period of not less than 10 years. At the end of that period, the assets revert to the donor, making him a kind of Indian giver. The second part of the plan consists of a custodial bank account for Junior. The income from the trust is emptied out into this bank account at least once a year to take advantage of a minor's favored income-tax treatment.

Let's see how the scheme might work in actual practice. Grandfather happens to have $20,000 worth of stock that pays almost 5 per cent in dividends. He puts the stock into trust. Since the gift tax on this is under Grandfather and Grandmother's combined exemption, he pays no gift tax on it. The annual income of more than $900 in dividends goes into Junior's bank account. Since Grandfather doesn't collect this income, he pays no income tax on it. Junior must declare the $900 or so income. But he can take advantage of the regular stock dividend exclusion of $100—which reduces his taxable income to less than $900. Then he takes his minor's exemption of $900, which brings his taxable income to zero. Over the 10-year period of Grandfather's Indian-giving trust, Junior receives a total of some $9,000—plus another $1,000 or so in savings account interest—without anyone paying taxes on it at all. Not even Junior's father gets nicked. So long as he provides more than half of his son's total support, he can continue to claim Junior as a dependent and take his regular $600 deduction. Such a combination as this is extremely tricky to set up, and anyone intending to use it should seek sound professional advice.)

How to find the money

If rich grandfathers are rare, so are parents who can hit the college expense bull's-eye from 18 years away. Few youngsters can go serenely off to enroll, with money for the full four years ready to be drawn on. They go anyway. They get the money from a variety of sources: their savings and current earnings, loans, in some cases special work-study programs and scholarships, but mainly parents' income.

You see how the problem is managed when you learn how other

parents have managed it. The best way to start is to talk to the guidance counselor at your high school and then to the financial-aid officer at the college your youngster is planning to attend. They are excellent sources of information themselves and can lead you to other up-to-date sources. They know how the costs vary from school to school, how to go about getting loans and scholarships, what the chances of part-time jobs are and how much a student can be expected to earn.

The first question you want to settle is: What will those four years really cost? It can be far less than the average $10,000. All states and many cities have publicly supported systems of higher education, among them some of the world's most prestigious centers of intellectual achievement. For residents of the city or state, tuition is cheaper than it is in an equivalent private school, and it may be free. The low charges of the famous University of California system actually lure residents to that state; this attraction is frequently cited in advertisements recruiting employees for firms located there. Smaller and lesser known public colleges—such as the many two- and four-year community colleges that have sprung up across the country—also provide good basic education at minimum cost.

If there is a college or university right in your own community —or within easy commuting distance—you could probably lop off about half of that $10,000 by continuing to board and room Junior at home rather than in some distant campus dormitory and refectory. It may not be as much fun for him to be hanging around home another four years, but he'll be gone soon enough as it is.

Even if you are unable to reduce the cost of college, that $10,000 price does not have to be anted up all at once. Neither is $2,500 a year due in an annual lump. At nearly all schools the bill is broken into at least two payments, and at some it is subdivided further. Many colleges offer the services of the Tuition Plan, Inc., which finances educational costs on the installment plan just as though you were buying a car. You can arrange to pay monthly and even to spread the payments over more than the four years your child attends the school. You have to pay financing charges, just as you do when using most kinds of credit, but the rate may be lower than that of a bank loan. Spreading out the payments eases Father's burden, but it can be effectively reduced only if Junior shifts part of it onto his own shoulders.

Working his way through college

A few glib young men and women still earn all their college expenses peddling encyclopedias or housewares door-to-door. Not everybody has such talent, but nearly all young people work at least during summer

mers. When labor is scarce, as it has been, they do fairly well, typically earning about $1,000 a summer. Even if half the total is spent for such teen-age necessities as dates, clothing and car expenses, that leaves $500 to put into the college kitty.

Full-time jobs during the school year are discouraged by most college authorities. But part-time jobs are often available, at least in urban areas, through a centralized office on campus (the financial aid officer is the one to ask). The pay is usually low, perhaps $1 or $1.50 an hour, and 15 hours a week is about all a student can work without interfering with his studies. Even so, that means another $500 or so to add to summer earnings.

There is also a special college work-study program, underwritten by the federal government, that helps provide students from low-income families with jobs in nonprofit agencies. The students are chosen on the basis of need. They may work no more than 15 hours a week while classes are in session, but can put in 40 hours a week during vacations. They earn at least the prevailing minimum wage.

With reasonable luck in finding jobs, an average student should be able to contribute toward his own education about $1,000 a year —that is, approximately 40 per cent of the total required. An even

The strings on scholarships

Scholarship aid—now largely based on need—makes the big difference in the financing of college years, as these two actual case histories demonstrate. Although both students' school expenses—slightly more than $4,000 —and summertime earnings were similar, their scholarships—and their family's contributions—were not. Student A, whose parents had another child and an income of $9,000, got an $1,800 scholarship. Student B, an only child in a family with an income of $16,000, received $200.

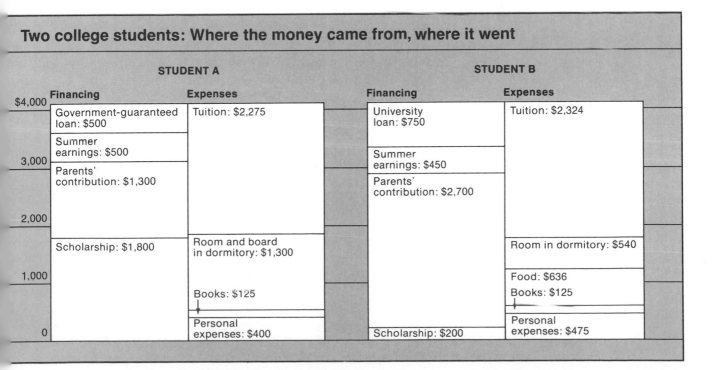

Two college students: Where the money came from, where it went

greater contribution is possible for those students whose abilities qualify them for special programs that combine college education with well-
paid jobs in industry.

The co-op courses

Many firms ranging from small companies to giants like IBM and
the Ford Motor Company have formed an alliance with the colleges
to share in the training of promising students—and in the expense of
educating them. Let's say that Jerry is interested in chemical engineering as a career. After he finishes his freshman year, Amalgamated Chemicals agrees to take him on as a part-time employee while
he attends college—if he stretches his college years to five years instead of four. The reason is that he must now spend from four to six
months of each year working full time at an Amalgamated plant, and
has only six to eight months for college classes. He will not only learn
a good deal about his future career, but he will be paid the regular
wages due an adult worker for that job. There are no strings attached. If Jerry decides when the five years are up that he likes the people over at United Chemical better than the ones at Amalgamated,
he is free to move on. But if he sticks with Amalgamated, he will
begin his career with a leg-up in seniority, probably a higher salary
than if he were starting from scratch, and a good deal more practical
knowledge of his profession and his company than the average college graduate has. For detailed information about colleges that take
part in the Cooperative Education Program, send a stamped, self-
addressed envelope to the National Commission for Cooperative
Education at 52 Vanderbilt Avenue, New York, New York 10017.

Where the scholarships are

It used to be that any all-A student could expect a college to rebate
part of his tuition with a scholarship. Those days are gone. Youngsters
still have to be bright to win scholarships, but now they also have to
be poor. Really poor, not just poor like ordinary folks. Most schools require detailed financial statements from the parents of applicants for
scholarship aid, and they make grants according to need.

The picture is not entirely bleak, however. The rigorous requirements for need apply mainly to scholarships underwritten by the
institutions themselves and by the federal government. Many states
offer scholarships for which children of middle-income families are eligible. There are many local scholarships underwritten by service
clubs, the PTA, alumni groups, churches and high schools.

The time to start checking on these is while Junior is still in high

school; 11th grade is none too soon. High-school guidance counselors are the first source of information, particularly about locally sponsored scholarships. College financial-aid officers—they expect to be queried well in advance, too—know state and nationwide sources. There are also books that list detailed information; two are *Financial Aids for Students Entering College* by Oreon Keeslar (Wm. C. Brown Company, New York) and *33 Ways to Meet the Spiraling Cost of a College Education* by J.K. Lasser (Cornerstone Library, New York).

Buying an education on time

All the usual arguments against borrowing money (and some special ones besides) apply to college loans. But in the hard-nosed view of a cost accountant, borrowing to finance higher education is a very profitable deal. The costs are modest and the return fantastic, simply because a degree is worth a great deal of money. College graduates earn an average of 65 per cent more than high-school graduates.

It is worth borrowing to invest in education even if Dad has to refinance the mortgage on the old homestead or pay the fairly steep interest rates that banks charge for personal loans. This is seldom necessary, for much better terms are available if Junior borrows the money on his own. A large assortment of governmental and private agencies sponsor student loans with favorable interest rates and very generous repayment plans. In some instances, a large part of the loan never has to be repaid at all.

The best sources of specific information on student loans are again high-school counselors and college financial-aid officers. Among the best deals available are loans made under the terms of the National Defense Education Act of 1958. Under this act, an undergraduate who can prove that his education would otherwise place a financial burden on his family can apply for a loan of up to $1,000 each year. The government puts up 90 per cent of the money, but the student applies for it through the financial-aid officer of his college. The interest rate is only 3 per cent per year. Repayment starts nine months after his graduation. He then has up to 10 years to pay off the loan. If he goes into teaching as a profession, 50 per cent or more of the loan may be canceled. And he is allowed up to three years of service in the armed forces, the Peace Corps or VISTA, during which no repayments need be made and no interest is charged. (If he spends three years in each, repayment will not start for nine years.)

In addition to these Defense Act loans are loans made by local institutions, primarily banks, but guaranteed by the state or federal government. Under this Guaranteed Loan Program, any student accepted

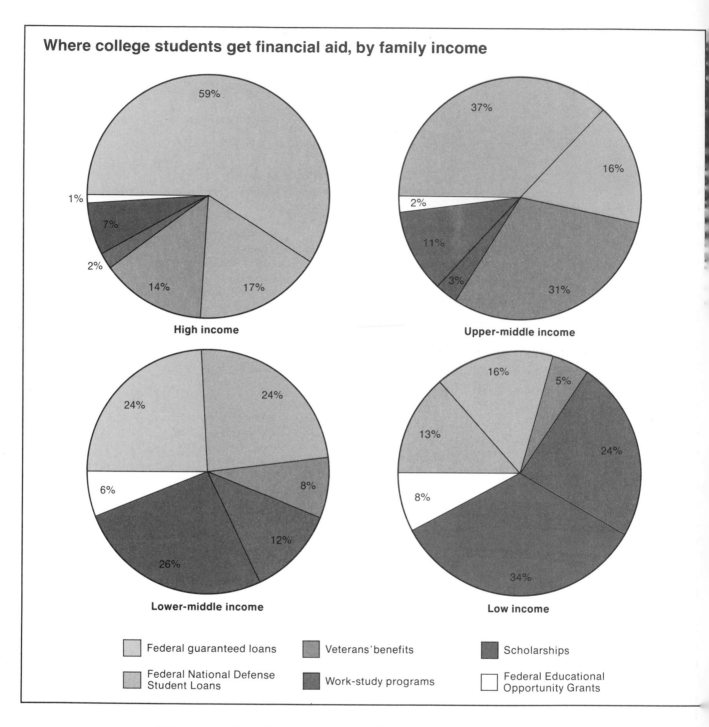

Where college students get financial aid, by family income

High income
59%
1%
7%
2%
14%
17%

Upper-middle income
37%
16%
2%
11%
3%
31%

Lower-middle income
24%
24%
8%
6%
12%
26%

Low income
16%
5%
13%
24%
8%
34%

Federal guaranteed loans   Veterans' benefits   Scholarships

Federal National Defense Student Loans   Work-study programs   Federal Educational Opportunity Grants

Where student aid comes from

Family income determines not only how much financial help a student can expect but also the source likely to provide it. Students from low-income families get most aid from scholarships and the government-subsidized work-study plan (part-time paid work in nonprofit agencies); few use veterans' benefits or loans. Scholarships and work-study jobs are fewer but loans and GI benefits more plentiful for the next higher economic group. Upper-middle-income students depend heavily on GI benefits. Well-to-do students get few scholarships and rely on government-guaranteed loans.

by a college can borrow up to $1,500 per academic year. The interest rate charged the student has been much less than the rate on ordinary personal loans. (Unless the student's family is quite well-to-do the government pays the interest for nine to 12 months after graduation, when repayment begins.) These loans must be applied for at the local lending institutions.

Among the private organizations sponsoring student loans is United Student Aid Funds, Inc. It will lend up to $1,000 a year for three years at 6 per cent interest. Repayments are not required until five months after graduation, and can be spread over three years. There is also an additional moratorium of three years for graduates serving in the armed forces, the Peace Corps or VISTA.

While these student loans are among the country's top bargains in borrowed money, their availability is often limited when inflation causes an economic squeeze. With the exception of loans made under the National Defense Education Act, the actual money in each case is provided by a local participating bank or other private institution, and it comes out of whatever funds the institution happens to have on hand for making loans of all kinds. Since the fixed rate of interest that the lending agencies are permitted to charge on a student loan is usually below the going rate for other types of loans that they could be making, the agencies do not always have enough money available to accommodate all of the students who have applied. Some banks are more willing to help than others, and the guidance counselor or aid officer often knows which ones they are.

Whether the times make college loans easy or difficult to come by, they generally turn out to be inconvenient to pay back, even more so than most borrowed money. The reason is the timing of the repayment. If Dad pays off the loan, he must do so in his middle years. That's a particularly bad time to be in hock, for his family responsibilities should then be expected to lighten so that he can put money into retirement funds. If Junior pays off the loan, he must do so in his young adult years. That's a bad time, economically, for him too. He's just getting started, and any extra money should be put aside to prepare for heavy responsibilities to come—a wife, a home. And some should be available for enjoying those brief swinging years.

Though borrowing is justifiable and economical, it should not often be necessary. Junior's resources and Dad's together ought to cover a college education—if some starting funds have been laid by in earlier years. Being prepared to pay for college, as much as solving any other financial problem, depends on careful, long-range planning and difficult decisions on personal values.

10
Income tax

Are you paying
too much?

It is entirely possible that a majority of the country's taxpayers regularly overpay their federal income tax—that is, put themselves down for more than they are legally required to pay. For obvious reasons, there are no official statistics on how many overpay, but the guesses of tax experts range from one in three to well over half. Probably as good an estimate as any comes from H & R Block, Inc., whose staff prepares more than five million individual returns yearly in the company's 3,000 offices, the largest operation of its kind in the country.

"It's our experience," says Henry W. Bloch, company president (the spelling of the firm's name has been simplified), "that roughly three out of four new clients have been overpaying, because they simply are unaware of all the credits to which they're entitled. The tax code has become so complex that making out your own return today is like trying to repair your own television set. Unless you're a professional, the results will usually leave something to be desired."

Even if you have your return prepared by a professional, you'll have to tell him what tax savers you believe you're entitled to, and you'll need records, receipts or other data collected during the past year to support your claims. If only to know what to collect you will have to become something of a professional yourself. You'll want to know about the strategies you can use to shelter income or estate assets from tax liability (*Chapters 14 and 15*), but those are long-range protections. They can't provide a quick defense against the financial danger that strikes each year when you sit down with a bundle of forms to settle your accounts with the tax collectors. You're on the firing line; the time for strategy is past; now is the time for tactics.

A good tax manual will lead you through the confusion of tax forms. (One of the best is the government's own "Your Federal Income Tax," available at district Internal Revenue Service offices or from the Superintendent of Documents, Washington, D.C. 20402, for less than a dollar.) But at certain points you can save money particularly easily if you know how. Most of these tax-reducing points relate to deductions, exemptions and exclusions—the sums that you are permitted to subtract from total income and thus cut the amount subject to tax. And it's not just a matter of knowing which ones to claim but of knowing how to claim them. The small savings add up, and some of these potential savings are not so small.

STANDARD DEDUCTION VS. AN ITEMIZED LIST
Possibly the most common reason for overpayment of income tax, reports the Block organization, is yielding to the temptation to accept the quick-and-easy way of computing income tax. As anyone who

has ever figured his own tax knows, you aren't really forced to itemize the deductions—for charitable contributions, medical expenses, interest payments and many other items—that you are permitted to subtract in arriving at your taxable income. The government will let you subtract a "standard deduction": 10 per cent of total income but not exceeding $1,000. If, instead of listing deductions separately, you choose to use this standard deduction, as 57 per cent of taxpayers do, making out your income tax can be as simple as filling out an application for a driver's license. But using the standard deduction can be an expensive, if easy, way out.

Typical of standard-deduction taxpayers is the newly married couple with a relatively low income and a simple, uncomplicated financial statement. Half a dozen entries on the front of Form 1040 tell everything they have to tell, and the standard 10 per cent deduction is considerably more generous to them than they could be to themselves by itemizing deductions. At this point in their lives their actual deductible expenditures total less than the lump sum of the standard deduction. But it isn't long before they begin to furnish and equip a household (largely on credit), acquire a car, pay doctor and hospital bills as children arrive, buy a house. With each of these steps their allowable deductions increase, but the habit of using the simple standard deduction may run well past the point at which they could save by itemizing and totaling their own deductions.

As they will find out when they buy a house, almost any homeowner supporting a mortgage can itemize deductions to his own advantage, accumulating more than the $1,000 maximum that the standard deduction allows. His two major deductions will be property taxes and the interest on his mortgage loan. Especially in the early years of a mortgage, when most of each monthly payment goes toward interest charges, interest alone will frequently exceed the standard deduction. For example, a 6½ per cent, 25-year loan of $20,000 calls for a monthly payment of $135. Out of the first month's payment, more than $108 represents interest—and five years later the interest is still almost $100. During all this time the homeowner has a deduction of $1,200 or more a year for this one item.

If at first glance it does not appear that you have enough deductions to equal or surpass the government's standard deduction, look again. The mortgage example above is obvious and most homeowners are not likely to overlook it. But many other deductions are more subtle. Every one you can find is important because it whittles away your tax bill at a rate corresponding to the top of your tax bracket. Suppose your return shows net taxable income of $12,500, and the

formula for calculating the tax due reads: "$2,260 plus 25 per cent of the excess over $12,000." The tax owed is $2,385, which means you're paying an overall 19.1 per cent of your net income as tax. However, the excess over $12,000—your last $500 of income—is being taxed at 25 per cent. Any additional deductions you find serve to reduce the top $500, and thus every $4 of deductions would mean $1 less tax to pay. So hunt carefully; there is a long list of possibilities.

What's deductible

These are the major deductions that most taxpayers can claim:

■ Interest—not just mortgage-loan interest, but any charges for the use of borrowed money or credit: interest you pay for auto financing, charge accounts, loans of any kind. In fact, whenever you pay for something in installments, you can usually deduct "assumed interest" of 6 per cent of the average unpaid balance during the year, even if no interest charge is explicitly stated. If you pay a college student's tuition in installments, for example, you can assume you're paying 6 per cent interest on the diminishing balance even though no such charge appears on your statements. To figure out how much this deductible interest comes to, set down in a column the unpaid balances at the beginning of each month during the calendar year. Add them up. Multiply the total by the decimal .005. That's the interest you're assumed to have paid unless you can prove you have paid more.

■ State and local taxes. Most are deductible, provided they're really taxes. You cannot deduct fees and charges for licenses—auto, hunting, dog tags, etc.—not connected with your business, or excise taxes on jewelry, cosmetics, phone bills, or on cigarettes or alcoholic beverages. But, state and local taxes being what they are today, this leaves a lot of taxes that can be deducted: real-estate taxes, school taxes, personal property taxes, state and city income taxes, sales or use taxes, and state (not federal) gasoline taxes.

The instructions that come with your federal return include guideline tables on state sales and gasoline taxes. You can deduct the amounts they indicate without detailed supporting records. However, it may be to your advantage to ignore the tables and figure the amount of tax you have paid according to your own personal records. The gasoline tax table, for instance, assumes that you get about 14 miles to the gallon. If you drive a gas-eater, you can knock quite a few dollars off your tax bill by keeping a careful record of how much gas you actually did buy during the year—but be prepared to prove it with sales slips. Guidelines on deductions for sales tax may also prove to be niggardly for some families. In one case, a New York City family that

began keeping every sales receipt and cash register slip found it was paying nearly three times as much sales tax as the guidelines allowed. The effort of savings sales slips, of course, can be more than it's worth. But if you use the guidelines, don't forget that you are allowed to add the tax you pay on a large purchase, like a car.

■ Contributions. Many taxpayers fail to claim deductions they're entitled to because they think only contributions to a church or to charitable organizations such as a Community Chest or the Salvation Army are deductible. You can deduct for gifts to most religious, charitable, scientific, literary or educational organizations. Nonprofit organizations that exist for the purpose of preventing cruelty to animals or children, combating crime, improving public morals, or furthering any worthy public purpose generally qualify for deductible contributions. So do agencies of either federal or state governments that promote the public good—highway safety programs, urban redevelopment, civil defense. Hospitals, libraries, and veterans organizations also qualify providing they are nonprofit. Your list of deductible contributions may be longer than you suspected possible.

What you give need not be money; it can be property as well. If you donate furniture, appliances, clothing or the like, make a list of the items and ask the organization to give you a receipt. Be conservative when you evaluate them, though; used furniture and clothing, as the Internal Revenue Service well knows, are not worth much. If your contribution is a large one, the organization will generally give you its own appraisal of value. There is a special way of getting a hefty tax break on donations of property. Let's say you want to give $500 to a college. At the same time you decide to sell the 25 shares of United Camelsaddle that you bought at $8 a share five years ago; it's now selling at $20. Suppose that in your income bracket the tax on the profit would be $54; you'd net only $446. But you can give your college the stock and take credit for a full $500 contribution, which, of course, entitles you to a tax deduction of $500.

Another deduction for contributions often missed is that allowed for transportation costs when you make trips to an organization's offices or facilities in order to donate your services. Also deductible is the cost of stationery, postage, phone calls or any other money of your own that you spend serving a qualified charitable organization.

■ Medical expenses. Frequently missed: the relatively new change that allows you to deduct half the premiums you pay for medical and hospital insurance. On other hospital and doctor bills, you get no tax credit until after you subtract 3 per cent of your adjusted gross income from the total expenses; the family with an income of $12,000 and med-

cal expenses of $359 gets no tax deduction, and gets only a $1 deduction when expenses reach $361. This 3 per cent rule does not apply to the expense of medical insurance like Blue Cross-Blue Shield. If, for example, your employer is taking $20 a month from your paycheck for such insurance, you can list half of that yearly $240 as a separate, straight deduction. The rule is: Half of the premiums that you pay, up to a maximum of $150, is your deduction; the other half is treated the same as any other medical expense. It has to be true medical or hospital insurance; the kind of insurance that replaces pay lost while you're sick does not qualify. But take a good look at paycheck stubs to see what's withheld for medical insurance. You may be overlooking a good-sized deduction.

Also frequently missed: transportation costs in connection with medical care. Unless you live next door to your doctor or dentist and walk over for appointments, it costs something going and coming. Many taxpayers neglect to keep a record of the cost of medical transportation, which is a legitimate deduction. You can claim actual out-of-pocket expenses if you use public transportation or cabs, or choose between a mileage allowance or gas-and-oil cost if you drive.

Actually, there is a wide variety of medical deductions many people overlook. The cost of items ranging from arch supports to wigs may qualify if they really are prescribed medical necessities. But you can't tell the players without a program; on pages that follow is a list of potential medical deductions.

EXCLUSIONS: INCOME THAT ESCAPES TAXES

Not all the items that can reduce your tax bill are deductions. Another section of your return is headed "Adjustments to Income." These also offer the possibility of important savings because they represent income you need not count when calculating your tax. Keep adjustments in mind in the event that you (a) receive pay from your employer while off the job because of illness, or (b) move to a new residence because you are changing jobs.

Exclusion of sick pay

Within limits you can consider money paid you while you were sick as income you didn't receive. The limits are these: Your employer, first of all, must have a regular policy of continuing wages or salary during absences due to illness or injury. The policy does not have to be in writing, merely a regular practice. Then, whether or not you can exclude sick pay from your taxable income, and how much of it you can exclude, depends on two things: the percentage of your regular pay

Medical deductions to check

Lots of things besides doctors' bills count for medical deductions from your income tax. Many people miss them. This list, prepared by H & R Block, Inc., is by no means complete —no list ever can be. But it does give a good idea of the sort of things that can be considered a tax-deductible medical expense.

you received while sick and whether or not you were hospitalized.

In the official instructions for Form 1040 is a complicated-sounding formula for figuring the exclusion if you're being paid more than $75 or $100 a week, but if you ignore this and simply follow the line-by-line steps on IRS Form 2440, which you must file if excluding sick pay, you'll have no difficulty. Among the forms shown in this chapter is an example showing how it worked out for one taxpayer, out of the office three weeks with a broken leg. His regular pay is $110 a week; company practice is to give its employees 75 per cent of their regular pay

Abdominal supports
Air conditioner when prescribed by a doctor for an allergy or difficulty in breathing
Ambulance
Anesthetist's fees
Arch supports
Artificial eyes
Artificial teeth

Autoette, or golf cart, when prescribed by a doctor (but not if used to travel to job or business)
Back supports
Blood tests
Blood transfusions
Braces
Cardiogram
Chiropodist's fees
Chiropractor's fees
Christian Science practitioner's fees
Contraceptives (by prescription)
Convalescent home (for medical treatment only)
Crutches

Dental fees
Dental hygiene
Dental X-rays
Dermatologist's fees
Diathermy
Drugs
Elastic hosiery (by prescription)
Electric shock treatments
Eyeglasses
Fluoridation unit in home
Gum treatments
Gynecologist's fees
Health club (or similar institution) fees where the exercises, rubdowns, etc., are prescribed by a physician as necessary treatments to alleviate physical or mental defects or illnesses
Hearing aids and batteries
Heating devices (therapeutic)
Hospital bills
Hydrotherapy (water treatments)
Injections

Installation cost of stair-seat elevator for incapacitated person
Insulin treatments
Invalid chair
Iron lung
Lab fees
Medicines
Metabolism tests
Neurologist's fees
Nursing care
Obstetrician's fees
Oculist's fees
Optician's fees
Optometrist's fees

Oral surgery
Orthopedic shoes
Orthopedist's fees
Osteopath's fees
Oxygen mask
Oxygen tent
Patent medicines
Pediatrician's fees
Physician's fees

while sick, so he drew $82.50 a week for the three weeks he was out.

He is allowed to exclude $225 of his sick pay; his "adjusted gross income" is reduced by that amount, so this taxpayer, who is single and takes a standard deduction, pays $45 less tax.

Moving expenses

With almost one family in five moving every year, many because of job relocations, the number who qualify for the moving-expense tax saver is enormous. Yet, according to the Block organization, many peo-

Physiotherapist's fees
Plastic surgery (other than to beautify)
Podiatrist's fees
Postnatal treatments
Practical nurse's fees or those of other nonprofessional nurses for medical services only, including medical care of elderly persons unable to get about or subject to "spells" (not for care of healthy persons or small children)
Premiums for that part of any health and accident policy that provides reimbursement for your medical expenses
Premiums for free-choice medical plan
Premiums for group clinical-care plan
Premiums for group hospital plan
Premiums for health policy
Premiums for hospitalization
Premiums for medical service cooperatives
Premiums for medical care costs paid to a college as part of tuition bill (if separately stated on the tuition bill)

Premiums for voluntary federal Medicare insurance (Part B)
Prenatal treatments
Prescriptions
Psychiatrist's fees
Psychoanalyst's fees
Psychologist's fees
Psychotherapy

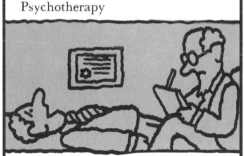

Radium therapy
Reclining chair (if prescribed by physician)
Registered nurse's fees
Sacroiliac belt
Sanitarium and similar fees
Seeing-eye dog and its maintenance
Sickroom supplies
Special mattress and plywood bed board, where prescribed

Special school costs for handicapped children
Spinal fluid tests
Splints
Surgeon's fees
Tooth extractions
Transportation connected with illness
Trusses
Ultraviolet-ray treatments
Unlicensed practitioners' fees, where such services are not illegal
Vaccines
Vitamins, tonics, etc., prescribed by a doctor (but not as food supplement or for general health)
Wages and board of nurse (including Social Security taxes on her wages)
Wages of a guide for a blind person
Wheelchair
Whirlpool baths

Wig (if advised by doctor as essential to mental health of person who lost all her hair from disease)
X-rays

The Treasury Department considers moving a business expense, a tax saver frequently missed by graduating students who are going to their first jobs.

ple evidently don't know that IRS considers moving expenses one o the costs of getting the job and lets you take them off your income a a kind of business expense. This assumes, of course, that you bear th moving expenses yourself; there's no deduction if your new employe pays your moving expenses.

The rule is that the new job location must be at least 20 miles far ther from your old home (measured in a straight line) than the ol job location. And the new job has to be a permanent job. If you hol it less than 39 weeks, you'll have to make an adjustment when you fi out the following year's return.

This tax saver is frequently missed by graduating students wh are going to their first jobs. It's available not only to those who ar changing jobs, but to anyone who has to move because of job lc cation. He can deduct from the income earned in the year of the mov the cost of travel to the new location, transportation of his belonging and meals and lodging along the way. Details are on Form 3903.

CREDITS: SUBTRACTIONS FROM THE TAX

Under still another heading on your tax return comes a more direc type of saving, tax credits. They are powerful reducers because the cut down not your taxable income but the actual amount of tax yo pay. Instead of saving $1 for $4, as a deduction or exclusion migh credits reduce taxes dollar-for-dollar. When you qualify for a $25 ta credit, that means you pay $25 less tax.

Most taxpayers will usually be affected by only two possible ta credits: (1) federal fuel tax, and (2) retirement income.

In addition to state motor-fuel taxes, which are legitimate tax de ductions, you pay a 2 per cent federal tax whenever you buy a gallo of gasoline or diesel fuel. These taxes are not deductible as suc They are allocated to build federal highways. Therefore, if you don use your gallon of gasoline or diesel fuel to operate some kind of v hicle on the highways, Uncle Sam says with commendable consistenc that you shouldn't have paid the tax, and you're allowed to recover when you file your tax return.

This benefits the operators of such nonhighway equipment as ai planes, boats, power mowers, snow blowers, gasoline-powered too and stationary engines. It isn't a large item for most taxpayers, but you throw a couple of hundred gallons of gas a year into a boat ar other equipment, you will cut about $4 off your tax payment by clain ing your credit on Form 4136. Farmers who use quantities of gasolii in their tractors and other equipment are well aware of this tax r bate; there is a sample in this chapter.

Retirement-income credit is something that everyone who is about to retire or has retired should be aware of, as it can substantially reduce the tax he must pay after he passes 65 years of age. What's meant by "retirement income" is money received from annuities, pensions other than Social Security, interest, dividends or rents; it does not cover pay received for work that is performed after retirement age is reached. The credit is generally 15 per cent of such income, though it may be reduced or eliminated entirely in certain circumstances. Like other tax credits, it is subtracted directly from the total tax due the government, giving you a dollar-for-dollar saving on any credit for which you qualify.

Unfortunately, both the general instructions and the computations are complicated. It takes a head for figures and a good deal of patience to work your way through the retirement-income credit, even with an assist from one of the income-tax workbooks written in layman's language. There is one set of rules when both husband and wife qualify for the credit, another when only one qualifies, and special rules for community-property states. Most taxpayers will need professional assistance for this one, at least the first time, but it can be important enough as a tax saver to repay the cost of a professionally prepared return many times over.

EXEMPTIONS: TAKE A DEPENDENT TO LUNCH

Henry's elderly parents have as income only their joint Social Security benefit of $1,200 a year. To meet living expenses, they need $230 a month, which comes to $2,760 a year. Their son contributes the difference, $1,560 a year. Can he claim either parent, or both, as a dependent, to give him an exemption to subtract from his taxable income?

A dependency exemption can be an important tax saver, and a lot of taxpayers fail to claim one they're entitled to because they're not aware of the rules. Before you claim this exemption, however, make sure the rules back you up, and keep good records. Because this is one of the easiest tax reducers to fake, tax examiners take a long, close look at dependency exemptions.

In deciding whether he can claim one or both parents as dependents, Henry refers first to the five tests that must be met:

■ Gross income test. A dependent must have a "gross income" of less than $600 during the tax year. This does not include Social Security benefits, but it does include gross income from rental property—before deducting expenses. (A child is excepted from this test.)

■ Support test. More than 50 per cent of a dependent's support must be provided by the person claiming the exemption.

■ Citizenship or residence test. A dependent must be a citizen or resident of the U.S., Canada, the Canal Zone or Mexico during some part of the tax year being reported.

■ Joint return test. Anyone who files a joint return is not eligible.

■ Relationship test. The dependent must either be related to the taxpayer fairly directly (aunts and brothers-in-law are among those included, but not cousins), or must be a member of his immediate household (not including anyone who works for him). If husband and wife file a joint return, the dependent may be related to either of them—not necessarily to both.

Henry is concerned about the first and second tests. First, does each of his parents have a gross income of less than $600 a year? Since their income is solely from Social Security, it isn't taxed and is not counted in gross income. Thus the first test is passed.

The Social Security benefits become a factor in determining how much support Henry is providing, under the support test. It is assumed that his parents, husband and wife, pooled their Social Security income to pay for common living expenses, and hence benefited equally from the $1,200 received. As support, each receives $600 a year.

The $1,560 a year that Henry contributes is also considered to provide equally for their support. For tax purposes, Henry is contributing $780 a year to each parent—more than the $600 from Social Security, hence more than 50 per cent of the support of each. He can claim both of them as dependents: two $600 exemptions. For his contribution of $1,560 a year, Henry reduces his taxable income by $1,200.

It's obviously wise, whenever support of relatives is involved, to arrange things so that the five tests of dependency are met, if at all possible. For example, Ralph's father, a widower, has some $14,000 worth of stock that pays blue-chip dividends, and a couple of thousand in a savings account, the yearly interest from which puts the father's income slightly over the $600 limit. Ralph, who's sweetening Dad's pocket money by $1,800 a year, can't claim him as a dependent, though he's contributing more than 50 per cent of his total income from Social Security, investments and savings. But suppose Ralph suggests that his father sell enough of his stock to buy a couple of tax-exempt bonds. He might then have $60 or $70 less "gross income" for tax purposes, and meet the gross income test as a dependent. On the lower-yield investment the father may sacrifice $15 or $20 a year, but the son realizes a $600 dependency exemption and saves perhaps $150 on his own income tax bill. "To make up for your loss," Ralph suggests to his father, "let me take you out to lunch once a month. We'll both come out ahead financially, besides having an excuse to go out

together oftener." In this case, it pays to take a dependent to lunch.

Note that there are a number of circumstances in which an individual may meet the less-than-$600 test on gross income, even though actual income is higher, if a portion of the income is exempt from taxation. Included in such exempt income, in addition to Social Security benefits, are life insurance proceeds paid on account of death, armed-forces family allotments, the nontaxable portion of annuities or pensions, nontaxable pensions of disabled veterans and welfare payments, to name the most common. However, all actual income—tax exempt or not—must be counted in computing the sum that the dependent contributes to his own support, under the support test.

Support doesn't have to be furnished by check or money order. It can be contributed in the form of food, lodging, clothing and other cost-of-living items, if the dependent is living under your roof. Among the items counted as support are the cost of medical and dental care (including premiums on health insurance but not on life insurance), personal care, entertainment (including the cost of alcoholic beverages for an adult) and transportation.

Transportation does not, however, include the cost of a car. This, along with life insurance premiums, falls in the category of "capital expenditures," which are not considered a part of support. If Dad needs a car, let him buy it out of his Social Security checks; you give him money to use for his everyday needs.

When you're lodging a dependent in your own home, you determine the value of the room or rooms occupied on the basis of "fair rental value"; find out what comparable houses in the neighborhood, or comparable neighborhoods, are renting for, then prorate on the basis of space occupied. In addition to space, make allowance for furnishings, electricity, gas, water and telephone.

There is one case in which you can claim a dependency exemption without contributing more than 50 per cent of an individual's support. For example, two sons and a daughter contribute to the support of their parents—no one of them providing more than the required 50 per cent. By agreement among them, one who has contributed more than 10 per cent may claim the exemption if together they contribute more than 50 per cent. To take advantage of this arrangement, a special "Multiple Support Declaration," Form 2120, usually must be filed; a sample is shown on page 290.

Although a complete accounting of expenditures in support of a dependent is not expected with your return, it may be asked for later. If you are questioned you'll receive IRS Form 2038 in the mail; you may want to get one to use as your own guide. The tax men won't ob-

Text continues on page 294

Formidable forms that cut taxes

Besides the basic Form 1040 for reporting your federal income tax, the government requires a host of satellite forms to describe special circumstances. These forms can save you money, but many people are so intimidated by the specter of added paper work that they don't file the forms and pass up tax reductions they are legally entitled to. Most of the added forms are straightforward and simple to fill out. To show just how simple, examples of those mentioned in this chapter are reproduced here and on the following two pages.

FORM 2120 (REV. SEPT. 1962)	U. S. TREASURY DEPARTMENT—INTERNAL REVENUE SERVICE **MULTIPLE SUPPORT DECLARATION**	For instructions see other side.

During the calendar year 19*68*, I contributed more than 10 percent toward the support of *CATHERINE JONES* _____, for whom
(Name of individual)

I would have been entitled to claim a dependency exemption but for the fact that I did not contribute more than 50 percent of his (her) support.

I understand that he (she) is being claimed as a dependent on the income tax return of *GLEN JONES* _____
(Name)

12 W. 4TH ST. OMAHA, NEBRASKA _____, and
(Address)

I declare that I will not claim his (her) exemption on my Federal income tax return for any taxable year beginning in such calendar year.

Frank Jones _____   *200   00   0000*
(Signature)   (Social security number)

4/13/69   *803 E. 78TH ST. NEW YORK, N.Y.* _____
(Date)   (Address)

Who's dependent on whom

A dependency deduction may require this form. When an aged parent, say, is supported by more than one child, one of the children may claim the parent as a dependent—but only one. Which one must be decided by common agreement among all. The others must file waivers, Form 2120, with the return of the taxpayer who makes the claim.

That extra effort

Although the government does not require you to itemize a claim for dependency support to the extent of the form reproduced at the right, it's not a bad idea to do so anyway. Dependency claims —so easy to make but so hard to substantiate —are red flags to tax examiners. By filing a more complete statement than the law calls for, you may forestall troublesome requests for other documentation. (This form is one used by H & R Block, Inc., tax consultants; the others reproduced on these pages are official IRS forms.)

STATEMENT OF DEPENDENCY SUPPORT

F_____ HS_____ K_____
CC_____ WS___(T)___

NAME OF DEPENDENT (A) **SALLY JONES**   AGE: **68**   (B) _____ AGE: _____

1. NAME AND ADDRESS OF OTHERS WITH WHOM DEPENDENT LIVED
(If dependent entered Armed Forces show "AF" and date of entry)

	RELATIONSHIP TO DEPENDENT	MONTHS
A.		
B.		

2. IF DEPENDENT IS YOUR CHILD AND YOU WERE SEPARATED OR DIVORCED FROM THE OTHER PARENT SHOW:

DATE OF SEPARATION _____ DATE OF DIVORCE _____ WAS THE CHILD IN YOUR CUSTODY? ☐ YES. ☐ NO.

IF "YES" STATE PERIOD: FROM: _____ TO: _____ IF "NO", DOES THE DECREE OF DIVORCE, OR OF SEPARATE MAINTENANCE

OR A WRITTEN AGREEMENT SPECIFY THAT YOU ARE TO RECEIVE THE DEPENDENCY DEDUCTION? ☐ YES. ☐ NO.

IF "YES", FURNISH COPY.

NAME AND ADDRESS OF OTHER PARENT OF EACH DEPENDENT	AMOUNT OTHER PARENT CONTRIBUTED TO THE SUPPORT OF DEPENDENT (DO NOT INCLUDE ARREAR PAYMENTS FOR PRIOR YEARS)
A.	$
B.	$

IF DEPENDENT IS MARRIED, IS DEPENDENT FILING A JOINT RETURN? A. ☐ YES. ☐ NO.   B. ☐ YES. ☐ NO.

3. IS DEPENDENT A MINOR AND NOT YOUR CHILD? ☐ YES ☐ NO. IF "YES", GIVE NAMES AND ADDRESS OF PARENTS, IF LIVING.

IS DEPENDENT MARRIED? ☐ YES ☐ NO. IF "YES", GIVE NAME AND ADDRESS OF SPOUSE.

A. _____

B. _____

4. SHOW AMOUNTS RECEIVED BY AND FOR EACH DEPENDENT: **5. DEPENDENT'S INCOME NOT USED FOR SUPPORT:**

	A.	B.		A.	B.		A.	B.
WAGES AND SALARIES	$	$	RENTAL INCOME $	$		SAVINGS - INVESTMENTS $		$
SOC. SEC. BENEFITS	450		SELF EMPLOYMENT			CAPITAL ITEMS **CHAIR**	100	
V. A. BENEFITS						WITHHOLDING TAXES		
CHILD SUPPORT						GIFTS		
AID FOR DEP. CHILDREN								
DIV. AND INTEREST			TOTAL	450		TOTAL	100	

6. MONTHLY HOUSEHOLD EXPENSES

	TAXPAYER'S RESIDENCE	SECOND RESIDENCE
A. FOOD	$ 125	$
B. RENTAL*	120	
C. UTILITIES & PHONE	30	
D. TOTAL	275	
E. NUMBER OF OCCUPANTS	5	
F. COST PER OCCUPANT	55	
G. LINE F X MONTHS APPLICABLE	12	

*Rental is actual rent paid or fair rental value of residence (furnished). If dependent owns residence in which taxpayer lives, the rental value of the lodging must be offset in computing the amount spent by taxpayer for dependent's support.

Offsetting Amount: $ _____

7. SUPPORT ITEMS

		A.	B.
FROM PART 6 LINE G	TAXPAYER'S RESIDENCE	$ 660	$
	SECOND RESIDENCE		
CLOTHING ($ 60 /) PERS. GROOMING ($ 15 /)		75	
EDUCATION ($ /) SPEND. MONEY ($ /)			
MEDICAL-DENTAL (INCL. INSURANCE PREMIUMS)		305	
CARE OF CHILD OR OTHER (DISABLED) DEPENDENT			
TRANSP. ($ 30 /) RECREATION ($ 100 /)		130	
CONTRIB. ($ 79 /) MISC. ($ 50 /)		129	
OTHER (SPECIFY):			
TOTAL SUPPORT		1299	
AMOUNT CONTRIBUTED BY TAXPAYER - - - - -		949	
AMOUNT CONTRIBUTED BY OTHERS INCLUDING DEPENDENT (4 – 5) - - - - - -		350	

DECLARATION

I (we) hereby declare that the above information is true, correct, and complete to the best of my (our) knowledge.

John A. Jones   _Mary A. Jones_
Signature   Signature

1040-4

FORM 4136 (Rev. Sept. 1968)
U.S. Treasury Department
Internal Revenue Service

Computation of Credit for Federal Tax on Gasoline and Lubricating Oil

Attach this form to your income tax return for calendar year 19**68**
or other taxable year beginning .... 19...... ending .... 19......

Name (as shown on page 1 of your income tax return)						Identifying Number
FRANK HAROLD						300-00-0000

Type of Use	Gasoline			Lubricating Oil		
	Number of Gallons Used (A)	Rate of Tax (B)	Column (A) Multiplied by Column (B) (C)	Number of Gallons Used (D)	Rate of Tax (E)	Column (D) Multiplied by Column (E) (F)
1 Nonhighway:						
a. Farm		.04	$		.06	$
b. Motorboat	120	.02	2.40	2	.06	.12
c. Aviation	400	.02	8.00	10	.06	.60
d. Other (specify) LAWN MOWER	20	.02	.40		.06	
2 Local transit system*		.02				
3 Totals			$ 10.80			$ .72
4 Total income tax credit claimed (sum of line 3, columns (C) and (F))						$ 11.52

*Attach a statement with the information required under section 6421 of the Internal Revenue Code and Regulations thereunder. List qualifying "lubricating oil" (see Instruction D) in line 1d column D.

FORM 3903
U.S. Treasury Department
Internal Revenue Service

Moving Expense Adjustment

(Attach this statement to your individual income tax return)

1968

(See instructions before completing this form)

Name as shown on page 1 of Form 1040	Social Security Number
JOHN NEWCOMB	100 00 0000

Did you receive an allowance or reimbursement from your employer for any expenses related to this move which were not actual travel expenses for you and members of your household, or transportation expenses of your household goods and personal effects? (See instruction 5.) ☐ Yes ☒ No

Dates of move	Departed	Arrived
	APRIL 27, 1968	APRIL 30, 1968

(a) What is the distance from your **former** residence to your new business location? **2430** miles

(b) What is the distance from your **former** residence to your **former** business location? **4** miles

NOTE: The moving expense deduction is not allowed unless distance (a) is 20 or more miles farther than distance (b) (see instruction 1). However, any reimbursement must be included in income reported on your return.

Name and address of employer at old location
A & B. EXPORTERS, 1 W. SMITH ST., LOS ANGELES, CALIF.

Name and address of employer at new location
LAWRENCE IMPORT CO., 1640 W. 30TH ST., NEW YORK, N.Y.

Address of old residence
18 W. JOHNSON ST., LOS ANGELES, CALIF.

Period of employment in new location (see instruction 7)	Total number of weeks
From MAY 1, 1968 to PRESENT (4/15) 1969	50

SCHEDULE OF EXPENSES

1 Travel expenses:	
(a) Railroad, airplane, boat, etc., fares	$ 145
(b) Meals and lodging en route	47
(c) Automobile expenses (attach schedule)	
(d) Total travel expenses (add lines 1(a) through 1(c))	192
2 Transportation of household and personal property (see instruction 3)	847
3 Total moving expenses (add lines 1(d) and 2)	$ 1039
4 Reimbursement for this move (other than amounts included on Form W–2) (see instruction 6)	—
5 If employer's payments (line 4) are less than moving expenses (line 3), enter the excess expenses here and on page 2, Part III, line 2, Form 1040	1039
6 If employer's payments (line 4) are larger than moving expenses (line 3), enter the excess payments here and on page 2, Part II, line 7, Form 1040 as "Excess moving reimbursement"	

Recouping your gas tax

The federal government levies a special tax on gasoline and lubricating oil. This revenue is earmarked for highway maintenance. So if you use gas and oil in some manner other than on the road, you are entitled to a refund. The claim is made on the form at the left.

Moving costs—a business expense

With the form shown here you can deduct the cost of moving to a new job —both the cost of transportation and the cost of moving your personal belongings. There are some restrictions: The new job must be at least 20 miles farther away from your former home than the old job was. And you must hold the new job for at least 39 weeks.

When sick pay doesn't count

If you were absent from work because of sickness or injury, you may not have to pay taxes on all the wages you received during that period. The formula for computing what sick pay is taxable and what is not is complicated, but if you follow the step-by-step procedure on Form 2440, shown at the right, you shouldn't run into any trouble.

FORM **2440**
(Rev. Sept. 1968)
U.S. Treasury Department
Internal Revenue Service

Statement to Support Exclusion of Sick Pay
For taxable year ....

Attach this Statement to your Income Tax Return, Form 1040

Name of taxpayer ROBERT MARTIN

Period of absence from work
From NOV. 20, 1968, to DEC. 11, 1968

Were you hospitalized (bed patient) at least one day during this period? ☒ Yes ☐ No

Regular weekly rate of wages $ 110.00

Number of workdays in your normal workweek 5

Nature of illness or injury BROKEN LEG

Name of employer GRAND, INC.

Payer of sick pay, if other than employer

Part I.—GENERAL

1 Total workdays in this period of absence for which you were paid	15	
2 Workdays in the first 30 calendar days for which you were paid	15	
3 Workdays after the first 30 calendar days for which you were paid (if any)	0	
4 Total amount received as "sick pay"		$ 247.50
5 Daily rate of "sick pay" (line 4 divided by line 1)		$ 16.50

Part II.—USE THIS PART IF SICK PAY IS 75% OR LESS OF YOUR REGULAR WEEKLY RATE OF WAGES

1 Number of workdays from line 2, Part I	15	
2 Limitation: If you were not hospitalized, enter the number of workdays for which you were paid in the first 7 calendar days of absence. If you were hospitalized, enter ZERO. .	0	
3 Balance (line 1 less line 2).	15	
4 $75 divided by the number of workdays in a normal workweek (maximum daily rate)		$ 15
5 Enter the amount on line 5, Part I, or line 4, Part II, whichever is smaller		$ 15
6 Multiply the amount on line 5 by the number of days on line 3 . . . . NOTE: Omit lines 7, 8, 9, and 10, if your period of absence was 30 calendar days or less.		$ 225
7 $100 divided by the number of workdays in a normal workweek (maximum daily rate after the first 30 calendar days)		$
8 Enter the amount on line 5, Part I, or line 7, Part II, whichever is smaller		$
9 Enter the number of workdays from line 3, Part I		
10 Multiply the amount on line 8 by the number of days on line 9		$
11 Enter the amount shown on line 6		$ 225
12 Total "sick pay" exclusion (line 10 plus line 11). Enter here and on line 1, Part III, page 2, of Form 1040 .		$ 225

Part III.—USE THIS PART IF SICK PAY IS MORE THAN 75% OF YOUR REGULAR WEEKLY RATE OF WAGES

1 Daily rate of "sick pay" from line 5, Part I.		$
2 $100 divided by the number of workdays in a normal workweek (maximum daily rate)		$
3 Enter the amount on line 1 or 2, whichever is smaller		$
4 Number of workdays from line 3, Part I		
5 Multiply the amount on line 3 by the number of days on line 4, for your "sick pay" exclusion. Enter here and on line 1, Part III, page 2, Form 1040.		$

16—80182-1   GPO

ject, however—and your chances of being questioned will probably be reduced—if you attach to your return a statement such as the one shown in this chapter, used by one tax service.

Double exemptions

In addition to the exemptions you can claim for dependents, you are also entitled to one or more for yourself and usually your spouse. The "more" part of these personal exemptions applies only in special circumstances and depends partly on the calendar. A taxpayer is entitled to an additional $600 personal exemption for himself in the tax year during which he or she reaches age 65. It applies to the full year, even if you turn 65 on the last day of the year. And, by IRS definition, you turn 65 on the last day of the year if your birthday is January 1. The double exemption continues to apply in subsequent years.

The calendar rule also applies to the additional personal exemption allowed to blind persons. Not only the totally blind get the exemption, but those who are "legally blind" according to an IRS definition of blindness. An exemption claimed for legal blindness must be supported by a statement from a doctor or optometrist.

If your spouse dies any time during the year—up to and including the last day—you can take his or her personal exemption for the full year. But if you're divorced, even as late as December 31, you can't take your spouse's exemption although you provided full support for the entire year.

DON'T OVERPAY THE TAX WHEN YOU SELL YOUR HOME

Many a homeowner is lax about sharpening his pencil to figure tax liability when he makes a profit selling his house. Most know about the rule concerning reinvestment of the proceeds: you don't pay income tax on the profit if you put it all back into another house within a year. But that's only a partial truth. The tax on profit is only deferred. You need never pay up so long as you keep buying more expensive houses. But if the day ever comes when you sell and buy a less expensive house, or no house at all . . . *whomp!* All the untaxed profits that have been accumulating over the years suddenly get taxed.

The rule on deferment, to begin with, is that you must buy another residence within 12 months, paying as much as, or more than, the "adjusted sales price" that you got for your old one. If you're building instead of buying, the replacement period is extended to 18 months, but construction must begin within 12 months, and you must occupy your new home within the 18 months. (There are special concessions for members of the armed forces and taxpayers 65 or over.)

The profit—if there is one—is not taxed in the same way as ordinary income. It's a "capital gain"—money made through the sale of property such as real estate or securities. If it is a long-term capital gain—you owned the property more than six months before selling —it is taxed at a lower rate than that used on ordinary income. But even this cut-rate tax often need not be paid on a house sale if you correctly count all elements in the sale.

Keep a record of improvements

How do you avoid overpaying the tax—deferred or not—when you make a gain on the sale? You really should begin on the day you buy your first house, or even before then, by keeping a complete record of all expenses in connection with the purchase, subsequent occupancy and use, and finally the sale. For instance:

The Hanleys bought their first house in a well-chosen neighborhood where property values appreciated during the next dozen years. Their purchase price was $21,500; now they've sold the house for $27,700. That gives them a gain of $6,200 that will have to be reported sooner or later. For people in the Hanleys' tax bracket, that means $775 they'll have to part with as tax, either now or at some future reckoning—unless they can show they did not actually realize that much gain on the sale.

Taking out their carefully kept records, they start with the purchase 12 years ago. They consult IRS Document No. 5447, "Tax Tips for Homeowners," which says "[certain] items which are charged to you at settlement or closing are added to the cost of your home and are a part of your original basis. These items include attorney fees, abstract fees, utility connection charges, surveys, transfer taxes, title insurance, and any amounts that may be owed by the seller but which you agreed to pay, such as back taxes. . . ." Their old closing statement tells them they paid an attorney's fee, cost of survey, abstract of title, title insurance, utility connection charge, and $243 in back taxes —a total of $595.25 they can add to their "basis"—the investment they made in the first house.

In figuring gain or loss on sale of a residence, basis is everything. Forget the stated purchase price except as a point of departure. It's an obsolete figure by the time you walk away from the closing, since inevitably you'll pay some extra costs in acquiring the house. Those extras are part of the actual outlay for buying the house. Thus, although the Hanleys' purchase price was $21,500, after all the checks had changed hands at the closing, it had cost them $22,095.25 to receive the keys. That figure was, at that moment, their basis.

When is profit not a profit?

Proposition: If you sell a house for more than you paid for it originally, the "profit" is what the accountants call a capital gain and you will have to pay tax on it. Right? Not necessarily! The Hanleys (*see text*) bought a house for $21,500 and sold it 12 years later for $27,700—a difference of $6,200 —yet they figured that they made no real profit:

Purchase price	$21,500
Closing costs	595
Landscaping	1,260
New driveway, etc.	1,477
Street assessment	752
Pre-sale repairs	487
Broker's fee	1,662
Attorney's fee	170
Total	$27,903

The last figure, $27,903, represents the Hanleys' true capital expenditure on their house during the 12 years they owned it. So instead of making $6,200 on the deal, they lost $203. Result: no tax.

One of the Hanleys' first major expenses after settling in was $1,260 for landscaping. That is, according to the tax code, an improvement (as distinguished from maintenance or repair). An improvement adds something to the house—to its value. In effect, the Hanleys had bought an additional $1,260 worth of house. So that was added to the basis. So were the costs, as the years went along, of blacktopping what had been a gravel driveway, of putting in a yard light, flagstone patio and walks, and of adding a split-sapling fence along the rear lot line. All this, along with the landscaping, had increased their basis to something more than $24,800.

Moreover the Hanleys found in their records the bills and canceled checks for the special assessment for street improvements —$62.70 a quarter for three years. That raised their basis to around $25,500, since special assessments also constitute improvements.

Again, just before they sold the house, there were the bills for "fixing-up expenses"—the painting and repairing that they did before putting their house on the market. Ordinarily repair and maintenance of this kind is not a tax-deductible expense. However, when you're prettying up a house to sell, it is; the work must be done within a 90-day period prior to the date on the sale contract, and paid for within 30 days after the sale. The Hanleys counted $487 of such expenses in getting the house ready to sell.

Finally, there was a real-estate broker's commission of $1,662 and an attorney's fee of $170, both part of the basis—which had now risen to $27,903.65. Lo and behold, they hadn't made a gain of $6,200 on the sale after all. They had, in fact, a loss of $203.65. But you don't get a tax credit for losses on sales of residential property. You always pay tax on a gain, but the gains may not be offset by losses.

Note that the Hanleys' $200 loss on the sale was not a bit of tax chicanery achieved with a sharp pencil, but a genuine loss. In addition to the original purchase price, there was $6,403.65 that had come out of the Hanleys' bank accounts during the 12 years they owned their home. They had bought that much more house over the years—$27,903.65 worth, all together—which they sold for $27,700. A genuine loss. But at least they didn't make the mistake of paying a capital gains tax of $775 on their loss.

HOW TO CUT YOUR TAXES BY PLANNING AHEAD

There are some tax savers that require long-range planning beyond the filing away of receipts and canceled checks. You can often cut tax payments substantially with year-ahead scheduling of certain deductible expenditures. For example:

The Bermans' daughter needs her teeth straightened—about $1,500 worth, the orthodontist estimates, and he can start the work in about four weeks, around November 15. "Make it right after the first of the year, instead," says Berman. This delay is a simple bit of tax planning that will probably save the Bermans $40 or $50. How? Let's say they'd pay the dentist $250 in November and December, if he started the work in mid-November as suggested. The Bermans had accumulated, earlier in the year, another $150 in doctors' and dentists' bills, giving them total medical expenses of $400 for the year. But Berman must subtract 3 per cent of his adjusted gross income of $14,000, or $420—leaving him no medical deduction at all. He'd be taxed on that $250 worth of tooth-straightening. By arranging to spend the $250 with the orthodontist next year instead, when he can expect total medical bills to be well over the 3 per cent hurdle, Berman will get the full benefit of a $250 deduction.

That's only step number one. The Bermans look around for other deductible expenses they can bunch up next year. A $40 doctor's bill that arrives in the second week of December can be paid on January 2. The monthly mortgage payment, due on the 23rd, can be a week late just this once, producing an additional $41 in interest that can be thrown over into next year. Berman also intended to buy a new car a year from next spring, now he decides to move his plans up three or four months and buy the car in December, giving him a big addition to his deduction for sales tax. No doubt he can find other opportunities for bunching deductions in the year ahead.

What's the advantage of bunching? Let's say the Bermans can normally itemize $1,300 in deductions. With two children as dependents, the tax on their $14,000 income comes to $1,886.

Now assume, unlikely though it is, that the Bermans can manage to defer the whole $1,300 of this year's deductions to the following year and take instead, this year, a "standard deduction" of $1,000. (Remember that you are legally entitled to a standard deduction even if you did not actually spend a penny for the items it is meant to cover.) Their tax payment this year is $1,952. But next year, with deductions of $2,600, it's whittled down to $1,600. That's a total tax for the two years of $3,558—roughly $200 less than they would pay if they itemized their regular $1,300 in deductions each year.

The same kind of tax strategy can sometimes be applied to the deferment of income, particularly when the income hinges on a decision to sell property. The tax strategy of the investor gets to be a course of study for advanced students—but almost any taxpayer, with ordinary attention to planning his tax year, can realize agreeable savings.

JOINT RETURNS

Unless both husband and wife have substantial incomes, filing a joint return almost always lowers the amount of income tax to be paid. The reason is simple: The government assumes that the total income is divided equally between them, no matter who actually earned it. Thus, each half falls into a lower tax bracket than would be the case with an individual return. If a husband has an income of $12,000 and a wife an income of $3,000, for example, the joint return credits each with $7,500. In effect, an individual tax is figured on that tax bracket for each, then the two sums are added together to arrive at the total tax due. In practice, you reach the same goal simply by figuring the tax with joint-return tables.

Half of the joint-return savings can be achieved by an unmarried individual who, in his home, supports at least one relative. He simply claims the head-of-household benefit and uses that tax table.

FOR WHOM THE AUDITOR CALLS

One thing you should plan on is the possibility that you will be called in for an eyeball-to-eyeball IRS audit of your tax return. If your "adjusted gross income" exceeds $10,000, you have about one chance in nine of being among those taxpayers so honored. The summons doesn't necessarily mean that there is something suspicious about your return; the computer may simply have picked your number.

The notice that you are about to have to prove your claims is polite enough. A date is usually specified when an IRS examiner will hear your nervous explanations, but you are free to ask for another date if that will be more convenient. (Also possible is a house audit —you will be visited at home—or a mail audit—you will be asked to send in your supporting evidence.) The audit notice will usually tell you what category of your return is in question—exemptions, deductions, capital gains or whatever.

So you collect the relevant canceled checks and receipts and make your way to the examiner's office. As you wait your turn among sober-faced citizens in like predicament, you can take comfort from one fact: of the more than 70 million individuals filing tax returns each year, only a few hundred are indicted for income tax evasion. Less comforting is this fact: almost three of every five taxpayers audited find they must dig up some extra cash for Uncle Sam.

The audit will be a polite interview, not an inquisition. It may take only a few minutes—if you have documentary proof supporting your claims. Your opinion of what is reasonable counts for little. But if you have been reasonably honest and can substantiate most of the

items in question, the auditor, knowing averages, is likely to be surprisingly willing to give you the benefit of the doubt.

In the event that an IRS computer has its eye on you, how long should you keep records? H & R Block advises three years from the date when the return was due to be filed. If your returns are being audited farther back than that, you need a tax attorney as much as you need canceled checks.

But nobody—not even the IRS—wants you to pay one cent more tax than you're legally required to. You are expected to take advantage of all the opportunities for saving that the tax code makes available. The proof of that fact is the rack of helpful booklets and pamphlets you'll find in your local Internal Revenue Service office—many of them free, others available at a nominal cost, but all of them offering advice and help in getting your tax bill down to just what you owe, and no more. That rack is a good place to start if you want to develop a semi-professional knowledge of tax strategy and tactics, and quit overpaying the government every April 15.

11
Savings
The fine art
of putting
something aside

Larry and Carolyn found the Financial Wizard seated on a stool at a high desk, furiously covering large sheets of foolscap with figures. "Yes, yes," he said. "What is it? Come, come; I don't have all day."

"If it's not asking too much, sir," said Larry, "they told us that you know how to—that is, you know the, the. . . ."

"The secret!" snapped the Wizard, whirling around and pointing his long quill pen at them. "That's what you want, isn't it? You want to have money. Some money in the bank. Is that right?"

"We're not asking how to get rich," Carolyn offered. "It's just that we're going along, making ends meet, but not ever seeming to get ahead—and we *would* like to put something aside until we reach the point that we're what you might call, uh. . . ."

"Loaded?" asked the Wizard.

"Well," Larry said, "we're not really greedy."

"Just something cozy to fall back on?" asked the Wizard. "A little cushion? Is that it?"

Carolyn and Larry nodded agreement. "But like you said," Larry added, "we need to know the secret. We want to be able to feel more secure about money. But we just can't seem to save anything. We honestly don't know how to save."

"Easy as pie," the Wizard said. "How much do you make?"

"Ten thousand," said Larry.

"All right, you," he commanded, pointing at Larry. "Fish around in your pocket and hand me $1.50. And you," he said turning to Carolyn. "Shake down your purse and give me the same amount." Then, when he was holding their $3 in his hand, the Wizard fixed his eyes on them. "Can you spare this right now? It would not ruin your day to give it up?" They hesitated briefly, then shook their heads. "And you can part with the same amount tomorrow?" Carolyn looked at Larry, who shrugged his shoulders and then nodded. "And you could do the same thing the day after tomorrow—and the day after that and the day after that? Every day?"

Larry and Carolyn hesitated. "Remember," barked the Wizard, "you say that you want to save; you want to feel secure. Well, $3 a day is about $1,000 a year. That's a substantial amount of money. But if you're really concerned about adding to your financial security, it's a reasonable amount. Nothing magical about that figure, of course. Some people with your income save more, some less. Now, are you serious about this or aren't you?" Carolyn nodded first; then Larry.

"All right," the Wizard sighed, handing the money back. "That's all there is to it." He picked up his quill and began to scratch away at a pad on his desk, murmuring half to himself and half to his visitors

as he did so. "Put aside $3 a day—$21 a week—take it to some bank or savings and loan that pays good interest and shove it across the counter to them. Do it every week. Regularly, without fail. At the end of five years you'll have a nice little total of $6,117.04."

Larry and Carolyn exchanged smiles. The Wizard went on figuring and muttering. "At the end of 20 years, if you decide to keep it untouched that long (I don't advise it!), you'll have all of $36,801.81. Minus my fee for giving out the secret, of course."

How does your money grow?

Like most people who have never really tried to save, Carolyn and Larry were rather surprised by the amounts the Wizard came up with. But he was correct in his figuring. It was the miracle of compound interest that made the money add up that way. (The Wizard assumed 5 per cent, compounded semiannually.) When you put your cash in a savings account, the money starts to grow as soon as the institution makes its first interest payment. Then that small amount of interest begins to draw its own interest. This steady accumulation of "interest paid on interest"—which is what compound interest means —allows the entire account to grow at an accelerating rate. Growth is very slow at first. But then, like rabbits, your dollars gradually begin to multiply, too, as the interest piles up and you continue to add your own deposits to keep the process going.

As you can see from the graph reproduced on page 304, time is the key element. At the end of five years, when you would have plunked a total of $5,460 into the account in weekly deposits, you would have a total of $6,117 on hand—meaning that you had accrued $657 in interest. At the end of 20 years you would have deposited four times as much money—$21,840—but you would have a total of $36,801 in your account, over 20 times as much interest. Compound interest is the driving force behind all the savings plans discussed in this chapter.

The reserve everybody wants

Larry and Carolyn were not alone in their concern over savings. According to a study by the University of Michigan, less than half of the nation's families had $500 or more squirreled away in some kind of savings; 39 per cent had none at all. Even among families with incomes of over $15,000, one family in five had no money put aside for a rainy day. It was not because they did not want to save, however, says Professor George Katona. "They believe they are unable to save," he concluded. But the answers revealed that most people felt bad about their predicament and wanted to do better. "The accumulation of sav-

The first and perhaps most compelling reason for saving money is to provide yourself with an emergency fund—a cushion of dollars.

ings," the professor observed, "still represents a highly valued goal."

And indeed it should. The first and perhaps most compelling reason for saving money is to provide yourself with an emergency fund —a cushion of dollars. Just as surely as you need fire insurance on a house, you need insurance against financial damage caused by the unexpected. To cite a rather extreme example, here is an actual case from the files of a financial counseling service in the East: Arthur D. was the father of a teen-age son who had disappeared from home and was next heard from on the West Coast in the hands of the police. Mr. D. flew out and spent two hectic weeks straightening out the trouble—which included a $600 settlement with the owner of a damaged car. Air fares, legal costs, and two weeks of hotel and restaurant bills added up to another $900—in all, some $1,200 more than Mr. D. had in cash and savings. Mrs. D. raised the difference by borrowing from relatives. After his return, Mr. D. got a personal loan, secured by the family car, and borrowed against his insurance, raising enough to repay the emergency loans. The financial counseling service helped arrange a moratorium on the mortgage payments and an extension on other debts. The D.s finally got back on their feet after a year of austerity living. But it was a close and costly call.

Here's an even unhappier case from the records of a referee in bankruptcy: Arnold F., a shopkeeper, was on vacation with his wife on the Gulf Coast when she suddenly had to be hospitalized. Insurance covered about $1,200 of the expenses, but five weeks of hospital bills amounted to nearly $3,000. Other expenses added $1,000 more. Because the F.s were from out of state, the bills had to be settled before they could leave for home. This wiped out both personal-savings and business accounts. When Mr. F. returned to work after a long period of neglected business, he found that he was in a severe bind. Suppliers had cut off his credit, and in the end the shop went under. There was no rescue for the F.s as there had been for the D.s.

Another reason for saving is to provide money to buy the costly things you want. Early on, you'll probably be saving to make the down payment on a home of your own (*Chapter 7*). Later, if you simply must have a boat while the kids are still young enough to enjoy it with you, chances are you'll never make it unless you start making yourself put the money aside. And if you discipline yourself to put away regular amounts for a car, you'll be able to get a new one every few years for cash—saving perhaps $500 or $600 in finance charges (*Chapter 4*).

Many people also look on savings as an investment, money at work piling up a nest egg for retirement. It is true that small sums regularly put away over many, many years in a savings account will

build into a very respectable amount; Larry and Carolyn's $3 a day grew to nearly $37,000 in 20 years, and if they continued the practice for 40 years they would end up with a grandiose $135,500. This sounds great. But it fails to take into account inflation, which, if it continues at its recent pace, would shrink the purchasing power of the savings by more than half in 40 years: the $135,500 would really be worth only about $61,000. Other forms of investment (*Chapter 12*) more closely follow basic changes in the economy (and also pay higher returns than savings accounts); these may be better choices for truly extra

How interest multiplies savings

"Interest paid on interest" is what makes money grow in a savings account. But it does take time. As the chart shows, regular deposits plus interest pyramid slowly at first, then grow faster and faster as the years pass. Daily deposits of $3 would build to about $36,801 in 20 years. A miser hiding the same $3 daily in a mattress for 20 years—forgoing all interest —would end up with only $21,840, a little over half as much.

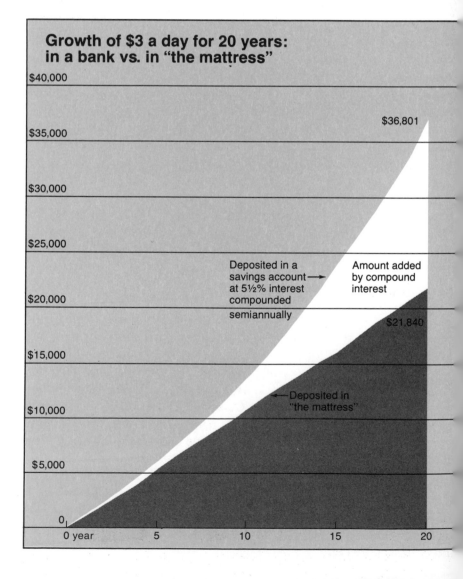

Growth of $3 a day for 20 years: in a bank vs. in "the mattress"

$40,000

$35,000 — $36,801

$30,000

$25,000

Deposited in a savings account → at 5½% interest compounded semiannually

Amount added by compound interest

$20,000 — $21,840

$15,000

←Deposited in "the mattress"

$10,000

$5,000

0

0 year   5   10   15   20

money—surpluses beyond the emergency reserve—that can be put away for needs of the distant future.

Inflation and rates of return should also be considered when building up funds for children's college education. If you are foresighted and strong-willed enough to carry out a regular, no-exceptions plan for setting aside college money, starting long in advance—when a child is born, say—that money might be invested in the kind of program used for retirement purposes. Over the long haul, inflation and return rate make a big difference. But if you are like most people, and cannot begin reserving college funds until a few years before they are needed, they might as well be treated as simply another form of savings for a costly purchase. In those few years, the money may not grow much from compound interest, but it can't shrink much either.

HOW TO MAKE YOURSELF SAVE

It's not the reasons for saving that trouble people, as Professor Katona's survey demonstrated. It's the method that bothers them. The plan the Wizard prescribed for Larry and Carolyn sounds easier to follow than it really is. The high cost of raising, sheltering, educating and amusing a family discourages people from saving at the very time in their lives when they should be knuckling down and getting started. Yet savings must be started early in life. There's no need to be a penny-pinching spoilsport about it, but money is indeed very slippery stuff. If you do not quickly form a habit of setting some aside regularly, it will always slide through your fingers.

One of the best methods for building up a savings account is to split a pay raise—or any other increase in income—between your spending funds and your savings. Don't try to put the entire raise into savings; human nature doesn't work that way. Reward yourself, too. But if you have managed to live on your income before you got the raise, you can't really use the excuse that "there's nothing left for savings" when that extra money starts coming in.

Raises, unfortunately, don't come often enough. But there are some tricks you can play—on yourself and your money—to see that a certain percentage of any income goes automatically into savings each month. The principle is simple and virtually foolproof: If you haven't got the money, you can't spend it. This means diverting the money at its source. There are a number of ways to do it:

Payroll deductions. Many companies have a savings plan to which contributions can be voluntarily made. You can ask the payroll department to deduct a specified amount from each of your paychecks and deposit it directly in the company savings plan.

■ Bond-a-month. If your company does not have a savings plan of its own, you can usually ask the payroll department to deduct a certain amount from each check and use it to buy U.S. Savings Bonds.

■ Direct deposit. For a two-step method of withholding money from yourself, ask the payroll department to send your checks directly to your bank for deposit in your checking account. At the same time, ask the bank to transfer a stipulated amount from the checking account directly into a savings account or U.S. Savings Bonds.

■ Increased withholding tax. As a fairly desperate last resort, you can arrange to increase the amount of money withheld from your checks for income-tax purposes. Just reduce the number of dependents you claim as exemptions on the form you fill out for your payroll office. This has nothing to do with the number you actually claim when you later file your tax return, but it obliges the payroll department to increase the amount of withholding it deducts each payday. Then, when you do file your return, claiming your actual exemptions, the over payment will be refunded to you by the government. This is a way to accumulate savings for those who lack will power to put money aside any other way. But it is wasteful because the surplus that piles up during the year is not earning any interest.

These savings methods work because you never get your hand on the money. Many people also view as forced savings the money they are compelled to put into home-mortgage and life-insurance payments. The payments are forced, all right. No one, no matter how easily he rationalizes skipping a savings-account deposit, lightly misses a mortgage or insurance payment. But how much of that money represents real savings is debatable.

When you pay the premium on a "cash-value" life-insurance policy, you add to a sum the insurance company keeps set aside for you. That money belongs to you and earns interest *(fairly low; see Chapter 5)*. But the trouble is in getting your hands on it. If you tried to utilize that money for some purpose other than the insurance it was intended to provide—by borrowing against the cash value of the policy to pay off a debt—the insurance protection would decline in value. If you didn't pay off the "loan," your heirs would.

There is a different kind of argument over the savings value in mortgage payments. True, each payment reduces the principal of the loan and brings to you ownership of another small portion of your home. After many years of payments you own a lot of house *(Chapter 7)* that you could sell for a lot of money. But is that money available for any use you choose, as true savings are? Most people do not sell a house to realize cash, but rather to make it possible for them to buy another

other home. They cannot use the money to take a trip to Europe or pay college tuition. If you can rent housing for no more than it is costing you to buy it, there is real question whether the house payments constitute savings or just expenses.

No matter what method you use to divert some money into savings, the real trick is to divert enough so that you accumulate worthwhile sums. Don't fool yourself with pseudo savings, such as filling gallon jars with coins or emptying your pockets of loose change and tossing it into the umbrella stand. These schemes fail because they cannot accomplish anything more substantial than allowing the saver to buy a few extra bags of peanuts.

At the beginning, you will find it easier to save if you do it for some specific purpose, such as setting up that emergency fund. As soon as you feel you have enough put aside for that purpose, you can shift your focus to a new goal—set your heart on something you really want but can't afford unless you save for it. A vacation in South America, a backyard pool, a ski lodge, a boat. Keep on saving for whatever it is that makes you really g-r-o-a-n with desire whenever you think of it. One good by-product of this kind of saving-for-spending is that it will force you to be more methodical and self-disciplined in your day-to-day spending habits.

Then, as your savings mount, you will find that diverting money from present spending to future spending becomes less and less difficult and more a matter of habit. What's more, you will also discover that there is a saving syndrome involved: Once you get into the habit and have accumulated a respectable sum of money, you will be motivated to save just because it feels so good to have a surplus on hand.

WHERE YOU PUT IT MAKES A DIFFERENCE

If learning how to save requires you to train yourself in living habits, learning where to deposit your savings requires you to educate yourself a bit in the mysteries of banking. What goes on behind that shiny counter determines how much your savings do for you.

Thousands of institutions scattered across the land would be happy to take your money and put it to work. There are four main types, but they vary so widely in their functions, their methods of operation and the ways in which they handle your money that the proper choice among them can mean extra dollars to your credit.

■ Commercial banks. They carry out the bulk of financial transactions in most communities and offer the widest variety of services. If you have a checking account, you are already associated with a commercial bank, for these are the only banks that provide this service. Commercial

Where savings are put

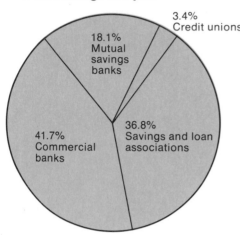

3.4%
Credit unions

18.1%
Mutual
savings
banks

36.8%
Savings and loan
associations

41.7%
Commercial
banks

Data: Federal Reserve System

Americans, having given up saving money in a cookie jar since deposits began to be insured against bank failure by the government, stash their cash in four major kinds of institutions. Commercial banks, which hold 41.7 per cent of all U.S. savings, pay the lowest interest rates, but offer such banking services as checking accounts and personal loans. Savings and loan associations, with a third of deposits, specialize in savings accounts and pay higher interest. Mutual savings banks also pay high interest, but they are chartered in only a handful of states and so attract only a fifth of the nation's savings. Credit unions generally pay the highest interest, but you can make deposits only if you are a member of the sponsoring organization; the unions receive only 3.4 per cent of deposits.

banks also maintain savings accounts, many of them handle family estates and investments, and they make mortgage loans, auto loans, personal loans and business loans of all kinds.

■ Mutual savings banks. These are banks that specialize in savings accounts and use the deposits chiefly to make mortgage and home-improvement loans. They do not deal in auto loans or the usual personal loans, nor do they provide checking accounts. Banks of this type are found in only 18 states; they are located principally in the Northeast, but there are a few in the Northwest and the North Central states.

■ Savings and loan associations. Also known as savings associations or as building and loan associations, these institutions are not banks at all but associations of people who pool funds and lend the money out to other people who wish to build or buy a home. The S&Ls, as they are often called, do not perform the usual banking functions. Indeed, to emphasize their difference from banks, federal charters and many state laws require that a person who puts his savings into an S&L be issued "shares" in that organization and that he be referred to not as a depositor but as a "shareholder." The return he receives on his savings is referred to as dividends rather than as interest.

■ Credit unions. These are also associations of people who pool their savings. But in this case the membership is limited to people with some common bond or interest—such as employees of a certain company or members of a farm group, church, labor union or fraternal society, or even of professional groups like actors and writers. The members acquire shares in a union by putting their money into what are referred to as "share accounts." The union then uses this money to make short-term loans to its members.

■ U.S. Treasury. A major repository for savings (almost $5 billion each year in the late 1960s), the United States Treasury Department sells interest-bearing U.S. Savings Bonds to the public through post offices, banks and company payroll-savings plans.

There are three main considerations to keep in mind when deciding which of these institutions should hold your savings: (1) How safe is it? That is, what happens to your money if the institution goes broke? (2) How available is your money? That is, how long will it take you to get it back if you need it? And (3) How much return will you get on your money? That is, how rapidly will it grow?

How safe would your money be?

With the possible exception of credit unions, there is really not much difference on this score among the institutions with which you might deal. U.S. Savings Bonds, of course, are the safest of all—as safe as

the U.S. government itself, and safer than cash. Cash can be lost or accidentally destroyed. But if you keep a record of the serial numbers of your bonds, you can easily replace them if they are lost.

Banks are almost as safe as savings bonds. Deposits in nearly all commercial banks (97 per cent) and most savings banks (60 per cent) are insured by a U.S. government agency, the Federal Deposit Insurance Corporation (FDIC). At the end of 1968, of the 14,199 U.S. banks of all types, 13,822 were insured. This means that if the bank should fail—which is unlikely—the U.S. government would pay back your personal deposits or transfer the money to a financially sound institution. Deposits of an individual are insured only up to a maximum of $15,000, and multiple accounts of one depositor are added together to establish the amount of insured deposits. If you happen to have a checking account balance of $12,000, for example, and a savings account in the same bank containing $4,000, you have $1,000 that would not be insured if that bank happened to fail. But if you also have a joint account, shared by your wife, it would be insured separately up to the $15,000 maximum. She could also have her own insured account, giving the two of you deposit insurance totaling $45,000. In the unlikely event that a husband and wife have more than $45,000 in bank deposits, the remedy is to use more than one bank.

All you have to do to make sure that your money would be safe in any particular bank is to look for an FDIC decal on the window or on a counter placard. If the bank is not covered by federal insurance, it probably is covered by state insurance. If you do not see the FDIC decal, ask. There is no reason to take a chance.

As a group, savings and loan associations are not altogether as safe as banks. Some are vulnerable to the ups-and-downs of the mortgage market and may occasionally find themselves in a financial squeeze that could imperil your account. Another U.S. government agency, the Federal Savings and Loan Insurance Corporation, or FSLIC, insures the funds in S&Ls that operate under federal charter —which accounts for approximately one third of them—and in many of the state-chartered associations. Insured accounts represent nearly 97 per cent of all S&L accounts. So look for the FSLIC seal in the window as proof that your account there will be protected by the U.S. government, or ask if the association comes under state insurance protection. If the association is insured, your money will be safe.

Strictly from the standpoint of relative safety, credit unions come last on this list. The funds entrusted to them are not insured, and a fairly large number of them are liquidated each year for such reasons as a decline in interest among members, the lack of trained personnel to

Signs of safe savings

The old fear that a lifetime's savings might be wiped out by bank failure has been eliminated by two government insurance programs, signified by the seals above. The decal at top indicates that funds in the savings and loan association displaying it are backed by the Federal Savings and Loan Insurance Corporation (FSLIC). Deposits in banks are insured by the Federal Deposit Insurance Corporation (FDIC), which issues the lower decal.

manage the union, or the decision of a few large shareholders to pull out, thus weakening the fund. However, the laws regulating credit unions require periodic inspection of each union's books by state or federal examiners, the setting aside of adequate reserve funds to cover bad loans and the bonding of all personnel who handle the money. The credit union record is not bad. While approximately 5,000 federally chartered credit unions went out of business between 1934 and 1968, more than 80 per cent of them paid off members in full and a few were able to add on some profit.

How fast can you get your money out?

If you are like most people with a savings account, you are concerned not only that your money will be safe but also that you can get your hands on it quickly when you need it. There is no point in saving for a rainy day and then having no umbrella when the cloudburst comes. In most commercial banks, mutual savings banks and savings and loan associations, your money is available when you ask for it. In theory, an S&L can require 30 days' notice before letting you draw out your money; after all, that money is out on loan somewhere. But this requirement is rarely enforced. The same thing applies to banks. The fine print in your passbook probably says the institution requires 30 to 60 days' notice before handing money over, but there is no record in banking circles that this regulation has ever been invoked.

Credit unions are sometimes slower about giving a member back his savings. Theoretically, the money is available on short notice; and in the best-run credit unions it is. But not all unions are run with equal efficiency, and you might have to wait for a day or two if you happen to belong to a union that has an inexperienced staff.

Savings in U.S. Savings Bonds are the least available. They cannot be redeemed at all for 60 days after purchase, they yield no return if cashed in the first six months, and you pay a penalty through a reduced return if you cash them in before the stipulated "maturity" date. The full "equivalent rate" is paid, providing $100.64 in redemption value for a bond that cost $75 to buy, for example, only if the bond is kept over the years to maturity.

What return will you get?

The third point to consider in selecting a place for savings is the rate of return itself. It varies surprisingly, differing widely from city to city, state to state, institution to institution, even between seemingly identical banks located next door to each other.

The maximum rates of interest (or dividends) that savings in-

stitutions can pay are set by federal regulations. But they don't all pay the maximum. They are not required to pay that much; they are simply allowed to. And there is not one maximum, but several different ones, each of which may be affected by bookkeeping methods:

■ Some types of savings institutions are permitted to pay higher interest or dividends than others.

■ Certain geographical areas may be allowed to pay higher interest rates or dividends than others.

■ The legal ceiling for interest rates may be higher in the case of special kinds of savings accounts.

■ Various institutions compute their interest payments in different ways, and this can affect your return sharply.

To see how rates can differ at various institutions, let's look at the range of interest rates in effect during the late 1960s. Commercial banks were offering the lowest rate, 4 per cent. S&Ls were paying 4¾ per cent throughout most of the country. Mutual savings banks were offering 5 per cent. And the maximum legal dividend rate permitted for the credit unions was 6 per cent.

But that was not the end of the story. Though the S&Ls were paying 4¾ per cent through most of the U.S., they were allowed to offer a rate of 5¼ per cent in California, Nevada and Alaska. The reason for giving these three Western states extra latitude was the scarcity of capital in those areas. The "West Coast S&Ls" were allowed a competitive advantage over the rest of the country in the nationwide scramble for money, and many of them campaigned vigorously by mail for accounts from the rest of the U.S.

The rate of return can vary widely among credit unions. A union that is efficiently managed—and many of them are—can sometimes afford to top the maximum rate in order to attract capital. The most profitable among them manage to get around the legal ceiling on rates by paying their members a "premium," which amounts to an extra dividend from profits. One enterprising credit union in New York paid members who had funds on deposit a 3 per cent premium on top of its regular 6 per cent dividend; that year each member made a total of 9 per cent on his money.

U.S. Savings Bonds—"Series E" bonds, Freedom Shares and "Series H" bonds—generally pay a lower return than other savings. During the period when savings banks were offering 5 per cent, the equivalent rate on "Series E" bonds rose reluctantly from 4.15 to 4.25 per cent. This is not really interest in the same sense as the return on other savings; the equivalent rate represents the bond's yield if it is held to maturity. If it is cashed in earlier, you receive a lower

rate of return. Up to a year and a half after purchase of a "4.15 per cent" bond, for example, you received only 57 cents more than the $18.75 purchase price, the equivalent of 2 per cent compounded semi-annually. The longer you held such a bond, of course, the nearer your yield came to the advertised equivalent rate. You reached the maximum when the bond matured.

A special form of saving that pays premium interest is a "time deposit"; this is a bank account you agree to leave untouched for a stipulated period of time. The standard rate a bank pays is predicated on the assumption that a depositer may withdraw his money at any time—thus depriving the bank of the funds it needs to carry out its business of making loans. But if a depositor is willing to promise to leave a substantial account intact for a specified period—from a month to a year or longer—the bank can plan its investments accordingly, realize a higher return on them and pass on some of that profit in the form of increased interest. When the going rate for commercial-bank savings accounts was 4 per cent, the same banks were offering 5 per cent for large time deposits. The S&Ls, which were paying 4¾ per cent in most of the U.S. for a regular account, were offering 5¼ per cent on time deposits. Commercial banks issue certificates of deposit—called CDs—against time deposits; S&Ls issue "savings certificates." Time deposits are useful only if you have a sizable chunk of

U.S.: an ungenerous banker

"Series E" U.S. Savings Bonds are a sound, safe investment in the nation's future, but they don't pay well in interest. A $100 bond cashed in after four years earns only $12.56, or 3.91 per cent interest, well below the usual savings-bank rate. The top return is 4.25 per cent, and to get that you have to keep the bond to maturity before cashing it.

Actual interest rate on $100 "Series E" U.S. Savings Bond (purchase price $75)

Time held	Redemption value	Amount of interest	Rate of interest
½ to 1 year	$ 75.84	$ .84	2.24%
1 to 1½ years	$ 77.28	$ 2.28	3.02%
1½ to 2 years	$ 78.80	$ 3.80	3.32%
2 to 2½ years	$ 80.40	$ 5.40	3.51%
2½ to 3 years	$ 82.08	$ 7.08	3.64%
3 to 3½ years	$ 83.84	$ 8.84	3.75%
3½ to 4 years	$ 85.68	$10.68	3.84%
4 to 4½ years	$ 87.56	$12.56	3.91%
4½ to 5 years	$ 89.48	$14.48	3.96%
5 to 5½ years	$ 91.44	$16.44	4.00%
5½ to 6 years	$ 93.44	$18.44	4.04%
6 to 6½ years	$ 95.52	$20.52	4.07%
6½ to 7 years	$ 97.68	$22.68	4.11%
At maturity date	$100.64	$25.64	4.25%

money you can leave alone for a while. The minimum amount at large commercial banks at the end of the 1960s was $25,000, but some institutions would take $1,000 or even $500.

What difference does the interest rate make?

The variation in interest rates on savings seldom exceeds 1 per cent and is often no more than ¼ per cent in one locality. Is it worth worrying about? Let's assume you have $1,000 to put into a savings account. The commercial bank where you do business is paying 4 per cent interest, compounded quarterly. Another institution down the street is offering 4½ per cent, also compounded quarterly. Would it be worthwhile to move your money for that extra ½ per cent or not?

Years $1,000 is on deposit	Amount of interest accumulated when the rate is:	
	4 per cent	4½ per cent
1	$ 40.60	$ 45.76
2	82.86	93.62
3	126.82	143.67
4	172.58	196.01
5	220.19	250.75
10	488.86	564.38

Earning an average of $7.50 a year on $1,000 left for 10 years might not make it worth your time to close the 4 per cent account, haul your money to a new bank and open a 4½ per cent account.

But let's continue our comparison shopping. You discover still another institution, clear across town, that is offering 5 per cent instead of 4. Now the compound-interest table looks like this:

Years $1,000 is on deposit	Amount of interest accumulated when the rate is:	
	4 per cent	5 per cent
1	$ 40.60	$ 50.94
2	82.86	104.49
3	126.82	160.75
4	172.58	219.89
5	220.19	282.04
10	488.86	643.62

Here, the difference begins to become significant. To start off with, there's a difference of $10 a year: 4 per cent of $1,000 is $40,

and 5 per cent is $50. Over a 10-year period, therefore, you might expect the difference to come to 10 times $10, or $100. Actually, the difference is $154.76, the effect of compounding 1 per cent over 10 years.

And if you choose to put money in a savings account for the long haul—25 or 30 years or more—even an extra quarter of a per cent of interest is worth shopping around for.

Quarterly vs. semiannually

Since compounding of interest multiplies your money faster and faster, it would seem that faster compounding would accelerate the growth still more. It does—somewhat—and institutions boast if they compound quarterly rather than semiannually. Actually, most depositors will not have many local choices. A man in Muscatine, Iowa, for example, or Decatur, Georgia, might discover that all of the savings institutions in town followed the same procedure: they compounded interest semiannually and that was that. At the same time, in California or New York City, the supply of money might be so scarce and institutions so competitive that many of them would be compounding interest quarterly or even monthly.

Occasionally, this hectic competition for deposits can verge on the ludicrous. At the height of the "credit crunch" of 1966, a number of banks and S&Ls were trying to lure depositors with the news that they were compounding interest on a daily basis. It remained for a bank in Detroit to offer the ultimate: a system it referred to as "continuous compounding." The bank's computer presumably had rolled up its sleeves and was calculating and compounding interest on deposits "every minute of the day."

What difference does this really make? Assuming that the rate of interest remains at 5 per cent, here is what the earned interest would have been on a $1,000 deposit compounded at various intervals:

Years $1,000 is on deposit	Interest accumulated when compounding is:			
	Annual	Semiannual	Quarterly	Monthly
1	$ 50.00	$ 50.62	$ 50.94	$ 51.16
2	102.50	103.81	104.49	104.94
3	157.62	159.69	160.75	161.47
4	215.51	218.40	219.89	220.89
5	276.28	280.08	282.04	283.36
10	628.89	638.62	643.62	647.01

Even after 10 years, the difference between compounding interest

semiannually and quarterly—the two most common practices—is only $5. The frequency with which the interest is compounded is not really all that important; it does not matter nearly so much as the *rate* of interest involved.

Why it pays to keep your eye on the bookkeeper

What does make a big difference in running up the numbers in your passbook—more than the rate of interest and the frequency of compounding put together—is something you may never have thought about. That is the method of bookkeeping used to keep track of your earnings. Two institutions, A and B, may both pay exactly the same rate of interest and they may both compound at the same intervals. But A, by using a method of bookkeeping different from the one used by B, can pay twice as much on savings as B.

The arithmetic is simple enough. If you have $1,000 on deposit from the first day of the year right through the last day, one year's interest is $50. But since we're compounding semiannually, at the end of the first six months you get credit for half that, $25. Now you have a balance of $1,025. A full year's interest on this amount is $51.25, so interest for the second six months is half that, or $25.62. Add this sum to a six months' balance of $1,025, and you have, at the end of the year, a total of $1,050.62.

And that's the way it should come out at any savings institution in the country paying 5 per cent interest compounded semiannually, if you have one sum on deposit all year long. Complications enter when you make deposits and withdrawals during the year.

Suppose you started the year with $1,000 on deposit, as above, and on July 1 you happened to get a look at the record of your account. If it were an old-fashioned ledger sheet (instead of the computer tape most banks now use) it might look like this:

DATE	WITHDRAWAL	DEPOSIT	INTEREST	BALANCE	INTEREST MEMO
JAN. 1				1,000.00	24.79
JULY 1			24.79	1,024.79	

So you rush to the bank, march up to the president, grasp him firmly by the lapel and say: "Hey! What happened to my 21 cents? I'm supposed to get $25 for half a year's interest, not $24.79!"

The president, disengaging your fingers from his lapel, replies: "No, sir, you see, we're on an actual-day basis. There are 181 days in the first six months of the year, so the interest on your account is fig-

ured as $1,000 times 5 per cent times 181/365, which comes out to $24.79. Don't worry; you'll make it up in the second half of the year."

And you will. You'll be credited with $25.83 after December 31 which brings you out at $1,050.62, right where you're supposed to be. (That's if you stay in all year. The bank picks up a few nickels on the slackers who pull out during the year.)

Not so bad thus far. But the plot begins to thicken if you start causing trouble by making deposits and withdrawals. Let's say you start the year, as before, with a balance of $1,000. When March 1 arrives you deposit another $1,000. Then on June 1—three months later to the day—you withdraw $1,000.

Again the arithmetic seems simple enough. That original $1,000 was on deposit throughout the first six months, so it earns half a year's interest, $24.79. In addition, you had $1,000 on deposit for three months, so it should earn half of half a year's interest, or $12.39. On July 1, therefore, you should be credited with $24.79 + 12.39 = $37.18. Right? Wrong.

Again you take a look at your ledger sheet after the bookkeepers get through posting your interest on July 1, and you see:

DATE	WITHDRAWAL	DEPOSIT	INTEREST	BALANCE	INTEREST MEMO
JAN. 1				1,000.00	
MARCH 1		1,000.00		2,000.00	
JUNE 1	1,000.00			1,000.00	24.79
JULY 1			24.79	1,024.79	

You march up to the president once more: "Sir, I'm afraid some one has made another mistake. You see, I started the year with . . ." and you explain the whole thing to him very carefully.

The president nods. "I can see how you might think that," he says understandingly, "but you must realize that if you bring some money in here one day, and then come back and draw it out a few days later, that's not really of any use to us. We have to have funds on deposit here long enough so that we can lend them out to our borrowers. That's how *we* make our money, you know. So, as you will see if you read what it says right there in your bank book, we pay interest only on the highest continuous balance. In your case, the highest amount that was continuously on deposit in your account during the six-month period was $1,000. Therefore, your account earned interest of $24.79, as we correctly indicate."

You look a little dubious, but you have to take an expert's word

or such things; so you tell the president you're sorry for having bothered him and you go back down the street to earn some more money
to put in the bank. And, sure enough, by the following January 1,
you're doing better, and by mid-year your ledger sheet, just before
the interest due is entered, looks like this:

DATE	WITHDRAWAL	DEPOSIT	INTEREST	BALANCE	INTEREST MEMO
JAN. 1				1,000.00	
APRIL 1		1,000.00		2,000.00	
MAY 15		1,000.00		3,000.00	
MAY 20	1,000.00			2,000.00	

You whistle cheerfully as you figure to yourself: "Let's see—
$1,000 for the entire six months; that's $24.79 worth of interest. Another $1,000 from April 1; that's half of six months, so add $12.39.
Then there's that other $1,000 from May 15 to May 20, or four days;
that's 4/181 times $24.79 or—umm, 55 cents. All together, I've earned
$37.73 as interest in six months. Not bad!"

Well, we're afraid you've forgotten what the president told you
last year, but let's watch as the bookkeeper posts your interest:

DATE	WITHDRAWAL	DEPOSIT	INTEREST	BALANCE	INTEREST MEMO
JAN. 1				1,000.00	
APRIL 1		1,000.00		2,000.00	
MAY 15		1,000.00	.	3,000.00	
MAY 20	1,000.00			2,000.00	24.79
JULY 1			24.79	2,024.79	

It's true, of course, that you had a good deal more money in
your account this year than last. It's also true that for half of the interest period involved you had a total of $2,000 in your account—at
all times, never any less. And for a short period you had all of $3,000
in your account. But you must remember that your bank is not paying interest based on the highest balance, but on the highest continuous
balance. Now, what was the largest amount that was on deposit for
the entire six months? That's right: just $1,000. So you earn interest
again only on that $1,000. The figure of $24.79 is still correct.

It would not make any difference, actually, if somehow you managed to add a whopping $50,000 to your account and kept it there for
almost six months. You would still receive interest only on the high-

est continuous balance, or that original $1,000, unless you made a spe-
cial arrangement. (In banking circles highest continuous balance is
often referred to as "low balance." The two terms mean exactly the
same thing, but "highest continuous balance" sounds better.)

The bankers' alphabet soup

You decide to be toughminded, and you draw your money out, grum-
bling about "putting my money where they'll pay interest on what
I've got in the account." You march into the bank across the street
and ask belligerently if they pay interest on the low-balance method.

"No, indeed, sir," the vice president says. "We use the FIFO system—which means 'first in, first out.' Let me explain. Ah, I see you
have a ledger sheet from our competitor across the street. Now here
on May 20 you made a withdrawal of $1,000. The question naturally
arises as to which $1,000 you withdrew. Was it the $1,000 you had in
the account on January 1? The $1,000 you deposited on April 1? Or
the $1,000 you deposited five days earlier, on May 15? . . . What is it?
. . . No, sir, I can't see that this has any resemblance to the questions de-
bated by the medieval theologians. It seems like a perfectly sensible
question to me. And the FIFO method we use supplies the answer.
The $1,000 you withdrew was the 'first deposit' put in the account
during this particular interest period; that is, your April 1 deposit.

"Here's how it works. Against this first item, we enter an interest memo which assumes that your opening balance of $1,000 is
going to remain in the account for the entire interest period."

DATE	WITHDRAWAL	DEPOSIT	INTEREST	BALANCE	INTEREST MEMO
JAN. 1				1,000.00	24.79

"Then, when you make this deposit on April 1, we again anticipate that it will remain in the account to the end of the interest period. That would be 91 days, and 91/365 of $50 is $12.47. We add
that to the $24.79 that we anticipate will be earned and show the
total in the second interest memo like this."

DATE	WITHDRAWAL	DEPOSIT	INTEREST	BALANCE	INTEREST MEMO
JAN. 1				1,000.00	24.79
APRIL 1		1,000.00		2,000.00	37.26

"The same with your May 15 deposit, with 47 days of anticipated
interest, or $6.44. Adding that to the $37.26, we have an interest
memo entered for $43.70."

DATE	WITHDRAWAL	DEPOSIT	INTEREST	BALANCE	INTEREST MEMO
JAN. 1				1,000.00	24.79
APRIL 1		1,000.00		2,000.00	37.26
MAY 15		1,000.00		3,000.00	43.70

"Now we come to your withdrawal on May 20. FIFO tells us that you withdrew the $1,000 first deposit—the one of April 1—so that in effect you didn't make this deposit at all. We simply subtract the $12.47 which we anticipated it would earn."

DATE	WITHDRAWAL	DEPOSIT	INTEREST	BALANCE	INTEREST MEMO
JAN. 1				1,000.00	24.79
APRIL 1		1,000.00		2,000.00	37.26
MAY 15		1,000.00		3,000.00	43.70
MAY 20	1,000.00			2,000.00	31.23

"And since you have no further activity in the account to the end of the interest period, $31.23 is in fact the interest credited July 1."

DATE	WITHDRAWAL	DEPOSIT	INTEREST	BALANCE	INTEREST MEMO
JAN. 1				1,000.00	24.79
APRIL 1		1,000.00		2,000.00	37.26
MAY 15		1,000.00		3,000.00	43.70
MAY 20	1,000.00			2,000.00	31.23
JULY 1			31.23	2,031.23	

That looks more like it. But by now you're a ruthless comparison shopper, so you thank the VP and head for the next savings institution down the street. There you find an assistant VP who tells you that here they use the LIFO method—last in, first out. "It seems perfectly obvious to me that it's the last deposit that comes out first," he explains. "If you were stuffing dollar bills into an olive jar, and then started taking them out, which one would come out first? The last one you'd put in, of course."

When this method is used, the bookkeepers treat your May 15 deposit as the one that had never been made, for purposes of figuring interest. That *would* have earned $6.44, so this amount is subtracted when you make the withdrawal: $43.70 - 6.44 = 37.26. Where they

use the LIFO method, you're $12.47 ahead of the low-balance method —about 50 per cent better off.

Your next stop is at an institution where the head cashier informs you that here they use the FIFO method: "Ah, one version of it, that is," he elucidates. "Some people think a withdrawal removes the first deposit to come into the account during the interest period. That's all wrong, of course. We're not talking about an olive jar, but a tube that's open on both ends—and naturally you put money in at one end, and take it out at the other."

"Do you mean . . .?" you ask, your eyes narrowing.

"What we call the 'first funds.' The first money you come to, when you make a withdrawal, is the money that was already there when the interest period begins."

"My $1,000 that was in the account from way back last year?"

"Of course. What else?"

"My $1,000 that is going to earn $24.79 for the six months?"

"That *would* have earned $24.79. But of course you withdrew it."

"So you'd subtract the $24.79 from the last interest memo?"

"That's right."

"And the interest I get for the six months is $18.91?"

"I believe . . . yes, we could let you have that extra penny."

You now trudge down the street, muttering darkly, for a visit to one last place. Here a brisk young man in a button-down collar tells you that their method is DD/DW—"day of deposit to day of withdrawal." What does that mean? "Just what it says," he explains. "If you deposit $1,000 in the account, keep it there 20 days, and then draw it out, it's earned 20 days' interest."

You hand him your now dog-eared ledger sheet. "Figure it out for me, doing it your way."

He takes out a vest-pocket computer, pushes a couple of buttons and says: "You lost 42 days' interest when you withdrew the $1,000 that's $5.75. The account earned $37.95."

"Sold!" you say, and hand him your satchel of money.

So there you have five methods of crediting the depositor with interest, all based on 5 per cent compounded semiannually, but resulting in quite a range of earnings on the same account:

FIFO (First funds)	$18.91
Low balance	24.79
FIFO (First deposits)	31.23
LIFO	37.26
DD/DW	37.95

In other words, the day-of-deposit-to-day-of-withdrawal method would give you nearly twice the earnings that you would get from an institution using the first-in-first-out-first-funds system.

A survey of banking practices in the 1960s showed that slightly more than half the commercial banks were using the low-balance method of recording interest. The American Bankers Association has spoken with disapproval of this practice. "Though it provides the bank a cost advantage," says the A.B.A., "it penalizes the customer. It could tend to discourage deposits and encourage customer dissatisfaction with the harsh penalty of interest loss due to withdrawals near the end of a period." FIFO, which also works to the bank's advantage, is also widely used. It, too, imposes a heavy penalty on a customer who makes a withdrawal during an interest period, and is not favored by the A.B.A., which says, "It can be seen that FIFO tends to discourage withdrawals. It may also discourage customers."

The same survey showed that approximately 10 per cent of the nation's banks use the DD/DW method. However, it is used by nearly all banks in the major metropolitan areas, where competition for depositors' dollars is especially keen. Since the method of crediting interest is by far the most influential factor in determining how much your savings earn, it may pay those who live in rural areas or in smaller cities to bank by mail. If nothing but low-earning methods are available in your own locality, watch bank advertisements in the financial sections of newspapers from nearby metropolitan areas. You might be able to double your earnings on savings by going a little afield.

Grace days and bonus interest

Grace days are also something you can take advantage of to increase earnings—considerably, sometimes. You may see bank advertisements that say "deposits received by the tenth of the month earn interest from the first of the month." In other words, the bank is permitted to allow you interest on deposits before they are actually received. How long before is the grace period. It is usually 10 days but varies with the bank and also with banking regulations.

Banks not using the day-of-deposit-to-day-of-withdrawal method of crediting interest usually credit it only on amounts of deposit from the beginning of the month. If you make a deposit during a month, it won't be picked up for purposes of figuring interest until the first of the following month. For the employee who gets a paycheck during the first 10 days of a month, or a businessman making frequent deposits, selecting a bank that offers the maximum number of grace days can add quite a bit to earnings, since a full month's interest

would be paid on money that otherwise would earn no interest that month.

Bonus interest also affects earnings. As an example, one savings bank that advertises 5 per cent interest on savings explains in smaller type that it actually pays regular interest of 4½ per cent, but pays an additional ½ per cent interest as a bonus on funds that stay in the account to the end of the quarter. If your savings are in an institution that pays bonus interest, you may find it feasible to delay withdrawals until the quarterly bonus is paid.

A very special case: how to make more than the law allows
When you search for a safe and profitable place to put your savings, keep in mind that the amount of money you can deposit may make a big difference. Financial institutions, like most business enterprises, treat bigger customers better. You might turn out to be a big customer more easily than you think. Consider the case of Morton, whose firm has just transferred him from Ohio to New Jersey.

Morton is not rich, but he sold his house just before leaving Ohio and he has a check for $10,000 in his possession when he arrives in New Jersey. Ordinarily this money would provide the down payment on a new home in New Jersey, but Morton and his wife decided to rent for a year or two while they take their time finding exactly the house they want. Meanwhile there was that check for $10,000. Morton knew about time deposits. He knew that the maximum interest bank could pay on passbook savings, at that time, was 4 per cent while 5 per cent was allowed on a time deposit's CD (certificate of deposit). He wasn't averse to the house money earning an extra $100 year, so when he took his check into his new bank in Jersey, he asked one of the officers about CDs.

This happened to be a period when money was extraordinarily tight, and banks were having trouble coming up with the money their regular business customers wanted to borrow to meet routine commercial needs. The VP in the bank immediately looked interested. "How much did you have in mind?" he asked.

When Morton said $10,000, he asked "Would you like to put into brokered CDs?" That was new to Morton. "Explain, please."

The VP went on to say that the head of a small manufacturing company had been in the bank the day before, wanting a loan of $25,000. He was one of the bank's regular customers and had an excellent credit rating, so it hurt when they had to tell him that tightened reserve requirements had made loan money so scarce they were being forced to say "sorry" to some good customers. But the loan officer su

gested a way out. He asked the manufacturer, "Would you be willing to pay a premium if we can find the money?" "I wouldn't say I'm willing, but I'll have to," was the reply. "I need the financing."

The bank, acting as broker, had promised to search around for the money. Morton was the first good source it had found. And the deal it offered him was a brokered CD. If he was willing to tie his money up for a year, the bank would lend it to the desperate manufacturer at, say, 6 per cent. The bank would pay Morton the legal rate of 5 per cent, but the manufacturer would also pay Morton a special bonus; Morton agreed to 1¼ per cent. So for a year Morton's house money was earning a total of 6¼ per cent, $125 more than it could legally earn in a savings account.

No nationwide figures are kept on the amount of money earning premium interest through brokered CDs, for the existence of these arrangements is not officially recognized, either by the banks or by repositories of financial statistics such as the Federal Reserve Board. But if you should happen to run across one of these deals, it would be perfectly safe to enter into it. In theory, you would be lending your money—just as Morton did—to one of the bank's customers. In practice, however, your money is technically a time deposit in the bank. It is therefore insured up to $15,000 by the FDIC. You can't lose.

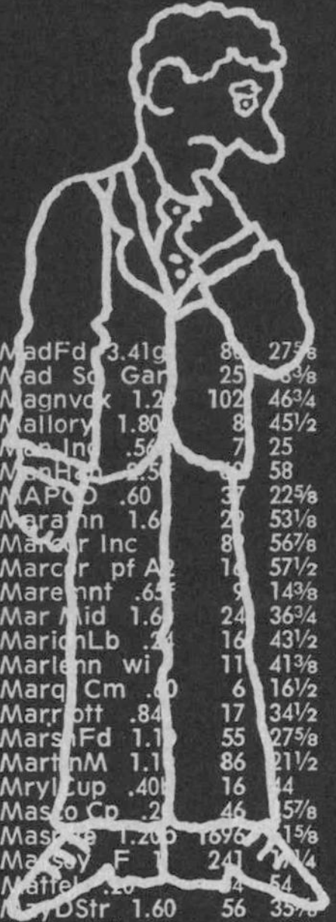

Column 1

High	Low	Stock	Sales	High	Low	Last	Chg
36¾	22½	GlfRes pf1.30	8	23⅜	23⅜	23¾	22¾ − ¼
27⅞	22⅛	GulfStaUt .96	1183	23¾	23¾	23⅛	23¼ − ½
81	73½	GulfSU pf5.08	z100	73½	73½	73½	73½ ...
70¾	60½	GulfSU pf4.40	z10	63	63	63	63 − ⅜
50¼	2	GulfWln .40a	604	25	26½	25	26¼+1⅛
203¾	98½	GulfW pf3.50	1	102	102	102	102 +3½
84	51	GulfW pf3.87	11	52	54½	52	54½+2
77¼	68	GulfW pf5.75	2	68⅜	68⅜	68	68
38½	22⅝	Gulton Ind	39	24¼	25	24	25 +1⅛
49	41¼	HackWat 2.20	4	41⅞	41⅞	41⅞	41⅞+ ⅛
48½	39⅞	HallPrt 1.40a	1	40½	40½	40½	40½ − ½
57	43¾	Halliburt 1.05	86	48⅜	48⅜	47	47¼−1¼
21⅜	13⅝	HamWat .31f	19	14⅝	15¼	14⅝	15¼+ ¾
38½	27¾	Hamm Pap 1	28	28¼	28¼	28¼	28¼ ...
23	17¾	Hammnd .70	22	18¼	18⅝	18¼	18¼ ...
48¾	35	HandlImn .68	13	36	36⅜	35⅞	35⅞ ...
34⅞	27½	Hand Har .72	33	28⅜	28⅜	28	28¾+ ⅛
44¼	23¾	HanesCp .90	27	23¾	23¾	23¾	23¾ ...
44⅞	40½	HannaM .30	7	41⅜	41⅜	41⅛	41⅜ − ¾
76	54½	Harcourt 1	6	61¼	61¾	61¼	61¼ − ¾
75¼	63	Harris Int 1	36	66	66	64¼	65⅛ − ⅝
27½	21	Harsco Cp 1	19	21½	22¼	21¾	21¾ ...
39⅛	33	HartSMrx .80	6	33¼	33½	33	33⅜+ ⅛
39½	24½	Harv AI 1.20	34	25½	25½	25⅛	25 − ¾
21¼	8	Hat Corp .40	2	10½	10½	10⅜	10⅜ − ⅛
37½	31	Hawli EI 1.32	12	32½	32½	32	32 + ⅛
29¼	20¼	Hayes Alb 1	12	21	21	20¾	20¾ − ¼
30½	19¼	Hazeltine Cp	25	25	25¼	24	24 − ¾
37½	21⅜	HeclaMng .70	66	23½	23¾	23	23¼+ ¾
34	28¼	Heinz HJ .84	46	30	30	29	29 − ½
23¼	14⅞	Helene Curt	28	15⅛	15⅝	15¼	15½+ ½
25¼	17¾	Heli Coil .60	33	20½	20½	20	20 − ¼
24⅜	17¼	HellerWE .60	124	18⅛	18¾	18⅛	18⅝+ ½
102½	76½	Heller pf4.07	55	78⅝	80⅝	78⅝	80⅝+2⅜
32⅛	20¼	Helme Pds 1	10	21¼	21⅞	21¼	21⅞+ ⅞
29	20⅞	HelmrhP .10	15	23¾	24¼	23¼	24¼+ ¼
10⅝	6¾	Hemisph Cap	13	7	7⅛	7	7⅛+ ⅛
10¾	9⅝	HemiInc .43g	4	9⅞	9⅞	9¾	9¾ ...
53⅝	38⅞	Herc Inc 1	50	39⅝	40¼	39¼	39⅛ ...
31⅛	25½	HershFd 1.10	17	26⅞	27⅛	26⅞	27⅛+ ⅛
39⅝	32½	Heublein .75	21	32¼	32⅝	32	32 − ⅝
95	75¼	HewPack .20	123	83½	83½	81¾	81¾−1⅝
37¾	21¾	High Voltage	987	22	22½	21½	22⅜+ ¾
70⅞	51¾	HiltonHotel 1	97	57	60½	57	60½+3⅛
44	23¾	Hitco .15	174	26⅜	27⅝	26	27¼+1¼
53½	42¼	Hobart Mf 1a	2	43¼	43¼	43	43 ...
28⅜	15½	Hoff Electrn	89	24¾	25⅜	24¾	25⅛+ ¾
47¾	40⅞	Holidy Inn	138	41¼	41¾	40¾	41½+ ¾
70	48	HolidA 1.70b	3	64¼	64¾	64¼	64¾+ ¾
37¼	23⅛	HollySug 1.20	11	23⅞	23¾	23¾	23¾ − ⅛
46	27⅞	Homestke .40	62	30	30½	29¼	29¾ − ¾
140¾	107¾	Honewyl 1.20	47	129½	130⅜	129½	130¼+2
47¼	32½	Hoov Bl 1.20a	7	34	34	33⅝	33⅝ − ¼
21	13	Hotel Cp Am	27	16½	16¾	16	16¼ ...
24	17¾	Houd Ind .80	21	17¾	18	17¾	18 + ¼
27⅞	20¼	Houg Miff .40	6	22⅛	22¼	22⅛	22⅛ ...
45⅜	37¾	HousehF 1.10	34	38⅝	39¾	38⅝	39¾+1⅛
136¼	116	HousF pf4.40	9	117	118	114	115 −1
69¼	59	HousF pf2.37	4	59½	59½	59½	59½+ ¾
47	37	HoustLP 1.12	42	37½	38	37⅛	38 − ¾
56	38⅝	HoustNGs .80	31	39⅛	39¾	38⅞	83⅞ − ¾
47¾	37½	HouGs pf1.50	3	38½	38½	38½	38½ − ⅛
28⅛	22½	How John .40	x31	23⅛	23¼	23	23 ...
37¾	27½	Howmet .70	34	32¾	33	32½	32¾ − ⅛
83½	67¼	HudsnB 3.40a	9	68	68½	68	68 + ¼
24¼	18	Hugh Hat .40	13	20¾	20¾	20¾	20¾+ ⅛
35¼	29⅝	IdahoPw 1.60	36	30½	30½	29¾	30 − ¼
19¼	14	deal Basic 1	51	14⅛	14¾	14	14⅜ ...
72½	52¾	III Cent 1.50	5	53¼	54	53¼	54 +1
79½	60¾	III Cen pf3.50	11	62	62½	61¾	61¾+ ⅝
41¼	33⅝	III Pow 1.80	35	34⅜	35	34⅛	35 + ¼
18¾	11⅝	Imp Cp Am	176	14¼	14¼	14	14 − ¾
52¾	30	NA Cp 1.40	113	31⅞	32½	31⅜	31⅝+ ¼
17¾	13½	Income Capit	10	14	14⅛	13⅞	14⅛+ ¼
11¼	9¼	In CCum .58g	1	9½	9½	9¼	9¼ − ⅛
42½	27¾	Indian Hd .60	36	28	28¼	27⅝	28¼+ ¼
55⅞	40	Ind Genl .80	160	51	51	50¾	50¾ − ⅝
31	25⅛	IndplsPL 1.50	14	26½	26¾	26⅜	26⅝+ ⅜
116	101	Ind PL pf6.25	2	100	101	100	101 ...
13	8⅝	InElMex .52g	6	8⅝	8⅞	8⅝	8⅞ ...
28⅛	24⅜	IndBancp .80	14	24⅜	24½	24⅜	24⅜ − ¼
55¼	41¾	IngerRand	38	41½	42⅜	41½	42 + ¼
46½	36	IngRd pf2.35	33	36½	37¾	36½	37¾+1¾
42⅝	33	Inland Stl 2	148	33⅛	33½	33	33⅛ − ¼
27¼	19½	InmontCp .76	31	20¼	20½	20	20½+ ¼
73¼	67	Inmont pf4.50	z410	68½	68½	67½	67½ − ¾
32½	22⅝	InsilcoCp 1	25	23	23	22¾	22¾ − ¼
52⅞	42¾	InspirtnCop 3	16	46½	47¼	46½	46¾+ ¾
49	38¼	Interco 1	43	38¾	38¾	38¾	38¾ − ¾
40⅜	30¾	InterlkSt 1.80	9	32¼	32⅞	32¼	32⅞+ ⅜
334¾	291¾	IBM 4	406	332½	339½	332½	337¾+6¼
57½	45¼	IntFlaFr .40b	12	49¾	50¾	49¾	50¾+ ¾
38	30	Int Harv 1.80	167	30¼	30¾	30	30⅛ − ⅛
23	17⅞	Int Hold 3g	19	18⅞	18⅞	18⅜	18⅜ − ¼
58	41¼	Int Indust	83	45	46	44¾	45¾+ ¾
75	56	Int Ind pf1.70	10	60	61	60	61 +2
24⅜	13⅞	IntMiner .25p	208	14¼	14¾	14	14½ − ½
36⅜	22½	Int Mng .20g	92	24	25	23¾	23¾ − ¼
41	31	IntNick 1.20a	153	36¼	36¾	36¼	36½+ ¼
46	34¾	Int Pap 1.50	148	38¾	39¼	38¼	38¼ ...
19¼	11⅜	Intl Rectif	25	12	12⅝	12	12⅝+1⅛
46⅜	32¾	Int Salt 1.40	8	32⅞	33⅛	32⅞	33⅛ − ¼

Column 2

High	Low	Stock	Sales	High	Low	Last	Chg
34¾	26⅞	MadFd 3.41g	88	27⅜	27⅝	27	27⅜ − ¼
12⅜	7⅛	Mad Sq Gar	25	8⅝	8½	8¼	8⅜+ ⅛
56¾	44⅛	Magnvox 1.2	102	46¾	47	46¾	46⅞+ ⅜
65¼	45⅜	Mallory 1.80	8	45½	45¾	45⅛	45¼ − ⅛
38⅞	23½	Mon Ins .5	7	25	25¼	24¾	25 − ¾
66¾	57¼	MngHtr 2.25	97	58	58¼	57¾	57¾ − ⅜
34	22⅛	MAPCO .60	3	22⅝	22⅝	22	22½ − ⅜
59¾	49⅝	Marathon 1.6	22	53⅛	53¼	52⅞	53¼+ ⅛
64½	46	Marcor Inc	8	56⅞	57⅝	56½	57¼ − ½
65	51	Marcor pf A2	1	57½	58	57¼	58
21¾	14⅜	Maremnt .65	9	14⅜	14½	14¼	14¼+ ⅛
35¼	30	Mar Mid 1.68	24	36¾	36⅜	36⅛	36⅛ − ⅜
52½	41½	MarionLb 1.2	16	43½	44¼	43½	44 + ¾
45¼	37½	Marlenn wi	11	41⅜	41⅜	41¼	41¾+ ¾
22¾	16	Marq Cm .60	6	16½	16½	16¼	16⅜+ ⅛
37⅞	31½	Marrott .84	17	34½	35	34½	34¾+ ¼
29¾	27½	MarsIFd 1.1	55	27⅝	28	27⅝	27⅞+ ⅛
28⅜	20	MartnM 1.1	86	21½	21⅞	21⅜	21⅛+ ½
49¾	41¼	MryICup .40	16	44	44	43¾	43¾+ ⅜
53	37⅜	Masco Cp .2	8	45¼	45⅞	45⅛	45¾+ ¾
69	55¾	Masonite 1.20	16⅞	61⅝	61⅝	61½	60¼−1⅜
25¼	16½	Massey F .24	17½	17½	17¼	17½+ ¼
51⅛	48⅜	Mattel 1.5	54	54½	53¼	53⅞+ ⅜
40½	33½	MayDStr 1.60	56	36	36⅜	35⅝	35⅜ − ⅜
48¼	38¾	Mays JW .80	3	41¾	42	41¾	42 + ½
32¼	25¾	Maytag 1	18	27	27⅜	26⅞	27 ...
44½	29⅜	MC AInc.60	28	30½	31¼	30⅜	31¼+ ⅝
36	22¾	McCrory 1.20	35	24⅝	24¾	24¼	24¼ − ⅜
87	79¾	McCrory6pf 6	z100	81	81	81	81 − ¾
92	69¼	McDermott 1	84	71½	71½	71	71 ...
35⅞	30	McDonald Cp	33	31	31	30⅜	30½ − ¾
49¾	27¼	McDonnD .40	453	29⅜	32½	29⅜	32½+3⅛
38¼	32¾	McGrEd 1.40	84	33½	33¾	33¼	33¾+ ¼
39½	33¼	McGHill .60a	8	33¾	34	33½	34 + ¼
11⅝	8⅝	McGrgDA .40	1	8⅞	9	8¾	8¾ − ⅜
131½	85	McIntyre 2	2	111	111	111	111 ...
45¼	28⅝	McKee 1.50	10	28	28	26¾	27¼−1⅜
65	42⅜	McLean .80a	15	43⅛	43⅜	43	43 − ¾
48¼	37¼	McLouth 1.60	25	40⅜	40⅜	39	39 −1¼
28¾	19	McNeil .70	15	18⅞	19⅜	18¾	19⅜+ ⅜
25	18⅝	McQuay .80b	72	24⅝	25⅛	24⅜	25¼+1½
33½	25⅞	Mead Corp	65	26¼	26¾	26¼	26¼+ ¼
65	50	Mead pfA2.80	3	49	49	49	49 −1
66½	51	Mead pfB2.80	7	52½	52½	52¼	52¼ − ¼
41	32½	MedusaC 1.20	3	33¾	34	33¾	34 + ½
60½	52¼	MelvSho 1.30	11	57½	57½	57¼	57½ ...
70	60½	Melv Sh pf 4	z110	60	61	60	61 ...
89¾	65	Memorex 1	82	82⅜	82½	81	81⅛ − ⅞
74¼	62⅜	MrecanS 1.40	2	64½	64½	64¼	64¼ − ¾
94¾	82½	Merck 1.80a	37	92½	92¾	92	92⅝ − ¼
71	67¼	Merck pf3.50	z80	67¾	67¾	67⅜	67⅜+ ¼
59¾	41½	Meredith 1	20	41½	42	40	40⅜−1⅛
12½	9½	MesabiT .33g	115	9⅞	10	9	10 + ¼
43	33⅜	Mesta Mch 2	3	33¾	33⅝	33½	33⅝+ ⅛
44½	27¼	MGM .60p	117	27¾	27¾	26¾	27½ − ⅜
53¾	23	Metrom .80	41	25½	26	25½	25⅝+ ¾
62¾	54½	MetEd pf3.90	z50	56	56	56	56 + ¾
60	42½	MGIC Inv .20	23	50½	51	50¼	50¾+ ⅝
19¼	15⅞	MichGasUt 1	23	16	16	16	16 ...
27¾	19¼	Mich Tube 1	4	19½	19½	19¼	19¼ ...
32⅞	21	Microdot .20g	46	21⅝	21⅝	21⅛	21⅛ − ⅛
26¾	12⅜	MidConIn .40	11	13	13¼	12¾	12¾+ ¼
24½	20¼	MidCnTel .88	7	20¾	20¾	20⅜	20¾ ...
25⅞	20⅞	MidSoUtil .88	46	23	23¼	23	23 ...
35½	26½	Midld R 1.40	65	27	27⅝	27	27 − ½
109	77¼	Midwst Oil 3	29	96	97¾	95¼	97¾+2¾
34½	23	MiehleGD .70	57	25¾	26¾	25⅝	26 ...
64⅞	54⅛	MileLab 1.20	9	60⅛	60½	60⅛	60½+ ⅛
40	24⅞	Milt Brad .60	47	25	25¼	24¾	25 ...
36¾	17	Minn Enterp	11	17¾	18	17½	17⅝+ ½
112¼	94	MinnMM 1.60	145	101	102½	101	101 ...
25⅞	21⅛	MinnPLt 1	7	21⅞	22¼	21¾	21½ ...
165	115	MissnCp 2.35	4	115	115	115	115 ...
28⅜	20	Miss Riv 1.20	49	20⅛	20⅝	20	20¾+ ½
36½	26¾	MP Cem 1.60	8	26½	26½	26¼	26¼ − ¼
26½	21¼	MoPubS .80b	8	21½	22¼	21½	22⅛+ ¼
69¾	51⅛	MobilOil 2.20	256	59¾	59⅝	58⅝	58⅝ − ¾
43	33½	Mohasco .60	11	36½	36⅝	35½	35⅞ − ⅜
47¼	31½	Monarch 1.40	21	31¼	31¾	29¾	29¾−1¾
61⅜	35⅝	Monogm Ind	122	40¼	41	40	40⅞+ ½
36½	30½	Monroe Eq *n	5	31⅝	31½	31½	31½ − ⅜
55⅞	44⅞	Monsan 1.80	108	45½	45¼	45	45 − ⅝
36½	29⅝	MontDUt 1.68	7	30½	30⅞	30¼	30¾+ ½
35⅜	27⅝	Mont Pw 1.68	11	29	29	29	29 + ⅛
24¼	15½	Moor McCor	24	16	16	15¾	15⅞ ...
59⅞	51½	MorganJ 2.40	36	52½	52½	52½	52½+ ½
40½	33	MorseSho .60	13	33½	33½	33	33½+ ¼
26	29¾	Mor-Nor .80	48	31½	31¼	31¼	31 ...
133½	102¾	Motorola 1	62	115¼	117¾	115¼	117 +2
54⅜	29	MtFuelS 1.68	6	29½	29¾	29½	29½+ ⅝
24⅞	22½	Mt St TT 1.24	72	23⅜	24	23½	23¾+ ⅛
46¾	30	MSL Ind 1.60	24	32	32	31½	31½ ...
30⅛	28½	Munsingwr 1	3	30	30	30	30 + ¼
35½	28	Murphy 1.20	6	28¼	28¼	28	28 ...
21	14¼	MurphInd .60	11	15½	15½	15	15 − ½
36½	26½	MurphOil .60	30	28⅛	28⅛	28	28 ...
61⅜	53½	Nalco Ch .60	47	58⅞	58⅞	58⅝	59¾+ ⅞
50½	40½	Narco Sci .60	11	45⅜	45⅜	44⅝	45 ...
35⅛	24¼	NashuaCp .44	31	40	40	40⅜	40¼+ ¾
47½	35½	NatAirlin .30	21	29½	29½	29¼	29¼ − ⅛
43½	29	NAviat 2.15g	14	29	29½	29	29¼+1
40⅜	20¾	Nat Bisc 2.20	41	52⅛	52½	51¾	51¾+ ⅛

Column 3 — S-T-U

High	Low	Stock	Sales	High	Low	Last	Chg
39¾	34	PitneyBw .68	31	35⅝	36	35½
103	78¼	Pit Coke .40	19	102½	102¾	101⅛
22	15⅜	Pit Forg .80	3	15½	15½	15½
63¾	48½	Pittston 1.20b	35	53⅝	54	53
72⅝	62¼	Plough .60	27	69⅝	69¾	68⅛
131	102⅝	Polaroid .32	465	118	119⅝	116¾
32½	23¾	Portec 1.20	6	23⅝	23⅞	23⅝
21¾	18	PotomEl 1.10	56	18⅜	18⅜	18⅛
50	44¼	Pot El pf2.44	2	44⅞	44⅞	44⅜
42	33⅜	PPG Ind 1.40	27	38	38	37¾
47¾	38⅝	PremrInd .90	2	40	40	39⅜
23	17⅛	PremIn pf.90	4	18⅛	18	18
94½	82	ProctGa 2.60	37	88	89	88
34¾	17¼	ProdRsch .28	13	17⅜	18	17¾
28	21½	PubSCol 1.06	39	22	22¼	22
37	30¼	PSvcEG 1.64	80	31	31⅝	30⅞
106½	100	PSEG pf6.80	z20	101¾	101¾	101¾
84	76½	PSEG pf5.28	z180	77½	77¾	76¾
80½	74½	PSEG pf5.05	z50	74¼	74¼	74¼
66½	61	PSEG pf4.18	z60	61	61	61
23⅝	21	PSEG pf1.40	12	21½	21⅜	21¼
49½	36½	Pub Sv Ind 2	25	3	8	39½	38
58½	50½	PSInd pf3.50	z60	51½	51½	50½
17½	15¼	PSInd pf1.08	z420	15½	15½	15½
17	15	PSInd pf1.04	z10	15⅝	15⅝	15⅝
15⅝	9½	PublkInd .75f	17	9⅝	9¾	9½
52¾	41½	Pueb Sup .48	29	47¾	48¾	47¾
24⅞	18⅝	PR Cem 1.10	6	18⅝	18⅝	18⅛
37⅞	31½	PugSPL 1.68	8	32⅜	32⅞	32⅜
60⅜	45	Pullman 2.80	13	45¾	46	45¾
33	25	PurexCp .80b	81	27¾	27¾	25¾
64	51½	Purolatr 1.60	7	59	59⅜	59
60¾	50	QuakOat 1.30	9	54	54	54
50½	37¾	QuakStO 1.40	5	43	43¼	42½
35	23⅞	Questor .50	10	24	24	23⅞
28½	21¾	RalstonP 1	99	23	23½	23
39¼	31⅜	RalstP pf1.20	2	32½	33	33
47¼	31¼	Ranco Inc .92	30	32½	32½	31½
45⅝	24	RapidAm .7	148	24¾	25¼	23¼
59¾	49	Raybestos 3	9	49	49	48⅛
67½	55	Rayette .60	6	60¾	61	60⅜
31	18⅜	Raym Int .80	15	20	20	19¼
50¼	30⅝	Raytheon .50	136	34½	35½	34⅛
48⅛	40⅜	RCA 1	220	41¼	41	41¼
108½	89	RCA cv pf 4	18	93	93	93
64	57	RCA pf3.50	z250	59	57½	59
26⅝	18	Reading Co	37	20⅛	21½	20
25	17⅞	Reading 1 pf	9	18½	19	18½
23⅞	17	Reading 2 pf	4	18⅛	18¼	18
48¼	16¼	RdgBates .25	1196	34½	38⅝	34⅛
81½	29½	RdgBt pf1.37	2	60⅞	61	60⅞
49¼	31¼	ReeveB 1.50b	3	31⅜	31½	31⅜
19½	14	ReichCh .50	38	14⅞	15¼	14⅜
17⅞	12¾	ReliabStr .60	7	13⅛	13⅜	13
61⅜	51¼	RelianEl 1.20	8	52¼	52⅞	52
86	73	RelianEl pf 3	3	74⅞	74⅞	74¼
57½	45¾	Relian fp1.60	2	46	46	46
53⅛	29½	Republic Cp	112	29⅛	30¼	28
53⅞	41⅛	RepublSt 2.50	43	41½	42¼	41¼
49¾	36½	Revco DS .40	9	39½	39⅝	39¼
38	27¾	RevereC 1.50	8	28½	28⅞	28
90⅝	75	Revlon 1.40	20	85⅝	86	85½
44¼	35¼	Rex Chn 1.50	11	35¾	35⅞	35⅜
45¼	33¾	Reyn Met .90	77	34⅝	36¼	34¼
0⅛	85	ReyM pf.450	2	86¼	86¼	86
50⅝	37¼	ReynTob 2.20	149	38¼	38¼	38
43¼	38¼	ReyTb pf2.25	105	39⅜	40⅛	39
34¼	20½	Rheingold .20	18	26½	26¾	26
32¾	23⅞	Richrdson .80	6	25½	26¼	25½
57½	46⅝	RichMerr .80	42	52	52	51
30⅝	22¼	Riegel Pap 1	14	25⅛	25¼	24⅛
34½	19⅝	RiegelT 1.20	14	20¾	21¼	20
23½	12½	RioGrand .60	29	12⅛	13	12½
13⅞	11½	RioGrn pf.80	33	11½	1	11½
31	25⅝	RivianaF .80	10	27⅝	2	27½
9½	7¼	Roan Sel Tr	346	7¼	7½	7
41⅜	34	RobshCon .70	85	36	37¼	36
38⅞	28¾	RobrtnH 1.10	7	29¾	30	29¾
42⅝	36	RobinsAH .40	4	38⅛	38½	38
11¼	34¾	Roch GE 1.20	17	28	28	27
41¼	34⅝	RochTel 1.10	11	36¼	36¼	35
35⅝	28	RockMfg 1.40	8	28½	28⅝	28
120	79	RohmH 1.60b	20	94½	95	94
39	28¼	Rohr Cp .80	133	29¼	29¾	28
38¾	30⅛	RollinsInc .18	10	36⅝	36⅝	36
25½	15¾	Ronson .50b	34	15½	15½	15
45¼	37	Roper Cp 1	2	39⅜	39½	39
35	22¼	RorerAm .70	26	23⅜	23¾	23
26	19	RoyCCola .54	32	20¼	21¾	20
56⅞	48	RoyDut 1.03g	468	50	50	49
—	—	RoyD fn1.03g	150	49¼	49½	48
25¾	15⅜	Royal Ind	42	15⅞	16	15
42¾	22⅝	RussTogs .68	14	25	25¾	24
45⅞	35½	Rubbrmd .96	6	37¾	38	37
30¼	17½	Rucker Co	77	20	20¾	19
39	30¾	RyderSys .50	28	33½	34⅜

S-T-U

38¾	25⅜	Safeway 1.10	i7	26¼	26⅝	26
38⅞	28⅝	StJosLd 1.50	23	33⅜	33½	32
57¾	40¾	StLSanF 2.40	4	41⅜	41⅜	40
38½	29¾	StRegisP 1.60				

12
Investor's guide
Making a
nest egg grow

Folklore abounds in stories of men and women who have built small investments into fortunes on the stock market. A 66-year-old post office employee salted away "at least" half a million dollars in stocks over the past 42 years, the press recounted not long ago, by investing only part of his mail carrier's salary. (He made the papers when he was arrested for evading payment of income taxes.) Investment manuals point out that if you had put $1,000 into Polaroid in the middle of the 1950s, the money would have increased to about $138,000 by 1966. And everyone has a friend who has a relative who has just made a killing by investing in a little-known electronics corporation that makes a tiny but essential part for bathyspheres.

Investing in the stock market can be made to sound ridiculously easy and profitable. At that point you should stop and think not twice, but three or four times. Before you can consider investing your money—taking certain calculated risks in the hope of gaining some meaningful return—you must have money that can truly be considered "extra." That means it is money left over after enough has been allowed for living expenses, after an adequate emergency fund has been established in a savings account, after your family's future needs have been fully provided for by life insurance. Even when these requirements have been met, you will want to compare stocks with other types of investment. Many people prefer to put their extra money into real estate, which has some advantages—stability, good return, tax breaks—but disadvantages as well, calling for sizable sums of cash, tying up assets, and consuming time for supervision.

Let's assume your extra money is modest, and you decide to start your investment program in the stock market. Certain key questions arise. How risky is it? Which stocks should you buy? Are bonds safer? How do you actually go about making a transaction? How much of your income can you safely afford to invest? For that matter, what exactly *are* stocks and bonds, in what ways do they differ and how are their prices determined?

The following account is fictional, but it explains why a corporation issues stocks, how they are sold and bid for, and why their value fluctuates. It also illustrates the difference between stocks and bonds, and we'll try to clarify such mysterious terms as "par value," "growth company," "dividends" and "price-earnings ratio." It won't turn you into a professional investor overnight—but it's a beginning.

Herb and Sal were a couple of young fellows with what sounded like a great idea, a patent on it, and a little bit of capital. Everybody they talked to said, yes sir, Autospandix sounded like just what the world needed. Herb and Sal could scrape up $5,000 each, but they cal-

culated they'd need $50,000 to get into production and reach a point where they'd start turning a profit.

So they needed other people's money to help finance the venture. The way out: take other people into their business with them. A lawyer drew up incorporation papers for Autospandix, Inc., and helped them issue stock, each share of which made the buyer an owner of a certain fraction of the company. That's what stock is; it is equity in the company, a share in everything it has any claim to: profits (and losses), machines, products, good name, buildings, even the typewriters and the pencils on the office desks.

Herb and Sal could have raised the additional $40,000 they needed by selling 40 shares of stock at $1,000 a share—or 80 shares at $500 a share—or 400 shares at $100 a share. All they needed were a few affluent relatives and friends. But that was not the way it worked out. While Uncle Gideon was good for $2,000, and a couple of others for $1,000 each, one of Sal's friends wanted a piece of the action for $20, and Herb's kid brother insisted he had to be a stockholder, though he had only $10. So it was decided that to start out, shares would be priced at $10, and they arranged for an issue of 5,000 shares. The handsomely engraved certificates said the stock had a par value of $10. Herb and Sal each spent their $5,000 on 500 shares of stock; each of them ended up owning 10 per cent of their company.

Shareholders expect a return on their investments—a share of the company's profits, usually in the form of dividends. If Autospandix had agreed to pay dividends on certain shares before others, these privileged shares would have been known as "preferred stock." In Autospandix, however, all shares had equal rights to a share of the profits; they were all "common stock."

Autospandix, Inc. scraped through the first 12 months, just getting into the black as the year ended. (It might have lost money, of course.) It closed the books on the next year with a profit of $2,500. The board of directors now had to decide what to do with the $2,500, and Uncle Gideon told the other directors:

"We can declare a dividend this year of 50 cents a share, which I suppose would make some of the stockholders happy. But as Herb and Sal have told us in their reports, the company is now producing all the units it can with present plant facilities—1,000 units a year. With the same production next year it would make a profit of approximately $3,000. But if we use this year's profit of $2,500 to buy additional production machinery, we should turn out 1,800 units a year and we could anticipate profits of about $4,500. That would be earnings of 90 cents a share, and speaking as a stockholder, I'd rather

have earnings of 90 cents a share next year than 50 or 60 cents—and 60 cents the year after, and the next after that. If we don't increase production, we'll never get much above that."

The other directors nodded, and voted to plow the $2,500 back into the company, leaving the stockholders without any dividends. Most of them understood that this is typical of an expanding business, a "growth company." Where there's enough of a market to soak up all the expanded production that can be financed, it makes sense to reinvest present profits in expansion rather than passing them out to stockholders as dividends and forgoing much greater profits in the years ahead.

Par value and market value

A month or two later one of the stockholders, Weatherspoon, needed cash and offered to sell his stock. "Well, I'm willing to do a fellow stockholder a favor if I can," said Armbruster. "I'll buy your stock."

"How much?" asked Weatherspoon.

"Why, $10 a share, of course," said Armbruster. "That's what you paid for it—and what it sells for. Says so right on the certificate: 'Par value, $10.' Why should it be worth more? Hasn't made any money for you, has it?"

"No, but it's worth more," Weatherspoon argued. "There was that 50-cent dividend that I didn't get. It went back into the company and bought more machinery—the company's worth more now than it was. And this certificate for 50 shares says I own one one-hundredth of the company. If the company's worth more, my certificate's worth more. At least 50 cents more—$10.50 a share."

Hefflefinger, another stockholder, had been listening and figuring. He knew that earnings of 90 cents a share were projected for the current year. In that case, even if he paid $11.25 a share, those 90 cents in company earnings would be an 8 per cent return on his investment this year, which sounded pretty good to him. "I'll give you $11 a share," he told Weatherspoon. "Done," said the latter.

Conclusion: The price of a stock, which is finally determined only by what investors are willing to pay for it, is generally based on a company's earnings—especially on projected earnings. And to many investors it doesn't make much difference whether the earnings are paid out to stockholders, in the form of cash dividends, or kept by the company as "retained earnings" to be plowed back into the operation. If they're retained, as Weatherspoon pointed out, they become additional company assets, increasing the worth of the company and hence of a share of stock.

Bonds—an assured income

By the end of the year, Autospandix had earnings of 90 cents a share, exactly as projected. Again Uncle Gideon thought the profits should all be kept as retained earnings and used to increase production, but now there were dissenting voices. Not everybody was so willing to forgo cash in hand—or so sanguine about the future of Autospandix. Mrs. Weasun remembered all too clearly the risks of stock investments. She had known hard times as a child after her father had lost his inheritance in the crash of 1929, and had seen her late husband's chagrin after he had plunged too deeply into promising new companies. But mainly she was interested in cash return.

"I think it's about time I had something to show for my investment," said Mrs. Weasun, "and if the chairman and the other members of the board can't see it that way, maybe we should elect a new board of directors." Others nodded.

"It's a shame not to be able to expand," said Herb, "because the market for our product is there. Right, Sal?" Sal agreed. "We can sell all we can make—five times what we're turning out now, 10 times—." He shrugged. "So," Herb went on, "we certainly need money to expand. We really need more than we'll get by reinvesting profits. And I'm certainly in sympathy with Mrs. Weasun and the others who want some income from their investment. I think they should be getting 6 per cent. Or more. Say 7 per cent." Mrs. Weasun beamed.

"So why don't we do this," said Herb. "We can issue bonds paying 7 per cent interest. Mrs. Weasun and the others who want money coming in every year can sell their stock and buy the bonds; we'll arrange to buy their stock at an agreed price, if they want to be sure of having buyers for it. We could issue"—he looked around the room—"$15,000 worth of bonds, and have more capital to expand than we'd get in three years by plowing the earnings back in every year. Issuing bonds is the most economical way to borrow that capital. The people who'd rather take a chance on sharing in the company's growth and future earnings can hold on to their common stock. The people who want an assured income from their investment now could get it with the bonds paying 7 per cent."

"How would I be sure of getting my 7 per cent?" Mrs. Weasun demanded. "Wouldn't it be just like those dividends I was supposed to get as my share of the earnings, but didn't?"

"Not at all," Herb told her. "When the company issues a bond, it has an ironclad legal obligation to pay you and the other bondholders your 7 per cent every year. You get paid before anybody gets anything else. You come in ahead of the owners of common stock. If there

isn't anything left over after we pay you, they don't get anything."

"But how can we be sure we'd be paid every year?" countered Mrs. Weasun. "What if the company has a bad year and says, 'Sorry, we don't have enough profit to pay interest on the bonds'?"

"Then the bonds would be in default," Herb answered, "and you and the other bondholders could sell all the assets of the company to get your money if necessary. Even if you had to have the sheriff auction off the company property, the sale would bring a lot more than the $15,000 needed to pay off the bondholders, plus whatever interest the company owed you."

"Well," said Mrs. Weasun, "the idea of getting 7 per cent every year sounds pretty good to me. I'm used to getting some return on my investments, and come to think about it, I *need* to get some return on my investments to balance my budget."

When Mrs. Weasun exchanged her shares of Autospandix stock for a 7 per cent Autospandix bond, she gave up her part ownership in the company to become its creditor. A bond is actually an acknowledgment of a loan, an obligation to pay at the end of a specified period (usually 20 years or more) a specified amount—its "face value" (usually $1,000). Because it will eventually be redeemed at face value, its cash worth over the years is reasonably stable; when a bond is bought or sold between the time it was issued and the time it comes due ("matures"), the price is usually fairly close to the fixed face value; this is in contrast to the price of a share of stock, which can vary greatly over a relatively short time.

Autospandix issued its bonds, raised the additional capital it needed, and in less than a year Sal had production up to 6,000 units; sales were up, profits were up, and earnings were building up to a rate of $3.60 a year. By now the people in the community who paid attention to such things were aware that Autospandix, Inc., was a lively, well-run, money-making operation. Wheeler, a fellow who consistently made money in the stock market, began to make inquiries about the company. There was no end in sight, he found, to growing sales and profits. With their patents, Herb and Sal had the market pretty well sewn up. They had both production and distribution well organized, management was strong, and it appeared they had not begun to satisfy demand for their product. They were getting to the point where they decided they should pay stockholders a nominal dividend, but they intended to put most of the earnings back into expanding production and sales. They had a course charted that would increase their production 50 per cent a year for the next four or five years —and after that, they hoped, grow at an even faster rate.

Back at his desk, Wheeler got out a piece of paper and wrote:

	Sales (units)	Earnings (net profit)	Earnings/Share
Year 1	6,000	$18,000	$3.60

Now, he said to himself, they're going to increase production—and sales—by 50 per cent a year. Earnings and earnings-per-share should go up at the same rate, at the least, and that means:

	Sales (units)	Earnings	Earnings/Share
Year 2	9,000	$27,000	$ 5.40
Year 3	13,500	$40,500	$ 8.10
Year 4	20,250	$60,750	$12.15

For a stock that's earning $12 a share, an investor who wants his investment to earn 10 per cent would pay $120 a share. "I heard that Bromley was talking about selling his Autospandix stock," said Wheeler. "I think I'd better go see him." He did, and found him talking to Hefflefinger about the stock.

"Come in," said Bromley. "Hefflefinger says he might be interested in buying my Autospandix stock. How much do you think it's worth per share?"

"I might go as high as $15," said Hefflefinger cagily. "Well, on second thought, maybe that's too high. Let's see, 90 cents of earnings went back into the company last year, and 50 cents the year before that. Add $1.40 on to what you paid for it, and that comes to $11.40. They're talking about raising earnings to $3 this year. I'd say about $14.50 a share is right."

"If you want to get rid of your stock," said Wheeler, "I'll give you $16 for it."

"Seventeen," said Hefflefinger.

"Twenty," said Wheeler.

"You're crazy," said Hefflefinger. "Twenty-two."

"Thirty," said Wheeler.

"Thirty-five," said Hefflefinger, breathing heavily.

"Fifty dollars," said Wheeler, taking out his checkbook.

"Done," said Bromley.

"You ought to be locked up," Hefflefinger told Wheeler as they left together. "You're dangerously insane."

"Wait and see what the stock's selling for in three years," Wheeler replied with a satisfied smile.

The P/E ratio

"The market," as they say, had now responded to the future prospects of Autospandix and established the price of the common stock, giving it what Wall Street calls a multiple. Divide the price Wheeler

paid, $50, by the stock's current earnings, $3.60, and you get approximately 14. This number is the stock's current price-earnings ratio, often shortened to P/E ratio, or simply multiple. In other words, the market, in the person of Wheeler, is willing to buy a share of Autospandix at a price 14 times greater than its current earnings.

If you are inclined to agree with Hefflefinger that Wheeler is dangerously insane for paying this kind of money for Autospandix, consider some recent P/E ratios for growth stocks:

Nytronics	43
Viewlex	54
Xerox	55
Varian	66
Rogers Corp.	80
Pacific Clay Products	103

Because these are growth stocks they all carry high multiples, in contrast to the P/E ratios of the staid and stable "blue chips"—for example: duPont, 22; AT&T, 15; General Motors, 14. So the multiple assigned to Autospandix by the market is really too low for a growth stock. That's only because Wheeler nosed around and got in on the ground floor. The multiple will go up when the other seekers after growth stocks hear about it and start bidding the price up.

A stock's multiple is a measure of how investors assess its future prospects. If Autospandix earnings continue to climb rapidly, and other investors take note and start bidding the stock price up, the multiple may go to 50—that is, the stock would then be selling at 50 times its current earnings per share.

A multiple of 50 does not represent a good immediate return; it's only about 2 per cent. (Wheeler, buying when the P/E ratio was 14, came in for a 7 per cent return on his investment.) When a rational investor buys a stock with a multiple of 50, he does so only because he is convinced that the company's—and the stock's—earnings will rapidly increase in the next few years. Present earnings do not concern him. Theoretically a stock's multiple should always be based on a rational estimate of its present and future earning capacity, but sometimes the ratio is merely a measure of speculative fever or of some such mysterious factor as the company's image.

In any event, the ratio only measures a moment in time. Wheeler was optimistic because he also knew Autospandix's earnings, and their steady growth was what had impressed him. Some companies have a long history of earnings growth; the market value of the stock grows proportionately. The earnings of other companies may show cyclical ups and downs with changes in business conditions but no long-

Earnings: a key to stock trends

Two well-known corporations, IBM and Bethlehem Steel, had radically different earnings records in the decade from 1959 through 1968. IBM's earnings per share grew steadily from $1.20 to almost $8, and the price of a share of stock rose from $60 to $320. As the decade closed, IBM stock was selling at a price 40 times earnings. Bethlehem Steel, by contrast, had earnings that fluctuated with industrial activity and showed no steady pattern of growth. The price of a share of Bethlehem stock dropped from $52 to $32. At the latter price, the stock was selling for less than 10 times its earnings.

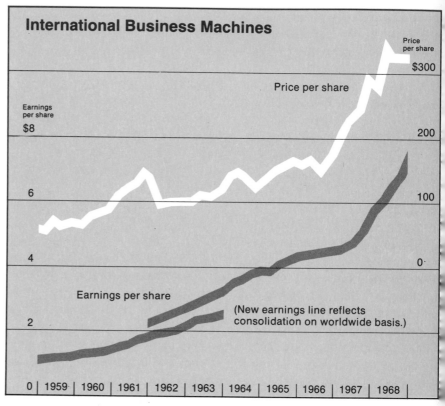

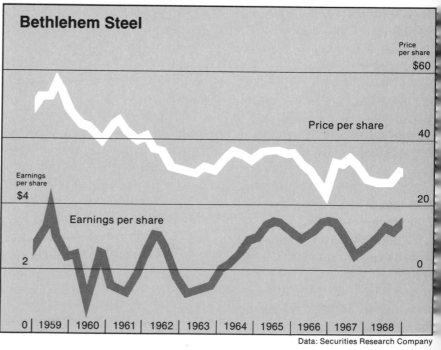

Data: Securities Research Company

term upward movement; the value of such a stock remains relatively stable, as the charts at the left indicate. You can obtain a historical perspective on a company's earnings per share by studying annual reports or such publications as *3- Trend Cycli-Graphs* (Securities Research Company, Boston), which charts prices, earnings and dividends over a 12-year period for 570 stocks.

What went on when Wheeler bought Bromley's shares of Autospandix isn't essentially different from what happens when shares of General Motors, for example, are traded in the regular stock market. The business of buying and selling stocks and bonds is essentially no more mysterious, in fact, than the extremely simplified story of Autospandix, Inc., and its stocks and bonds. True, there are many complicated variations on the simple theme, and after reading this elementary introduction no one should hock the family silver and commit the proceeds to the stock market. But the Autospandix story gives us a start on the two principal kinds of securities into which the world of market investments is divided: stocks and bonds. The next step is deciding whether you should invest in one or the other—or both—and how you should go about it. The choices depend not only on the risks you can afford to take but also on your income-tax bracket and on whether you expect current income or a future nest egg.

How safe is a "safe" investment?
Hefflefinger, by buying stock in Autospandix, and thus investing in equity, was sharing both a businessman's risk (that everything may go badly and everyone may lose his shirt) and his opportunity for profits (which may be high). There are many other ways you can become part owner of something and share the businessman's risks and opportunities. You can put up the money to open a grocery store, grubstake a gold prospector, buy a cattle ranch or underwrite a Broadway show, but most people invest in equity by buying common stock. To many people, however, equity investments seem overly risky.

Bonds and the risk of inflation
Owning the common stock of Autospandix made Mrs. Weasun nervous. She had invested $1,000 in the company, and in return she wasn't getting any money she could put in her purse. She was much happier with a bond that would pay her 7 per cent, $70 a year, year in and year out. Her income from her investment was fixed, and more or less certain, through good times and bad. Depressions may come, with interest rates dropping to 3 per cent, or inflation may

send interest rates up to 10 per cent. Mrs. Weasun still gets an un-varying $70 a year in fixed interest, 7 per cent of her original investment of $1,000, every year until the bond matures or she decides to sell it.

Fixed-income securities like bonds (and mortgages, discussed later in this chapter) are the traditional choice of the conservative investor. He views investing in stocks as fraught with risk. In contrast, as he sees it, nothing could provide greater safety than a high-grade bond. Invest $1,000 in a corporate bond paying 6 per cent, or in a government bond paying a little less, and years later $1,000 is there waiting for you. Meanwhile you've received a good rate of interest on your money, paid with certainty. Can there be any question but that this is a much safer type of investment than buying those chancy stocks?

Yes, there can. There is an important element of risk that this ultraconservative investor tends to ignore. It is the risk of losing capital through the erosion of inflation. If the value of a given sum of money dwindles over a period of years because of inflation, like a block of salt left out in the rain, the investor has suffered a loss just as surely as if stock he'd bought had dropped in price. This risk is a serious one. It has caused heavy losses to investors in the past and threatens to continue to do so in the future.

Although there have been short periods in American history when the value of the dollar has risen for a time, the over-all trend since 1820 has been ever downward. In the 20-year period from 1949 to 1969, the decline in purchasing power was so great that a 1949 dollar was worth only 67 cents by 1969. Assume you bought a 20-year, 5¾ per cent, $1,000 bond in 1949; 20 years later the maturity value of your $1,000 bond would have dropped in purchasing power to $670.

The shrinkage caused by inflation is worsened by a side effect. As your dollar lost purchasing power, income and social-security taxes rose to cover higher governmental expenses and they took an increasingly large bite out of your income (whether earned or from investments). For a middle-income family, this increased the inflation shrinkage of the dollar. To buy the same goods and services that you could get with $1,000 at the beginning of the period (1949), you would need $1,600 by the end of it (1969). Looked at another way, the $1,000 invested in the bond is then no longer worth $1,000 but has shrunk to about $560. And a 5¾ per cent interest rate no longer seems very good. The $57.50 paid each year as interest has gradually dwindled in real value to about $35, which is a return of 3½ per cent on the original value of the dollars invested.

These disturbing figures become even gloomier when you consider that inflation also affects the market price of a bond. If inflation push

es interest rates above 5¾ per cent, as it did, a bond paying this interest rate no longer seems so attractive. Other more recently issued bonds will pay more. If the bond is sold before maturity during such a period, it will bring less than its face value; the new owner, investing less than $1,000 but still getting $57.50 a year (5¾ per cent), earns interest on his investment at a rate above 5¾ per cent.

Bonds a safe, no-risk investment? What's the difference between making this sort of losing investment and buying a share of stock for $100 that you have to sell 20 years later for $56?

The values in bonds

Then why do people bother to buy bonds at all if they fare so badly in an inflationary period? One reason is that certain bonds provide income that is exempt from federal income taxes, which is appealing to investors in high tax brackets. The tax-exempt bonds are called "municipals" because they are issued by local governments or agencies —states, towns, turnpikes, bridge and tunnel authorities, school districts, in fact any unit of government other than federal. If you own a bond issued by a private company, Agglomerated Transit of San Simeon, paying 6 per cent interest, you must list the $60 annual interest on your income-tax report as ordinary income and you must pay tax on it. But if the bond is one issued by the incorporated village of San Simeon, paying 3¾ per cent interest, the $37.50 annual in-

Who should buy municipals?

You pay no federal income tax on the interest you earn from municipal bonds—bonds issued by a local government or public agency. Does that make them the investor's dream? Not necessarily. The return on municipals is relatively low when compared with that of most stocks. However, as the chart below illustrates, the higher your tax bracket, the more attractive municipal bonds become. For example, as the table shows, if your net taxable income is between $24,000 and $28,000, you reap the same net income from a municipal bond paying 4 per cent as you would from a taxable investment yielding 6.62 per cent.

Equivalent taxable and tax-exempt yields, by income bracket

If your net taxable income (joint return) is...	$8,000 to $12,000	$12,000 to $16,000	$16,000 to $20,000	$20,000 to $24,000	$24,000 to $28,000
a tax exempt bond paying...	is equivalent to a taxable investment paying...				
4.00%	5.27%	5.52%	5.78%	6.17%	6.62%
4.25%	5.61%	5.86%	6.14%	6.56%	7.04%
4.50%	5.94%	6.21%	6.50%	6.94%	7.45%
4.75%	6.27%	6.55%	6.86%	7.33%	7.86%
5.00%	6.60%	6.90%	7.23%	7.72%	8.27%
5.25%	6.93%	7.24%	7.58%	8.10%	8.69%
5.50%	7.26%	7.59%	7.95%	8.49%	9.11%
5.75%	7.59%	7.93%	8.31%	8.87%	9.52%
6.00%	7.92%	8.27%	8.67%	9.26%	9.93%
6.25%	8.25%	8.62%	9.03%	9.64%	10.35%
6.50%	8.57%	8.96%	9.39%	10.03%	10.76%

Data: J. B. Hanauer & Co.

terest you get is not subject to erosion by the federal income tax.

When it is to your advantage to invest in tax-exempt municipals depends on what the Internal Revenue Service calls your *taxable* income. The Wilsons—husband and wife and two children—have a *gross* income of $20,000. This is what Wilson's employer says he is being paid. ("Work for us, Wilson, and we'll pay you $20,000." —"That sounds good; I'll do it.") His take-home pay, of course, is considerably smaller. And his taxable income—assuming average deductions—may be only $15,600. This is something you have to watch. The people who push municipals always say: "This is how much you're ahead if you have a taxable income of $20,000"—and you think, "Why, I make $20,000; I should be buying municipals." Your taxable income, however, may be $17,000, or $15,000. But back to Wilson, with his gross income of $20,000, taxable income of $15,600. If Wilson bought the Agglomerated 6 per cent bond in 1969, he got $60, paid income tax on it of $21, kept $39. If he bought San Simeon 3¾ per cent municipals, he got $37.50, paid no tax on it, and kept $37.50.

If, however, Wilson had bought a municipal paying 4 per cent, he would have come out $1 a year ahead. He obviously has to sharpen his pencil and figure out what his taxable income is and how much he'll get to keep of a high-yield taxable investment as compared to a low-yield, tax-exempt investment.

As you can see, municipals are attractive mainly to the well-to-do. This is generally true of corporate bonds as well. The obvious advantages of bonds are the two that won over Mrs. Weasun:

■ Bonds provide steady, predictable income. Mrs. Weasun gets her check for $70 every single year.

■ Bonds can usually be sold at any time, if necessary, for something reasonably close to their initial price.

Less wealthy people can be attracted to bonds during certain periods. As your investments accumulate, you may find profit in putting extra cash into bonds at any time when they pay considerably more interest than your savings account.

T-bills: safety with (sometimes) good return

In periods of "tight money" the federal government's I.O.U.s—Government Treasury Bills or "T-bills"—may also offer an attractive alternative to the savings bank if you have sums of $1,000 or more to put away for several months. This was true in the spring and summer of 1969 when the shortage of money drove the yield on T-bills, which are sold in denominations of $1,000, $5,000, $10,000, $100,000, $500,000 and $1 million, to historic highs, and increasing numbers of

individual investors bought them. T-bills are like bonds in that they are redeemed for their face value after a specific period of time, 3, 6, 9 or 12 months. You can order T-bills by writing the Federal Reserve Bank of New York or one of the 12 Federal Reserve district banks, thus avoiding the purchase fee you would pay in dealing with a commercial bank. This gave a 1969 purchaser of a three-month, $1,000 T-bill a return on his money of as much as 7.46 per cent, a good deal more than his $982 would have earned in a bank in the same period.

T-bills are not always such a good buy. In about the same period in 1967, respective yields on three- and six-month bills were around 4 per cent. But in tight-money periods with some extra cash sitting around (many of the 1969 investors seemed to be stock-market investors who wanted to keep their money working but handy to put back in the market), anyone who likes to manage his money to eke out the last dollar is wise to check the quotations on T-bills. He can do this daily in *The Wall Street Journal* or ask his banker. Because the face-value redemption time comes closer and closer once the bills are on the market, newspaper quotations are listed by date of week of redemption. The banker will most likely ask the investor how long a period he wants to tie up his money for, then give him yield quotes. The shorter the time to redemption, the more the demand, therefore the costlier the bill and the lower the yield.

How risky are common stocks?

A model of a conservative approach to investing is provided by an organization managing $3 billion of assets, TIAA-CREF. The first half of the name stands for Teachers Insurance and Annuity Association. It was founded in 1918 to do something about the financial security of college teachers. TIAA started a retirement pension system for teachers, whose contributions were invested mainly in bonds and mortgages—fixed-income investments—as was considered proper in those years for maximum safety and assured results.

By 1952, it became evident to the directors of TIAA that fixed-income investments had failed. A report published 15 years later gave this account of their thinking: "Inflation . . . made it painfully evident that a guaranteed, level amount of income wasn't enough to give real security during retirement years. . . . Between 1940 and 1950 rising prices had cut the purchasing power of anyone living on a fixed income almost in half. But more moderate inflation can take its toll too. For example, the 1.9 per cent average yearly rate of price increase since 1950 had cut the purchasing power of fixed-dollar incomes 8 per cent by the middle of 1967."

Inflation-proofing retirement

One way to prevent money set aside
for retirement from losing value
because of inflation is to invest it in
the stock market. The Teachers
Insurance and Annuity Association
recognized this fact when they formed
the College Retirement Equities Fund
(CREF) in 1952. As the graph shows,
each share in this common-stock fund,
worth $10 at its inception, had risen
in value to more than $40 fifteen years
later (it earned substantial dividends
as well). Even when dividends are not
counted, the fund had done better for
its members than if it had put their
money into bonds or other fixed-
income investments.

Even mild inflation, then, can pose a serious problem. Investing
the teachers' contributions in equities was presumably the answer
—but the directors of the fund wanted to be as certain as was humanly
possible that equity investments could provide the assured and stable
income that the retired teachers needed. In an elaborate study, fixed-
income investments were compared with common stocks over the
period from 1880 to 1951. Various combinations were computed for
the 71-year period to provide TIAA with the answers it wanted: "How
would [a retired teacher] have fared in depression, in prosperity? In
war, in peace? In inflation, in deflation? How about a short or a long
working lifetime, a short or a long retirement?"

In every combination of conditions, the investor was better off
with part of his savings continually invested in stocks.

As a result of the study, the College Retirement Equities Fund
(CREF) was created. As a teacher contributes to CREF he acquires
"accumulation units," or shares in the fund. A report on the first 15
years of experience showed that the accumulation unit, worth $10.43
in the first month of the fund's existence, had increased in value to
$40.58 at the end of the 15-year period.

Probably the most elaborate study made of the hypothetical results that might have been achieved by long-term investment in
common stocks was conducted at the University of Chicago's Center
for Research in Security Prices. A computer was programmed with

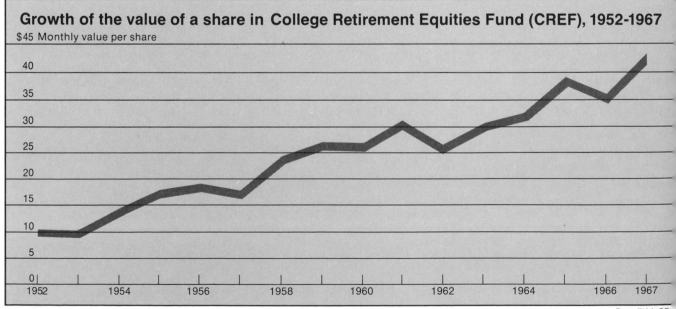

Growth of the value of a share in College Retirement Equities Fund (CREF), 1952-1967

$45 Monthly value per share

Data: TIAA-CR

40 years of prices, dividends and capital changes (1926-1965) for more than 1,800 stocks listed on the New York Stock Exchange. Runs were made through 820 different time periods in many combinations of those 40 years to see what happened to a hypothetical investor who had put an equal sum of money into each of the stocks.

He would have had a gain in 91 per cent of the 820 periods (and in 95 per cent of the periods if only the postwar years are analyzed). Over the entire 40 years, he'd have had an average rate of return of 9.3 per cent, compounded annually; in the 20 years after World War II his average rate of return would have been 12.6 per cent.

This study, taken with the similar TIAA-CREF study, indicates that despite up-and-down jiggles of the economy the prudent stock investor who is in for the long haul runs little risk of having his life's savings wiped out—and meanwhile earns a high rate of return. Common stocks look better than fixed-income securities like bonds when the many elements of risk—inflation, depression, war, variations in income —are taken into account. Does that mean everyone should sink all his savings in the stock market? Not necessarily. The directors of TIAA-CREF were cautious at first. When the equities fund, CREF, was established, it was at first stipulated that every dollar going into equities had to be matched by a dollar going into fixed-income investments; that is, a teacher could allocate no more than 50 per cent of his total pension contribution to the stock fund. But after 15 years of experience with the combination of fixed-income and equities investments, TIAA allowed teachers to put up to 75 per cent of their contributions into stocks. The rest is placed in stable investments.

How to buy stock

If you know somebody who wants to sell the stock you want to buy, theoretically you can make a deal directly with him, just as Hefflefinger did with Bromley. That doesn't happen often. Nearly always you need a middleman: a broker. You pay a modest commission for this service—the fee on a $1,000 transaction would be in the neighborhood of $17. The man you'll come to think of as "your broker" is likely to be one of a brokerage firm's "registered representatives," an employee who provides information and accepts your orders. The actual buying and selling for your account is done by someone else—one of the firm's senior officials who is qualified to deal in a formal security market. There are two main types of market where stocks change hands: one is the exchange, the other the over-the-counter market.

The exchange is the best-known securities market. The first one in America was born in the 18th Century under a buttonwood tree in

New York's Wall Street, where dealers in securities began meeting informally to buy and sell. This group formally turned into the New York Stock Exchange in 1792. The New York Stock Exchange, "the Big Board," is the best known, but there are other exchanges in New York and in many of the large cities of the country.

In all, the mechanics of a trade are the same. Brown and Jones are two men who live in widely separated parts of the country, have never met and never will, but are about to do business with each other. Brown has been talking to his broker about investing a couple of thousand dollars. National Chalkline seems a good choice if it can be bought for not more than $20 a share. The broker may have an electronic gadget on his desk that, after he punches a few buttons, will "give him a quote"—indicate the price—on National Chalkline. Or he may pick up his phone and ask his head office in New York for a quote, after which he tells Brown that the stock is "19 to a quarter." This means that, at the moment, there are offers to buy National Chalkline for $19, and offers to sell it for $19.25. The quote is not a fixed price like the one on a can of beans in a supermarket, but a high figure (that asked by those willing to sell) and a low figure (that offered by those willing to buy).

"All right," says Brown, "let's buy 100 shares." His order to his broker is an offer to buy "at the market"—that is, at the best price possible, probably between $19 and $19.25. But what the actual price will be is unknown at this point.

Meanwhile somewhere else in the country, our other man Jones has been telling his broker that he needs a couple of thousand dollars for his boy's college expenses, and thinks that his shares of National Chalkline might be the thing to sell. How's the market for it today? His broker gets the same quote: 19 to a quarter. "All right," says Jones. "Sell it." Jones, too, has made an uncertain commitment—to sell at the market, whatever that may be at the instant of sale.

The brokerage firm acting for Brown phones a message to one of its representatives at the New York exchange, telling him to buy 100 shares of Chalkline. This "floor trader" will close the deal.

The consummation of Brown's transaction involves certain elements of business in an Oriental bazaar. Trading takes place on "the floor"—one huge, very noisy room dotted with booths called trading posts. Each post is manned by "specialists" who among other duties serve as auctioneers of one or a few kinds of stock. The post where Chalkline is traded is now the destination of the representative of Brown's brokerage firm. "How's Chalkline?" he asks, as the representative of Jones's brokerage firm arrives at the post, having received

HOW TO READ A STOCK MARKET REPORT

Daily newspapers use abbreviations to report stock market activity. Not all papers report on the same markets or use exactly the same code, but the excerpts interpreted below, taken from *The Wall Street Journal*, are typical.

Securities traded on the N.Y. Stock Exchange

1 High-Low: Highest and lowest prices paid for the stock so far this year.

2 Stocks: Name of the company—usually abbreviated.

3 Div.: Amount of the quarterly dividend paid most recently on each share.

4 Sales in 100s: Number of round lots (100 shares each) sold that day. Odd lots (less than 100 shares each) are not included.

5 Open: Price at which the stock was first sold that day.

6 High: Highest price for that day.

7 Low: Lowest price for that day.

8 Close: Price at which stock sold in the day's last transaction.

9 Net Chg.: Difference between the closing price that day and the closing price at the end of the preceding business day.

	1		2	3	4	5	6	7	8	9

—1969—		Stocks	Div.	Sales in 100s	Open	High	Low	Close	Net Chg.
High	Low								
33½	21¼	Carlisle	.60	43	21	21⅞	20⅛	21⅛	− ⅛
81	73	Caro C&Oh	5	z210	73	73	73	73	− ½
40¾	33¾	CaroPLt	1.42	15	33¾	33¾	32¾	32¾	−1¼
44	31½	CarpTch	1.60	26	32¾	33	32¼	32⅜	− ⅝
43½	34½	CarrierCp	.60	123	37¼	38½	37¼	38½+	⅝
35½	30½	CarrGn	1.72g	2	31⅝	31⅞	31⅝	31⅞	− ⅛
23¾	16⅞	CarterW	.40a	106	19⅞	20⅛	19⅜	19⅝	− ½
22⅛	14¾	Case JI		43	15¼	15⅜	14¾	14¾	− ½
27	22⅜	Case pf A1.44		4	22⅛	22⅛	22	22	− ⅜
40⅛	31⅛	CastleCke	.60	160	31	31	29½	30¼	−1¼
54⅞	42¾	CaterTr	1.20	184	50¼	50¼	49	49¼	−1¼
19⅛	11	CCI Marqdt		126	11⅞	11⅞	11⅛	11¼	− ⅜
56½	35	CCI M pf1.25		2	36¼	36¼	36	36	.....
34¾	25⅛	Ceco Cp	.80	29	25½	25½	25	25	− ⅝

To follow the fortunes of Castle & Cooke, Inc., the huge Hawaiian manufacturing, food-processing and landholding concern, look for its abbreviation, CastleCke, and read across. The stock had been as high as 40⅛ and as low as 31⅛ this year (*left columns*), and appeared to be heading lower. The first sale this day was for only 31, some shares sold for as little as 29½, and the final sale of the day brought just 30¼—a drop from the previous day of 1¼ (*right columns*). A fair number of shares —16,000—changed hands (*center column*), showing that stockholders were willing to sell even at the lowered prices. An equal number of purchases had to be made, of course, the buyers possibly attracted by the 60-cent dividend.

Securities traded over the counter

1 Stock: Name of the company—usually abbreviated.

2 Div.: Amount of the quarterly dividend paid most recently on each share.

3 Bid: Price dealers are willing to buy at.

4 Asked: Price dealers are willing to sell at.

5 Bid Chg.: Difference between the bid price that day and the bid price at the end of the preceding business day.

	1	2	3	4	5

Stock & Div.	Bid	Asked	Bid Chg.
Consumers Nt	10¼	11	.....
ContAm Life 1	27	30	.....
Cont Mortgag	26¾	27½+	¾
Criterionln .20	54	56 −	½
Crum Frst 3½	7t	73 +	1¾
CrumFrpf 2.40	56	58 +	½
Eastern Lif In	9½	10½	.....
Empire Genrl	10½	11 −	½
Emp Life Am	3⅞	4¼	.....
Empl Grp 2.40	55½	56½	.....
EmpReinsur 2	73	74½−	½
Excel Inv .01d	4⅛	4½−	⅛
Excel NY .40	7½	8¼	.....
FamilyLife 5k	25	26	.....
FarmHoln .25	7¾	8¾	.....
FarmNWld .12	34¾	35¾−	1
Fidel Dep 1.52	50	52	.....
FideltyCp .20d	14½	15¼−	½
FideltyUn .17b	60	64	.....

Securities not listed on an organized exchange are traded "over the counter"—that is, between individual dealers. Newspapers reporting these stock prices list only the most active issues. Because not all are traded daily, the listings (*left*) show the prices dealers are willing to buy at (Bid) and the prices they are willing to sell at (Asked), rather than the prices of actual sales, as reports of exchange trading do (*above*). The third column, Bid Chg., shows the change from the previous day's bid. Thus, Continental American Life Insurance Company, abbreviated Cont Am Life, paid a dividend of $1 the previous quarter. If you wanted to sell it, you could get about $27 per share (Bid). If you wanted to buy it, you could for some $30 per share (Asked). The actual price would be between those extremes. There was no change in the bid price from the previous day.

by direct line the order to sell Jones's 100 shares. Both hear the specialist for Chalkline stock answer, "Nineteen bid, offered at a quarter."

Every broker has the obligation to get the best possible price for his client, whether it's a buying price or selling price. Brown's man could say, "All right, I'll buy Chalkline at 19¼," and fill Brown's order. But first he'll try to get the price down a little.

Jones's man, hearing that 19 is being bid for the stock, could without further ado have sold Jones's shares at $19—but he too must try to get a better price for his client, if he can. But he knows he can't get more than $19.25, since somebody is already trying to sell Chalkline at that price and finding no takers.

Brown's man, to see if he can get any action at a better price than 19¼, tries a bid of 19⅛ for 100 shares. Jones's man, considering this acceptable, replies "Sold 100 at 19⅛!"—and Brown and Jones, who've never met and never will, have concluded a $2,000 transaction between them—or, to be exact, one of $1,912.50. In addition, each pays his brokerage firm a commission of $26.13.

This is the mechanism referred to as the "auction market." Somebody has stock he's willing to sell, somebody else wants to buy it, and they haggle over the price until they arrive at a figure they will both accept. Notice that Brown did not buy stock from his broker, or from the exchange. He bought, through intermediaries, from an individual stock owner, Jones. When you buy a share of stock, there has to be an owner somewhere who is selling it. And when you sell a share, there has to be someone willing to buy it.

Bearing this in mind, suppose that someone wanted to sell his shares in a company because he had just heard the news that the president of the company had departed for Brazil with a couple of suitcases full of money, the treasurer was off to Pago-Pago with a snake charmer, and the chairman of the board had committed suicide. Several hundred other stockholders, also having heard the news, would be trying to sell at the trading post. Buyers would make successively lower offers as time went by. By the time they got around to the first piece of paper saying "sell 100 shares," the stock might have dropped 20 points below its earlier quote. You can't always be sure of what you can sell a stock for—or buy it for—regardless of what the quote was when you placed your order. You can, of course, specify your price —but then you cannot be sure when, or if, a trade will be made. One good argument for investing in the stocks of the biggest and best known companies is that large numbers of their shares are traded every day, and a buyer—or seller—can almost always make a transaction within a fraction of a point of the quoted market price.

To have its stock traded on an exchange, or "listed," a company must meet certain specifications: it must have issued a minimum number of shares, have a minimum number of stockholders, and be above a specified size in dollar value. The stocks of companies that cannot be —or do not want to be—listed on the exchanges are traded "over the counter" (OTC); these are the unlisted stocks. This second market for stocks has an undeservedly bad reputation with many people. "Over the counter" gets confused with "under the counter," and a notion exists that in this market many shady transactions take place. For technical reasons that we won't go into, the stocks of many leading financial institutions—multibillion-dollar banks and insurance companies—are traded OTC. It's true, on the other hand, that the stocks of a lot of lesser companies that can't make it on the exchanges, and for which there is a very thin market, are also traded this way. It's not by any means the flea market for junk stock, but you do find some odd ones here, and until an investor knows his way around the market he might do better by sticking to the more or less known quantities on the exchanges.

The OTC has no forum for trading—no building or room in which the traders can gather for the auctions that take place on the exchanges. A broker will shake the grapevine, using a telephone-telegraph system to shop around among other OTC dealers, to find who is offering the best selling price (or buying price). This is a "negotiation market," in contrast to the auction market of the exchanges.

To supplement this introduction to the workings of the market, you can get literature from the exchanges or the larger brokerage firms. A free booklet, "How to Get Help When You Invest," is available from Department TL, New York Stock Exchange, Box 252, New York, N.Y. 10005. And if one of the numerous offices of the brokerage firm of Merrill Lynch, Pierce, Fenner & Smith is near you, walk in and ask for a paperback copy of *How to Buy Stocks.*

When to buy stock

People talk about "getting in at the bottom," buying stocks when "the market is down." By "the market" they mean the average price of stocks. Individual stock prices fluctuate individually, and almost never do all prices rise together or fall together. The averages are literally only indicators of the state of the market at a particular time; to some professionals their patterns suggest future trends.

There are several different kinds of averages, such as the New York Stock Exchange Composite Index and the Dow Jones. (Actually there is more than one Dow-Jones average; what's usually understood

A barometer of ups and downs

When the stock market is said to be "up 10 points," what is usually meant is that the venerable Dow-Jones Industrial average went up 10 points. The DJI is based on the average prices paid for 30 blue-chip stocks; it has recorded up-and-down fluctuations of the New York Stock Exchange since 1896. General upward and downward movements of stock prices are symbolized on Wall Street by "bulls" and "bears"—the rising bull market of 1962-1966, when the DJI soared from less than 600 to nearly 1,000, was followed by a short bear market in which the average quickly dropped below 750.

by the term is the Dow-Jones Industrial average, or DJI, which is based on a group of 30 old-line, blue-chip stocks traded on the New York Stock Exchange.) Frequently one type of average may disagree with another, one showing the market up while the other indicates it is down. All the averages, taken over extended periods of time, reveal that stock prices, taken together, change in two characteristic ways. There are short-term, day-to-day fluctuations, and there are long-term movements that slowly rise and fall like great ocean swells, carrying the entire market up or down over periods lasting months or years—the bull markets (averages rising) and bear markets (averages falling). If you think the market is going to go up, you're "bullish"; if you think it's going to go down, you're "bearish." Recent years marked by bear markets were 1962 and 1966. In 1962 the DJI fell more than 200 points, a drop of nearly 30 per cent, and in 1966 a decline of about 26 per cent occurred.

But even in those bad years the investor who took a long view of the averages would have seen evidence of a continuing rise in stock prices. And if he followed this guide he would have done fairly well. Suppose in 1958 he had invested $1,000 in the 30 stocks that are averaged in the DJI; a decade later—despite the slumps of 1962 and 1966—this initial $1,000 would have become $1,881 (and this figure

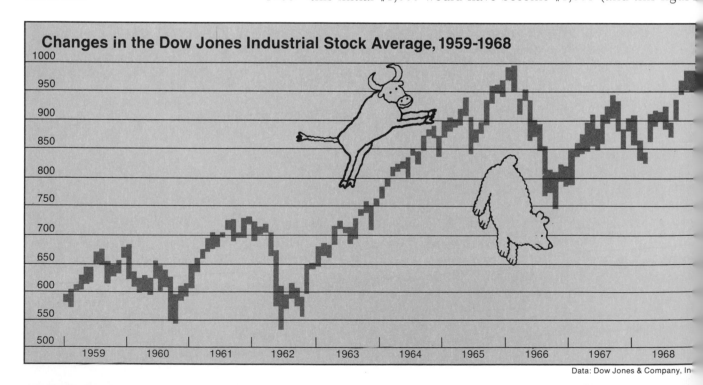

Changes in the Dow Jones Industrial Stock Average, 1959-1968

Data: Dow Jones & Company, Inc

doesn't take into account the substantial dividends his shares paid).

Unfortunately many small investors are misled by the averages. Those who are swayed by mob psychology, which may heavily influence averages on a short-term basis, almost inevitably buy too late and sell too soon. The mob doesn't buy until a roaring bull market has almost reached its peak and profit fever is at a high pitch. Then, stirred by tales of the money everyone is making in the market, the mob comes rushing up to climb on the bandwagon—just as the bandwagon tops the rise and starts down. And the reverse is true on the other half of the trip. Hopefully hanging on, to recoup its losses, the mob rides downhill with the bear market until hope finally gives way to the gloom and despair that have accumulated during the decline —thickest, of course, right at the bottom, which is where the mob finally gives up and sells out. The professionals are so certain the amateurs are always wrong that they watch for signs that small investors are selling heavily; then the professionals know it must be time for them to start buying, for the run uphill.

There is a better way to invest in stocks than following the mob. And it does not involve any attempt to outguess the market in its short-term variations. It does require close attention to long-term economic trends that over the years affect the value of stocks.

Dollar-cost averaging

The investor who keeps stolidly plugging away at a systematic investing plan, periodically putting his money into well-chosen equities through the minor ups and downs of the market, actually has working for him a phenomenon which is called dollar-cost averaging. It's a way of making money despite temporary declines in the market.

Consider a seven-month period during which the price of a stock declines 60 per cent—from 50 to 20—and then recovers. Let's say our investor puts $100 into the stock each month. During the decline and recovery he makes seven purchases, at the following prices:

$50
40
30
20
30
40
50
———

$260 ÷ 7 = $37.14—average price of the stock

**The trouble with too many
beginning investors is
that they are more interested
in tips than in facts.**

Since he bought at both high prices and low ones, each regular month-ly sum brought him differing numbers of shares:

Price per share	Number of shares purchased with $100
$50	2.0
40	2.5
30	3.3
20	5.0
30	3.3
40	2.5
50	2.0
	20.6

At the end of the seven-month period, after the price recovered to $50, the 20.6 shares our investor bought have a value of $1,030. He paid a total of $700 for them, and has gained $330.

That's a nice piece of change for a man who ignored temporary swings in the market and bought stocks on a systematic plan. His record looks even better if you compare it with that of the average buyer of the same stock during this period of decline and recovery. This average buyer paid the average price: $37.14. If he bought the same number of shares, he, too, owns 20.6 shares worth $1,030. But he paid $765 for them, and his gain was $265—25 per cent less.

Which stocks to choose

"The trouble with too many beginning investors is that they are interested in tips, not facts," says Robert Metz, a financial columnist for *The New York Times*. "Thousands of people who wouldn't trust a Fuller Brush man with a $5 order are aching to commit their life savings in stocks the names of which they can neither spell nor identify. If this sounds like a good way to lose money, it is."

Buying stocks blindly in the hope of making a killing is gambling, not investing. To invest in stock is to become a businessman. You are going into partnership with a businessman, or a number of businessmen, and you should go about it as knowledgeably as you would, we hope, if you were using your capital to buy a piece of land, put up a building and go into the business of manufacturing franistats. You would want to know a great deal about the financing of a business, the value of land and buildings, the potential market for franistats, the complexities of making them, and most of all, the abilities of the company's managers. The same sort of facts are needed if you are going to make prudent investments in stocks.

First, the investor is confronted with a great variety of terms and financial instruments. There is not just "stock," but a puzzling assortment of types of stock. It is also possible to borrow from a broker part of the purchase price of a stock, although such "buying on margin" is more common among speculators, who soon sell what they buy, than among investors, who expect to keep their stocks.

Next, the investor needs a keen sense of the shifting balance of demand for and growth in various businesses. For example, home building may slow down for two, three or four years. The construction industry's profits are then low and its stocks seem unattractive. But a backlog of demand is accumulating and a look at population statistics will tell the investor how many housing units are going to be needed in the next year or two. The demand for housing brings political actions; housing is subsidized, mortgage money is freed, construction is encouraged. Conceivably, construction stocks might then indeed be a sound investment. The potentials of different industries vary tremendously. During the seven years between 1961 and 1968—a period of prosperity—home furnishings stocks rose 483 per cent, while automobile stocks gained less than 40 per cent and steel stocks dropped more than 25 per cent.

Once you've put your finger on a growing industry, you still must evaluate the individual companies within the industry, identifying the ones that have the product, the management and the financial structure to take advantage of the growth opportunity. The electronics

Booms and busts: not universal
While one industry is advancing, another may be losing ground, for the fortunes of whole industries go up and down, sometimes quite independently of what is happening to the economy generally. And the fortunes of individual investors follow suit, depending on how well they have done their homework. During the eight years covered in the bar graph below, a period when stock market prices as a whole advanced 43 per cent, the home furnishings industry, for example, literally took off, with stock prices increasing nearly fivefold. At the same time, steel stocks dropped in average price some 30 per cent.

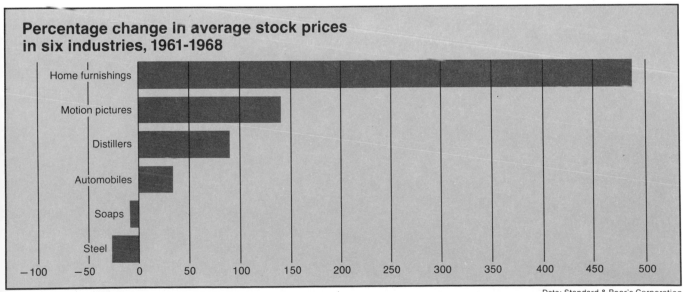

Percentage change in average stock prices in six industries, 1961-1968

Data: Standard & Poor's Corporation

industry, as an industry, boomed in the quarter century after World War II—but some electronics companies went broke.

And finally, once you've mastered the art of deciding which company's stock to buy, you'll find that knowing which ones to sell is just as important. There is almost no stock that you can afford to "put away and forget." The market history of even the solid old blue-chips is replete with examples of stocks that an owner should have sold a long time ago. For example, there was a time many, many years ago when New York ferry boat stocks were considered one of the safest investments in the world; Brooklyn was a booming suburb and all its residents would have to use ferries to get to and from jobs in Manhattan —that is, until the Brooklyn Bridge was built.

In effect, you have to evaluate each stock you own periodically, judging it as though you were trying to decide whether to buy it. Your decision to hold or sell it will be based on the same factors you weighed when you were looking for the right stock to buy.

When you sell, of course, you must take the broker's commission into account as a cost item, just as you do when you buy. And if your stock has increased in value, you will owe the federal government its share in "capital gains" tax, the amount depending on your tax bracket and on how long you have owned the stock.

Stock watching can become a more than sparetime occupation. You will need the advice of an expert.

Brokers and other pros

Newspaper and magazine articles provide essential information and general counsel for the investor, but most people want individual guidance. You can turn to a private investment counselor, who will take on all the work and make all the decisions; most such counselors concentrate on large accounts—$100,000 and up—but if you look hard you can find a few who will lay out the welcome mat even though you have as little as $5,000 in your pocket. Similar services are offered by trust officers of banks, but only half a dozen banks in the country accept individual investment accounts of $25,000 or less.

That leaves your broker. The ethics of his profession require him to guide you in specific ways. Before he opens your account he is supposed to inform himself about your financial affairs to the extent that he can responsibly counsel you on certain points. Should you invest in stocks at all—or should you first obtain more adequate insurance coverage, or a larger backlog of savings? How much can you afford to invest in stocks? What investment objectives are suited to you? Do you want immediate return or long-range growth? If you are subjected

**A key rule is diversify:
Don't put all of your eggs
in one basket.**

to a quiz on these matters when you approach a stock representative thinking he may become "my broker," that's an encouraging sign.

Whether his specific advice will be valuable is something else again. A broker may know his business thoroughly and yet not suit you. He may take a persistently conservative outlook and keep pushing pale-blue chips when you want at least a few aggressive growth stocks. Or he may try to argue you out of a solid, middle-of-the-road mutual fund and steer you into the new-issue firecrackers that double your money in five weeks—maybe.

Adding to the problems of the little guy is the tendency of brokerage firms to discourage small accounts. With more business than they can handle, they understandably prefer to weed out the least profitable accounts—those of investors with a few hundred dollars, who don't give a broker very much in commissions to repay him for the time generally needed to educate newcomers about the market. (This isn't necessarily true of all brokerage firms—some actively promote monthly investment plans for investors with small accounts.)

The problem of diversification

Even with the best professional guidance, the investor of modest means has to protect himself against the risks inherent in the market. A key rule is diversity: don't put all your eggs in one basket. You could, of course, start off with a few shares of U.S. Steel or Standard Oil of New Jersey, since there is very little chance that such hearties will fold up, or that you'll be wiped out by plummeting prices. But some of the most famous blue-chips have been so laggard over long periods of time that investors have carried them at little or no profit. You might as well bury your money in the back yard. This is not investing.

The prudent man selects a balanced group of stocks, a diversified "portfolio." He spreads his money among a select few companies, and among a select few industries as well. To diversify properly you need considerable capital; a conservative view may put it as high as $40,000. Obviously, few people have that kind of money. One way to handle the problem of diversification is to let somebody else do it for you: buy a share of a portfolio of stocks that is already diversified. That's what you do when you invest in a mutual fund.

Mutual funds: a piece of some big action

A mutual fund is a pooling of funds for investment. Let's say that the Smiths, Browns, Joneses and other families in a neighborhood decide to pool their capital and invest it in stocks. Twenty families contribute $500 each, creating a fund of $10,000 for investment. To indicate the

contributors' equity in the fund, each family is issued "shares," say 50 apiece; thus each share is worth $10 at the start. A part-time portfolio manager is hired, he invests the $10,000 wisely, and at the end of the year the portfolio has appreciated 12 per cent so that it now consists of stocks worth $11,200. The stocks also earned dividends; these, minus expenses of operating the pool, are divided up among the members, although part might also be reinvested in more stock.

If the fund were liquidated now, each share would be worth $11.20; this figure is the "net asset value per share." It's simply the fund's net assets, divided by the number of shares in the fund. The net asset value per share will increase and decrease proportionately with fluctuations in the total worth of the stocks owned by the fund; a share is partial ownership of all those stocks.

Now the Wilsons move into the neighborhood, hear about the investment pool, and want to participate. The shareholders, at this point, can go in one of two directions.

They can say: "Let's not let this get out of hand. We have 1,000 shares outstanding, which seems to be about the right size. Let's not issue any more shares. If somebody's moving out of the neighborhood and wants to sell his shares, he's free to sell them to anyone he wishes —but that's the only way that shares will ever be available for purchase." They have started a "closed-end investment company."

Or they might say: "The more the merrier. If the Wilsons want in, tell them to toss in their contribution, and we'll run off a certificate for another 50 shares. Same goes for anybody else who wants shares." Jones then rises and says, "Another thing. What if somebody moves out of the neighborhood and wants to sell his shares? Does he have to stay locked in until he can find somebody who is willing to buy them? I don't think he should. Why not let him turn them back into the fund—cash them in, so to speak—and get whatever the net asset value per share is at the time?" The shareholders vote "aye." They have decided to have an "open-end investment company," otherwise known as a mutual fund.

The open-end fund is open at both ends: the way in is open, and the way out is open. The financial structure of the closed-end fund, on the other hand, is similar to that of any company which, like Autospandix, issues a specified number of shares of stock in order to raise capital and thereafter lets buyers find sellers and vice versa, through the mechanism of the market. This is, in fact, how the shares of a closed-end fund are marketed. There are about 50 such funds; the shares of some are listed on the exchanges, while others are sold in the over-the-counter market.

The name "mutual fund" is now usually applied only to the open-end type. They have been around, after a fashion, for a number of years but it wasn't until 1940 that their mushroom growth started. The funds then in existence had total assets of about $448 million. Some 30 years later the total assets were about $55 billion—more than a hundredfold increase. In 1969 there were more than 600 funds in existence; more than a hundred of them were only a year old.

Shares in most of the large, well-known funds are sold by brokerage firms or special mutual fund sales organizations—in any case, by salesmen. They charge a commission, or "load," on every sale; typically 8.5 per cent is subtracted from the sum the investor hands over —which comes to roughly 9.3 per cent as other kinds of commissions are ordinarily figured and stated. The SEC, and some congressmen, have taken the position that mutual fund loads are too high. Spokesmen for the load funds counter the criticism by pointing out that a person investing small sums, under $250, pays about the same "load" for mutual fund shares that he would pay in "round trip" commissions for buying and selling stocks. (When you "sell" mutual fund shares, they are redeemed by the fund—there is ordinarily no cost to the investor.) Only on transactions exceeding $250 or $300 do the mutual fund's commissions begin to be much greater than the broker's fees would be for a round trip.

In addition, you also pay an annual management fee, deducted from dividends earned by the fund.

The mutual funds that charge commissions are classified as "load funds." There are a few funds that charge no sales commissions at all. These are the "no-load funds." A check for $1,000 for shares in a no-load fund buys shares with a net asset value of $1,000. Having 100 per cent of your investment capital working for you makes a difference as the years go by. Suppose you invested $1,000 in a no-load fund and another $1,000 in an 8.5 per cent load fund, each of which gave you 12 per cent a year return; after 15 years you'd be $466 ahead in the no-load fund—nearly half your investment.

Most no-load funds are adjuncts of investment counseling services. The profit to the inaugurators of the fund comes essentially from the business it generates for the investment counsel. Until recently most no-load funds have remained small and relatively obscure. No salesman comes knocking on your door to tell you about them. If you ask a broker about mutual funds, he is understandably uninterested in the no-loads, since he is neither invited to sell them nor paid for arranging the sale. To acquire shares in a no-load fund you have to spot their advertisements (usually small ones in the financial

pages of newspapers), write the fund for a prospectus,[1] and then make up your mind to send in your check without any help from someone sitting alongside you and offering you the use of his pen. You can get names and addresses of many no-load funds by writing the Investment Company Institute, 61 Broadway, New York, N.Y. 10006.

The high cost of front-end load

If you decide to buy shares in a mutual fund, load or no-load, you find a choice among several different systems of membership in the club. You can arrange for an "open account," buying as many or as few shares as you wish (usually above a minimum of $100 to $500 worth) whenever you feel like it. The return on your investment —which consists of both gains in capital and earned dividends—is usually paid in cash at regular intervals, like ordinary stock dividends. But some funds may, at your request, automatically plow the returns back into additional shares so that your investment grows by compounding, with returns accumulating from earlier gains, like an untouched account in a savings bank.

Many investors, determined to build good nest eggs, prefer to buy mutual funds on a "voluntary accumulation plan." After the initial purchase, you agree to buy additional shares at regular intervals (the amounts are sometimes stipulated, but often there is no minimum). Returns from dividends are usually reinvested automatically to help the nest egg grow faster. You can terminate your agreement to make regular purchases any time you wish; there is no requirement that you make a fixed number of purchases.

A third plan, sold to many low-income families, is an installment purchase scheme called the contractual plan. This arrangement requires much lower minimum investments than most voluntary plans, most frequently $25 a month. But the buyer signs a contract agreeing to make the investment regularly for a stipulated period, typically 10 to 15 years but in some cases 25 or 30. He is committing himself to a total investment over that time of perhaps $3,000 to $9,000. He can quit making his monthly investments any time he wants, but if he does so he loses much of his money because of the way the sales commissions are charged. Regulations limit such contractual plans to 9 per cent of the total investment stipulated in the contract, and as much as half of the total commissions may be deducted from the

---

[1]*Governmental regulations require that investors be provided with the prospectus before they make an investment. Some mutual fund companies may require you to sign a statement that you've read it when you place an order.*

amounts the investor pays in during the first year. Thus, a 15-year contract calling for $25 monthly investments involves a total investment of $4,500. Total commissions, at 9 per cent, would amount to $405; half of this, $202.50, can be deducted from the buyer's first-year payments of $300. Because such a large part of the sales commission is levied in the early part of the contractual period, these plans have become known as front-end load funds.

The disadvantage of front-end loading becomes clear when you consider what happens to our 15-year investor if he pulls out after one year. He has paid in $300 and gets back less than $100 (plus appreciation, if any). His percentage of loss decreases as the years go by, but there will always be some loss unless he completes the term of the contract. Funds selling contractual plans argue that this threat of loss acts as a strong incentive for the small investor to keep up his payments, whereas he might lack the self-discipline for it if there were no

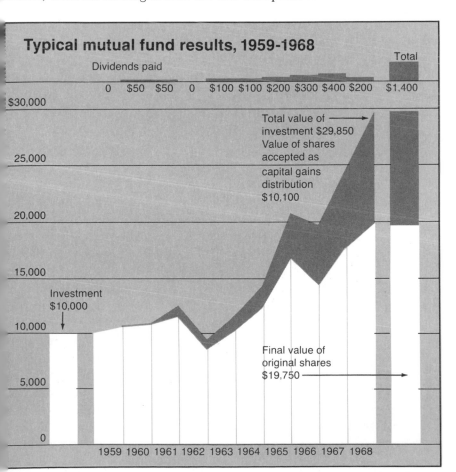

Portrait of a mutual fund
When you are appraising a mutual fund, search its sales literature for a chart similar to the one at the left. It tells at a glance how the fund has performed over a span of time, usually 10 years. In the hypothetical—but typical—fund charted here, a 1959 investment of $10,000 would have tripled by 1968. The original shares purchased for $10,000 would have increased in value to $19,750, as shown in white at the bottom of the chart. The value of additional shares distributed from "capital gains"—the profits the fund has made by buying and selling stocks—would have added $10,100, as shown in black in the middle of the chart. And cash dividends paid, represented by the black bars across the top of the chart, would have added $1,400 for a total return of $21,250 on the $10,000 invested.

threat. In any case, there is a built-in penalty in the front-end load plan, since the investor has relatively little money at work for him as an investment during the early period of the plan.

Getting rich in mutual funds

The sales literature for a successful mutual fund is almost guaranteed to stimulate visions of instant riches. The most tantalizing exhibit is a graph like the one on page 353, showing the long-term growth of an investment in the fund. It starts with an assumed investment of $10,000 ten years in the past and indicates how that multiplied to become $31,250 (including all dividends). That is indeed a real bundle, even when you stop to recall that (a) you didn't have anything resembling $10,000 to stash away 10 years ago, and (b) this 10-year period was one of almost unparalleled prosperity.

Over recent years mutual funds have done well. Regular investments—not of an imaginary $10,000 but of realistic sums—might have fallen short of making you rich but would have provided a comfortable nest egg. If you had made an initial investment of $500 and subsequent investments of $75 a quarter every quarter for 10 years in a typical no-load growth fund—neither high-flying nor ultraconservative—and reinvested all the returns, you would have $5,700 to show for your $3,500 investment. This is the equivalent of 8.4 per cent interest, compounded quarterly. If you had made the same deposits in a savings bank paying 5 per cent interest, compounded quarterly, your $3,500 would have grown to $4,562. Of course, you might not have been able to find a bank paying 5 per cent.

And yet mutual funds are not necessarily the secret of financial security. Some funds have given their investors 60 to more than 100 per cent return in a single year, and some have averaged less than the savings-bank rate over a 10-year period. For one thing, not all mutual funds have the same financial goals. They may aim for fast profit, or modest but sure income, or steady long-term growth or some compromise of these conflicting goals.

The first funds established invested in the kind of securities that a trust officer would prescribe to generate safe, dependable income for widows and orphans: bonds, preferred stock, and perhaps some very reliable old blue-chips that haven't missed paying a dividend for 75 years. This type is labeled an income fund, or, if it admits a cautious mixture of common stocks, balanced fund. Over the long term, returns have been relatively low.

More venturesome funds began to seek long-range growth of capital as well as current income, and they are now known as the growth

How different kinds of mutual funds increased their share values (1958-1967)

Type of fund	Objective	Variability of share value	Per cent increase in share value
Growth, small	Maximum growth of capital	High	404.3
Growth, large	Growth of capital	Generally high	320.8
Growth-income	Capital growth plus income	Moderately above average	245.4
Diversified stock	Capital growth plus income	Average	196.8
Diversified stock	Capital growth plus income	Below average	183.5
Balanced	Income plus some capital growth	Low	138.6
Income	Income	Low	162.5

Mutual funds, growth or income
The proper mutual fund to pick is the one whose investment objectives most closely match your own. Do you want to gamble on highly variable stocks that may rocket in value or drop like rocks? Or do you want to be conservative and settle for stocks not likely to grow much in value but with a good record of producing steady income in the form of dividends? There are mutual funds for either goal and there are others that combine the two in various proportions. This chart shows how funds with differing objectives increased their share values during the decade 1958-1967—a time when the market rose steadily. As was to be expected, the growth funds showed the greatest percentage increase per share—but at the greatest risk of loss of capital if the market had turned.

income funds. In the past few years the emphasis has shifted to the out-and-out growth funds, which invest almost exclusively in common stocks judged to have growth potential.

Many growth funds are quite volatile, that is they rise more in market upswings and drop more during declines than balanced funds. The investor who cannot afford a decline in income for a period of time should take a growth fund's record on volatility into account before committing his capital to it. The fact remains, however, that over the 10-year period from the end of 1957 to the end of 1967—which includes the two major market declines of '62 and '66—investors in the growth funds fared substantially better than those in any other type. In the reference annual "Investment Companies" (Arthur Wiesenberger Services, New York), figures covering these 10 years show that, on the average, growth fund shares increased their value at least twice as much as those of income funds (*see box*).

Averages, as noted earlier, can be misleading. One growth fund had a 725 per cent increase in share value, another had 237 per cent. An investor could have done as well as 237 per cent in some of the income funds. One ill-managed fund increased an investor's $1,000 to $1,390 during the 10 years—not quite as good as having it in a savings account at 3½ per cent compounded semi-annually, and not as safe. The moral is that you don't want to invest in a mutual fund simply because mutual funds, on the whole, have done quite well, or be-

cause investing in a mutual fund sounds like a good idea. Mutual funds come in all grades—good, average and poor—and the investor has to select one as carefully as he'd select individual stocks.

Don't be greedy. Funds that have shown spectacular profits —doubling or tripling their share values in a few years—are often the super-aggressive ones known as the "go-go funds." They are not so much investing as speculating. Read the prospectus carefully; the figures on portfolio turnover will give you a clue to the fund's policies. If a fund you are considering turns over 100 per cent or more of its holdings in a single year, caution is in order. Such a fund may be using your money to play the market, a very risky game indeed.

Generally, the 10-year record is a good indication of what you may expect from a fund in the future. If it is above average it is a sign that the people managing the investments know what they are about; it's hard to stay lucky for 10 years running. You will find this information graphed in the prospectuses of all funds. In recent years, publications comparing mutual fund performances have proliferated. They advertise in the financial sections of the major metropolitan newspapers—most heavily in *The New York Times* and *The Wall Street Journal*. The most comprehensive collection of information on mutual funds is "Investment Companies," usually known in financial circles as "the Wiesenberger report" after its former publisher. It sells for $45 a copy, but you can look at it free in the larger public libraries or in a broker's office.

Mutual funds provide a simple way to keep your capital growing in an expanding economy and thus protect yourself against inflation. They relieve you of tasks that the investor of modest means usually finds difficult to manage: research in economic trends, knowledgeable selection of stocks, supervision of sales and purchases, and most of all, diversification. Precisely because they take all the decisions out of the individual investor's hands, many people don't like them and prefer to buy stocks on their own. Either way, prudent investment in equities such as common stocks has proved, over the long haul, a reasonably safe and effective means of building a nest egg.

BECOMING A MAN OF PROPERTY

Investing in common stocks has attracted large numbers of ordinary people only in recent years. The old-fashioned way to make extra money work for you was to buy a piece of property and collect the rents. It's still a very good way. You see where your capital is going; the investment is a building you can inspect, not fractional ownership of an amorphous corporation whose business you don't understand.

and whose managers you have never met. Your money is protected against inflation, for rents go up, usually more steadily than stock prices. The return can be excellent—10 to 20 per cent or more.

Before you rush downtown to canvass the real-estate agents, though, remember that there are, naturally, drawbacks:

■ The investment will be sizable—for a not very impressive two-family house, perhaps $25,000 to $50,000, of which 20 to 40 per cent will probably have to be your own cash as down payment.

■ The investment is not a liquid one—if you need your money, selling the property takes time and could involve loss rather than profit.

■ You are buying a business and in most cases becoming its manager, with all the demands on time and skills that go with the role. It's you who get called up when a water pipe breaks at 3 a.m.; it's your property that is being damaged; and it's your job to get the plumber over to make repairs as fast as possible.

■ You can be caught in a financial squeeze if the property fails to attract desirable tenants at desirable rents, or if it requires extensive repairs *(see Chapter 7 on buying an existing house)*. Professional assistance in selecting and appraising property is well worth its cost.

How to make money in real estate by going into debt

Although a large proportion of amateur investors in real estate merely succeed in losing the family capital, or at best diminishing it, there are extraordinary opportunities for profit in real estate for those who know the ropes—and know which rope to pull on, and when.

The formula for profits in real estate is basically simple: (1) stay as deeply in debt as possible, and (2) make maximum use of the depreciation allowances you are permitted to take.

The first principle means that you use as little as possible of your own money and as much as possible of someone else's. The *Harvard Business Review* phrased it a little more elegantly: "[One] central source of profitability in real estate is the ability to use a great deal of borrowed money on a very modest equity basis."[2]

What this does can be seen in a grossly oversimplified example, assuming you buy a $30,000 two-family house to be used as a rental property. You rent each unit in the house at $250 a month, a combined total of $6,000 a year, and for the moment we'll forget about all your expenses except mortgage charges.

(A) You invest $15,000 of your own capital as down payment, giv-

ing you a one-half equity in the property, and get a mortgage loan of $15,000 to finance the rest of the cost.

(B) You invest $6,000 of your own money, for a one-fifth equity, and go into debt for $24,000.

First-year charges on the two mortgage loans (principal and interest) would amount to approximately: (A) $1,500; (B) $2,400. Here, then, is how the hypothetical return on your two investments would work out in these two instances:

(A)	
Gross rents	$6,000
Cost of mortgage charges	1,500
	$4,500
(B)	
Gross rents	$6,000
Cost of mortgage charges	2,400
	$3,600

And isn't it better to have $4,500 than $3,600? No, not when you have to invest two and a half times as much capital to get it. The important thing to an investor is yield, or percentage of capital returned, and the return in these two exaggerated instances is:

(A) 30 per cent

(B) 60 per cent

Sure, you say, 60 per cent. That's a fiction of course, for we didn't count expenses. You know how much it costs to heat your own home and keep it from falling apart at the seams; a bigger building is going to cost much more. True enough. But remember this is not your home; it's business property and the tax men take a different view of the expenses it entails.

On rental property, all operating expenses—heating, fuel, water, painting, repairs, etc., as well as property taxes—are business expenses. You subtract them from the gross rents and pay no taxes on them. But there's more you can subtract, and this is what makes real-estate investment potentially so profitable.

Let's take another look at the cash from that two-family house you bought for $30,000 with a $24,000 mortgage. Tax guidelines put the useful life of an average building at about 40 years. In theory, your building wears out over these 40 years, and at the end of the 480th month suddenly crumples in a heap and you have nothing left to show for your money but rubble. You are therefore allowed to recover one fortieth of the value of your total cost (including the mortgage) each year as a "depreciation" allowance—approximately

$750 if you use the "straight-line" method, $1,125 the first year if you choose the "declining balance" method. Let's use the latter.

To arrive at your taxable income, you subtract the following from the $6,000 received as gross rents:

Mortgage interest (principal payments excluded)	$2,040
Operating expenses and property taxes	2,850
Depreciation	1,125
Total deductible expenses	$6,015

Your tax return therefore shows that you operated at a loss of $15 for the year. That's right, a loss! You naturally pay no income tax —though you actually paid out of pocket only the mortgage charges, taxes and operating expenses, totaling $5,250, leaving you an in-pocket profit of $750 or a return of 12.5 per cent on your investment on which you pay absolutely no tax. In addition, you have your loss of $15, which you can subtract from any taxable income you might earn by shoeing horses, cutting out appendixes or whatever you do for a living when you are not managing real estate.

If this sounds apocryphal, the authorities advising developers in the *Harvard Business Review* make it sound no less so:

"Having realized abnormally large profits, via great leverage, in a successful real estate venture, the . . . entrepreneur can now shield most, if not all, of the earnings from income tax . . . [through the] relatively liberal allowances for depreciation and other expenses. . . . Frequently there is a loss in excess of the project cash flow which can be used to shield other profits from income taxes.

"But this is not the end of it . . . "

You mean it gets better? Absolutely. You take as much depreciation as you can, as quickly as you can, and then you sell the property —to another astute investor who then begins taking *his* depreciation allowances. Thus, as the *HBR* article continues, "the real estate investor can effectively have his cake and eat it too. When at the end of 10 years, for instance, he has exhausted the excess depreciation on the property he holds, he can sell it to another investor. The investor who purchases the property can then begin to depreciate the property again, at his cost basis, thus creating his own tax shield. And he can pass it on to still another investor when he, too, has exhausted the depreciation potential."

So all the talk you hear about the exceptional profits to be made in real-estate investments is true—unless you make a bad investment and lose a few buttons off your shirt, if not the whole shirt. It is easy

to spend so much money keeping up a building that you have real losses, not just paper ones. If you are not shrewd in your choice of a building and careful about maintaining it, you may find the high profits are hidden in the tax shields so well that you never find them.

Such profits almost never await the man who thinks of "investing in real estate" as picking up a vacant lot or two on the outskirts of town and waiting for the price to rise. There is a clear and important distinction to be made between real estate, meaning improved property, and land, meaning vacant or raw land. There is no tax shield in the latter instance, since land does not wear out and you may not depreciate it. There is ordinarily no current income from raw land. It just sits there and accumulates tax bills, which you pay every year while hopefully waiting for a buyer to come along and offer you more than you paid for it—plus accumulated taxes. When you buy vacant land you're gambling that this will happen. You may *invest* in real estate, but you *speculate* in land.

It's true that fortunes have been made by speculating in land, going all the way back to colonial days, and some of today's biggest fortunes are being made that way. But the land speculator (1) has a lot of money to begin with, and is in such a high income-tax bracket that the year-to-year real-estate taxes can be written off to a large extent, and (2) he buys land in large tracts which he has good reason to believe are in the path of development—or has ways of seeing to it that development comes his way to make the land more valuable.

The notion that any and all land has to increase in value because, as the cliché has it, the supply of land is limited while the population keeps increasing, is a demonstrable fallacy. Land is nowhere in shorter supply and in greater demand in the United States than on Manhattan Island. And, says Daniel M. Friedenberg, whose family has been in the real-estate business there for more than 50 years, "Manhattan has been a land investor's haven for 150 years." But only for those who knew which land to buy—for, as Mr. Friedenberg points out, "It is not generally realized, but the larger part of Manhattan's land is priced today below its value 40 years ago."

The strictures against speculating in land apply particularly to the purchase—as an investment—of "vacation and resort property" offered for sale by promoters. At best, the promoter has already milked the lots of as much profit as can be squeezed out of them. At worst, you'll find you've been defrauded into buying lots that are exorbitantly overpriced, snake-infested and, in many cases of recent record, actually under water. The postal inspectors and various attorneys-general put a number of these promoters out of business every year,

but they keep cropping up anew. When you buy a vacation-retirement lot by mail, sight unseen, you're simply asking to be defrauded.

The profits are in improved property, when you can make heavy use of someone else's money and take advantage of depreciation allowances and other tax shields. You can invest on a modest scale in single-family dwellings, two-flats, six-flats, etc., either as rental properties or for fix-up and resale. Or you can participate in the profits of shopping centers, big-city skyscraper office buildings and luxury high-priced apartment buildings as a member of a pool.

The real-estate investment trust, or REIT, makes use of pooled funds to invest in such real-estate properties in much the same fashion that mutual funds pool investors' money to purchase stock market securities. REITs are regulated by the federal government. There is one type that invests in equity in real-estate properties, and another, the mortgage trust, that invests in mortgages—a fixed-income type of security that is essentially different from equity investments. If the idea of buying a piece of the action appeals to you, information about REITs can be obtained from the National Association of Real Estate Investment Funds, 105 Mansfield Avenue, Darien, Conn.

Both real-estate and common-stock investments can provide good returns and protection against inflation. Whether you choose one or the other—or some of both—depends less on how much you can afford to invest than on your own temperament. Entrusting money to strangers is as alien to some people as being personally responsible to tenants is to others. But the point to remember is that both are investments—useful occupation for money that is truly extra. They cannot take the place of the essentials of financial security—sufficient life insurance to protect your family and an emergency reserve of cash safely tucked away in a savings account.

13
Your estate
Why it needs
planned protection

Many people think estate planning is only for the rich. If the life-insurance policies are up to date and the house and bank accounts properly taken care of, what else is there to worry about? Plenty, it turns out. A man of modest means may leave behind him assets of surprising value; $100,000 is not unusual. And the smaller the sum, the more important it may be to an heir—particularly a widow. Anyone who owns more than the shoes he is walking around in needs estate planning—or, more accurately, estate protection. He should have a carefully worked out program to make certain that his money and property go where he wants them to go and that their value shrinks as little as possible in the process. You will not achieve these objectives for yourself unless you:

■ Make a will. If you die intestate—without a valid will—what you leave must be distributed strictly according to the laws of your state; the law's way may not be your way and it can cause your family great hardship. Your estate will also be depleted by all sorts of fees and other expenses that could have been avoided.

■ Write a "letter of last instructions." This can be almost as important as the will itself. In it you can put information and advice your family will need that is inappropriate for the will itself.

■ Design your estate so that as little of it as possible will be reduced by taxes or suffer the delays and expenses of probate, a special court that must supervise disposal of a man's assets after he dies. Avoiding probate costs involves exploring the advantages of setting up trusts and of owning things jointly with your wife or grown-up children.

■ Get expert legal help at every step. Estate planning is complex, and "small estates are the most difficult to plan," says one specialist.

FIRST AND FOREMOST, YOUR WILL
The will is so crucial that failure to prepare one, or a seemingly minor lack of foresight in designing one, can visit terrible hardship on the very people it ought to protect. Take the case of Morton, a moderately successful man earning about $25,000 a year in his early forties. He and his wife had managed well. They had paid more than half the mortgage on their home; their bonus money every year had gone into well-selected stocks. They had only one financial problem: Morton's father had been in ill health and Morton supplied most of the money his parents lived on.

Then Morton died. The house and investments plus his life insurance brought his total estate to around $75,000, and the simple will he had executed years before, leaving everything to his wife, seemed adequate.

THE VAGARIES OF INHERITANCE LAW

If you die without a will, the inheritance laws of your state will parcel out your property and they will do so in a way that rarely conforms to your plans. In many states the laws are so antiquated and clumsy that they can make life miserable for your heirs; most remove at least part of the estate from the widow's control, handing it over to children's trustees or others. The list below gives a few examples of the many different ways the different states distribute property to the various kinds of survivors you might leave.

If you left a wife and one child:
■ Half the estate to your wife, half to the child.
■ One third to your wife, two thirds to the child.
■ Your wife gets the use of half the real estate during her lifetime, plus one third of the personal property. The child receives the balance of the estate.
■ Your wife gets a stipulated sum "off the top"—say, $2,000 in cash and all "intangible" property such as stocks and bonds. The rest of the estate is divided between wife and child.

If you left a wife and two or more children:
■ One third to wife, two thirds apportioned among children.
■ Wife and children take equal shares. For example, if there are four children, the estate is divided into fifths, with a fifth for the wife and for each child.

If you left your wife, your parents and no children:
■ All to your wife.
■ Your wife receives $5,000 off the top and half the residue; the balance of the estate goes to your parents.

If you left your wife and a brother:
■ All to your wife.
■ Your wife receives $10,000 off the top plus half of the rest of the estate; the remainder is divided among your brother and his descendants.

When a wife dies without having made a will, a surviving husband normally gets the same share under the law as would a surviving wife. Simply read "husband" for "wife" in the examples given above. It is evident that the laws cited above might well give a substantial share of an estate to people with no need for it—a rich brother or well-off parents—while a wife would receive much less than her husband would be likely to leave her.

But a couple of years after Morton's death his widow remarried. Soon she and her new husband began to wonder why they should keep on supporting Morton's parents. Hadn't Morton done enough, carrying the entire burden all those years? The support of the elderly couple fell to Morton's brother, a man with a small salary and a large family who could ill afford the extra expense. This brother had received no share of Morton's estate, and neither had his parents.

Morton simply hadn't thought through the possibilities the future might hold. But if a thoughtless will like his can be bad, no will at all can be worse.

Vernon also left everything to his wife—he thought. He had been saying for years, "We've just *got* to see a lawyer and have wills drawn," but he and his wife never got around to it. What he did was buy a form at a stationery shop, fill it in and sign it. The document was found among his papers after his death. But it would not pass legal tests of validity. So far as the probate court was concerned, Vernon died intestate and his estate had to be distributed according to state law.

The law then provided that one third of Vernon's estate had to go to his wife and two thirds to their four-year-old daughter. A major part of the estate consisted of an investment in a two-family house. Since it could not be divided in thirds, a court-appointed administrator was required to sell it and divide the proceeds. The building brought $30,000, several thousand less than if marketed without a forced sale, and much less than its value to the family as an investment. That sum was further reduced by the administrator's fee of $1,900. The court also appointed a guardian for the daughter, naming her mother. As guardian, the mother was strictly accountable to the court for conserving the child's inheritance until she reached 21—she even had to hire an accountant to prepare reports every two years. Legal controls on the daughter's inheritance were so rigid that the mother could invest it only in low-income bonds. The principal could not be used even to pay for the daughter's education unless her guardian-mother made successful application to the court, at considerable legal expense. The mother also had to post a bond of roughly $45,000, on which the premiums for the next 17 years would total $4,000.

'The law is a ass"

Inheritance law sometimes seems to deserve the famous epithet quoted above, uttered by Mr. Bumble in Dickens' *Oliver Twist*. Coldly logical, the laws can parcel out the property of the deceased with what may seem a total lack of common sense (*see box*). Yet these are the laws to which you consign your property when you fail to make a

An ancient phrase: "Last will and testament"

The famous old phrase above pops up in the first sentence of every will but is really an anachronism, for the word "testament" is wholly unneeded. It comes from an ancient mixture of English Common Law and Roman Law. In early English law—up to the time of Henry VIII—the document called a will followed Anglo-Saxon custom and disposed only of "chattels"; that is, movable possessions or everything except real estate. The "testament" was a separate document used to dispose of real estate. Its origin was Roman—the word is derived from the Latin verb meaning to testify. In modern law, a will can give instructions for the disposition of all kinds of property. But the old phrase "will and testament" lingers on, a curious bit of legalese.

will. Plainly Vernon's widow needed untrammeled use of his whole estate to support herself and her daughter. Instead, the law restricted her at every turn, and also cost the estate needless fees. Other laws impose even greater hardship. Imagine the tangle a widow with five young children would face if the law of her state said she and the children had to share an estate equally. She'd get one sixth of the money and each child a sixth—with each of the children's sixths having to be administered by a guardian in strict conformity with the law and the courts. As a trust officer at New York's Marine Midland Bank gently put it, "The law is less generous than husbands usually are."

The lack of a will has always caused so much trouble that as far back as the 18th Century the great English jurist Blackstone said "God's mercy is infinite but we cannot bury the intestate in consecrated soil." Yet a staggering number of people forget to make a will, or put it off until too late. Some 50 per cent of the estates probated in New York City, an area crawling with lawyers, involve no will. Even professionals procrastinate; one well-known lawyer who died intestate was Abraham Lincoln.

If the first rule in protecting estate and family is "Make a will now," the second rule is "Get help from an expert." The laws governing the manner in which wills must be drawn and executed are so complex that they seem preposterous. But they must be followed.

If a will is to stand up, certain words and phrases have to be used and certain actions performed in a prescribed sequence. One legal authority cautions that once the signing starts the witnesses should not move an inch lest a chair block from view the pen that is signing the document. On such grounds as this wills have been broken. Do-it-yourself wills are regularly thrown out of court because they weren't properly witnessed, or witnessed by someone named in the will, or because a wrong word was used. Even a "holographic will" —one entirely in the handwriting of the person making it—is not the sure-fire instrument many people think.

A properly prepared will does more than simply name heirs. It generally has several distinct sections (see pages 370-371); only one section, the "dispositive clauses," parcels out the property and assets to beneficiaries. Another, equally important, contains the "administrative clauses," which select the agents who make sure that the will's instructions are carried out. These include the executor, who administers the estate, and, if there are minor children, a guardian to look after their interests. A will may also include instructions that are unrelated or related only indirectly, to the central business of disposing of assets. It is so complex—and crucial—that you should put careful

thought into exactly what you want yours to accomplish. This homework is best done before you sit down with your lawyer to have your wishes translated into legal form and language.

Why wives are not the best executors

Most people name a friend or relative—generally the wife or husband —to administer their estates. It looks like the economical thing to do —professional executors charge fees, naturally. But when you consider the duties and responsibilities involved *(see box on page 368)* you may begin to wonder whether your wife, or Bill, your bowling partner, is up to the job. Of course, if Bill has an excellent head for figures and owns an efficient little business that almost runs itself, he would be an excellent choice. But if Bill is an average guy and as busy as most people, he might do only half a job—and that could be costly to your heirs. As for naming your wife as executrix, even if she's a competent businesswoman, she may be in no state of mind right after your death to make the decisions that have to be made immediately.

Aside from the factor of personal capabilities, there are other considerations in choosing an executor. One is continuity. If you name a friend, relative or business associate of approximately your own age and then live out a normal life expectancy, your executor will also be getting old, too old perhaps to act effectively. There is also the distance factor: If either you or your executor moves away any substantial distance, the separation can be very inconvenient. What if you died in Pennsylvania and your old pal Bill had moved to California, or was representing his company in South America?

One good solution is to name your lawyer, especially if his firm has younger associates who would provide continuity. Another possibility is to name your bank—or a bank—as executor; it must be one that includes a trust department. Contrary to general opinion, trust departments are willing to act as executors even for rather small estates and the expense is not crushing. In Iowa, for example, the cost for a $75,000 estate is less than $2,000. That fee brings expert attention from people who know the angles; what they can save on taxes and realize on the investment of assets may well offset the cost.

About 4,000 of the country's banks have the trust departments to provide these services and there's probably one near enough to you to serve. If you feel that a bank would be unduly institutional and impersonal, you can name as co-executor a friend or relative. Someone sympathetically representing the family's interests would thus have a voice in any major decisions the bank made.

If you do name an individual as executor, it's advisable to name

THE EXECUTOR'S DUTIES

A heavy burden falls on an executor, so think carefully before naming your wife or a friend. A lawyer or bank trustee is usually best able to handle such financial and legal details as these:

1 Review the immediate financial needs of survivors and arrange for living expenses.

2 Find proof of the deceased's legal residence; it is needed to start probate proceedings.

3 Determine if the house and other assets are adequately insured; buy more coverage if needed.

4 Make sure that no assets are ignored or forgotten; collect and scrutinize all financial records.

5 Retain a lawyer to file the will, and give him whatever records and information he needs.

6 See that insurance companies are notified and that everyone named in the policies is paid.

7 Locate the safe-deposit box and remove needed papers in the presence of the proper state official.

8 Notify state tax authorities of assets in estate, including cash in bank accounts. Obtain waivers from them so bank accounts can be drawn on.

9 Collect all money owed, including salary and company benefits such as bonus fund payments.

10 Deposit securities and other valuables as they are assembled in safe-deposit box or bank vault.

11 Examine the demands of all who say the estate owes them money; pay off valid claims.

12 Decide if it would be cheaper to deduct estate administration costs from the income tax or estate tax. Then calculate and pay all income taxes due.

13 Find the most economical way to compute the income taxes that will build up while the estate is being administered. Prepare returns; pay tax.

14 Prepare and file forms needed to settle federal and state inheritance and estate taxes.

15 Find out if estate owes or is owed money on real estate. Arrange for payment or collection.

16 Pay all legacies mentioned in the will and collect receipts; deliver each bequest to the proper person.

17 Manage the money in the estate in accordance with the will. Where there is latitude, consult the wishes and needs of the family, selling assets and making new investments as necessary.

18 Keep records to show all transactions, sending periodic detailed statements to everyone concerned.

19 Prepare all the detailed information needed for a final accounting to beneficiaries and to the court.

an alternate in your will in case your first nominee is unavailable or dies. Usually, too, you'll want to stipulate in the will that he or she is to serve without a bond, which is not only a nuisance but expensive.

In addition to an executor, you'll need a guardian if you have minor children. Otherwise a court will appoint one, and he would be restricted by state laws, be required to post a bond and so on. He should be chosen with even greater care than an executor, and an alternate, like an alternate executor, is advisable. What if you and your wife should die simultaneously in an auto accident—a catastrophe not unfamiliar in the U.S.?

A guardian is so important because his primary purpose is not to manage property but to manage human beings—to oversee the upbringing of children. Many people are prepared to name as guardians a sister and brother-in-law, or a sister and then as an alternate the brother-in-law. They do not often consider the possibility that the sister may die before they do, leaving the care of their children to a brother-in-law who is then a stranger to the family, perhaps even remarried. On the other hand, if the sister survives the parents for some years, the children will have been living in her household all this time—in that situation her surviving husband might indeed be the best alternate guardian. Contingencies such as this argue for thoughtful discussion with someone experienced in the problems of guardianship before anyone is named.

It is wise to notify anyone you intend to name in your will as guardian, executor or alternate of your intentions, and get his approval before the will is drawn.

Good witnesses stay put

Forethought in choosing the people who will witness your will can avoid a lot of trouble and expense in later years. Do not commandeer the nearest secretary or some casually known office associate. Courts may require a witness to testify when a will is probated: "Yes, Mr. Jackson was indeed the same person who signed the will, I saw him sign with my very eyes, he was of sound mind, and no one pressured him." When a witness has moved to another state he must be found and then flown in—at the estate's expense, of course. More trouble still is the vanished witness. How can your lawyer locate Susan and Gladys, a couple of secretaries you employed 10 years ago? Their addresses lead to bachelor-girl apartments where nobody remembers either Susan or Gladys. They, more likely than not, have married and changed their names, or moved to California, or run off to Europe with a pair of banjo players. The ideal witnesses are persons per-

Text continues on page 372

A WILL—ITS CLAUSES, ITS LANGUAGE

How a will is organized

A will's structure is as functional as a well-designed machine. The sample will below has been broken down into its distinct sections, each identified with its legal name at left below. The sections express the maker's wishes, describe how his wishes are to be carried out, and provide protection against fraud and error. The will shown here is a very simple one; you will need a lawyer to be sure your will meets your needs and legal requirements.

1 The opening recitation
This introduction always gives the name and address of the person making the will. Often, as here, it is also used to revoke all previous wills.

2 The administrative clause
This names the man (executor) —or woman (executrix)—who will see that the provisions are carried out and outlines the powers and duties he is to have. It can, as here, request that the executor serve without bond. It may also name substitute or coexecutors, trustees and guardians for minor children, and direct that funeral costs and debts be paid.

3 The dispositive clause
The heart of a will, this names heirs and what each gets.

4 The testimonium clause
The will's maker signs below this, before witnesses.

5 The attestation clause
This short statement completes the will. It attests that the will's maker was neither forced to sign nor misled into signing it in the belief that he was signing something else. The two or three witnesses whose signatures follow this clause—none of whom can be beneficiaries—must swear that the testator announced clearly he was signing his will, and that they saw him do so of his own volition.

THE ESSENTIAL CLAUSES OF A SIMPLE WILL

1 I, John Smith of 721 East 84th Street, New York City, New York, do hereby make, publish and declare this to be my last will and testament, and I do hereby revoke all former wills and codicils thereto by me at any time made.

2 First: I appoint as executrix of my will my wife; I request that she be permitted to serve without sureties on her bond and that, without application to or order of courts, she have full power and authority to sell, transfer, grant, convey, exchange, lease, mortgage, pledge, or otherwise encumber or dispose of, any or all of the real and personal property of my estate. I desire that my just debts, including the expenses of my last illness and funeral, be paid as soon as may be practicable after my death.

3 Second: I devise and bequeath all of my property, real and personal, of every kind whatever and wheresoever situated, and whether now owned or hereafter acquired, to my wife Joan for her own use and benefit forever.

4 In Witness Whereof, I have hereunto subscribed my name this 12th day of June, 1969.

John Smith

5 On the date last above written, John Smith, in our presence, subscribed the foregoing instrument and declared it to be his last will and testament, and requested us to witness it, whereupon we, still in his presence and in the presence of each other, have signed our names below. And we declare that at the time of the execution of this instrument said testator, according to our best knowledge and belief, was of sound mind and memory and under no constraint.

Rose C. Bradley   Roger F. Williams
George Jones

Dated at New York City, New York, this 12th day of June, 1969.

The arcane language of wills

Lawyers are noted for their complex jargon, and some famous examples appear in wills. But the language has a purpose: The terms have been defined over the centuries so that they have more precise meanings than ordinary language and are able to convey subtle distinctions. Below is a glossary of terms found in the will at left, plus a sampling of other unfamiliar terms your lawyer may use when he talks to you about a will.

Testator (Testatrix)
The person making a will.

Codicil
An addition or supplement to a will; if you revoke a previous will, you must revoke the codicils too.

Estate
All the property of the will's maker —including real estate, cash, stocks, bonds, life-insurance proceeds and personal possessions.

Convey
To give or sell property to another.

Encumber
To make property subject to a charge or liability. An executor given the power to encumber may, for example, pledge part of the inherited estate to get a loan.

Executor (Executrix)
The person named to carry out the provisions of a will and manage and settle the estate.

Coexecutor
A second person named to aid or, if necessary, replace the executor.

Trustee
A person named to manage trusts set up by a will.

Devise
To will real property—land and buildings—as distinguished from personal or other kinds of property. The person named to receive real property is a *devisee*.

Bequeath
To will anything that is not real property—personal belongings or stocks and bonds, for example. The property bequeathed is a *bequest* and the recipient is a *legatee*.

Administrator (Administratrix)
The person appointed by a court to perform the functions of an executor when none has been named.

Beneficiary
A person named in a will as a recipient of property.

Domicile
A legal home. A man may have many residences; his domicile is determined by "evidence of his intent"—where he votes, pays taxes and so on.

Issue
Children.

Probate
Court procedure determining if a will is valid and in order; a first step in settling an estate is to *admit* a will to probate. Also, the process of carrying out the instructions of the will in settlement of the estate.

Probate estate
The portion of an estate subject to review in a probate court; generally this is the property disposed of in a will, or by state law if no will exists. Some assets may escape the delays and expenses of probate. They include life-insurance proceeds payable to a named beneficiary, death benefits paid to survivors by employee plans, property owned jointly and assets in certain trusts.

Intestate
Lacking a valid will.

Holographic will
A will written entirely by hand by the person making it.

Nuncupative will
An oral will of personal property, made by a person during his last illness or by a serviceman during battle. Such circumstances are usually necessary if an oral will is to be accepted in court. Witnesses have to put such a will in writing as soon as possible and offer it for probate.

Exculpatory clause
A passage excusing executors of liability for any "act or omission," short of actual fraud, in connection with the administration of an estate.

Living trust
Property placed in a trust during the lifetime of the person establishing it. Also known as an *inter vivos* trust. It can be either *revocable*—the grantor can revoke the trust and take back the assets—or *irrevocable*, meaning the grantor has surrendered ownership and control. Sometimes life-insurance policies are made payable to living trusts, or a will provides that certain property is to be added to a living trust (a "pour-over" trust).

Testamentary trust
A trust created by a will so that it comes into existence only after the death of the person establishing it.

manently settled in the community, younger than you, and likely to
be easily identified and located a number of years later. The requirement for witnesses who will be readily available when needed is one
of many reasons for revising your will if you move out of state. Needless to say, a beneficiary should never serve as a witness.

His-and-hers wills

Many women shy away from considering the eventuality of widowhood. But it's usually wise to involve your wife in the planning of
your will. That way she'll know what your thinking was and why the
will's provisions read as they do. It is also essential that she have a
will of her own. Even if she has no substantial assets at present, she
may if she inherits yours; then her death intestate is likely to cause
more trouble than yours would.

You'll generally get bargain rates on a pair of husband-and-wife
wills that are drawn at the same time. However, authorities on wills
caution that the wife's will should be a wholly separate instrument.
The notion is abroad that you can simplify matters with a joint will,
which incorporates the instructions of both husband and wife, or with
mutual wills—separate documents that contain identical provisions.
Both are dangerous. They can create legal ambiguities, make it difficult for either party to revoke his or her will, and in some
circumstances result in higher taxes.

How to have the right will in the right place at the right time

Now that you've gone to all this trouble to have wills drawn for both
of you, let's take good care of them. Take them down tomorrow and
stick them in the safe deposit box, right? Wrong! A will is one important paper that should not be kept in a safe deposit box.

In most states the law requires that boxes be sealed upon the
death of the owner—even boxes held jointly by husband and wife, or
held by one with the other named as a deputy having the right of access. In such states nobody can get into the box until a representative
of the state tax commission is present to take an inventory of its contents. Sometimes a member of the family can get permission to open
the box and remove a will, in the presence of specified witnesses, but
don't count on it.

If you name a bank as executor, the bank will keep the original
will in its vault at no charge. Or the attorney who drew the will can
keep the original in his vault. A fireproof strongbox at home is a third
possibility but not a very good choice—the box can be hard to find,
its key or combination even harder. Nor are separate safe deposit

boxes for husband and wife, each containing the original of the other's will, a good choice. They cause problems in case of simultaneous deaths; then there are *two* wills sealed up in boxes.

Why wills go stale

Finally, no matter how expertly your will was drawn, or how well it has been safeguarded, it can be nearly worthless if you do not review it frequently and keep it up to date. In some circumstances it can be worthless. States have varied and even contradictory laws; a valid will in one state may be rejected by the probate court of another. But moving is only one reason for renewing a will. Here are 10 signals for will review suggested by the Bank of Delaware:

■ Parenthood. If a child comes after your will has been drawn, update the will. Otherwise the court might rule that you had neglected the new child's interest and award it a share of the estate even though you plainly intended to leave everything to your spouse.

■ Grandparenthood. The living, breathing reality of a new grandchild may shift family priorities.

■ Changing needs of beneficiaries. As children grow up and marry, some provisions made earlier become inappropriate. Advanced age or infirmity may change the needs of other members of the family.

■ Divorce or remarriage. A major change in your domestic status usually requires changes in your will.

■ Sale or other disposal of property mentioned in the will. Selling one residence and purchasing another can outdate a will. In fact, the sale of almost anything can cause trouble. Suppose you sell Grandfather's gold watch—after leaving it in your will to Cousin Dick. After your death the watch cannot be found. What is the court to do? It might, following a precedent set in a similar case, order the watch repurchased with some of the estate's assets and handed over to Cousin Dick even if he doesn't want it. A messy and needless bother.

■ Death of a witness, executor, guardian, trustee. You need a new one.

■ Family gifts. Any significant transfer of property to others in the family probably has tax implications, and wills should be revised accordingly when any such move is made. In any event, the donor's will should clearly state whether gifts made in his lifetime should be considered advances on legacies or not.

■ Family loans. If you lend money to a member of your family, your will should state whether any remaining debt should be canceled on your death. If there's only an oral "understanding" that the debt is to be forgiven, or repaid at some distant time, the executor may be duty-bound to collect at once.

■ New assets. Even small acquisitions have a cumulative effect that can outdate a will. Major changes—the establishment of a new business—should get immediate attention in the will.

■ Growth of the estate. This is "perhaps the most frequently encountered signal for will review," says the Bank of Delaware. If your estate grows significantly, you may wish to distribute it differently. Also, your tax picture may change, dictating other changes in your will.

The letter of last instructions

To a man who values his survivors' peace of mind, a letter of last instructions is as important as a properly drawn up-to-date will. It is generally addressed to a wife. It can be of immeasurable practical help to her at a time when she's grief-stricken and needs all the help she can get. It should say, in effect, "Now, look—here's how you get your hands on the cash you need quickly; here's where the insurance policies are; the first thing you should do is this," and so on. It is especially helpful if terms of the will are not effective immediately.

Among the instructions the letter can provide (*see check list on following pages*) are directions for funeral arrangements. These are sometimes put in the will, but it's more appropriate to leave such instructions for the letter, which lends itself to personal touches that would be out of place in a will. If anyone has been disinherited, a court might want to know why. The reasons can be stated in the will, but this may cause unpleasantness and even litigation. It's better to give them privately, in a letter available to the court. Since your executor also needs this information, he should have a copy. A letter of last instructions needs periodic review as often as a will, perhaps more often since the matters covered are more subject to change.

WHY IT PAYS TO GIVE YOUR MONEY AWAY

A will and letter of last instructions see to it that your estate is distributed the way you want it to be. Now you want to make sure there's something to distribute. Your bequests, unfortunately, can be badly shrunk by estate taxes and the expenses involved in legal proceedings. The worst effects on a modest estate are those of probate. This is the legal process that takes place after a man dies.

Initially the man's will, together with an inventory of assets and liabilities prepared by the executor, must be "admitted to probate." Then it is up to the probate court to find the will valid, to settle claims, to give heirs a chance to object to the will's terms, and, if all goes well, to direct the executor to carry out the terms of the will. If there is no valid will, the court names an administrator to serve as ex-

The way to protect assets is simple: Give them away while you're alive. Then, since they already belong to somebody else, they cannot be counted as part of your probate estate.

ecutor and distribute the estate according to the laws of the state.

Probate costs money—court costs, compensation for the executor or administrator, travel expenses if witnesses are called, charges for property appraisals, legal fees. The cost of settling a $10,000 estate that goes through probate may run as high as a whopping $1,350; a $75,000 estate can lose as much as $4,500. These bites often eat up small bequests—money left to grandchildren and the like. There is just nothing left for them, and the stipulations of the will cannot be carried out.

Almost as serious as these money losses are time losses. The probate estate is not turned over to the heirs until the legal proceedings are completed. A widow might be allowed a modest income from the estate, but generally the principal cannot be touched until the estate is settled. When it's a clean job with no problems, probate takes from six months to a year in most states; if there are complications, it can easily take three to five years.

It isn't always wise to avoid probate; sometimes the cost of doing so is greater than the cost of probate. But it usually pays to try to keep most assets out of the probate estate. The bulk of your estate may already be immune. Most of the money an average man leaves is insurance; so long as the policies are payable directly to a named beneficiary (and not to an estate) they are excluded from probate.

The way to protect other assets is simple: Give them away while you're alive. Then, since they already belong to somebody else, they cannot be counted as part of your probate estate, provided they were not given in anticipation of death. If you go about this properly, you can dispose of many assets and still retain control over their use. There are two main mechanisms for protecting an estate this way: joint ownership and trusts.

Most people already make use of joint ownership. Many married couples maintain joint bank accounts (for convenience; either party can use the account). This form of joint ownership is simple to set up, since the bank does the legal work for you. Homes and automobiles, too, are likely to be jointly owned. All these forms of joint ownership are useful estate protection. Establishing joint ownership of other assets, such as investments, may be a bit more complicated but it can be equally advantageous—if you go about it right. Remember, though, that joint ownership can be a financial disaster in case of divorce.

WHEN JOHN OWNS EVERYTHING BUT MARY DOES TOO

The paramount advantage of joint ownership is that property held this way—be it real estate, bank accounts, securities or whatever—becomes the unquestionable property of one of the joint owners when

Text continues on page 378

PUTTING YOUR AFFAIRS IN ORDER

Second in importance only to a carefully drawn will is what lawyers call a letter of last instructions. It should tell your wife and your executor first of all where to find the will, as well as other documents and records, but it should also give details on assets like bank accounts. Here is a check list of things the letter should mention:

1 Describe where copies of the will can be found and where the original is kept. Also give the names of all executors, trustees, lawyers or guardians involved, and explain any potentially puzzling provisions that the will may contain.

5 It is necessary to do more than simply list life-insurance policies. Provide such details as the location of the policies, premium receipts and dividend statement. Have you borrowed against any of your policies? If so, which ones, and where did you get the loan? If you have any annuities, write down where the contracts can be found. Do you own a policy on anyone else's life? Does anyone own one on yours? Don't forget company group insurance. Who is your life-insurance agent? What should your beneficiary do with the insurance check? (One widow carried it around in her purse for weeks; she had never seen such a sum before.) You might also mention any medical or disability insurance that might cover medical bills charged to the estate.

8 Put down all the relevant details about your house or other real estate. If you own your home, is the deed in your name or your wife's, or both? What bank holds the mortgage? Where is the deed? Where is a copy of the mortgage papers? Other papers you might locate are the title abstract, the title insurance policy, insurance policies on the house itself, any surveys of the property that may have been made. If you own real estate aside from your home, give the same information about it, along with the name of your real-estate and insurance brokers.

11 Make a list of your personal debts and of the friends or relatives who owe you money. Say precisely how you would want these matters settled. Do you want to forget that long-standing $50 Cousin Homer owes you?

12 The dealings with Uncle Sam will be far easier if you locate copies of your past tax returns, tell where current tax information can be found and in general give a brief account of how you stand with the Internal Revenue Service.

List essential personal papers and records and tell where they can be found. Your marriage certificate is important; so are birth certificates and (if you have them) citizenship papers, divorce or separation documents, and military service papers.

3 Describe where your safe-deposit box is, what it contains and who has access to it.

4 Describe where the family burial plot is and where the deed is located. You can also outline the sort of funeral you want and any arrangements for it you have already made.

List your checking and savings accounts and describe where checkbooks and passbooks can be found. In addition, you should mention which accounts are jointly held and who has the power to sign checks or make withdrawals. Above all tell your wife and executor where they can get quick cash—there will be lots of expenses.

7 Give the names and addresses of your employers both past and present, and outline the various employee-benefit plans you've belonged to, such as company group life-insurance policies, profit-sharing schemes, retirement funds. Also list any fraternal organizations or unions you have belonged to. They may provide death benefits or burial expenses. In addition, give your Social Security number.

9 List the stocks and bonds you own, where they are kept, when you bought them and how much you paid—these figures could have a big effect on estate taxes. For the same reason, single out the stocks bought by you from those bought by your wife, or bought for your children and registered in their names. If you have ever pledged stock as security for a loan, mention that. List any U.S. Savings Bonds you hold and name the beneficiaries. Give the name of your stockbroker.

10 List all your personal property and how you would like it distributed—especially your car: Say where the title and registration are, and give instructions about transfer of ownership if it is not jointly owned. List home furnishings and valuables; give details of insurance coverage and the name of the broker. Is any of this jointly owned; if so what?

3 If you have set up trust funds for your wife or children, outline all of the provisions and purposes of the trusts. Tell where the trust agreements are, give the names of the trustees and, if a lawyer was involved, give his name too. Also list any trusts under which you are named a beneficiary, or any trusts set up by others under which your heirs are beneficiaries.

14 List the names, addresses and telephone numbers of your parents, if living, and of any other relatives or close friends who should be notified. Also give the name of your employer, plus any close associates at work. Also include the names of any lawyers, accountants, brokers and the like not already mentioned.

the other one dies. For example, if you die, your wife becomes sole and outright owner of your jointly held automobile with unquestioned right to use it. The property does not—in fact, cannot—pass by will, does not become involved in probate and is not tied up during the settlement of an estate.

But it *must* be the right kind of joint ownership. There are three sorts of joint or plural ownership; you are letting yourself in for trouble unless you know the differences between "tenancy in common," "joint tenancy," and "tenancy by the entirety."

The first of these, tenancy in common, is not the kind you want if you wish to avoid probate. The reason is simple: If you own a share of some property under tenancy in common, your share automatically becomes part of your estate on your death—no matter what your will says. It therefore has to pass through probate.

The second, joint tenancy, is generally the kind you do want. It is characterized by a kind of legal metaphysics that says that *each* of the tenants owns *all* of the property. It follows (at least according to the logic of law) that you cannot "devise your interest"—that is, dispose of your part of the property in your will. It cannot be part of your estate since 100 per cent of it still belongs to your surviving joint tenants. Your will has nothing to say about it, nor do the laws of your state or the court if you die intestate.

Obviously joint tenancy serves your purpose if your intention is to avoid probate, while tenancy in common defeats it. And here's where you have to be very careful about terminology. If there is any ambiguity, the court may decide that you and your wife (or other heirs) were tenants in common rather than joint tenants, thus defeating your purpose. For example, it is not enough to sign the certificate of ownership of your car or savings account "John and Mary Smith." This does not unambiguously establish that you were joint tenants. It is generally wise to use the following form of words: "John Smith and Mrs. Mary Smith, Joint Tenants with Right of Survivorship, and Not as Tenants in Common." This ponderous form is not always mandatory; the simple rubric "John Smith or Mrs. Mary Smith" is generally acceptable for U.S. Savings Bonds. However, for stock certificates the full, wordy form is essential, since corporate stocks cannot be owned by one person *or* another. In any case, the laws governing jointly held property are complex and, from state to state, extremely varied, so it is highly desirable to have good legal advice when you are setting up any arrangement of this kind.

There is a third type of joint or plural ownership: tenancy by the entirety. This has the same probate advantages as joint tenants with

right of survivorship. But it is available only to husband and wife and neither one can independently sell or assign his or her interest to a third party. The latter provision means, put bluntly, that you're locked into the agreement. Tenancy by the entirety insures that the property will remain intact and will pass *in toto* to the survivor (except where divorce occurs). Some states do not allow creation of a tenancy by the entirety; others limit its use. Again, good legal advice is called for.

When you seek this advice don't be put off by a lawyer's unfriendly reaction. Professional estate planners are inclined to bare their fangs when they hear the phrase "joint ownership." This is probably because professionals often deal with large estates and at these levels joint ownership can cause tax trouble. Unfortunately, even for the less affluent it can create problems.

The worst one, probably, is that jointly owned property may be seized for the debts of either of the joint owners, or for legal judgments against him. If you're in a business or profession that requires you to take out large loans or makes you liable to damage suits, your family property may be better protected if it is in your wife's name. That way claimants can't get at it if you should die.

Another frequently voiced objection to joint ownership is that neither owner has exclusive control. If a husband wanted to dispose of a piece of property and his wife objected, he wouldn't be able to sell. Of course, if things got bitter, the husband could go to court and ask for a partition of the property. But then how would he sell his half? Nobody wants to buy half a house in partnership with a dissident female.

A fourth drawback to joint ownership is the annoying legalities sometimes involved when the survivor seeks title to property. For example, when notice of death is published, a bank usually stops payment on checks written by either party to a joint owner of the account, and the account cannot be drawn without a clearance from state tax authorities. Similar rules may tie up jointly owned securities, brokerage accounts and savings accounts. The surviving owner must file a return with the state inheritance-tax office, listing all property held either jointly or individually by the deceased, and only when the tax liability has been determined does the state issue certificates of clearance. The survivor must send one of these certificates, accompanied by proof of the other owner's death, to get the jointly owned assets transferred to him as an individual.

Securing the survivor's title to real estate can be tedious in some states, involving a court hearing. Local law can require a survivor to file a petition to terminate the other owner's interest in the joint tenancy. The court then orders an appraisal of the property and sets a

While you live, you control money in a trust savings account just as in an ordinary account. But when you die, the money goes to the beneficiary, bypassing probate. A father can juggle funds in as many trust accounts as he has children.

date for a hearing. At the hearing, after proof of death has been established and any tax due has been paid, the court awards the survivor sole title. Annoying as this procedure may be, it is still far shorter, and may be simpler and less expensive, than probate. On balance, then, for most people, joint ownership remains the best refuge for assets.

THE OTHER WAY TO AVOID PROBATE: TRUSTS

After joint ownership, the second best way to protect chunks of your estate from probate is through trusts. For many people, the word "trust" is a formidable echo from the era when trusts were synonymous with baronial wealth. It's still true that trusts and the wealthy are inseparable companions. Authorities differ on how useful a trust is in the management of a modest estate, in part because many trusts cost money. But there are many ways in which the trust principle can be put to use by almost anyone who's going to have something left over when he dies . . . or whose heirs will.

The principle of a trust is simple. You turn property over to a trustworthy individual (or institution) to be held and administered for the benefit of your beneficiaries—or of yourself. In some cases you can also be that trustworthy individual, so that you continue to control your own assets. But here simplicity ends. There are myriad varieties of trusts and they are governed by a body of law so large that it constitutes one of the legal specialties. Talk to a lawyer or the trust officer of a bank if you think a trust might be useful to you.

First of all, trusts can be divided into two basic kinds. One is the "testamentary trust," provided for in your last will and testament. The machinery is designed before you die, but it is not put into operation until your death gives the "go" signal. The other is the living trust—the machinery is designed, assembled and started while you're still alive. Living trusts are very useful, flexible instruments.

Among the simplest is the trust savings account, which earns the bank's regular interest. It protects your own savings account against falling victim to probate, and it is convenient for building a fund for a child. The bank takes care of the legalities.

You open such an account in your name, with yourself as trustee and whomever you want as beneficiary. While you live, you control money in a trust savings account just as in an ordinary account, depositing and withdrawing as usual. But when you die, the money remaining in the account goes to the beneficiary, bypassing probate. You can also establish a joint trust account; then the money does not go to the beneficiary until both owners have died. In most states, however, each trust account can have only one beneficiary. This means a

probate-wary father with substantial savings might juggle the funds in as many trust accounts as he has children.

These trust savings accounts are "revocable trusts." You can establish them and cancel them at will. The assets really remain yours to use as you wish, so long as you live. There are also "irrevocable trusts." The name means what it says; once you commit assets to one, you cannot change your mind. The assets are tied up for the duration of the trust, to be used only for the purposes specified in the trust. Despite this inflexibility, irrevocable trusts can be very useful, particularly in saving taxes. The assets in such a trust no longer belong to you, so you no longer pay taxes on the income they produce (the trust pays if the income is accumulated, or the beneficiary pays if it is distributed, but usually at a much lower rate than you would). The limitation is the federal gift tax, which may cost more than the potential income-tax savings.

Among the more useful irrevocable trusts are:

■ Deed of gift with power-in-trust. This is a very useful way to leave money to a child, since the interest the funds in the trust earn is not ordinarily added to your own taxable income. Yet you do retain a measure of control, since you can use the money for the child's benefit until he is old enough himself to exercise control. This kind of trust is easy to set up. The account is opened in the child's name, and one or more trustees—they can, but need not, be you and your wife —are named who have power to make withdrawals. You can stipulate the age at which the child is to be allowed to make withdrawals (it need not be 21), and until then you decide (within certain legal limitations) what uses of the money benefit the child.

■ Deed of trust. This is also an irrevocable trust, with accompanying tax advantages. Like the one above, it can be used when you want to be able to draw on the money for a child's benefit while he's a minor, and want to make sure he can't get his hands on the principal until he's reached 21 or some other age of reason. Here, too, the money passes to the beneficiary without going through probate—for the good and sufficient reason that it's no longer part of your estate.

THE TAX COLLECTOR COMETH . . . FOR SOME

When you're thinking about leaving your estate to your heirs reasonably unshrunk, you have to think about more than the costs of probate. Does it surprise you to hear that you have to think about inheritance taxes, too?

Doubtless not. But "think" is the right word in the case of most estates; you don't really have to worry unless your estate is going to be

pretty hefty. It will be heftier than you may guess, mainly because your estate for tax purposes is a lot bigger than your estate for probate purposes. The tax man counts nearly everything, including —despite misinformed notions to the contrary—jointly owned property not purchased by the survivor and life-insurance proceeds. Even so, the tax bite on an ordinary man's estate is usually small. This is because federal estate-tax law provides for rather generous exemptions and state tax rates (in most states) at least start out quite low.

Federal estate taxes automatically give you an across-the-board exemption of $60,000. If your estate does not amount to more than that, you can leave it to anybody you want, in any way you want, free of federal tax. Then there's another provision, the "marital deduction." Federal law permits a person to transfer up to half of his estate, tax-free, to his spouse. With a good-sized estate of, say, $200,000, it works this way: Half of that, or $100,000, is not taxed—if it is left to the spouse—because of the marital deduction. The remaining $100,000 is reduced by the $60,000 exemption—so only $40,000 is subject to tax. The federal estate tax on this amount is around $5,000.

State inheritance taxes vary widely in detail but seldom take a big bite from modest estates. One state begins collecting a small 2 per cent tax at $2,000 where the heir is neither spouse nor surviving child. Another allows a widow an exemption of $75,000. For the most part, state exemptions for a spouse are smaller than the federal ones, but state tax rates are low at the levels where taxation begins. At higher levels, part of the tax paid to a state can be taken as a credit against the federal estate tax, and the end result in some cases is that the shrinkage of the estate is essentially the same as if there were only the federal tax to contend with. Estate planning for tax protection, therefore, focuses primarily on the federal tax except for smaller estates subject only to state inheritance tax. The simple methods used to protect against probate costs don't always work against taxes.

Joint ownership is no help. The entire value of any property held in joint ownership has to be reported as part of the estate of the joint tenant who dies first—whether it is husband or wife. Arthur and Nancy have $35,000 worth of stock and mutual fund shares, all with ownership registered as "Joint Tenants with Right of Survivorship." For purposes of figuring the taxable estate of Arthur, if he dies first, the entire $35,000 will have to be reported. Further, if Nancy bought some of this stock with her own money, the burden of proving that is on her. If she can prove that $10,000 of her own money went toward the purchase of the securities, then only $25,000 is included in Arthur's taxable estate. Similarly, if Nancy should die first, Arthur will

have to produce records and documents to prove that it was his money that paid for the securities.

Since Arthur and Nancy don't have to worry about the federal estate tax until the family fortunes get above $120,000, this potential tax liability seems unimportant. Even if the sum climbed to $200,000, the estate tax would still be a pretty small part of the total. Probate expenses would be more, so why shouldn't they use joint ownership as much as possible and avoid probate?

The trouble begins when the survivor passes the estate on to other heirs. Let's say Nancy inherited $120,000 and did not have to pay any tax at all. And that she was a good manager and on her death left her inheritance undiminished to the children. But now there is no marital deduction from this $120,000 and therefore $60,000 of it *is* subject to tax. Federal estate-tax rates can change, but it's safe to guess that the tax on $60,000 will continue to be pretty hefty.

How can Nancy avoid having the estate she leaves shrunk by taxes? One way is by a special trust called a two-trust plan. Here's the way it works. Arthur, before he dies, sets up two trusts. Trust A would be large enough to take full advantage of the marital deduction. Trust B would include the balance of the estate. Income from both trusts would be payable to Nancy during her lifetime. In addition, the trustee would be empowered to pay principal from Trust A to her if she needed it. On her death, Trust A is dissolved, its remnants being added to Trust B. Trust B supports the children until they grow up, when it, too, is dissolved and its remnants divided among them. They would receive something in the neighborhood of $10,000 more on an estate of $120,000, mainly because Trust A is protected against estate taxes completely and Trust B is protected until its dissolution. And they would also have saved the cost of probate, thus offsetting the costs of the trust to some extent.

The tax man's interest in your gifts

The two-trust plan in effect gives money away while the donor is still alive. But only in effect because the mechanism doesn't begin operating until after his death. Outright gifts, which turn assets over to a beneficiary immediately, may be preferable since they avoid income taxes as well as estate taxes. The danger here is giving away more than you really can spare, just to avoid taxes. Always leave sufficient leeway for unexpected financial needs.

The federal tax men, for their own purposes, help you do this. They have rules to prevent you from giving your estate away wholesale. These are the federal gift-tax laws, which work, briefly, this way:

The basic provision, on which the others are built, states that you can give away $3,000 a year to each of any number of persons without incurring a gift-tax liability. You could, for example, give a sister, a brother and a nephew $3,000 each, a total of $9,000. But whenever gifts to any individual exceed $3,000 in any one year, you must file a gift-tax return—although you may still not have to pay a tax.

The reason is that in addition to the annual "exclusion" for each recipient, there is a lifetime exemption for the donor of $30,000. It can be used up a little at a time, year by year, or all at once in a single year. Suppose you wanted to give the sister, the brother and the nephew $5,000 each per year, a total of $15,000 annually. Your gift-tax return would show that $9,000 of this was excluded from taxation; the rest would be charged against your lifetime exemption. You used up $2,000 of the exemption on each of the three—$6,000 of it in all. After five years of such gifts, the lifetime exemption would be exhausted and you would pay gift tax on any amount over $3,000 given to any individual.

Beyond these allowances, there is a marital deduction that is taken in the same way as the marital deduction on the estate tax. One half of the value of a gift from husband to wife, or from wife to husband, is tax free. Thus John gives his wife Mary $6,000 this year. Half of it is covered by the marital deduction, the remaining $3,000 by John's annual exclusion of $3,000. He can, year after year, give Mary $6,000 without paying a gift tax.

How much more than $6,000 a husband can give a wife (or vice versa) before incurring gift-tax liability depends on how the gifts are spread out. John could give Mary $9,000 a year for 20 years, using up $3,000 of his lifetime exemption each year until the $30,000 lifetime exemption was reached. Gifts would total $180,000, free of gift tax, estate tax and probate costs. But if all Mary's gifts from John were received in one year, the limit before taxes would be $66,000. The marital deduction frees half of this, $33,000, from tax. John's lifetime exemption covers $30,000 of the remainder, leaving a balance of $3,000 —which is just covered by the annual exclusion.

There is one other restriction—if gifts are made within three years of death, recipients will have to prove they were not made "in contemplation of death." If this can't be proved, the gifts become part of the taxable estate.

The tax rules are even more favorable to gifts made jointly by husband and wife. The amount of a joint gift can be divided between husband and wife, each taking separate exemptions or exclusions, even though the gift comes exclusively from funds of one and the other

makes no contribution to it. Parents can thus give a son or daughter $6,000 a year, file returns showing each gave $3,000, and pay no tax.

There are other rules. Generally the gift must have "present interest"—that is, the recipient must get immediate use or benefit from it. If funds are placed in a joint savings account, for example, only amounts withdrawn by the joint tenant (your wife, your son) count as gifts.

Gift-tax laws also affect real estate. If you and your wife buy a home and title it jointly, the half you give her *can* be considered a gift if you wish, and if you file a gift-tax return. Or you can delay the gift until you sell the house. Then, if you divide the proceeds, half her amount qualifies as a gift. But the gift can be reduced by any amount she can prove she contributed to the original purchase price. If you die while owning the house jointly, there is no gift tax on it, but there may be an estate tax. It's all very complicated. Consult an expert.

For the average family, gifts are an excellent way to avoid estate taxes, since gift exemptions and exclusions are so large that gift taxes are seldom a problem. Even if gifts exceed the exemptions and exclusions, and tax has to be paid, estate shrinkage is still minimized since gift-tax rates are much less than estate-tax rates.

These are only a few highlights of a complex subject, omitting many technical and complicated aspects of the federal estate and gift taxes. (Many states have inheritance or estate taxes, and there are more than a dozen states with their own gift taxes, the rates varying widely.) But if the shoe looks as if it might fit, try it on—with an expert bootmaker in attendance to make sure it really does.

14
Retirement

An independent
income for
the future

Financial planning for retirement years depends on whose retirement you're talking about—yours, or somebody else's. They are two distinct problems, but the changing age profile of the U.S. population makes it increasingly likely that a family may have to take both into account in its financial planning.

During the decade of the 1950s the segment of the population aged 65 and over increased by 3 per cent each year. It increased by another 2 per cent a year during the '60s. Thus, by 1970, the nation had an unprecedented 20 million in this age group. And a total increase of 50 per cent in the number of over-65 Americans was projected for the period 1960 to 1985. All of this adds up to a new and important element in the financial plans of the working-age family: In an increasing number of cases, there will be a responsibility to help support older members of the family.

It would be nice to be able to assume that Social Security will take care of the old folks now and you later on. But you may think differently after you consider the following figures on the increasing gap between Social Security benefits and the cost of living for retired couples. In the first column are the average Social Security benefits paid to a worker (and his wife) who retired in 1950, the changes reflecting successive increases authorized by Congress during the 17 years. In the second column is the amount of money the government believed Social Security beneficiaries really needed to live on—the Retired Couple's Budget for a Moderate Living Standard developed by the Bureau of Labor Statistics.

	Monthly Social Security payments	Monthly budget for a moderate living standard
1950	$ 75	$149
1959	98	255
1966	104	344
1968	118	370

The steadily widening gap between the figures in those two columns has to be filled by money from someplace—investments, savings, cash support from younger family members, earnings. Where this money comes from makes an important difference, for some funds, oddly enough, turn out to be easier to use than others. A number of retirement-fund sources are favored by the government with indirect tax subsidies; other sources may be penalized by government regulations. The source that most people turn to, unfortunately, is among the economically least desirable: work.

Earnings that can't be kept

A survey of the Social Security Administration showed that of the income of all persons 65 and over, about one dollar in three came from earnings. Among those most able to work—couples aged 65 to 72 —the proportion was even higher, their earnings making up almost half their income.

The trouble with having to depend on earnings to supplement retirement income stems from the regulation limiting Social Security benefits paid those who also collect wages or salary. Some or all benefits may be canceled, depending on how much is earned. A retired person may earn up to $140 a month and still receive full benefits. He may earn 12 times $140—$1,680—during the year and still receive full benefits for the entire year, regardless of how much is earned in any particular month. (That is, he could earn the whole $1,680 in one month and receive full benefits for that month.) When annual earnings go over $1,680, though, he loses 50 cents of Social Security benefits for each dollar earned. A second restriction occurs when his earnings pass $2,880. After this, the loss becomes totally nullifying—one dollar of benefits for each dollar of earnings.

As an example of how this works, look at what happens to Andrews, who retired on Social Security benefits of $1,800 a year plus whatever he can make as a part-time clerk. Here's how he fares as his earnings increase from $1,680 to $2,500 a year:

Earnings	Social Security payments	Benefits lost	Income
$1,680	$1,800	None	$3,480
1,800	1,740	60	3,540
2,500	1,390	410	3,890

Not too bad so far. But see what happens when earnings pass $2,880:

2,880	1,200	600	4,080
3,500	580	1,220	4,080
4,000	80	1,720	4,080
4,080	None	1,800	4,080
4,081	None	1,800	4,081

In this range, he does a lot of work for nothing. Once he begins losing benefits dollar-for-dollar, he can't increase his net annual income until he's done enough "free" work to equal the amount of his Social Security benefits. (There has been sentiment in Congress for liberalizing the amount of earnings allowed before Social Security benefits are

It's income from savings, investments annuities, trust funds or outright gifts that puts money in the pocket after you retire. All these keep cash coming in that does not reduce your Social Security benefits.

lost. Your local Social Security office can tell you whether the Retirement Test has been changed.)

However, the rules do not mean that Andrews could not have any income at all above $1,680 without losing benefits. Look at his friend Roberts, who also does part-time work that pays $1,680 a year, but in addition receives an annual income of $1,820 from investments. With $1,800 Social Security added, Roberts' total annual income is $5,300, and he keeps every bit of that $5,300.

Why does Roberts get $1,220 more than Andrews? Because a person drawing Social Security benefits can receive an income of any amount from dividends, interest, rents, annuities, pensions or sales of property, and lose none of his Social Security benefits. So long as none of it is earned money, it doesn't reduce benefits.

The moral is obvious. Whether you are planning your own retirement or that of someone you will have to help, it's income from savings and investments that puts money in the pocket after you retire. So far as the Social Security rules are concerned, this nest egg can take any form—savings account, mutual fund shares, annuities, trust funds or outright gifts. All these keep cash coming in that does not reduce your Social Security benefits. To the Internal Revenue Service, however, the form of the retirement fund does matter. All forms get valuable tax assistance, but in different ways.

TAX-SHELTERED SAVINGS ACCOUNTS

Even so simple a retirement fund as a savings account can be fattened if you take advantage of tax rules. Putting away *x* dollars per week steadily builds up a respectable sum, although inflation may shrink its true value (*Chapter 11*). Wilson, for example, awakens at age 45 to the realization that time is marching on. He can accomplish quite a bit with $5 a week. Deposited in an account paying 5 per cent interest compounded quarterly, the weekly five becomes about $13,000 in his passbook at retirement age, 20 years later. Paid back out of the same account in installments, it will give him $1,200 of retirement income each year for about 16 years.

But income taxes could alter that rosy picture considerably. If Wilson was in the 25 per cent tax bracket all the time he was saving, he'd have about $2,000 less at age 65 simply because of the taxes on the interest that his retirement fund earned while it was on deposit in the bank. He need not pay those taxes immediately, however, if he sets up the bank account right.

Several of the larger banks across the country offer "deferred-income" savings accounts. These are for long-term deposits, on which

Federal Reserve Board regulations allow higher interest rates than for regular savings accounts. To open such an account, Wilson must agree not to touch either principal or interest before the end of a stipulated period. In effect, he collects no interest until the end of that period, and there is meanwhile no income tax to pay. (The Internal Revenue Service has raised objections to some types of deferred-income accounts. Before you sign up for one, ask an officer of the bank whether the IRS has questioned it.)

The object, of course, is to defer the interest income until retirement puts Wilson in a lower tax bracket, when the bite will be gentler. But with this type of account, you can't always defer long enough. The individual bank sets the term of deposit, usually seven to 10 years. Such an account, therefore, provides Wilson with a tax shelter only if he starts it just a few years prior to retirement.

If Wilson wants to get his retirement program under a tax shelter at the very beginning, when he is many years from retirement, a trust account will do the job. Bank-account trusts are the easiest to set up, since the bank provides standard trust forms. But other trusts —of real estate, stock, annuities or any other assets—are equally effective tax shelters. Establishing one is a short chore for a lawyer. The trust must be irrevocable; that is, the assets going into the trust must be given away completely and beyond recall. Wilson could give his $5 a week away to his wife. He would open a "deed of trust" account for his deposits, naming his wife as beneficiary and himself as trustee. The money no longer belongs to him, and neither does the interest it earns; Wilson pays no tax on it. The income will be taxed to the trust, which is treated as a separate taxpayer. Until the interest mounts up to around $2,000, the trust has no tax to pay. Thereafter, it is usually taxed in a lower bracket than is Wilson. He arranges for his wife to begin drawing on the trust at whatever age she will be when he retires. She will then pay tax on her income from the trust, but again it will be in a low tax bracket.

If instead of planning for his own retirement, Wilson is faced with the need of helping an elderly relative, he could make even more effective use of a trust to provide tax-sheltered retirement funds. Take, for example, the case of the Letwins.

USING A TRUST TO EASE THE BURDEN

Letwin is a middle-echelon executive in a West Coast industrial firm. He has a typical family problem. His 66-year-old mother-in-law, a widow, receives about $1,900 a year from Social Security plus $480 from insurance, not enough by itself for her to live on. The $1,200

An association for the retired

Back in the mid-'40s a California high-school principal, Dr. Ethel Percy Andrus, learned what it was like to be a retired teacher on a teacher's meager retirement income. She devoted her life thereafter to bettering the teacher's lot. Out of an organization for which she was responsible—the National Retired Teachers Association—grew the American Association of Retired Persons. It offers a health-insurance plan to supplement Medicare coverage; auto insurance (in most states) for those who have been denied coverage because of age; low-cost prescription drugs; and consultations on retirement housing in any geographic region. Aside from such mundane attention to the economics of retirement, the AARP concentrates on the mental and psychological welfare of its members. Be forewarned, if you join, that you'll be exhorted to get up out of the rocking chair and engage in stimulating activities—for example, the AARP's Institutes of Lifetime Learning, offering continuing education geared to the interests of retirees, and a travel program that now takes several thousand AARP members yearly to near and far corners of the world. It's all in line with the conviction of the late Dr. Andrus that retirees should "get their lips moving again" (and their minds). You can get information about AARP membership by writing to the association at 1225 Connecticut Avenue, N.W., Washington, D.C. 20036.

Economics of living in retirement

Where to live and how to enjoy life on a restricted income are among the major problems for most retirees, and they are complex ones, social and psychological as well as financial. To help solve them, there are a number of retirement handbooks and directories of living facilities for retirees. Representative of these publications are:

Best Places to Live When You Retire, by Helen Heusinkveld and Noverre Musson (Frederick Fell Publishing Co., New York, 1968).

Resort/Retirement Facilities Register, edited by George Stromme (Drake Publications, San Francisco, 1967). Published in four geographic editions covering the United States: California, Northwestern, Southern and Northeastern.

The New Guide to Happy Retirement, by George W. Ware (Crown Publishers, New York, 1968).

The Retirement Handbook, by Joseph C. Buckley, third edition revised by Henry Schmidt (Harper & Row, New York, 1967).

a year contributed by the Letwins keeps her in moderate comfort.

The Letwins last year filed a joint return on $15,700 of taxable income, putting them in a bracket where it takes $1,600 in before-tax income to give them the $1,200 a year of spendable dollars they contribute to Mrs. Letwin's mother. But Letwin has found a better way of providing his mother-in-law with that $1,200 supplemental income than writing out a check every month and putting it in the mail. By making use of a trust, he turns over the $1,200 without letting it get tangled up in his taxable income; instead of needing $1,600 to provide $1,200, he does it with the equivalent of $1,200, thereby saving his family the sum of $400 a year.

Letwin is able to do this because he was fortunate enough to come into an inheritance that generates about $1,200 a year. He had planned to set the inherited assets aside for his own retirement—until a lawyer friend explained how he could save on taxes by giving the inheritance to his mother-in-law temporarily. In the end the assets would return to Letwin, so he would still have them when he needed them for his older years. This is how he was able to do it:

Letwin placed the inheritance assets in a trust with his mother-in-law as the beneficiary. So long as he surrenders completely, for the duration of the trust, ownership and control of the assets except for the benefit of the beneficiary, and so long as the trust cannot accumulate surplus income that will revert to Letwin, the tax laws concede that the assets are no longer his. He will not have to pay taxes on the trust income. It will be taxed either to the trust or—to the extent that the income is paid out each year to the beneficiary—to the mother-in-law. She pays no income tax on her own yearly income of $3,580; neither her Social Security benefits nor her insurance money is taxable. She reports as taxable income only the $1,200 received from the trust; since her personal deductions and exemptions add up to more than that, no tax is due.

Setting up a small trust of the type Letwin uses is relatively simple and inexpensive. Technically it is a "Clifford trust"; in such a trust, the assets must belong to the trust for not less than 10 years or until the death of the beneficiary, whichever is sooner. If his mother-in-law is still living at the end of the 10 years, Letwin will renew the trust for another 10-year period; in effect it lasts for her lifetime. On her death the trust will be dissolved and whatever assets remain will revert to Letwin. Meanwhile, he acts as trustee, with considerable discretion in managing the assets for his mother-in-law's benefit. The extent of his control is shown in the legal language of the trust form.

Letwin signed a so-called indenture declaring that he gave and as-

Where to retire cheaply

The cost of living varies from city to city for retired couples just as for the young, but in a pattern that is startlingly different. The elderly, unlike their prosperous juniors, find New York less expensive than Seattle or Hartford, and Los Angeles less expensive than Indianapolis. One reason is retired couples' low budgets, which average half those of younger families and may be heavily influenced by a few specific factors: lower taxes, special discounts and services for those over 65, or a climate mild enough to cut expenses for heat and winter clothing. The justly famed climate of Honolulu is not enough, however, to make up for the cost of shipping goods from the mainland; that city has in recent years had the nation's highest living costs, for the retired as well as for the working young.

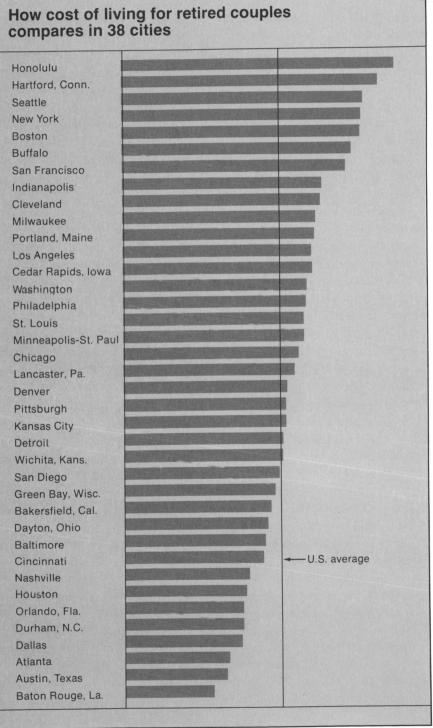

How cost of living for retired couples compares in 38 cities

Honolulu
Hartford, Conn.
Seattle
New York
Boston
Buffalo
San Francisco
Indianapolis
Cleveland
Milwaukee
Portland, Maine
Los Angeles
Cedar Rapids, Iowa
Washington
Philadelphia
St. Louis
Minneapolis-St. Paul
Chicago
Lancaster, Pa.
Denver
Pittsburgh
Kansas City
Detroit
Wichita, Kans.
San Diego
Green Bay, Wisc.
Bakersfield, Cal.
Dayton, Ohio
Baltimore
Cincinnati ←——U.S. average
Nashville
Houston
Orlando, Fla.
Durham, N.C.
Dallas
Atlanta
Austin, Texas
Baton Rouge, La.

Data: U.S. Department of Labor, Bureau of Labor Statistics

signed 500 shares of XYZ fund "to my trustees, hereinafter named, in trust, to hold the same in trust for my beneficiary"—his mother-in-law—"until the death of the beneficiary or the end of 10 years, whichever shall occur first." Upon termination of the trust by reason of either, "I direct my said trustees to convey, transfer, pay over and deliver the principal of the trust fund hereby created unto the Grantor" —the grantor being Letwin himself. As for the trustee who was being directed to do all this, "I nominate, constitute and appoint myself and_____ Trustees under this indenture of trust" to serve without bond. As trustee, Letwin was empowered by the indenture to "retain . . . sell or redeem such shares of the fund as may be necessary to make the payments provided for . . . to invest and reinvest the income dividends and capital gains distributions of any part thereof . . . in additional shares of the fund . . . and to perform all other acts as shall be necessary or deemed advisable for the proper execution of the provisions of this indenture."

It's apparent that giving assets to a trust in this way and for this purpose is not a fearsome surrender of control. Letwin continued to do exactly what he would have done to manage the assets in any case. The only restrictions were that he could not sell the shares or use the income for his own benefit until the trust was terminated, and he could not accumulate income in the trust for distribution to himself after termination—his mother-in-law had to receive whatever income was produced.

Savings realized with this type of short-term trust are proportionate to the grantor's tax bracket. If the Letwins had been reporting $24,000 of taxable income instead of $15,700, they would have needed $1,875 of pre-tax earnings to contribute the $1,200 of support, and would have saved $675 instead of $400.

Trust income paid to anyone in this fashion for support is removed from the grantor's tax liability *except* when the payments are made to someone he is legally obligated to support. This means, with a few exceptions, his wife, his minor children and his own parents. In some instances even his own parents can be beneficiaries of such trust income if, for example, they have enough resources of their own to free him from a legal obligation to support them.

While trusts and deferred-income savings accounts provide excellent tax shelters for retirement funds, they are not always practical for people of modest means. For one thing, the tax saving may not be as great as you think. Particularly if you are thinking of supporting a relative by a trust, you must remember that by doing so you may lose him as a tax-deductible dependent (*Chapter 10*). As a rule of thumb, if

you contribute more than $600 to support someone, you save on taxes if you let that support be furnished from trust income rather than from your own personal income.

A much more crucial disadvantage of tax-sheltered retirement funds is their freezing of assets you might need. To gain the tax advantages you must give up your right, at least for a time, to use the money involved. If Letwin decided, a year after he set up the Clifford trust for his mother-in-law, that he really wanted to use that inheritance as the down payment on a new house, he would be out of luck. He could not touch a penny of the trust fund for such a purpose. To get at the money he would have to dissolve the trust, not an easy thing to do. First he needs his mother-in-law's permission. Then he must pay all accrued income tax plus possible penalties for late payment.

Tax protection can add significantly to the value of retirement funds, but you first need the funds to protect. Any asset will usually serve—not just savings accounts and stocks but real estate, patents, even diamonds or a collection of rare china; if it's a good long-term investment, it's probably a good investment for retirement. Certain investments, however, are planned to meet particular needs of retirement. The best known of these is the annuity.

Annuities for a fixed retirement income

Wilson, when he set up the special savings account to be drawn on only after retirement, was establishing his own private annuity. He contributed regularly to a fund that, many years later, would begin paying him regular sums. Not many people can discipline themselves to bank $5 a week, never touch any of it for 20 years, and then draw it out only a bit at a time. So formal plans—annuities—to push them into this sort of regimen have been developed, mostly by insurance companies, although an annuity need not include life insurance.

Annuities come in a bewildering variety of forms, but are basically no more complicated than Wilson's special savings account. How far the accumulated fund will go depends on (a) how much has been accumulated as principal, (b) the interest earned by the principal and (c) the size of the income installments that are to be paid out upon maturity.

If you have a principal of $10,000, it will obviously provide payments of $1,000 a year for 10 years if it's simply kept in a cardboard box and doled out. But if it's on deposit at 4 per cent interest (a rate common on annuities), you can withdraw $1,000 for the first year's payment and have $9,000 left on deposit, which will earn interest of $360 before the next payment is due. There is still $9,360 to dis-

Text continues on page 398

HOUSING

Should you sell your home when you retire?

In out-of-pocket expenses, you may be better off to stay put. One study shows that older people who own their own homes spend about 20 per cent of their incomes on housing, while those who rent spend over 25 per cent. However, the capital tied up in your house could be at work producing extra retirement income; $25,000, say, in a relatively safe investment program could return $150 to $200 a month. Also, the family house may be larger than you need, hence expensive to heat; you may have to hire someone to do maintenance and gardening chores; you may want to move to an area where living costs are lower or the climate more temperate. But the comfort of familiar surroundings and nearby friends may outweigh all dollars-and-cents aspects of the equation.

When should you sell?

Not till you pass 65, if you can hold off, since older people get special tax breaks. Inflation has probably

HEALTH INSURANCE

How much help will you get from Medicare?

Medicare, the federal health-insurance plan for the elderly, has two parts. The first, hospital insurance, is free and works like this: The patient pays for the first $44 of hospital bills, but then Medicare picks up the rest of the cost of most hospital services (not doctor's bills) for the first 60 days of hospitalization. For up to 30 days more it meets costs that exceed $11 a day (which the patient pays). The second part of Medicare covers doctors' bills inside a hospital or out. It costs $4 a month and must be applied for in advance through the Social Security Administration. This may be done

INVESTMENTS

Should investments change after retirement?

Unless you are very well fixed, retirement years probably require secure investments that produce regular income rather than riskier investments that promise quick growth. Among securities that have traditionally served this purpose are stocks in the food, banking and utility industries, which pay fairly constant dividends and offer some protection against inflation; and bonds and annuities, which pay fixed incomes but lose value during

SOCIAL SECURITY

How will early retirement affect Social Security?

If you start collecting at 62 rather than 65, payments are smaller, so the total if you live a normal life span is the same both ways. The method of figuring your payments—explained on page 123—depends on earnings over the years. (In 1969 the average monthly benefit for a couple was $150.) To allow time for processing, you should file a benefit claim at least three months before you plan to retire.

made your house worth more than you think, and if you sell it and do not replace it, or replace it at a lower cost, all the profit made through value inflation is taxable. If you wait till after 65, the tax on such a capital gain is greatly reduced or eliminated altogether.

What about refinancing a mortgage?

You can still have your home to live in and also have money to put into income-yielding investments by refinancing the mortgage—even if it is not paid off. But if you must pay $7\frac{1}{2}$ per cent on the newly borrowed mortgage money, make sure you can do better than that with the investments. Refinancing may also involve several hundred dollars in new closing costs.

Should you buy a house in a retirement village?

Not without investigating carefully, and certainly not sight unseen. A small home in one of the communities specially planned for the elderly generally costs between $10,000 and $25,000, and mortgage financing is usually simple to arrange. Living costs, however, are not low;

one estimate places them at about $300 a month per couple, not counting mortgage payments. One fact to be noted: Retirement villages tend to appear in outlying areas where land costs are low. This means living in relative isolation. If you prefer the stimulation of living among people of all ages, a city apartment in a modern condominium or cooperative might be a better choice.

Can you get a mortgage at age 65?

It may not be easy. You will probably have to make a larger down payment than a younger person and agree to pay off the mortgage in seven years or less. The reason is not strictly financial. A sound mortgage loan is fully covered by the value of the property for young and old alike, but no banker likes the prospect of foreclosing on an elderly widow. If you do assume a mortgage, try for a prepayment clause that lets you pay the balance at any time without penalty, especially if the mortgage carries a high interest rate that might be a temporary reflection of a tight money market.

starting three months before the month of your 65th birthday and up to three months after, or during the annual enrollment period. The patient pays the first $50 of medical fees during any one year; Medicare pays 80 per cent of the remaining expenses specifically covered by the plan. There are a number of exclusions, but they are minor compared to the potential benefits.

What other health insurance should you have?

"Over-age" health-insurance policies are expensive and frequently are hedged with restrictions and exclusions. Be sure you read and understand every provision before you buy. Look for a policy that will cover large,

unexpected medical expenses, such as extended nursing care—not one designed to plug the relatively small gaps in Medicare protection; such "first-dollar" insurance is rarely worthwhile. You can reduce the rate you will pay by excluding the first 30 days of an illness from any coverage at all. Check carefully to determine when payments begin and end if you become totally disabled. If you have health-insurance coverage where you work, find out if it is convertible to a policy you can keep after retirement. And check the provisions of your regular insurance policies; they may include special allowances for medical emergencies.

inflation. There are also mutual funds planned to produce income through dividends rather than capital growth. Many retired people invest in real estate—the return can be very high and it has historically gone up with inflation—but this amounts to going into business, with all the problems and risks that such a venture entails (*Chapter 6*).

When should you buy or sell?

If you are holding any stocks on which you have a

capital loss, it may pay for you to dispose of them before you retire so that you can get the maximum income-tax credit. But stocks that have gained substantially in value probably should be held until after you have retired, at which time your income will presumably be lower and the tax bite less painful. Even then, it may pay for you to sell the stocks gradually over a period of several years to keep income taxes as low as possible.

What benefits does a wife receive?

At retirement age she gets half her husband's amount unless she qualifies on her own. In that case, she may take either her own benefit or the one based on her husband's, whichever is larger, but not both. A widow's pension starting at 62 is $82\frac{1}{2}$ per cent of her husband's retirement benefit (she can start at 60 at a reduced rate). If she is already drawing her own, she may receive a second monthly check for the difference.

Is everybody eligible for Social Security?

Except for some people who already collect railroad retirement or civil service benefits and also never held a job requiring them to pay Social Security taxes, virtually everyone retiring after 1965 is entitled to a federal old-age pension, no matter how rich he (or his family) is. Anyone who reached 72 before 1968 may be entitled to a special monthly payment even if he never paid into the Social Security fund.

tribute, which will last longer than nine years. How much longer is shown by annuity tables giving the "present value of $1 per annum" at various rates of interest:

	Interest rate			
Years	3½%	3¾%	4%	5%
10	8.317	8.213	8.111	7.722
11	9.022	8.880	8.760	8.306
12	9.663	9.523	9.385	8.863
13	10.303	10.142	9.986	9.394

If you want $1 per year for 13 years, from principal on deposit at 4 per cent, you would have to begin with a sum having the "present value" of $9.986. A $10,000 principal would therefore provide $1,000 a year, not for 10 years, but for slightly more than 13 years.

When you buy an annuity from an insurance company, essentially all the company does is find out how many years it would have to pay you an income by looking up your life expectancy in its mortality table. It gets the amount needed to fund your annuity by going to its "present value" table, like the one above.

There is an advantage in letting an insurance company do the job for you, rather than paying yourself an annuity out of your own funds. You may miscalculate on how long you are going to live. If you fool the mortality table and live to be 106, the insurance company continues paying you and makes it up on the next customer who gets hit by a truck when he is 67. But if you're operating your own annuity fund you may run out of principal, ending the annuity, before you die. It has been said that life insurance is protection against dying too soon and the annuity is protection against living too long.

The first annuities were calculated strictly on the basis of the mortality table, the income was paid until you died, and that was it—the shorts balancing off the longs. But people who didn't understand the beauty of pure statistics objected; they might collect only a small fraction of the amount paid in. The "straight life" annuity, as this basic arrangement is called, dwindled in popularity. More sophisticated contracts were developed. For example:

■ Installment refund. You get the income for life; if you die before collecting all you have paid in, the remainder is paid to your beneficiaries in continued installments.

■ Cash refund. You get the income for life; if you die before collecting all that you have paid in, your beneficiaries get the remainder in a lump sum.

■ Installments certain. You get the income for life; but it is also guaranteed to continue for 5, 10, 15 or 20 years to your beneficiaries if you die before the end of a specified period.

■ Joint and survivorship annuity. You get the income for life; so does your co-beneficiary, for so long as he or she lives.

Needless to say, these all put the insurance company in hock for more benefits, or at least more potential benefits, than a straight-life annuity would. Therefore, the more sophisticated contracts either (1) cost you more to buy or (2) result in lower monthly benefits for the same premium.

How to buy an annuity

An annuity can be purchased in one of two ways: (1) You are going to be 65 in a few weeks, so you ask the insurance company, "How much will you charge to pay me $100 a month for life?" Then you make a lump-sum payment and get an "immediate annuity." (2) You are 40 years old when it occurs to you that you will want some retirement income in 25 years. So you ask the insurance company, "What's the premium, for the next 25 years, on an annuity that will pay me $100 a month for life, beginning at age 65?" Here you are asking about a "deferred annuity." (A deferred annuity is often sold in a package with life insurance; the combination is called a retirement-income policy.)

The cost, in out-of-pocket dollars, is going to be less for the deferred than for the immediate annuity, since the insurance company has the use of your money for 25 years. But by the same token, you have to count as part of your cost the earnings you lose from the money you do not have for 25 years because you are giving it to the insurance company. As a third alternative, one that requires no cash payment at all, most insurance companies will let you apply the cash value of an insurance policy to the purchase of an annuity. Typically, $1,650 of cash value will, at age 65, buy an annuity of $10 per month for the rest of your life.

It is difficult to compare annuity costs, either between types of annuities or between annuities and other methods of providing retirement income, because of the great variety of ways in which annuities are packaged and sold. There is, moreover, quite a range of costs between different insurance companies. Take the example of a single-premium immediate annuity, purchased at age 65. The cost of getting $10 per month for life can range from about $1,575 to $2,100. It is even more difficult to compare the cost of a formal annuity with that of a personal fund you set up yourself in a savings account. For one

To make up for inflation the insurance industry has developed what it calls the "variable annuity." You buy dollars for future delivery, but the hope is that the number of dollars delivered will vary in a way to counterbalance inflation.

thing, you don't know how long you will live. Mortality tables[1] on which insurance companies base annuity costs assign a life expectancy of about 14.4 years to a 65-year-old man. He could guarantee himself $10 a month for that long by just putting $1,700 in a shoebox and doling it out month by month. If he set up his own private fund by depositing it somewhere at 4 per cent interest compounded semiannually, he (or his heirs) could collect the $10 a month for 21 years—but then it would stop. If he used the $1,700 to buy a formal annuity, the $10-a-month payments would keep coming no matter how long he lived.

One of the main criticisms of annuities designed for retirement has been that they provide a fixed income that cannot increase to counterbalance inflation. When you buy an annuity you buy dollars for future delivery; on the delivery date those dollars may not be worth as much as they were when you bought them. In response to this problem the insurance industry has in recent years developed what it calls the "variable annuity." You still buy dollars for future delivery, but the hope is that the number of dollars delivered will vary—in a way to counterbalance inflation.

THE VARIABLE ANNUITY

Premiums for a variable annuity, instead of going into what amounts to a savings account with a fixed rate of interest, go into an investment fund much like a mutual fund *(Chapter 12)*. The pooled premiums are invested by the insurance company in a portfolio of common stocks, but your share of the portfolio is represented by "accumulation units" rather than mutual fund shares.

By the time you retire you have acquired a certain number of accumulation units. Thereafter you have that number of units, gaining no more but drawing income based on them. As the value of the stocks in the company's portfolio varies, each unit will be worth more or less, and income will vary accordingly. If stocks have a bad year, income may decrease; in good years it may go up. Most variable annuities, however, will probably be based on a combination of stocks and bonds that will tend to level off extreme fluctuations, up or down. The main attraction is that if inflation continues, the investment in stocks will, it is to be presumed, keep the value of an accumulation unit growing, just as the value of shares grows in a carefully selected mutual fund.

---

[1] *The insurance industry does not use the same table for life insurance as for annuities. A life insurance table says you are likely to die sooner; the annuity table says you are likely to live longer.*

The problem with the variable annuity, up to about 1970, was that only a few insurance companies offered it. Their sales costs were relatively high and the annuities were consequently quite expensive in terms of potential return to the buyer. As more insurance companies develop variable annuities, lower costs may make them an attractive choice for retirement income.

RETIREMENT INCOME FROM A MUTUAL FUND

If a variable annuity is so similar to a mutual fund, why not simply use a mutual fund investment as a retirement nest egg? Why not indeed. Mutual funds provide a convenient way to build up substantial sums. Their values have grown, in recent prosperous years, at a rate much faster than annuity interest (a conservative mutual fund return, compounded, has been about 12 per cent annually). And they have tended to provide greater protection against the ravages of inflation than annuities do.

The men who peddle mutual fund shares were not slow to respond, and they have devised a scheme especially for retirement income called a systematic withdrawal plan. Most of the larger funds offer these plans, which require a minimum investment of $5,000 to $10,000. The fund automatically reinvests all profits, and periodically liquidates enough shares to provide the amount of income you've set for yourself. Income is not guaranteed for any period of time; when the principal is used up, payments stop.

But the principal need not be used up—it could conceivably even grow while income payments continue—if you choose your fund carefully and don't demand payments that are too large. The chart on page 402 shows a 10-year record of an aggressive but not wild-eyed mutual fund, with an initial deposit of $10,000, followed by withdrawals of $600 a year. A shareowner using a systematic withdrawal plan could have taken a regular income from this fund without touching the $10,000 he initially invested—in fact, he would have doubled his money in these 10 years. Obviously, the fund would have grown at a much faster rate if there had been no withdrawals. Withdrawals sacrifice compounding—profits paid on earlier profits. When you keep draining off part of the growth for income, there's less to grow on and hence less growth. It was quite feasible, however, to draw an income of 6 per cent of the principal each year from this fund. In the first three years, for example, the total increase in share value was $3,000. An investor who drew out only $600 each year, or 6 per cent of the initial investment, would have had enough principal still invested to take care of the fourth year—a bad year in the market, when the

value of the account declined almost $2,500. He still wouldn't have been invading his principal—in fact, he could have had substantial growth of principal despite market declines in 1962 and 1966.

Just remember that there are going to be poor years in the market, and you can't draw out all your growth during a single year if you want to preserve the principal. But there are also going to be good years like 1965, when the fund in the example shown enjoyed an appreciation of about 25 per cent—and as the principal builds up well above the original investment, you can draw on it for a trip to Europe or whatever else makes retirement years more enjoyable.

One attractive feature of this arrangement is that a retired family can draw its income and still leave the principal intact, unlike an an-

Income from a mutual fund

The systematic withdrawal plan offered by many mutual funds seems to let a retired person have his cake and eat it, too, since it can pay out regular monthly income while keeping an initial investment growing—at least in a booming economy. The chart shows how such a plan would have worked for a man who invested $10,000 in 1959, arranging to take out $50 every month thereafter but otherwise reinvesting all profits. He got his check for $50 automatically each month for the following 10 years, and—despite the market drops of 1962 and 1966—never had to dip into the starting investment for income; in fact his principal more than doubled over that generally prosperous decade.

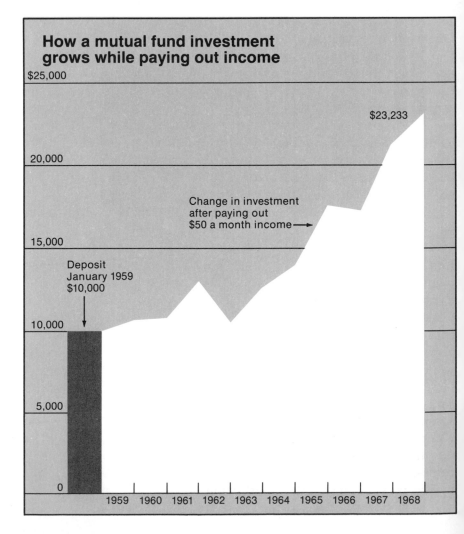

How a mutual fund investment grows while paying out income

Change in investment after paying out $50 a month income →

Deposit January 1959 $10,000

$23,233

nuity, which uses up the investment as it is spread over the years of your life expectancy. While it's still true that you can't take it with you, if you want to have something to leave, this is a way to do it.

THE KEOGH PLANS' EXTRA MONEY

One of the best ways to set up retirement income is one many people neglect to take advantage of. It involves the "Keogh plans," which divert money away from taxes and into your own retirement account. The government's effective gift to you can be large—for every $100 of spendable dollars you put aside, the government may kick in close to another $100. Yet only about 5 per cent of those who qualify for the special treatment afforded by the Keogh Act are making use of it —probably for the simple reason that most of the remaining 95 per cent don't know about Keogh plans, or don't realize that they qualify for the plans' benefits.

In general, if you have any income that's not subject to withholding taxes, that portion of your income, however small, probably can be put in Keogh plan funds. Keogh plans are almost universally used by doctors, lawyers and owners of stores. But any income from self-employment makes you eligible. If you do work at home on your own—writing articles, preparing someone's tax return, serving as a consultant—the fees you are paid are all considered self-employment income. Proceeds from the sale of housewives' needlework —even earnings from Junior's paper route—qualify.

These plans permit you to set aside as much as 10 per cent of your annual income from self-employment, up to a maximum of $2,-500, and deduct the entire amount from your taxable income. Furthermore, there is no tax on the return earned by your Keogh plan funds until you begin to make withdrawals after retirement, when presumably you'll get lighter tax treatment. So there's a double benefit: the immediate tax saving each year on funds that you contribute to your Keogh plan, and the fact that you have all of your investment and its accumulated earnings, undiminished by taxes, at work earning more money. The growth rate of an untaxed fund will be substantially higher than the growth rate of one subject to taxes. Anyone contributing the maximum of $2,500 a year and realizing only a modest 4 per cent yield on his retirement fund would have tax savings of roughly $27,000 over a 20-year period.

If Keogh plan contributions are also deductible on your state income-tax return, the tax advantage is even more important. An individual earning $25,000 a year and putting $2,500 a year in his plan would be in a tax bracket in which the immediate saving on fed-

One of the best ways to set up retirement income involves the "Keogh plans," which divert money away from taxes and into your own retirement account. Any self-employment income qualifies—even earnings from Junior's paper route.

eral income tax would be about $900 each year. If he was a resident of New York, his saving on state and federal taxes combined would come to about $1,200. In effect, he'd be putting aside $2,500 of retirement money at a cost of only $1,300.

There are a half-dozen types of Keogh plans approved by the Internal Revenue Service. Contributions can be invested in a special issue of U.S. Retirement Plan Bonds. They can also be used to purchase certificates similar to bonds issued by certain registered investment companies. For other types of investment, your fund must have a custodian—a device designed to insure that the fund is not used as a temporary tax dodge.

The principal disadvantage of a Keogh plan, to be considered before you embark on one, is that your savings are frozen until you're at least 59½ years old—the earliest you can begin drawing on your funds without penalty except in case of total disability. If you tap the fund early, you pay all accumulated taxes at once, plus a penalty, and you're barred from participating in a Keogh plan for the next five years. Another consideration is that an "owner-employee" who employs others full time must include them in the plan, after three years of service, and make for them the same percentage-of-salary contribution that he does for himself.

If you want to set up your own private Keogh plan for investing in stocks and bonds, you have to set up a trust (a chore for a lawyer specializing in that field of law), arrange for administration of the trust by a corporate trustee such as a bank or trust company (they generally want customers to have $50,000 or $100,000 to work with), and get individual approval of your plan from the IRS. Obviously, there aren't many Keogh plans of this "bank-trusteed investments" type. The most popular plans make use of insurance or mutual fund shares, bought from a company that has an IRS-approved master plan; then it's as simple as signing a printed form and sending the IRS another form announcing that you're enrolling.

An ordinary annuity, endowment or life-insurance policy requires the use of a bank custodial account. But if contributions are applied to the purchase of nontransferable, level-premium retirement annuities or life-insurance policies, you can buy directly from the insurer without the need of a trust or custodial account.

Contributions of $1,500 a year to a Keogh plan beginning at age 30 would total $52,500 by age 65. For an individual in a 25 per cent tax bracket meanwhile, the John Hancock Life Insurance Company points out, "$13,125 of this would have been 'contributed' by Uncle Sam in the form of tax deferral." With the full, untaxed amount avail-

able for purchase of a retirement annuity, it might be possible for him to end up with a life income of as much as $800 a month.

The cost of maintaining a Keogh plan is nominal. Where a custodial account is involved, there's ordinarily a custodian's fee of around $5 a year, and frequently charges of $1 or so for each contribution and for each withdrawal after retirement age. Against that, consider the potential benefits. A boy with a paper route might want to set up a Keogh plan if someone would sit down and do a little compound-growth arithmetic with him. Joe is making $9 and change a week from his route; say $40 a month. He's allowed to put up to 10 per cent of his year's earnings—$48—into his Keogh plan. With some professional help, he picks a mutual fund that gives him, for the rest of his working life, the annual growth averaged by all mutual funds over the past decade—about 15 per cent. Joe is now 15 years old, so his $48 has 45 years to grow and multiply. Anyone care to guess what Joe's $48 would be worth when he's 60 years old? The answer is so unbelievable that you'd better work it out for yourself. A sum of money increased by 15 per cent a year will roughly double every five years: Joe's original contribution becomes $96 in five years, $192 in 10 years, etc. Double his $48 nine times, and believe your eyes if you get a five-figure answer. It may not enroll many paper boys in Keogh plans, but it should be a persuasive example to their fathers, arguing that they should get their own fund started as early in life as possible.

ACKNOWLEDGMENTS

The editors of this book wish to acknowledge the help of the following persons and institutions: American Automobile Association, Washington, D.C.; Milton Amsel, Director, Press and Editorial Division, Institute of Life Insurance, New York City; James I. Avignone, Huckin & Huckin, Englewood, N.J.; Mildred Bebell, Professor of Education, Southern Colorado State College, Pueblo, Colo.; James L. Bowman, Program Director, College Scholarship Service, Educational Testing Service, Princeton, N.J.; Joseph F. Bradley, Professor of Finance, Pennsylvania State University, University Park, Pa.; Raymond J. Brienza, Director of Financial Aid, New York University, New York City; Jody Carr, Huntington Woods, Mich.; Arthur Cashman, Director of Education and Research, New York State Credit Union League, Inc., New York City; Walter H. Clemens, Vice President, Johnson & Higgins, New York City; David Clurman, Adjunct Assistant Professor of Real Estate, New York University, New York City; Donald P. Cole, Assistant Professor of Economics, Drew University, Madison, N.J.; Robert J. Connor, Feature Editor, *Mechanix Illustrated*, New York City; Jack Crestol, Tax Manager, Lybrand, Ross Bros. & Montgomery, Inc., New York City; Robert Dubuss, Assistant Treasurer, The Dreyfus Fund, Inc., New York City; Edgar R. Fiedler, Manager, General Economics Department, National Industrial Conference Board, New York City; Alan S. Fields, Investment Advisor, Hornblower & Weeks—Hemphill Noyes, New York City; Flow-of-Funds Section, Federal Reserve System, Washington, D.C.; Bernard N. Freedman, Economist, Board of Governors of the Federal Reserve System, Washington, D.C.; Bernard Gelb, Associate Economist, National Industrial Conference Board, New York City; Fred Giancola, Chase Manhattan Bank, New York City; Paul M. Giddings, New York City; George J. Grueneberg, Bank Examiner, New York State Banking Department, New York City; Celeste Hemingson, Information Representative, Social Security Administration, New York City; Gary Hendricks, Assistant Study Director, Survey Research Center of the Institute for Social Research, The University of Michigan, Ann Arbor, Mich.; Harland W. Hoisington, Director of Financial Aid, Columbia College, New York City; Insurance Information Institute, New York City; Norman W. Jack, Manager, Industry Procedures, American Society of Travel Agents, Inc., New York City; Martin Karlin, Economist, U.S. Department of Labor, Bureau of Labor Statistics, Region II—New York; Robert H. Kastengren, Field Relations Director, Runzheimer & Co., Rochester, Wis.; Joseph P. Klock, Philadelphia, Pa.; William N. Leonard, Professor of Economics, Hofstra University, Hempstead, L.I., N.Y.; Charles M. Lucas, Economist, Federal Reserve Bank of New York, New York City; Joan Lyons, Associate Research Manager, *Merchandising Week*, New York City; John A. Marlin, Assistant Professor of Economics, The Bernard M. Baruch College, New York City; Catherine E. Martini, Director of Research, National Association of Real Estate Boards, Washington, D.C.; Morton H. Meisler, Chief, Branch of Information and Advisory Services, U.S. Department of Labor, Bureau of Labor Statistics, Region II—New York; Bert Mogin, Director of Post-Secondary and Special Education Programs Division, Office of Program Planning and Evaluation, Department of Health, Education and Welfare, Washington, D.C.; Edwin R. Murphy, Manager, Research Department, Standard & Poor's Corporation, New York City; Robert W. Murray, Jr., Public Information Officer, Federal Housing Administration, Department of Housing and Urban Development, Washington, D.C.; New York State College of Home Economics, Cornell University, Ithaca, N.Y.; Joseph O'Connell, Veterans Administration, Washington, D.C.; Mitsuo Ono, Chief, Consumer Income Statistics Branch, Population Division, Bureau of the Census, Department of Commerce, Suitland, Md.; Thomas W. Phelps, Scudder, Stevens & Clark, New York City; Jane Ritter, National Industrial Conference Board, Inc., New York City; Evelyn Scheyer Travel Service, Inc., New York City; Emmett Spiers, Consumer Income Statistics Branch, Population Division, Bureau

of the Census, Department of Commerce, Suitland, Md.; Edwin L. Stoll, Director of Public Relations, National Association of Real Estate Boards, Washington, D.C.; John van Steenwyk, New York City; Eliot N. Vestner, Jr., Special Counsel to Superintendent of Banks, New York State Banking Department, New York City; Ralph H. Wherry, William Elliott Professor of Life Insurance, Pennsylvania State University, University Park, Pa.; Larry R. Winters, City Manager, H & R Block, Inc., New York City; Marianne Witschy, Consumer Income Statistics Branch, Population Division, Bureau of the Census, Department of Commerce, Suitland, Md.; Edward D. Zinbarg, Vice President and Chief Economist, Prudential Insurance Company of America, Newark, N.J.

BIBLIOGRAPHY

*Available in paperback

H & R Block, *Income Tax Workbook*.* Macmillan. Annual.

Brosterman, Robert, *The Complete Estate Planning Guide*. McGraw-Hill, 1964.

Britten, Virginia, *Personal Finance*. American Book Company, 1968.

Cohen, Jerome B., and Arthur W. Hanson, *Personal Finance*. 3rd ed. Richard D. Irwin, Inc., 1964.

The Consumers Union Report on Life Insurance.* Consumers Union, Mt. Vernon, N.Y., 1967.

Cooley, Leland Frederick, and Lee Morrison Cooley, *The Retirement Trap*. Doubleday, 1965.

Crane, Burton, *The Sophisticated Investor*.* Rev. ed. Simon & Schuster, 1964.

Donaldson, Elvin F., and John K. Pfahl, *Personal Finance*. 4th ed. The Ronald Press Company, 1966.

Engel, Louis, *How to Buy Stocks*.* 4th ed. rev. Little, Brown, 1967.

Jackson, Charles R., *How to Buy a Used Car*.* Chilton Book Co., 1967.

Katona, George, *The Mass Consumption Society*. McGraw-Hill, 1964.

J. K. Lasser Tax Institute, *Your Income Tax*.* Simon & Schuster. Annual.

J. K. Lasser Institute, *J. K. Lasser's Managing Your Family Finances*. Doubleday, 1968.

J. K. Lasser Tax Institute and John D. Cunnion, *How to Get the Most Life Insurance Protection at the Lowest Cost*.

Business Reports, Inc., 1968.

Margolius, Sidney, *How to Make the Most of Your Money*. Meredith Press, 1969.

Margolius, Sidney, *Your Personal Guide to Successful Retirement*. Random House, 1969.

Masteller, Kenneth C., *How to Avoid Financial Tangles*.* American Institute for Economic Research, 1965.

Merritt, Robert D., *Financial Independence through Common Stocks*. 4th ed. Simon & Schuster, 1969.

Murray, Robert W., Jr., *How to Buy the Right House at the Right Price*.* Crowell-Collier, 1965.

Neal, Charles, *Sense with Dollars*.* Doubleday, 1968.

Nuccio, Sal, *The New York Times Guide to Personal Finance*. Harper & Row, 1967.

O'Neill, Barbara, *Careers for Women after Marriage and Children*. Macmillan, 1965.

Phillips, E. Bryant, and Sylvia Lane, *Personal Finance*. 2nd ed. John Wiley, 1969.

Rodda, William H., and Edward A. Nelson, *Managing Personal Finances*. Prentice-Hall, 1965.

Rose, Jerome G., *The Legal Adviser on Home Ownership*. Little, Brown, 1967.

Smith, Adam, *The Money Game*. Random House, 1965.

Watkins, A. M., *How to Avoid the 10 Biggest Home-Buying Traps*.* Meredith Press, 1968.

Wilder, Rex, *The Macmillan Guide to Family Finance*. Macmillan, 1967.

INDEX

x

PRODUCTION STAFF FOR TIME INCORPORATED
John L. Hallenbeck (Vice President and Director of Production), Robert E. Foy and Caroline Ferri
Text photocomposed under the direction of Albert J. Dunn